Temporal Variables in Speech

JANUA
LINGUARUM   Series Maior 86

Studia Memoriae
Nicolai van Wijk Dedicata

edenda curat
C. H. van Schooneveld
Indiana University

Temporal Variables in Speech

Studies in Honour of Frieda Goldman-Eisler

edited by
Hans W. Dechert · Manfred Raupach

Mouton Publishers
The Hague · Paris · New York

ISBN 90 279 7946 4

Preface

From June 13–17, 1978 the Kassel interdisciplinary Workshop "Pausological Implications of Speech Production", sponsored by the University of Kassel (Gesamthochschule), the City of Kassel, the State of Hessen in cooperation with the German Academic Exchange Service (DAAD), and the German Fulbright Commission, took place in Schloß Wilhelmshöhe. It was the result of a common effort of the Kassel Psycholinguistic and Pragmalinguistic Research Group (KAPPA) and the St. Louis University Group. Its object was to deal with an area of psycholinguistic research which was felt to be a desideratum.

During 1977 and 1978, researchers in various countries were informed and invited. The abstracts of their proposed papers were collected in advance and sent to all participants, since discussion was thought to be the main object of the Workshop.

The proposed topics and abstracts were the guidelines for the organization and grouping into five sessions, according to the salient themes.

With a few exceptions, the order in which the papers are presented in this volume reflects the organization of the Workshop. We do realize, of course, that other, perhaps even more adequate ways of structuring the material would have been possible as well. The paper on Sign Language by Grosjean and the statement on formal approaches by Ballmer were written at the request of the participants during the final discussion and thus added to this volume.

Baars' edition of the final discussion was based on the transcripts provided by us. It is an effort to reflect the main lines of argument and avoid redundancy. This résumé also seems to indicate that a learning process took place during the Workshop.

Three special lectures during the Workshop were open to all members of Kassel University and the public. The ones by Chafe and Di Pietro are found in this volume. Kałuża's lecture on "Time and Tense in Modern English", however, does not appear here; it has already been published in the *International Review of Applied Linguistics,* 17 (1979) 2.

A great many people have contributed to this volume. First of all, the participants of the conference themselves, who provided us with their manuscripts in a relatively short amount of time. Some of the articles are identical with the papers read at the Workshop, some are revised versions considering points made during the discussion following their presentation.

Dafydd Gibbon from the University of Göttingen and Nora Johnson as native speakers of English have kindly assisted us in eliminating irregularities found in contributions by some of the non-native participants, including our own. Gabriela Appel had compiled a "Pausology-Bibliography" for all participants. Together with Christa Meuser and Hildegard Blessmann she was very helpful in editing the Bibliography at the end of this volume. We owe thanks to Richard Wiese for the assistance he gave us as editors.

Frieda Goldman-Eisler, London, had agreed to attend the Workshop and present a paper. Due to a sudden illness, it was not possible for her to come, which was sorely regretted by all at the Workshop. It has been the unanimous desire of all its participants to dedicate this volume to Frieda Goldman-Eisler. This, we feel, indicates best the spirit of the Kassel Workshop.

Kassel, December 1978

H. W. D.   M. R.

Contents

Third section: Conversational aspects

Fourth section: Prosodic aspects

Final discussion

Participants

Bernard J. Baars, Dept. of Psychology, State University of New York, Stony Brook

Thomas T. Ballmer, Sprachwissenschaftliches Institut, Ruhr-Universität Bochum

Geoffrey W. Beattie, Dept. of Psychology, University of Sheffield

Hans-Georg Bosshardt, Psychologisches Institut, Ruhr-Universität Bochum

E. Keith Brown, Dept. of Linguistics, University of Edinburgh

Andrew Butcher, Queen Margaret College, Edinburgh

Wallace L. Chafe, Dept. of Linguistics, University of California, Berkeley

Mark Cook, Dept. of Psychology, University College of Swansea, Swansea

Vivian J. Cook, Dept. of Language and Linguistics, University of Essex, Colchester

Anne Cutler, Dept. of Experimental Psychology, University of Sussex, Brighton

Hans W. Dechert, OE Sprache und Literatur, Gesamthochschule Kassel

James Deese, Dept. of Psychology, University of Virginia, Charlottesville

Alain Deschamps, Dépt. d'Anglais, Université de Paris VIII – Vincennes

Robert J. Di Pietro, Dept. of Linguistics, Georgetown University, Washington, D.C.

Raimund H. Drommel, Romanisches Seminar, Universität Köln

Marc Faure, Sprachenzentrum, Universität Trier

Borge Frøkjær-Jensen, Audiologopedic Research Group, University of Copenhagen

David A. Good, The Psychological Laboratory, University of Cambridge

François Grosjean, Dept. of Psychology, Northeastern University, Boston

Hede Helfrich, FB Psychologie, Justus-Liebig-Universität Gießen

Alan I. Henderson, Dept. of Psychology, University of Southampton

Elisabeth Hofmann, Jugendwerk Gailingen

Henryk Kałuża, Dept. of English, Wrocław University

Heinz Klatt, King's College, London, Ontario

Wolfgang Klein, Projektgruppe für Psycholinguistik der Max-Planck-Gesellschaft, Nijmegen

Jens-Peter Köster, FB Sprach- und Literaturwissenschaft, Universität Trier

Sabine Kowal, Berlin

John Laver, Dept. of Linguistics, University of Edinburgh

Bogusław Marek, Institute of English, M. Curie Skłodowska University, Lublin

Barry McLaughlin, Dept. of Psychology, University of California, Santa Cruz

Paul Meara, Language Research Centre, Birkbeck College, London

Carl Mills, School of Languages and Literature, University of Tromsø

Daniel C. O'Connell, Psychology Dept., Saint Louis University

Janina Ozga, Institute of English, Jagiellonian University, Kraków

Karl H. Pribram, Dept. of Psychology, Stanford University

Manfred Raupach, OE Sprache und Literatur, Gesamthochschule Kassel

Wolfgang Wildgen, Institut für Allgemeine und Indogermanische Sprachwissenschaft, Universität Regensburg

DANIEL C. O'CONNELL and SABINE KOWAL

General introduction

DANIEL C. O'CONNELL and SABINE KOWAL

Prospectus for a science of pausology

Uh ... we ... we ... I ... uh. Our interdisciplinary workshop on Pausological Implications of Speech Production has now been solemnly inaugurated with a filled pause, four silent pauses, a repeat, and a false start – though not a false start, we hope, in any more general sense.

It is both an awesome responsibility and an honor to be requested to give an introductory and – it is to be hoped – a keynote address for this workshop on the pausological implications of speech production. Sabine Kowal and I wish to add our own welcome to the rest of our colleagues to the welcome from our hosts from the Gesamthochschule Kassel, Professors Hans Dechert and Manfred Raupach.

It is indeed a privilege to address all of you as colleagues. We are not unaware of the fact that representatives of various specific disciplines have joined us for this workshop, nor of the distances traveled by many of you to be with us. In fact, we would like to dwell for a moment on the variety of native languages, nationalities, and scientific disciplines represented in this gathering. All of us know how disastrous a scientific workshop can be when the non-native speakers of the workshop language are not given adequate consideration. It would indeed be a paradox – and a travesty of all the sciences of speech and language which we represent – were we to fail to exercise the clarity of articulation, the evenness of pace, the exactness of diction needed by colleagues for whom experience with the English language is different from our own. I am reminded of an experience with a fellow Jesuit priest from Malta. After his Christmas sermon in a rural Kansas parish, U.S.A. – in the queen's own English – the local pastor said of him, "Too bad Fr. Mario has trouble with his English". No, Father, trouble only with the Kansas twang!

We come too from a variety of scientific traditions, disciplines, systems, theories, and languages. Many words, phrases, and expressions have variant meanings from one of us to another – possibly including the key concepts of this workshop, pausology and speech production – although we all share an interest in temporal aspects of speech. From the very beginning we must face the fact that such heterogeneity can either be a challenge to openness, learning, inquiry, and progress on the one hand, or a stumbling block of isolation, failure to communicate, and the perpetuation of whatever *status quo* we begin from. Only good will, openness, and complete intellectual integrity can make a scientific building block of such a stumbling block. Perhaps we could sum it up by saying that we have not come to market to show off and sell our wares, i.e. to give the right *answers*; but rather we have come back to school to find out what the questions are and to learn from one another. Personally, I would be very happy to hear the expression "I don't know" frequently during the next few days.

These comments have been meant to pinpoint both the interdisciplinary and the workshop aspects of our several days here in Kassel. A key concept in this regard, and one which has been repeated frequently by Dechert and Raupach in their preliminary announcements is that of discussion. We have not come hundreds or thousands of kilometers only to give canned speeches which only the speaker himself listens to, and copies of which could be mailed to you by airmail for a dollar. Quite the contrary, each of us must bring his own research material to bear on the theme of the conference: the pausological implications of speech production. And we must all – graciously and with good humor – bring one another back to this central theme. Given such an effort to maintain a unified forward thrust, we have an historic task and a momentous opportunity before us.

If you will allow us for a moment, we would make an historical analogy with general psycholinguistics. In the early nineteen fifties, the term psycholinguistics was little known and less used. It had first been introduced in the late nineteen forties. The Indiana Conference planned by Osgood and Sebeok (1954) became the historic occasion for the christening of the new science. And although 1978 will likely never be as illustrious because of pausology as the date ninety-nine years earlier – or one year later – because of Wilhelm Wundt, still the science of pausology awaits the formative influence of creative minds. We have a great opportunity.

It might be instructive for us to look backwards for a moment to ask where pausology has been up until now. In this respect, it is hardly coincidental that the co-authors of this introductory presentation are representatives of the German and English languages and of German and American institutions of higher learning. To our knowledge, pausology has been from its beginnings almost entirely represented in German and English studies. Heinrich von Kleist, the German dramatist and philosopher, as early as the early nineteenth century, laid down pausological principles in his "Über die allmähliche Verfertigung der

Gedanken beim Reden", – "On the gradual working-out of thoughts in speaking".

But in our own time, it has been before all others another German, working in English and in England, who has been the modern pioneer of the science of pausology (though without using the term pausology). It is a source of great personal disappointment to us that Frieda Goldman-Eisler cannot be with us today because of her delicate health. The Kassel workshop should stand as an historical credit to her years of research in the field of pausology. In fact, the reason Sabine Kowal and I are here today is that an air-freight error left me bookless in Berlin in 1968, but for one monograph, Goldman-Eisler's (1968) *Psycholinguistics: Experiments in spontaneous speech,* which I thereupon well nigh committed to memory.

Pausology should have been christened along with psycholinguistics and as a component part of the latter in the early nineteen fifties. But Lounsbury's (1954) section of the Osgood and Sebeok report, though it provided a number of hypotheses to researchers such as Maclay & Osgood (1959), has never been influential toward the formation of a science of pausology. Conceptually, he was dependent upon the originating or parent sciences. Nor has anyone in the intervening years conceptually clarified the status of a science of pausology, much less developed a theory of pausology.

Without wishing to track through the past quarter century of psycholinguistics, we think some notion of the neglect of both speech production and real-time variables in the psychological research of recent years is important for us to keep in mind. One could consult any of the standard texts. Two of the most recent are particularly informative. Clark & Clark (1977) disregard the vast majority of the research in pausology and categorize pauses as speech errors, disruptions, and disfluencies; and all this despite the fact that they devote a chapter to speech production. Similarly, Palermo (1978) mentions only a few studies under the generic heading "Rhythm" and nothing more recent than Martin (1972). Nonetheless, there has been a steady stream of research, not only by psychologists, but in areas such as communications, linguistics, speech pathology, and aphasiology.

But more germane to our present purposes, how can we characterize the research represented by our own abstracts, the research traditions we bring with us to the workshop? First of all, there are some notable absences. Neglected are studies of developmental speech production, of emotional or expressive speech, and of dialogue and multilogue. Such limitations are of course inevitable in any group of participants and need not reflect a conviction that these are not fertile grounds for pausological research. It would be even more regrettable if the absence of affective and emotional variables reflected some abortive effort to study cognitive variables in their absence – and therefore in a vacuum. One is reminded of the introductory statement in Ulric Neisser's (1967) *Cognitive psychology,* where he sets out to do just that, and of his concluding statement in the same book, where he admits that it can't be done.

What *is* represented in the abstracts is a broad spectrum of research which very well fulfills the purpose and finality of pausology, namely the psychological explanation of speech production – with special emphasis on its real-time aspects.

We can all be grateful that Chafe's abstract reminds us as to why we study pauses – not for themselves, but to come upon a theory of speech production. We would add to this: to come upon a theory of speech perception as well. But since the actual term pausology hardly appears in these abstracts, the focal emphasis needs to be expressed. Before we leave Chafe's abstract, however, let us quote an important sentence: "[...] spontaneously created language constitutes the primary data, and hesitations are welcomed as overt, measurable indications of processing activity." We happen to agree with this and wish to hear it much discussed during the next several days. It asserts obliquely that most of us are still concerned in our research with the non-primary data, data produced not spontaneously, but elicited by a variety of experimental materials and in a variety of artificial stimulus situations.

Along the lines of theory construction indicated by Chafe is the abstract of Baars. His Competing Plans Hypothesis is an excellent presentation of the theoretical centrality of *tempus utile* or available time. There should indeed be a trade off between time and errors under the constraints of real-time speech production.

We could not help thinking of the emphasis placed on serialization by Karl Lashley as we read Bosshardt's abstract. Speech production is essentially ordering in real time – serialization. The importance of suprasegmental constituents of this process cannot be overestimated. Closely related to this is the work of Butcher on the perception of artificially induced pauses as a function of intonation pattern rather than as a function of their position in syntactic structure.

The relationship of pause and other suprasegmental aspects appears as a topic in Cutler's and Ozga's abstracts respectively. Whereas Ozga offers some intriguing approaches to the relationship of pause and pitch variations, Cutler is concerned with misplaced emphasis. Nearly all recent researchers, including Lenneberg (1967) and Goldman-Eisler (1968), have deliberately neglected the variations of articulation rate due to syllabic prolongation and other on-time phenomena. A closer look seems now to be in order, with the promise of lawful and functional findings regarding variations of articulation rate.

Ballmer poses an equally central problem: the relationship of pause categories to linguistic categories and their role for a theory of grammar. Beattie reminds us that pauses must ultimately be related to and integrated with nonverbal behaviors such as gaze if we are to explain speech production, particularly in terms of encoding units.

We have already hinted at the importance of dialogic research. Butterworth and Good's research on hesitancy as a conversational resource seems to point in the same direction.

Cattell (1885) had suggested ninety-three years ago that pausological measures would clearly be useful to test foreign-language learning. It is nothing less than astounding that so little has been done in this regard. Our hosts, Dechert and Raupach, have set about remedying the situation in their research on English and French second-language learning. In a similar vein, Meara's abstract compares native speakers and learners of Spanish. Grosjean in his abstract asks an incisive question as to whether our research on pauses gets at a significantly predictive part of the variance and what formula might be optimally predictive.

One of the questions raised by Henderson's abstract is the extent to which a natural language foreign to experimental subjects can be used to throw light on speech production and speech perception in the language of those subjects.

In commenting briefly on the abstracts of Hofmann and Klatt, we think it important to keep in mind that the pathological speech of aphasics is still in need of extensive research and that it can throw light also on normal speech production. At a much more moderate level of error rate Laver and McLaughlin make use of errors for the construction of models for native and second-language speech production respectively. Laver also calls our attention to an empirical fact which has been again and again forgotten even in the recent history of pausology: "Listeners are expert in mentally editing the speech they hear." Indeed, this is one of the most important reasons for instrumental physical measurement of pauses, rather than use of perceptual judgments of secretaries or even trained observers.

Finally, Wildgen's abstract conceptualizes speech production within a theory of catastrophes or sudden shifts in dynamic.

In the hope of insuring that our workshop be an "anastrophe", rather than a catastrophe, i.e. a sudden shift of dynamic in a *felicitous* direction, we have made the preceding brief comments on the workshop abstracts which were at hand by the end of May 1978, excluding our own. We hope the commentary will give a better focus to our forthcoming discussions and that it reflects the state of the science, as we feel the abstracts themselves do.

Nonetheless, this introduction must also serve – or attempt at least to serve – a prospective, or if you will, prophetic function for the science of pausology. At long last, then, we would like to offer a definition of pausology for your discussion in the workshop: *Pausology is the behavioral investigation of temporal dimensions of human speech.* To comment briefly, behavioral investigation asserts an empirical science, but does not mandate a behavioristic framework. The term behavioral does, however, imply that the primary performance of interest to the science is genuine speech production, not reactions to demonstration stimuli, not isolated sentences, not nonsense strings or syllables, not numbers, not speech sounds as such, but human discourse in the oral mode. Nor does the term human speech assert that there is genuine non-human speech, but is intended only *in sensu aiente et non negante.*

Occasionally pausology is still thought of, if at all, by some psychologists and undoubtedly by some others as methodologically soft or trivially redundant. Perhaps there is still need for an *apologia pro scientia pausologica.* Surely there need be no defense made for a scientific investigation of human speech behavior as such, since it reflects better than any other overt behavior the cognitive and affective processes of mankind. And all human speech goes on in real time. The question that remains is whether temporal dimensions of speech *reveal* the higher processes of human mental activity. The empirical evidence at our disposal indicates that they are both reliable and lawful indicators of such processes. Traditionally these temporal measures have included primarily those introduced to the literature by Maclay & Osgood (1959). Their categories of silent or unfilled pauses, filled pauses, repeats, and false starts still remain basic to the science. In our own research, we have found that speech rate, articulation rate, and a number of other derived measures are useful additions. Parenthetical remarks too have a special role as "time savers" in human speech and are to be included. Nor is there any reason why the preceding list need be considered closed to any future entries which may prove useful.

The behavior of listeners is not *per se* speech behavior. Nonetheless, it is speech related and determines in many ways what a speaker says and how he says it. In this respect, therefore, speech perception plays an important role in pausology.

As we indicated in the original title of our abstract, a look into the future is definitely in order: Where is the science going? What is being neglected? What needs to be changed? What facts have been adequately established? What findings need to be questioned, reviewed, or confirmed?

One thing seems abundantly clear: If we are to speak to one another, we must speak a common language. By no means do we refer to English, but rather to a common nomenclature. The terminology of pausology has been plagued by multiple meanings, theoretical overtones, implicit assumptions, and simple inconsistent usage. The familiar term "hesitation", for example, implies a deficiency in speech or a disturbance of speech, whereas hesitation phenomena may indeed be a necessary accompaniment of spontaneous speech precisely for purposes of efficient and clear expression, as Baars pointed out in his abstract. The conventions and methods have varied too. It is certainly true that a science with completely standardized methods is static, if not moribund; but a modicum of methodological comparability from experiment to experiment and laboratory to laboratory is long overdue in our science. During the present workshop, we will have an excellent opportunity to discuss some of these measurement problems with the various equipment firms which have joined us for the occasion. It is not too much to hope that we could agree upon some generally acceptable measurement conventions.

We suspect that many of us are attracted by the richness of spontaneous speech produced in naturalistic settings and at the same time frightened off by its complexity. If we are ever to transcend the trivialization which has beset modern psychology, however, we must find a way of engaging meaningful human discourse in all its multifaceted, dialogic, and multilogic reality. Until now, the vast majority of pausological research has been limited to formal laboratory situations which are representative of very few speech genre in natural settings. Even the laboratory studies have given us clues that very slight changes in speech settings induce notable changes in speech behavior. The sensitivity of speech behavior in everyday life to subtle changes of cognitive and affective processes is a given; we need only be alert enough to capture them.

Nonetheless, the laboratory studies have been a necessary step toward the development of pausological methodology. And despite the importance of extensive observation, methodological development remains a primary need. As I insisted recently with William Russell in replying to a vast research proposal which emphasized the collection of children's speech corpora, corpora are not the problem at all; what to do with them in terms of methodology and goals *is* the problem.

The various interdisciplinary relationships of pausology have been and will remain delicate and controversial. But suffice it to say that "my dog's better than your dog" usually says a great deal more about personality – and character – than about real dogs. Pausology is not a better or worse science than phonetics, linguistics, speech pathology, or neurology. Rather, science is itself an honest, open, intelligent habit of mind that concerns itself variously with learning about empirical reality. All of us must concern ourselves with the acceptance of relevant empirical facts and at the same time must not be seduced by theories from a sister science which subserve the purposes only of that specific scientific discipline. Such a delicate balance of independence and dependence is not easy for the youngster who must stand on someone's shoulders even to see the parade of modern science march by. Pausology is the junior member of the team, for whom a modest stance of learning from others remains most becoming.

Still, pausological theory must be pausological. Its goal is the understanding of a behavior — which defines it as psychological. And the behavior is human speech studied with respect to its temporal dimensions. This is not to say that temporal dimensions provide an adequate base for a general theory of speech production. Nonetheless, they must be investigated with a certain amount of scientific autonomy and focus, i.e. pausologically.

A number of people have criticized pausology for being atheoretical, in particular Boomer (1970) and Fillenbaum (1971). We have felt this lack very strongly ourselves, but we feel that a recent personal communication from Rochester (1978) says it much better than we could — and we agree:

> [...] with some exceptions, I don't believe that more experimentation is needed now. I think that the "field", if one can use that term, is in a difficult position at this time because there is a gaping hole right in its center — the hole where theory or models should be.
>
> Every time I read another paper about pauses — even if the experimentation is excellent — I feel this need more strongly. I think that right now, in this field, a strong theoretical direction is essential. And I don't know how to make such a theory.

We don't know how either, even though we have been working in this direction for some time now; but perhaps as a group we can make significant progress in filling this theoretical vacuum.

Finally, with respect to various types of regional and international cooperation, we take the position, for purposes of discussion at least, that the scientific world does not at this time need another journal. We are of the conviction that new ideas for methods of communication, support, and publication are bound to come from this workshop, which is itself the best example to date of the sort of development to be wished for.

We would like to take this opportunity finally to express on the part of all of us who are invited participants of this workshop our gratitude to Professors Dechert and Raupach and their staff, both for the invitation to participate and for the long hours of work they have dedicated to its preparation.

For the rest, thanks for listening and, "An die Arbeit!" We will consider that we have done our job well only if vigorous and open discussion characterizes all the remainder of this workshop.

FIRST SECTION

General aspects

Chairman   JAMES DEESE

KARL H. PRIBRAM

The place of pragmatics in the syntactic and semantic organization of language[1]

Introduction

In *Languages of the Brain* (Pribram, 1971, Chaps. 17, 18 and 19), I made some preliminary proposals concerning the relationship between human language and the functional organization of the brain. These proposals were based on clinical experience with aphasic patients and on the analysis of the structure of language by Charles Peirce (1934). The proposals were incomplete in many respects and raised problems that have persistently plagued me in trying to understand linguistic processing by the brain. The current conference thus presents an opportunity to enlarge on the earlier views which have been especially enriched by attendance at a conference on the origins of speech and language sponsored by the New York Academy of Sciences in 1976, by an interdisciplinary conference on the nature of human language sponsored by the Society for the Interdisciplinary Study of the Mind in 1978, and by the participants of this conference on 'pausology'.

Perhaps the most important problems concern the relationship between brain organization and Peirce's categories of semantics, pragmatics and syntactics. The connection between semantics and syntactics appeared to be relatively easy to establish: grammar and meaning mutually imply each other much as partitions on a set determine the organization into subsets (Pribram, 1973 a). Thus, no separate brain locus would be expected to distinguish disturbances of semantics from those of syntax.

Two problems immediately arise from this formulation: one, it is incomplete since it ignores pragmatics; and two, it contradicts the clinical observation that semantic aphasias more often follow parietal lesions while agrammatism is found most often in patients with more anteriorly placed damage in the temporal lobe or adjacently at the foot of the central fissure.

The problems concerning semantics, pragmatics and syntactics are intimately related to another set of distinctions that Peirce makes, i.e., those that characterize signs and symbols. Signs refer to icons, i.e., images that outline or caricature the sensory input. Signs may also become indices that point to, categorize or classify that input into groups, i.e., sets and subsets. Symbols, on the other hand, are tokens that bear only an indirect and completely arbitrary relationship to the events or objects symbolized. In *Languages of the Brain* I focused on this distinction between the direct, deictic nature of iconic and indexal signs and the indirect tokens that compose symbols as fundamental. However, the criticism has often been voiced that signs are also tokens, and furthermore, that in *Languages,* Peirce's differentiation between icon and index was not pursued.

These difficulties are compounded by the generally held opinion by philosophers, linguists and cognitive psychologists that signs and symbols are hierarchically related. Peirce is not altogether clear on this issue, but in *Languages of the Brain,* sign and symbol are conceived to originate from the operation of separate neural systems: signs are processed by the posterior convexity of the brain, symbols by frontolimbic formations. Thus, the neuropsychological formulation has been at variance with accepted linguistic conceptualizations.

Finally, in *Languages of the Brain* I suggested that the ordinary distinction between nouns and verbs in terms of nominalization and predication is in error. Both nouns and verbs are seen as nominalized: verbs refer to nominalized actions while nouns refer to objects, the difference between objects and acts being their relative stability over time and place. Predication is defined neuropsychologically as expressing a relationship, a proposition, a belief about how objects and acts have become momentarily related. Predication, therefore, demands syntax, in English, for example, the use of only a restricted range of verbs such as "is". Linguists, on the other hand have tended to identify predication with action per se and to consider all verbs as predicates. Verbs are thus instrumental, procedural referents to actions of objects referred to by nouns.

One may be tempted to ignore these differences. After all, differences in disciplinary approach may well produce different analyses. But, if understanding human language is to be of a piece, the different approaches ought to shed light on a commonality of problems, and the discrepancies listed above should be resolvable. The following attempt toward resolution is made in this spirit.

Linguistic processing: A proposal

Resolution of these issues rests on the following proposals: 1) Icons and indices are processed by the posterior convexity of the brain. 2) Icons are images and when an arbitrary representation is made of an icon it is called a sign. 3) *Image processing* and sign (significant) communication is ordinarily processed primarily by the right hemisphere. 4) Indexing involves *information processing* and when an arbitrary representation is made of an index it is called a symbol. 5) Information processing and symbolic communication are ordinarily processed primarily by the left hemisphere. 6) Since indexing often, though not always, subsumes imaging, symbols are often, though not always, hierarchical to signs. 7) Image and information processing is semantic. 8) The frontolimbic forebrain is concerned with expressing the relationship of the organism's internal state to that which is being communicated. 9) Expressive communication molds language and is responsible for its modifications.

Semantic processing: Image and information

Note that in this formulation the distinction between image processing (iconicity) and information processing (indexing) rests on hemispheric specialization. The evidence for such specialization has been repeatedly reviewed (e.g., Dimond & Beaumont, 1974) and has become common knowledge. Less well articulated are the relationships between image and information processing and the construction of linguistic signs and symbols. As Peirce makes clear, icons and indicants bear a direct relationship to what is being signified. In today's parlance, images (see e.g., Paivio, 1971) and information, considered as alternatives (see e.g., Miller, 1953) are also rather directly derived from sensory input. Signs and symbols, on the other hand, are higher order categorizations, which can become arbitrary with use. This arbitrariness stems from the modification of language by expressions of internal states that give form to the language.

The hierarchical nature of linguistic processing is most likely derived from the beginnings of hemispheric specialization and later from the audiovocal nature of human language. There is considerable evidence that initially primate communication proceeded by establishing a reciprocal relationship between icon and index using visual-gestural mechanisms. Thus, apes have been taught to indicate their communications by American Sign Language (e.g., Gardner & Gardner, 1969) and the cave paintings of early man suggest considerable skill at iconic symbolization. A plausible scenario of the origins of *speech* might be that frustrations with visual-gestural communication due to darkness in caves, distance, or other awkward circumstances became expressed in vocalizations which then became differentiated into tokens for the unseen gestures. In this fashion, the expressions became signs and symbols initially standing in lieu of icons and indexes and then supplanting them because of their overwhelming adaptive advantage. In short, the expressions became words.

It is likely that these first expressions of frustrations were related to actions and were, therefore, verbs. Verbs are words that denote actions (Miller, Galanter & Pribram, 1960, Chap. 14). "A hole is to dig" a child will tell you and an aphasic patient will gesture only "to dig". Later in evolution verb words became nominalized and objectified. Thus, whether one wishes to call words symbols or signs is a matter of convention. Because the meaning of words is ordinarily processed by the posterior convexity of the *left* hemisphere and because indices are usually hierarchical to icons, it does seem most appropriate to call them symbols as is the custom in linguistics and philosophy (e.g., Morris, 1946) and not signs as in *Languages of the Brain*.

Pragmatic procedures: Language formation

But by what mechanism are these higher order arbitrary signs and symbols achieved? The proposal made here is that pragmatic procedures involving the functions of the frontolimbic forebrain continuously modify icon and index once vocal expression becomes involved in the communication. The limbic systems are primarily concerned with monitoring the states of the organism that are expressed as hunger, thirst, sex, etc. (for review see Pribram, 1971, Chaps. 9 and 10). In addition, the intensive aspects of pain and temperature are regulated by these systems (see Pribram, 1977c). These basic functions are reflected in higher order processes as establishing the needs and desires, i.e., the bases for the utilities that determine what reinforces the organism's behavior (see e.g., Douglas & Pribram, 1966; Pribram, Douglas & Pribram, 1969; Pribram, 1977a). In essence, therefore, these systems establish an internally determined pragmatic *context* within which the organism approaches the world about him.

The limbic forebrain shares regulation of context-dependent behavior with the pole of the frontal cortex which can be considered as the "association" area of the limbic systems (Pribram, 1958). The functions of the frontal cortex make possible the distribution of behavioral responses according to the probability that the behavior will be reinforced (Pribram, 1961). Thus, frontal cortex participates in determining the utilities which, as noted above, organize the context within which an organism approaches his world. (Utilities are defined in economic theory as derived multiplicatively from desires and probabilities.)

Linguists and psycholinguists have up to now paid little heed to the pragmatics of language. The line of evidence and reasoning pursued here suggests that pragmatic procedures are derived from processes that establish desirabilities and the probabilities of reinforcement given a particular state of desire. The linguistic expression of such pragmatic processes would therefore be episodic, i.e., would be dependent on momentary state. Some mnemonic mechanism must also be involved since state change is monitored and outcome (reinforcement) probability estimates are made. Cognitive psychologists often refer to such mnemonic processes as short term but more recently, and accurately, the process has been identified as "episodic" memory (Tulving, 1970, 1972) to distinguish it from longer term, more universally applicable semantic stores.

Forming a language: The role of pausing and parsing

In non-human primates, lesions of the frontolimbic forebrain but not of the posterior convexity, interfere with the performance of a task which can be used as a model for relating episodic, context dependent constructions to linguistic processing. This task is the delayed alternation procedure during which a subject is reinforced for alternating his responses between the two boxes. During the interval between opportunities for response an opaque screen hides the boxes. The screen is kept in place for from 5 sec. to a minute or longer depending on how difficult one chooses to make the task. When the interval between opportunities is equal, subjects with frontolimbic lesions invariably fail the task; i.e., they seem to forget which box they previously chose, successfully or unsuccessfully. When, however, the intervals between opportunities are made unequal though regular – e.g. 5 sec. before box one must be chosen and 15 sec. before box two is the correct choice – then the deficit is quickly overcome (Pribram & Tubbs, 1967; Pribram, Plotkin, Anderson & Leong, 1977).

The reason for performing the above experiment was that it seemed as if a monkey failing the alternation task were in much the same situation as a person hearing or reading a paragraph in which letters and words were separated by equal intervals. Thus, MARESEATOATSAND-DOESEATOATSANDLITTLELAMBSEATIVY is unintelligible until parsed into words. In general, chunking (Miller, 1956; Simon, 1974) has been found to be an essential processing mechanism when the limits of competency are involved (Pribram & McGuinness, 1975).

It is remarkable that the same parts of the brain are responsible for the operations that determine context by way of pragmatic procedures and those that determine the *pauses* necessary to parsing utterances, i.e., expressions into words. This identity of neural substrate suggests that *pauses* in speech provide the contextual cues within which the content becomes related to the speaker's state: his mood, his momentary desires and probability estimates of success in meeting those desires. From these contextual cues, therefore, signification and symbolization derive – pragmatic processing *forms* (gives form to) the linguistic production. Pauses, inflections and the dynamic range of speech form the context in which the content of the communication occurs. This idiosyncratic aspect of language formation may therefore be responsible for the rapid transformation of a language into dialect by an intimate group and thus the variety of languages used by man.

Further, this relationship between pragmatics and the *form* of language expression may underlie the process of predication. Making words into sentences would be unnecessary unless a statement about state, about desire and belief (probability), etc. were at stake. Thus, predication stems from pragmatic procedures while nomination, i.e., making words more universally meaningful, results from semantic image and information processing.

Syntactics: The motor aspects of language

What then is the role of syntax? Syntax must reflect both the pragmatic form of language and its semantics. Neurologically, both the frontolimbic forebrain and the posterior convexity of the brain are directly connected to such subcortical motor structures as the basal ganglia which are known to regulate postural and sensory sets (for review, see Pribram, 1977b). These basal structures are, in turn, intimately connected with the centrally located motor cortex which organizes skills.

Over the past three decades, a great deal has been learned about the hierarchical nature of processing information by the use of symbols (e.g., Miller, Galanter & Pribram, 1960). The construction of programs that make serially operating computers into effective data storage and retrieval mechanisms has shown that such programs must categorize data into items which can be universally retrieved and are thus essentially context free. Hierarchies of such context free items (bits → bytes → words) are then compiled into assemblers which in turn are the elements of more complex programming languages.

More recently, cognitive psychologists interested in simulating human experience and behavior have found that exclusive reliance on such hierarchical organization does not reflect the full nature of human perception, action, and communication. Even the relatively simple process of compiling demands arbitrary decisions that are specific to the "episode" or situation, e.g., the particular computer in *use*. More and more, these investigators have resorted to the construction of "procedures", episode specific program *clusters* that can be flexibly switched into an ongoing program whenever a situation so demands (see Miller & Johnson-Laird, 1976; Winograd, 1977; Schank & Abelson, 1977). As noted earlier, in primates, evidence has accummulated to support the hypothesis that the frontal cortex operates such a context sensitive noticing mechanism and becomes, in this sense, therefore, the executive organ of the brain (Pribram, 1973 b).

Conclusion

The import of this recent attention to context sensitive, pragmatic procedures in all cognitive operations, does not exclude psycholinguistics or neurolinguistics. In a sense, this paper has summarized a set of conceptualizations that has benefited substantially from recognition of the role of pragmatics, its definition in terms of current issues, and the possibility of constructing a reasonable model of the brain processes involved. Pragmatics has thus proved the key concept in resolving a set of issues and problems that grew from an interest in relating semantics to syntax. Pragmatics provides the context and form within which image and information become meaningful. Syntax must thus be accountable to both hierarchical, essentially context free semantic considerations, and to episode specific, context sensitive procedures. Brain mechanisms exist for semantic processing in its posterior convexity and for procedural organization in the frontolimbic systems. Syntactic collation becomes the burden of the motor systems to accomplish, for the linguistic act is little different in this respect from the achievement of other actions (Pribram, 1971, Chaps. 16, 19).

Note

1. Conversations with Thomas Ballmer during and after the conference and discussions during a course on neurolinguistics presented at Gesamthochschule Kassel were especially helpful in clarifying many of the problems discussed herein. Whatever their merit, the ideas expressed are therefore deeply indebted to these sources and to those who organized the conference and lectures and to Ernst von Weizsäcker who personally and financially supported the possibility of my attendance. My thanks are also due to Diane McGuinness who helped in the preparation of this manuscript. She was especially involved in clarifying the roles of sign and symbol in language construction.

JOHN LAVER

Slips of the tongue as neuromuscular evidence for a model of speech production

In 1951, Rulon Wells put forward three descriptive laws for slips of the tongue. He suggested the First Law in the following terms:

> *A slip of the tongue is practically always a phonetically possible noise.* The notion of phonetic possibility is most easily explained by examples. There are lots of noises that could perfectly well be English words, though they are not: "scrin", "scring", "scrill", "scriffly", "sny", "mip", and so on. Then there are a lot of noise that could not be English words, either because they contain un-English sounds (e.g. "loef" – with "oe" pronounced as in French "l'oeuf" or German "Löffel") or because they contain English sounds but in un-English combinations (e.g. "ktin", "pmip", "ksob", where none of the letters are silent). [...] A few exceptions to this First Law have been recorded; but exceptions are so exceedingly rare that in the present state of linguistics they may be disregarded (Wells, 1951: 26).

It is thus clear that by 'phonetically possible' Wells meant 'phonologically possible in the language concerned'. The exceptions to his First Law are either sub-phonemic errors which break orthodox phonetic realization rules, or they are structural errors that violate constraints on segmental sequence. Discussion here will be limited to this first, sub-phonemic type of error. We must also leave unresolved Wells' contention that such errors seem to be very rare in spontaneous speech. It may be that their apparent rarity is actually an artefactual product of the observer's perceptual system, in that listeners tend to edit the speech they hear into canonical form, sometimes to the point of not being consciously aware of even quite blatant errors by the speaker (Boomer & Laver, 1968: 3).

Sub-phonemic errors do sometimes occur, however, and they can give us important insights into the nature of neurolinguistic units in speech production, and of strategies of neuromuscular execution of speech programs. It would take an inconveniently long time to collect a reasonable corpus of these errors from spontaneous speech. This paper describes an experiment designed to provoke sub-phonemic errors of vowel quality in a laboratory situation, and offers some initial conclusions about the relationship between the neurolinguistic representations of vowels and the muscle systems available for their implementation. The following account gives a brief outline of the preliminary analysis of the results of the experiment.

PUSS (Programming Unit for Stimuli Sequencing) is an electronic device built in the Phonetics Laboratory of the University of Edinburgh, the principle of whose design was suggested by Donald Boomer. PUSS controls the random sequencing of two stimuli, and the durations and intervals of their presentation to subjects. The stimuli in this case were two lights, below each of which was a stimulus-word of the form P_P, with a medial vowel taken from the list of stressed vowels in Received Pronunciation of British English (Jones, 1962). This gave a set of ten words (the retracted half-open central vowel found in "cup" was omitted) as follows: PEEP, PIP, PEP, PAP, PARP, POP, PORP, PUP (with the vowel found in "push"), POOP and PURP. Articulatory positions for these ten vowels are given in Figure 1.

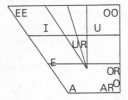

Figure 1. *Cardinal Vowel diagram of the articulatory position of the ten stimulus-vowels PEEP, PIP, PEP, PAP, PARP, POP, PORP, PUP, POOP and PURP.*

The subject's task was to pronounce the stimulus-word as accurately as possible immediately on presentation of the corresponding stimulus-light. The rationale of the experiment was to push the subjects just beyond the limits of their accurately-controllable performance, in order to explore any regularities in the consequent effect on accuracy of vowel production. The hypothesis underlying the experiment was that the incidence of error should reflect neuromuscular dissimilarity in the production of the vowels concerned.

The material for the experiment was made up as follows: the words were arranged in 48 pairings, six consisting of PIP-PEEP, PEEP-PIP, PUP-POOP, POOP-PUP, POP-PORP and PORP-POP. The remaining 42 consisted of all possible pairings of PEEP, PEP, PAP, PARP, PORP, PURP and POOP, with any left-right reading effect being cancelled by having both possible sequences of each pairing. The 48 pairs were then divided into six groups of eight pairs, with each group including one pair from the first six mentioned and seven pairs from the last. Each group of eight pairs was then presented, after two practice trials, to one of six adult, male speakers of Received Pronunciation. Each pair of words formed the material for a 30-second trial, with the stimuli being presented by PUSS initially for .3 second each, with an interval between stimuli of .3 second. After 15 seconds, the presentation rate was increased, with each stimulus lasting for only .2 seconds, with an inter-stimulus interval of .2 seconds. Each subject's performance was tape-recorded under studio conditions on a Revox A 77 recorder, and analyzed auditorily, spectrographically and oscillographically.

In addition to the main experiment, a supplementary group of seven pairs of words was presented to one of the same subjects, to check on the possible interaction of short vowels, both with each other (PIP-POP, PIP-PUP and POP-PUP), and with other vowels (PIP-PEP, PIP-PARP, PORP-PUP and PUP-PARP).

The P_P frame was chosen for the stimulus-words in order to facilitate segmentation, to minimize formant-transitions for convenience of spectrographic analysis, and to allow ease and speed of performance by the subjects, for whom the lingual gesture for the vowel would thus be articulatorily uncontaminated by consonantal requirements.

Most of the subjects were able to maintain adequate performance of vowel quality during the first 15 seconds of each trial. The increased presentation-rate of the last 15 seconds of the trial produced a number of errors. These fell into four categories: two sorts of diphthongs, one in each direction between the target-vowels (thus competition between PEEP and PARP gave rise to both "PIPE" and "PIARP", as it were); a monophthong of a quality intermediate between the two targets – often of a quite un-English quality; and a monophthong of the right articulatory quality but the wrong phonological length. Figure 2 gives examples of the articulatory correlates of some of these errors.

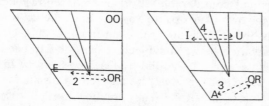

Figure 2. *Cardinal Vowel diagrams of the articulatory positions of some target vowels and errors. 1 = labialized front vowel produced by competition between PEP and POOP. 2, 3 and 4 = diphthongal errors produced by competition between PEP and PORP, PAP and PORP, and PIP and PUP respectively.*

Errors were often shorter than either target would have required, of lower loudness, with inefficient (breathy, whispery or creaky) phonation, and with a longer voice onset time for the initial plosive. The support

such findings give to notions of internal monitoring of the pre-articula-
tion stages of neurolinguistic programming (Laver, 1970; 1977b) is
strong.

All errors, together with sample target vowels performed by the same
speaker, were edited onto a data-tape with an electronic segmenter. The
auditory quality of all vowel-errors was then plotted on Cardinal Vowel
diagrams (Jones, 1962), and broad-band 4 KHz spectrograms were
made. An oscillographic print-out of the speech waveform of the subject's recording was made, on which was also included a synchronized
recording of the PUSS output controlling the two stimulus-lights, to
allow measurement of response-latencies. The discussion that follows is
based on the auditory analysis that was performed.

Because the purpose of the experiment was to examine the characteristic degradation of performance when the required task was beyond
the comfortable attainment of the subjects, it is important to make clear
the definition of "error" used here. With stimuli following each other so
fast, it was not possible to be sure which was the stimulus to which the
subject was currently responding. This difficulty was compounded by the
tendency of subjects to stop momentarily after detecting (and often
trying to correct) an erroneous response. In the analysis of the recorded
tapes, many wrong responses may well have escaped notice, so long as
the performed vowel was a satisfactory version of either of the target
vowels, regardless of whether it was in fact a 'correct' response or not.
"Errors", therefore, are to be understood here as meaning any performance of a vowel other than one of the two prescribed target vowels,
either in terms of vowel quality or of vowel quantity.

Nearly all pairs of vowels interacted to produce errors. Subjects
regarded the experimental procedure as a challenge to their articulatory
skill, and devoted considerable effort and concentration to avoiding
error, so that the overall error-rate was low. Each subject was exposed to
approximately 560 stimuli, over the eight trials per subject. Total numbers of errors varied between subjects, from 6 to 21. The most erratic
performance on a single 30-second trial yielded 6 errors, in response to
the 70 or so stimuli of the trial. The differential results for the various
vowels are therefore not strong. They are, however, provocative. Out of
the 55 trials, only seven pairs of vowels failed to produce errors of vowel
quality. These seven were: PEEP-PIP, PIP-PEEP, POOP-PUP, PUP-
POOP, PORP-POP, POP-PORP and PUP-POP. The first six of these,
strikingly, are pairs involving long-short vowel contrasts of considerable
articulatory similarity, with their order of presentation balanced to prevent a left-right reading effect. The zero-error finding is made stronger
in these instances by the fact that in no case were the two pairs concerned in the same long-short contrast presented to the same subject.

Leaving out of account PUP-POP (and noting that POP-PUP was not tested), we can ask the question "Of all the competing pairings of vowels, why should only PEEP-PIP, POOP-PUP and PORP-POP (ignoring their order of presentation) resist what Hockett (1967) would have called this tendency to blend?" The physiological conclusion that comes to mind is couched in terms of the neuromuscular control of vowel articulation. If we consider what muscle systems might be responsible for the production of particular vowels, then the vowels in PEP and POOP, for example, are obviously performed by largely different systems. If, in indecision, the speaker issues simultaneous neuromuscular commands to both systems, then some intermediate vowel will be the consequence, as the mechanically-joint product of their simultaneous muscular contraction. This is plausibly what happened in this experiment, where, hesitating between PEP and POOP, the speaker pronounced "POEP", with a vowel similar to that in French "peu". The finding that a diphthong is sometimes the outcome is then explicable as a matter of the time-course of the issuing of the commands to the different muscle systems con-

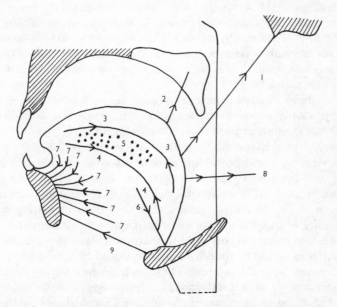

Figure 3. *A schematic diagram of the location and action of some of the muscles responsible for vowel production.*

1. *Styloglossus m.*
2. *Palatoglossus m.*
3. *Superior longitudinal m.*
4. *Inferior longitudinal m.*
5. *Transverse lingual m.*

6. *Hyoglossus m.*
7. *Genioglossus m.*
8. *Middle pharyngeal constrictor m.*
9. *Geniohyoid m.*

cerned. If the command for PARP, for instance, precedes very slightly that for PEEP, then "PIPE" will be the result; if the reverse happens, then "PIARP" will be pronounced. The alternative explanation for such diphthongs would be that an error of wrong vowel-choice is detected sensorily and very quickly corrected in mid-syllable. This would, however, fail to explain the monophthongal mistakes of intermediate qualities between the target vowels.

If we consider the three vowel-pairs that resisted erratic performance, PEEP-PIP, POOP-PUP or PORP-POP, then it is not implausible to suggest that each of the members of any of these pairs is performed essentially by the same muscle system as the other member of the pair, the muscles being contracted merely to a different degree. POOP and PUP, for instance, are reasonably thought of as being executed by a muscle system in which the styloglossus muscle is the chief protagonist component (see Figure 3; cf. Figure 1).

The muscular responsibility for PEEP and PIP is more complex, but although more muscles are probably involved, their co-operative effect is to distinguish between the two vowels in terms of greater or less movement along the same oral radius. To some extent, this is also true of PORP and POP. In this hypothesis, blending errors of these vowel pairs would not normally occur, because it is improbable to think of the brain as sending out simultaneous but contradictory neuromuscular commands to the same muscles.

The findings described here lend some support to a view of vowels having primarily a motor representation, and minimizes the role played in vowel production by auditory feedback control.

The hypothesis that multiple muscle systems are active in the production of blending errors of the sort discussed above is clearly amenable to testing by electromyographic techniques. But if electromyographic experiment sustains the hypothesis, and if replication experiments uphold the differential error-results, then here is an interesting example of a finding from speech-error data enriching general phonetic theory. The principle being put forward, of neuromuscular compatibility in the production of different speech segments, would be applicable to many other areas of phonetic interest. These include the study of co-articulatory phenomena, of natural classes in phonology, of physiologically-motivated sound-change, and of physiologically-based constraints on the progression of language-acquisition and of second-language learning.

E. KEITH BROWN

Grammatical incoherence

In recent years there has been some considerable interest in 'slips of the tongue'. Boomer & Laver (1968) define a 'slip of the tongue' as an "involuntary deviation in performance from the speaker's current phonological, grammatical or lexical intention". Slips "involve units of varying size, from segments to sequences of segments, to whole syllables and words, on the phonological level; on the grammatical level units include morphemes and whole words, and, more rarely, higher order constituent groups". "The deviation", they claim, "is almost always detected, not always consciously, by the speaker, and corrected". Greatest attention has been devoted to those slips of the tongue that Boomer and Laver, I would judge, would analyse as being at the phonological level, or as involving the phonological level, and the most frequently discussed examples are those that involve some overt distortion of word form. Thus, for example, the vast majority of what Fromkin refers to as "errors" and lists in the appendix to her valuable collection of papers *Speech Errors as Linguistic Evidence* are of this sort; even those in what she describes as "ungrammatical utterances".

I am not sure whether the data I would like to consider would be classified as involving 'slips of the tongue' in terms of the definition given above. I shall refer to it as involving 'grammatical incoherence'. This term implies that the competence grammarian would characterise the syntactic surface structures involved as "ungrammatical". There is, however, no implication that there is any necessary semantic or communicative incoherence.

Speech of this sort does not typically involve distortions in word form. It does involve 'higher order constituents' – the 'clause' or 'sentence', insofar as these units can be identified in speech. It is of far more frequent occurrence than are 'slips of the tongue'. It characteristically passes uncorrected by the speaker. Whether it is undetected or not is, I believe, probably impossible to demonstrate; certainly it does not appear to involve more hesitation, pausing and the like than grammatically coherent speech. Similarly, it does not appear to be detected by the hearer, or, if it is, it does not generally seem to impede comprehension. Nor is it clear to me that it can, in any very straightforward sense, be held to involve 'deviance from the speaker's current ... grammatical ... intention'. Finally, I would hypothesise that typically it is not at variance with the speaker's cognitive intention. I would suggest that it is this last hypothesis coupled with the fact that grammatically incoherent speech does not involve distortion of word form that accounts for the fact that it passes uncorrected and does not apparently impede communication.

As an example of the sort of speech I mean, consider the following utterance. My fifteen year old daughter was stroking our cat, who is moulting, and holding up a hair asked:

1. How long do you suppose a life of a fur has?

Note that there were no pauses, no hesitations, no self-correction and no obvious sense of anomaly. Note furthermore, that there was the confident expectation of having conveyed a comprehensible message, a confidence that, in the circumstances, was not misplaced. This utterance illustrates two somewhat different kinds of grammatical incoherence – one associated with the selection of the item *fur,* and the other with the syntactic structure of the sentence as a whole. Let us consider each in turn.

First, the problem of fur. As a mass noun, this should not occur with an indefinite article. Since the speaker was holding a hair, we might suppose that fur was a 'replacement' for some other lexical item, *hair* perhaps, or a phrase ?*a piece of (the cat's) fur.* Subsequent enquiry elicited the information that while she was indeed in a sense talking about a particular hair, that hair was representative of the cat's 'fur' as a whole, and at an even greater level of abstraction was a representative of 'fur' as a generic category. It transpired that she had been learning about the 'life span' of human hair at school! Thus, there seems to have been a 'blending' of the generic and the particular at a very abstract level. This, you might think, is properly reflected in the surface blend *a fur.* We are not dealing here with a simple substitution, but with a surface form that might be analysed as capturing some of the complexity of the thought processes that can lie behind speech. This is not unlike what poets have done at a conscious level for centuries (cf. Empson's *Seven Types of Ambiguity*) and stylistics has fortunately progressed beyond the stage at which poetry was considered to be full of 'deviant sentences'. Part of the difficulty is that no single surface structure quite captures the complexity of the cognition behind the utterance. I shall refer to such blends as 'cognitive blends'.[1]

Let us now turn to the form of the sentence as a whole. Disregarding, for a moment, the interpolated *do you suppose,* we might perhaps analyse it as a blend of grammatical characteristics from some set of well-formed structures. These might include the following:

2. How long a life does a hair have?

(Note the constituent *How long a life,* the inverted interrogative form with DO support and, in final position, a form of HAVE)

3. How long a life has a hair?

(Again, the constituent *How long a life,* and the *has* form of HAVE)

4. How long is the life of a hair?

(Note the constituent *How long,* and also the phrase *the life of a hair*).

If we now consider the interpolated *do you suppose,* we observe that like (2), (3) and (4), it involves an inverted interrogative form, and that like (2) it involves DO support. For full grammaticality it can only be inserted at a constituent break:

5. How long a life, do you suppose, does a hair have? (cf. 2)
6. How long a life, do you suppose, has a hair? (cf. 3)

or

7. How long, do you suppose, is the life of a hair? (cf. 4)

Let us now return to the original utterance:

1. How long do you suppose a life of a fur has?

Observe first that the cognitive structure of all of the well-formed versions of (1) – i.e. (2–4) – is either the same or almost identical. This is perhaps reflected in the fact that the items which would receive phonetic prominence in these sentences are *how long, life,* and *fur.* These items also occur in the same order, and are similarly phonetically prominent in the grammatically incoherent (1). They are, of course, the principal 'semantic carriers' in the utterance. In all versions of the utterance the 'function words' (*do, a,* etc.) are phonetically non-prominent. It may perhaps be hypothesised that whatever machinery monitors cognitive well-formedness is satisfied with an appropriate sequence of phonetically prominent items, and pays little attention to the syntactic detail which causes the grammatical incoherence. This raises the question of how independent cognitive and syntactic monitoring may be held to be, and is a question to which I return later.

If we turn to consider the grammatical form of (1) a number of questions arise. To begin with we may ask ourselves why it is that grammatically incoherent speech of the sort illustrated seems to pass so frequently without self-correction or any other overt recognition of anomaly, when 'slips of the tongue' are very frequently corrected. Individuals apparently have far greater tolerance of grammatical malformation than they do of distortions of word form, and judgements of grammatical niceity are notoriously variable – a fact which has long been recognised by descriptive linguists even with respect to the written language. This leads one to suggest that the systems that monitor grammatical well-formedness do not have access to the same kind of well-formedness constraints as the systems that monitor word form. Some scholars have suggested that in the case of 'slips of the tongue' there is a late monitoring function that checks word form by reference to a lexicon of some sort. It is surely inconceivable to suppose any analogous process with syntactic form (checking syntactic form against a list of well formed structures!). Indeed attempting to account for the incoherence of examples like (1) in terms of a blend of surface structures seems to me to run into considerable difficulties. If it is structures that are blended then the *structures* at issue must be something like those shown in (2–7); but then we must postulate a very complex mechanism for producing the blend, since words from all of (2–7) are selected to produce (1), and the total structure of (1) does not correspond to any of the well formed (2–7). It is perhaps less complex to hypothesise that what is involved is a set of abstract grammatical *processes*. The process involved I have represented as 'interrogative inversion' (shared by 2, 3); DO support (shared by (2) and the interpolated *do you suppose*); the formation of the correct form of *have* (shared in different ways by 2, 3); the formation of constituents (shown by 2, 3 and 4). Suppose that some monitoring function is satisfied if the appropriate processes have been carried out – and in a sense, as you can see, they have: we have *DO* support (but only once in *do you suppose* rather than twice), we have interrogative inversion, we have a form of *HAVE,* and we have the interpolation of *do you suppose* at a place that is consistent with some appropriate constituent break.

Exactly how one might formulate such processes is not at all clear. A formalisation in terms of a 'standard theory' transformational grammar would seem to be able to account for some data of this general type (cf. Fay, forthcoming, for some discussion), but it is not clear to me that such an approach would always be very fruitful, and in the particular example at issue does not seem to be very insightful. This is perhaps because models such as that appealed to by Fay are 'competence' models, and such models may not be the most suitable for use as a description of 'performance'. That being said, however, it does seem that a 'process' approach is more fruitful than a 'structural' approach. (cf. for some pertinent comments on this Quirk, 1972: 123ff.).

In the example at issue, and this seems to be typical of many such examples, all the different grammatical structures available seem to be in free variation, so that no communicative difference would ensue if one rather than another is chosen: in a sense it hardly matters that the structure uttered shares the characteristics of a variety of well-formed structures. Cases like this do not seem to involve the blending of several slightly different cognitive structures, as I would argue what I have called cognitive blends do, rather they appear to involve the incompatible selection of abstract grammatical characteristics of a number of different surface forms that do not in themselves have any clear communicative difference. I shall refer to such structures as involving 'process blends'.

In both types of incoherence so far discussed, we may suppose that the incoherence arises from the fact that the speaker has available a number of conflicting 'plans': the incoherence arising from the selection of some features from each plan. Not all instances of incoherence seem to be amenable to such a general description. For example, consider utterances like:

8. It's about the police I'd like to talk about.
9. Now + in one of last week's + er Sunday papers + somebody wrote in and said that er the BBC should be + taken up on the Trades Description Act ...

It is the repetition of the preposition that is at issue. In both cases the source of the difficulty is not hard to pinpoint, and it is clear in such cases that the utterances could not appropriately be accounted for in the same way as was discussed with respect to process blends and (1). In the case of (8) one may hypothesise that the speaker announces a topic, using a conventional structure for this – he starts a cleft sentence: *It's about the police*. But by the time he comes to articulate the rest of the sentence, the details of English surface grammar (in this case the cohesion between *talk* and *about*) force him to repeat the preposition and lead him to grammatical incoherence. It may be observed that:

10. It's about the police I'd like to talk.

seems itself somewhat anomalous, and the well-formed:

11. It's the police I'd like to talk about.

does not seem to have quite the same force as the original utterance, since the clefted constituent is the NP *the police* rather than the PP *about the police*.

Two observations are relevant here. Firstly it would not seem unreasonable to hypothesise that the speaker has a relatively complete, though perhaps sketchy, cognitive structure in mind, but that a syntactic form for the whole of this structure has not been formulated before the utterance begins. The 'skeleton + constituents' model that Clark &

Clark (1977: 248–9; 262–4) propose seems appropriate here (cf. also the type of model proposed in Fry, 1969). Topicalisation of one constituent leads the speaker into incoherence, since he has topicalised a constituent that cannot be successfully formed into a grammatical utterance.

The second observation is that incoherence of this kind cannot realistically be accounted for in terms of the blending of some set of well-formed structures, since no competing set of structures can be found. It is impossible to set up an 'ideal delivery' or set of 'ideal deliveries' (cf. Clark & Clark, 1977: 261) in such cases, since as the discussion has tried to show, there is no fully grammatical 'ideal delivery' that quite captures the speaker's communicative intention.

I shall refer to incoherence of this type as 'topicalisation incoherence'. It is a type of incoherence that is common in all kinds of topicalised structures. We have been talking here of the topicalisation of prepositional phrases, consider also, however, question sentences (where we may analyse the *wh*-word as topicalised):

12. Who would like me to throw a piece of chalk at him + if anyone would.

and relative clauses (where we may analyse the relative pronoun as topicalised within its constituent):

13. For my birthday I was given a model aeroplane + which when you wind up it flies.

As with the intrusive preposition in (8) we find intrusive pronouns in (12) and (13) and may hypothesise the same sort of cause.

A different type of incoherence may be found in utterances like:

14. That is a suggestion for which I am all.

The problem lies with the cohesion between *all* and *for,* the attempt to topicalise *a suggestion,* and the inappropriate fronting of *for* in the relative formation. If *for* had not been fronted then all might have been well (or at least better!):

15. That is a suggestion I am all for.

but perhaps the analogy of well-formed structures like:

16. That is a suggestion for which I am grateful.

forces the error. It is pertinent to observe that (14) cannot reasonably be held to involve a blend – since it is not clear what could be involved in the blending. One might hypothesise that a grammatical process, which in many cases causes no problem (cf. 16) has here been wrongly applied. This supports the notion of the cognitive reality of grammatical processes argued for in the discussion of (1) earlier. I will refer to incoherence of this sort as 'process incoherence'.

Another type of incoherence that can be illustrated with prepositions involves cases where structures involving prepositions are co-ordinated, or where a prepositional phrase is interpolated. This often leads to incoherence either in the selection of the prepositions or in some associated structure. Consider examples like:

17. A loss of wages about the overtime + about thirty five pounds a week.

One might suggest that the first *about* is an anticipation of the *about* in *about thirty five pounds a week*. I suppose one could postulate an 'ideal delivery' on the lines of: *a loss of wages from overtime of about* ... but this approach is questionable since it may not reflect the speaker's intention. *About* may have the sense of 'in the matter of' (cf. *I want to see you about working overtime*). There is also the problem of the ellipsis, if that's the right way of considering the matter, of *of*. What seems to be at issue here is incoherence caused by co-ordination. Let us refer to this as 'co-ordination incoherence'. Incoherence of this type is similar to that suggested with topicalisation incoherence in that one may hypothesise that the speaker has not processed his speech forms sufficiently far ahead to anticipate grammatical problems that will arise from a particular co-ordination.

A pattern that frequently emerges in this sort of grammatical incoherence is that of three clauses A, B and C. A and B are coherently structured, as are B and C, but the whole sequence A B C is not. Here is an example:

18. ... if the Right Honourable Gentleman could tell me + what was involved in spraying a bus queue with machine gun fire + that kills people and injures people + what that is supposed to do for the future of the community on either side + I just cannot sum up ...

As with other types of incoherence, no self-correction ensues. If we were to hypothesise as to why this may be, we might perhaps take a cue from studies of speech perception. Bever (1972: 105) summarises some recent research as follows:

'During a clause we accumulate information and hypotheses concerning its potential deep structure; at the end of the clause, we decide on the structure of what we have just heard' (Abrams & Bever, 1969). More recent research has suggested that once its internal structure is decided on, the external representation of a clause is erased from short term storage. The surface structure of sentences in running texts is forgotten after only a few clauses (Sachs, 1967 [...] While immediate recall of the *meaning* of the first clause of a two clause sentence is virtually perfect, free recall of the exact words is distinctly worse than recall of the exact words in the second clause (Jarvella, 1970; Jarvella & Herman, 1972) [...] The following picture of speech perception emerges from these studies. During a clause a listener isolates major phrases and projects a possible internal organisation for the semantic relations between the phrases. At the end of each clause a structure is assigned, and the external form of the clause is erased from immediate memory.

If this should be true of perception, might it not be equally true of production? Perhaps it would be amenable to experimental testing, though I am not aware of anyone who has tried to test it.

A somewhat different type of incoherence can be illustrated in the following (from a phone-in-programme):

19. You also realise of course that apart from denying + certain people who can't actually go to matches + the right to see it + and enjoy it + you are also denying smaller teams + the chance to get the money + that television eh + brings to the game.

It is the use of *it* in lines 2 and 3 that is at issue. There is clearly no anaphor for this pronoun in the verbal text. One would need to hypothesise that some 'mental referent' is available to the speaker: 'football' or the like. Note that while no communicative difficulty results, there is grammatical incoherence. This sort of pronominal usage is not uncommon in unscripted conversations. A similar instance involves an example like the following, where the 'same' pronoun may in two sucessive mentions have two distinct referents:

20. A: I just like to have friendly discussions and + you know + pass over purely your + own views of + you know + what you want to talk about.
    B: I mean + they they don't even show you what + I mean + when we get RE + when we had it in first year + and second year + the man that gave us it + ...

In cases of this sort surface grammatical incoherence can result, and I will, therefore, refer to it as 'referential incoherence'. This is not entirely a happy term however, since in the majority of cases, as in those shown, there is no referential obscurity or communicative difficulty, and the grammatical anomaly will pass without notice. This is not, of course, to deny that there are occasions when referential obscurity results and this may need to be corrected by either the speaker or his interlocutor (cf. Grimes, 1975, for discussion of similar examples).

The last type of incoherence I'd like to mention briefly involves lexical selection. Goldman-Eisler (1968) has shown that there is a relationship between pause behaviour, either filled or unfilled, and lexical choice. It has been hypothesised that one of the functions of pausing is to enable lexical searches to be carried out:

21. I don't think any policeman wants a + wants a medal for + for eh the profession which he's in.

Lexical selection of this sort can lead to incoherence – of a type we may refer to as 'selection incoherence'.

22. I feel that the press eh eh in a lot of cases give us a a bad publicity.

The problem once more involves 'count' nouns *(a bad public image)* and 'mass' nouns *(bad publicity)*. Uncertainty in selection causes grammatical anomaly, but no communicative difficulty.

I have tried to identify a number of different types of grammatical incoherence. It is obviously true that these do not form anything like a complete taxonomy (one could easily think of other types of incoherence) and they are not mutually exclusive (in that some examples may be held to result from more than one type of incoherence). On the other hand I believe these types of incoherence are sufficiently different to warrant a variety of descriptive labels.

I identify two types of 'blending': 'cognitive' and 'process' blends. In the case of cognitive blends, we may hypothesise a blending of a number of slightly different cognitive structures, each of which would have a distinct surface realisation: cf. discussion of *a fur* from (1). In the case of process blends I suggest there is a single cognitive structure which may be realised by a number of surface forms and the resultant utterance is a blend of the processes that lead to these different forms (a blend, note, of the processes, not the forms themselves); cf. discussion of the syntactic form of (1).

I identify three types of incoherence I do not believe can be analysed in terms of 'blending': 'topicalisation' incoherence, 'co-ordination' incoherence and 'process' incoherence. In the first, incoherence results from the topicalisation of a constituent that the structure chosen cannot appropriately topicalise (example 8). In the second case, co-ordination leads to incoherence (example 17). In both cases we may hypothesise that the structure has not been pre-planned sufficiently far ahead. The third type of incoherence is the result of the misapplication of some grammatical process (example 14).

My final two types of incoherence are 'referential' and 'selectional' incoherence. In the former case pronominal reference leads to surface ungrammaticality; in the latter case lexical selection leads to incoherence.

As I said at the beginning of this paper such incoherence is of a type that apparently escapes the monitoring systems, it does not in general cause communicative difficulty and it does not, in general, result in self-correction etc. Various obvious characteristics of conversation may account for this. I would like to mention three.

Firstly, conversation is typically made up as it goes along. There must be some pre-planning, but this pre-planning must vary from the very specific to the very general. Anticipatory slips of the tongue (cf. Boomer & Laver, 1968; Fromkin, 1971) would seem to suggest some highly specific pre-planning and this has led scholars like Laver (cf. 1977a) and Fromkin (cf. 1971) to postulate rather specific models of speech production. There is also, however, evidence for less specific pre-planning. Difficulties that arise in what I have called 'selectional incoherence' suggest that the speaker sometimes has only the most general idea of what is to be the specific lexical item to be selected as, say, the object of a verb. Similarly, 'topicalisation' incoherence suggests that the speaker selects a topic before fully planning the linguistic form of the topicalised construction as a whole. The sort of model of speech production postulated by Fry (1969) would seem to be more appropriate to account for this incoherence than the rather more 'static' models of Fromkin, etc. mentioned above.

Secondly, conversation has to do with the communication of meanings (and I mean 'meanings' in a wide sense to include 'social' and 'attitudinal' meanings as well as 'cognitive' meanings (cf. Lyons, 1977)). I have previously quoted Bever's observations on the hearer's comprehension of speech in which he hypothesises that surface form is 'forgotten' once a meaning has been assigned to it, and suggested that this is likely to be as true for the speaker as it is for the hearer. If this is so, it would account for 'co-ordination' incoherence. Providing the meaning is coherent, then perhaps the speaker is literally unaware that his syntax is incoherent.

My third obvious generalisation is that conversation is interactive. The speaker must rely on the hearer to reconstruct for himself the meaning that he wishes to convey. The hearer must use a variety of strategies for this, including his powers of inference. Evidence of this ability is shown in one participant in a conversation 'shadowing' another –

23. ... but I remember I took the decision (to wear) yes if I wear those I'll feel better (the bracketted *to wear* is the other participant in the conversation).

Some of Goldman-Eisler's experiments seem to bear this out (Goldman-Eisler, 1968). I suggest that communicative confusion is avoided in the cases of referential incoherence for this reason.

One would like to hope that in time we may be able to establish a taxonomy of such incoherence rather in the manner that other scholars have achieved a taxonomy of tongue slips. It seems to me, however, that the behavioural evidence of grammatical incoherence is of a somewhat different sort from that seen in 'slips of the tongue'. It may be that perception of grammatical form and hence the nature of the monitoring processes involved is of a different nature from that of tongue slips, perhaps because such incoherence does not involve distortion in word form. I believe, however, that grammatical incoherence will provide as interesting a 'window on the mind' as do tongue slips.

Note

1. In his closing remarks, the Chairman of the final session of the Workshop uttered the following (with no pause etc.):
   [...] the organisers of the conference have done an incredible amount of job [...]
   We might analyse this as an example of a cognitive blend expressing a sentiment with which the participants would doubtless agree!

BERNARD J. BAARS

The competing plans hypothesis: An heuristic viewpoint on the causes of errors in speech

Scientific study of the "inner workings" of the complex and high-speed processes of speech production has long been thought difficult, in the absence of direct experimental control over covert processes in the planning and execution of speech. For this reason both psychologists and linguists since the 1890s have used collections of speech errors to gain some insight into this otherwise inaccessible system (e.g., Meringer, 1908; Freud, 1901; Fromkin, 1973). However, one cannot make causal inferences about spontaneous speech errors, and for this reason we have conducted a research program to develop a number of new techniques for inducing complex, high-level and predictable errors under conditions of excellent experimental control. As a direct consequence of these methodological advances we have found new evidence regarding (1) the planning of serial-order action, (2) covert editing of speech plans, and (3) the first rigorous demonstrations of the existence of 'Freudian slips'.

In this paper we attempt some generalizations from the research program. It appears that all laboratory methods to date for eliciting speech errors work by (1) *inducing competition* between alternative plans for production, and (2) *restricting the time* available for choosing between the alternatives and for resolving internal errors. This approach is called the Competing Plans Hypothesis and using it we have been able to induce spoonerisms, word-blends, subject-object reversals, and word-switches between the phrases of a sentence. It is clear that the resulting errors need not *look like* a product of the two competing plans. For example word-blends have traditionally been considered the result of internal competition between two lexical items for the same place in an utterance, and indeed we can create experimental competition between words that result in such blends. But spoonerisms and word-exchanges, which do not look like fusions, can also be produced by means of internal competition. Thus spoonerisms (which involve a switch of phonemes) can be induced by creating competition between two *word*-orders, and an exchange of words can be elicited by confusing subjects about the order of two *phrases*. It may be generally true that an order conflict between higher-level units will result in an exchange of subordinate ones.

The Competing Plans Hypothesis (CPH) is compared to other possible causal theories for speech errors. The Weak Causal Hypothesis would claim that errors result from random noise in the system, and the Wrong Plan Hypothesis that the error is introduced from the top down. Both hypotheses are heuristically uninteresting. Stronger claims are made by a Derivational Cut-Off Hypothesis (such as is currently proposed by Fay, forthcoming), and a Stage Desynchronization Hypothesis (Fry, 1969; Reich, 1975). Where possible this paper attempts to compare these types of theory to the CPH.

The preference for the CPH rests on the following grounds. (a) It is consistent with known properties of complex executive systems including human motor systems; (b) It has considerable, and growing, experimental backing; (c) It has been proposed in one form or another by a number of previous workers for more restricted cases, and (d) It can be related in a very natural way to the literature on pauses in speech. Finally, (e) the CPH leads to a viewpoint of speech production which differs considerably from the standard 'hierarchical' approach; one which I believe is more valid, interesting, and workable than the conventional view. That is, the CPH leads to a conception of *normal* error-free speech as inherently involving a consideration of alternative plans for production which are reviewed and edited prior to speaking. The system naturally contains ambiguities which are resolved most of the time by context-sensitive sub-systems. Indeed one could defend the proposal that *any* system faced with solving the problems of speech production will occasionally emit errors. Speech errors thus reflect a positive and useful property of a workable, complex, fast-acting and context-sensitive action system; they are the price we pay for our ability to express ourselves so well.

I. Introduction

A. The study of errors in speaking is, curiously enough, in its second infancy without ever having passed through an intervening period of maturity. The 1890s saw strong interest develop in slips of the tongue as a way of investigating the speech production system, part of the great *Sprachpsychologie* movement that came out of German psychology and linguistics primarily. Wundt, Paul, Meringer, J.H. Jackson (in a related tradition) and ultimately Freud made major contributions to our thinking about speech breakdowns, only to be ignored in most academic work in psychology and linguistics for the first half of the twentieth century. The year 1951 saw the publication of two influential papers that suggested a revival of interest in these problems: Lashley's paper on the problem of serial order in behavior, and Wells' essay on "predicting slips of the tongue" (see Fromkin, 1973). This interest has since increased, especially by MacKay's work in psychology (1970, 1971, 1972, 1973, 1976, forthcoming) and Fromkin's papers in linguistics (1968, 1971, 1973).

Current indications are that this trend is becoming more and more widespread (e.g., Garrett, 1975; Motley, 1973; Fromkin, forthcoming). There is increasing experimental interest in eliciting predictable speech errors under known conditions (MacKay, 1971; Baars, 1977; Baars, forthcoming; Baars & Motley, 1976; Baars, Motley & MacKay, 1975), and this work is now being extended to more kinds of speech errors.

B. In spite of the tentative character of the information we have to date, there is already enough of it to make some sort of heuristic framework necessary. This essay is intended to present such a unifying viewpoint for our current knowledge. Undoubtedly it will change as more information becomes available, but I believe the time has come to make explicit what we know to date, and how we can organize this knowledge.

I will argue that speech errors may best be viewed as an overt manifestation of *ambiguity* in an output system (Greene, 1972); i.e., there are *competing plans* (each of which may be correct) which have failed to be reconciled prior to execution. This view fits well with a more general conception of the speech production system as an actively planning executive system, generating alternative plans for conveying different shades of meaning. The competing plans may both be linguistically correct, differing only in some semantic or stylistic way which would normally tend to create a preference between them. The anomalous plan that results from a fusion of the two original plans may become overt when there is a *failure to edit* (due to lack of time, attentional load, and so on); nonetheless, an overt error need not appear as a perfect fusion between the two plans, because some reconciliation processes may have started to apply to the anomalous plan prior to utterance. We now have good experimental evidence for exactly these processes in the cases of spoonerisms, word-exchanges in compound sentences, and blends.

The Competing Plans Hypothesis (CPH) is a causal hypothesis which suggests what may have triggered the error, but does not necessarily predict the final form of the error. That implies that it does not conflict with other hypotheses about errors which do concern themselves primarily with error patterns, such as MacKay's Incomplete Specification Hypothesis and Fromkin's Disordering Hypothesis. Unfortunately, there are not many well worked-out models that deal with the proximate cause of errors, as CPH does. Some examples of alternative viewpoints will be developed and discussed in the following section.

II. Some possible causes of speech errors

What gives rise to speech errors? I would like to consider this question apart from the more usual one that asks "What accounts for the ultimate *form* of the error?" – since an answer to the first question may well open up the second one to experimental investigation. First of all, it must be conceded that the question may not have a unitary answer: Different errors may have different causes. Worse than that, any one error may be caused in more than one way; we have experimental evidence to indicate that spoonerisms, for example, can be elicited in at least *two* ways (Baars & Motley, 1976). But let us put all such complications aside for the moment to consider the problem in the abstract.

A. The Random Cause Hypothesis. Perhaps the weakest general theory of speech errors might suggest that like any control system, the speech production system has some level of random "noise" which could occasionally rise above a response threshold to trigger a random error (Dell & Reich, 1977). Along with Meringer (1908) and all subsequent writers on the subject, we might object that "das Versprechen ist geregelt" – errors appear too systematic to be accidental. A more sophisticated proponent of such a Random Cause Theory of speech errors might then proceed to argue that, true, the error as it *appears* is systematic due to rule-application and so on, but the proximate *cause* of the error may have been random. Indeed, this argument could be carried through almost indefinitely if its hypothetical proponent were stubborn enough, and it could not be refuted by *post-hoc* argumentation at all. The only way to test the Random Cause Theory is to actually cause errors to occur in situations where random noise is controlled.

The main point I would like to make about the Random Cause Theory is its infertility – it is not necessarily an unreasonable theory, but its heuristic value is almost nil unless one could think of a way to manipulate noise in the speech control system. Its chief function here is to create a back-drop for stronger proposals, which are also more testable.

B. Incorrect Input Hypothesis. Again, let's consider another hypothetical suggestion, which may be called the Incorrect Input Hypothesis. This simply states that the input to the speech control system receives an incorrect plan and carries it out as it would any other plan. Obviously, the question arises in what sense this would be considered an error at all – certainly when people make deliberate errors this is distinguished from involuntary ones. Work in our laboratory indicates that when people are asked to make *voluntary* speech "errors", a different pattern emerges from the one that is observed in the real world. For example, when people are asked to voluntarily create spoonerisms from targets such as "fried soup", they will say "sried foop". But the initial /sr-/ does not exist in English, and is hardly ever reported in natural errors, nor is it ever observed in our experimentally elicited spoonerisms (e.g., Baars & Motley, 1976).

C. Derivational Cut-Off Hypothesis. Speech errors may be caused by a perfectly normal plan that is being developed, but which is caused to be executed before it is completely ready. Thus one may be forced to perform lexical insertion before some obligatory "neg movement" transformation, and the result would be a negative particle in the wrong clause, such as in the hypothetical example (adapted from Fromkin, 1973):

Intended: People don't agree that it's well-formed, ———→
Error: People agree that it's not well-formed.

(i.e., the abstract "neg" has remained in the embedded clause, incorrectly).

In general, the Cut-Off Hypothesis implies that such errors would occur if one somehow hurried the process of speaking, and it is true that the number of errors does rise when people are made to speak fast (as Wundt found out in the first recorded experimental manipulation of speech errors). However, any hypothesis that assumes one needs a minimum "time-to-completion" or "time to edit" would make the same prediction. To test this notion properly, one would have to propose some detailed production grammar in which certain sentences needed to go through, say, a particle-movement and others did not. Then one could see how people err on the two different sentence-types when they are made to speak fast.

Until recently it was true to say, as Fromkin did in 1973, that "no one suggests that transformations are actually applied in the production of an utterance." However, Fay (forthcoming) cites a number of errors which could be so interpreted. Alternative explanations come readily to mind however, so that it is difficult to decide the question one way or another.

D. Stage Desynchronization Hypothesis. There are two interesting proposals of this kind (Fry, 1969, in Fromkin, 1973; and Reich, 1975). The basic notion is that speech production proceeds according to the traditional levels of structural analysis, but that in a performance model, each level must be offset in time so that processing of some element occurs earlier at a semantic level than at a syntactic one, etc., down to the motor commands (Fig. 1, after Fry, 1969). In a sense, then, some such notion is taken to be necessarily true, given the general conception of speaking as a translation of meaning into articulation.

For example, one might be planning the next clause even while one says a word in the first clause. If one plans too far ahead, processing load may force a "skip" in the plan that is currently being executed. Conversely,

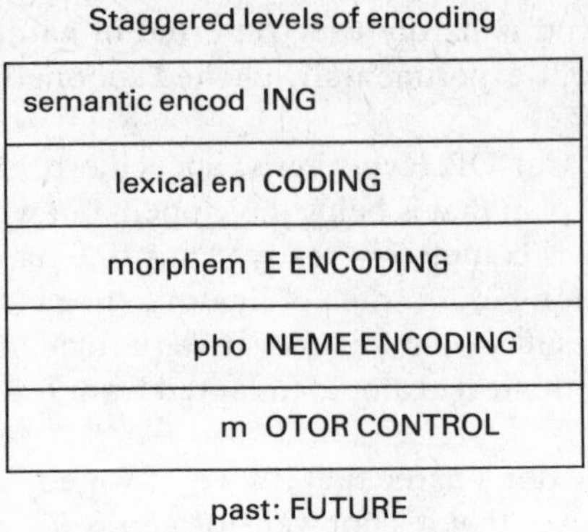

Staggered levels of encoding

semantic encod ING
lexical en CODING
morphem E ENCODING
pho NEME ENCODING
m OTOR CONTROL

past: FUTURE

Figure 1

one may forget that a plan has already been executed and do it twice, and so on.

According to Fry, "the time-lag between programs is variable, (but) it is probable that in normal error-free speech the range of variation is not very great and it is quite likely that any individual speaker has a preferred set of time-relations which he likes to keep to, within certain limits. When for some reason the time-relations change rather abruptly, perhaps because the time-lag has become uncomfortably large, then errors may occur which are triggered off by the new relation between one programme and another. If this happens, for example, between the phoneme programme and the morpheme and lexical encoding, there may be ANTICIPATION ERRORS at the phoneme level [...]". It is not quite clear to me why only a *single* phoneme would be anticipated if the whole level shifts.

All theories, without exception, have to account for anticipations and perseverations, so some sort of device for producing temporal shifts is needed. A scanner, operating over elements in a buffer memory is a common solution (MacKay, 1973, and others). It would be interesting to specify exactly in what ways Stage Desynchronization might differ from such a device. Perhaps there would be different buffers for each stage, overlapping in such a way as to permit interactions between stages.

The strongest evidence cited by Fry for Stage Desynchronization seems to come from *contractions,* such as [achievl] for "achievement level", and [asubtle yourself] for "observe subtlety yourself".

It seems to me that Stage Desynchronization can be reconceptualized in the following way. For any element in the output string there is a contingent series of control decisions that preceded it. The intended motor movement in the word "bad" must have been programmed at some point prior to its utterance. But prior to the initiation of the motor program there must have been a phonemic programmer (with phonotactic checks, and so on), and prior to that, some sort of lexical retrieval, etc. Each of these programs outputs a plan to some succeeding program, and it must *lose control* of that plan as it is passed on (though the buffer may retain a copy of the plan for checking by feedback from the lower level). If we throw a ball at a basket, we lose control over the ball not just at the time it leaves the hand, but prior to that by the amount of time which it would take to feed back and adjust for any errors. This would seem to be true for all levels of control. It may be for this reason that spoonerisms, for example, clearly violate semantic control, partly violate lexico-syntactic control, and virtually never violate phonotactic and motor control. The nature of this error seems to partition the traditional structural levels rather well. Therefore these stages should differ in terms of their "points of no return". Semantic control should be relinguished before lexico-syntactic control – at least if editing mechanisms do not cycle the control upward again. Such editing must always add more time to the process, however. It should be possible to test this kind of idea rather directly by means of experimentally elicited errors.

Although stages of programming would seem to be needed in every complete theory, one may question whether the Stage-Desynchronization Hypothesis can account for many errors when compared to a scanning hypothesis, which also deals with temporal order shifts. A rigid adherence to stages probably does not work well for the speech control system, and when Reich (1975) introduces a rapid alternation between stages as a feature of his theory, one wonders if there is any difference left between this model and others. There is considerable need here for interaction between proponents of superficially different theories, so that agreed-upon tests can be performed.

E. The Competing Plans Hypothesis. The Competing Plans Hypothesis (CPH) depends upon certain basic notions:

1. that very often in normal speech production, multiple plans are developed although only one is to be ultimately used;

2. that sometimes two correct plans of this kind will be forced into execution before one is clearly favored over the other;

3. that this may cause a "fused" plan for production, which is anomalous, and

4. that this anomalous plan may fail to be edited in time. For the purposes of this paper I would like to consider a "plan" as a *representation* of a reasonably complex action, existing prior to the action, and feeding into some set of programs and sub-goals which can carry out the action in detail. An "intention" is simply a conscious and reportable plan, which also serves as a superordinate plan to other, unconscious plans.

It should be obvious by now that I consider CPH the most attractive causal "umbrella hypothesis" for speech errors. There are a number of reasons for this:

a. It is consistent with known properties of complex executive systems in general, and the human nervous system in particular;

b. It has a considerable, and growing, amount of experimental backing, and is heuristically valuable in suggesting further methods of inducing errors;

c. If true, it will give us an opportunity for experimentally testing various forms of incomplete rule-application on the anomalous "fused" plan, which may provide deeper insight into the nature of the human production grammar;

d. Historically, the CPH has been widely suggested in the speech error literature under a variety of rubrics and limitations, so that this paper is really making explicit and general a thought which is quite old and very widespread;

e. The CPH leads to a viewpoint of speech production which is considerably different from the usual "derivational" approach; one which, I believe, is more valid, interesting, and workable than the conventional view;

f. It relates in a very natural way to other phenomena in speech production such as pauses;

g. Finally, Dell & Reich (1977) have proposed a simple and effective computer simulation based upon the idea of "spreading activation in a relational network", which resembles in some important respects the model proposed here.

Let me discuss some of these points in some detail.

Properties of complex executive systems. Greene (1972) has pointed out that working control systems have a great number of properties in common, regardless of their specific purpose. One of these is the use of subsystems separate from central executive control. A general in an army may want to give an overall direction to his subordinates, who, in turn, will translate it into a number of more specific commands, all the way down the line. The general certainly does not want to tell an infantry soldier to put one foot in front of the other, and this is so not merely because of limits to human memory and attention that do not permit the general to know and attend to everything. Rather, Greene argues, there are *in principle* limits on centralized control, so that in many different control systems the initial plan is not *fully* elaborated, focusing rather on "ball-parks" and leaving the elaboration and detailed execution of lower-level plans to subsystems. The problem is that while this is an efficient form of organization, it also permits certain problems to occur. Lower-level plans might contradict each other.

In the case of our general, if he directs a division to move along a road, lower-level elements may have to decide which regiment will move first along this limited-capacity channel (the road), because the higher-level command was not, and cannot be, explicit in every respect. Thus ambiguities arise as an inevitable consequence of complexity in control systems. In an extreme case of ambiguity, such tactical conflict may have to be "kicked upstairs" again, and become strategic in nature. However, cycling upward like this takes time so that the execution of the action is delayed, and lower-level forms of reconciliation would seem to be preferable.

To give some idea of the generality of this problem of ambiguity in control systems, let me cite some very disparate examples given by Greene (p. 304). "A person can perform the same action in many different ways; for example, he can write with his arm held high or low or loaded with a weight, or even with a pencil held in his teeth, and although his muscles move differently in each case, the same handwriting always results. An infinity of motions can lead to a single result [...] Surely [the] brain does not store [...] all the possible configurations of all his hand muscles [...] The nervous system avoids this storage through a style of motor control whereby *subsystems having many degrees of freedom* are governed by a central control system having a few degrees of freedom [...] The highest control center selects an appropriate combination that almost fits what it wants to do, and transformations at lower levels shape these combinations into a better approximation of the desired action". MacNeilage (1970) makes much the same point regarding the enormous flexibility of the speech production system.

The postural reflexes of the cat have been researched extensively and reveal the same control pattern:

> When a cat turns its head to look at a mouse, the angles of tilt of its head, and flexion and torsion of its neck will tune spinal motor centers in such a way that its brain has only to command "Jump!" and the jump will be in the right direction. In particular, the tilt and neck flexion combine additively to determine the degrees of extension of fore and hind limbs appropriate to each act of climbing up or down, jumping onto a platform, standing on an incline [...] These postures must be set as the act begins; for if they were entirely dependent upon corrective feedback, the cat would have stumbled [...] before the feedback could work. *A few of these reflex patterns of feedforward are adequate for the approximate regulation of all feline postures and movements required* [...] The cat's brain is thereby relieved of having to control all muscular degrees of freedom, for they are regulated by the lower centers.

A very different example can be given that is solved by the same principle:

> "Computer simulation of a distillation column accurately modeled by a forty-second order differential equation, showed that feedback alone could not

compensate for fluctuations of input composition [...] However, inexact feed-forward, computed from a crude second-order model of the column, compensated well enough so that feedback could maintain almost perfect stabilization of the output. The feedforward had only to bring the state of the system "into the ball-park" [...]"

"[...] Typically, pre-existing structure can substract out complexity, so that simple devices will work that could not handle general inputs [...]" (For this reason, one might expect to find *context-effects* in output systems as well as input. The effect of expectancy on speech errors is illustrated by the phonolog-ical-bias technique of eliciting speech errors, described below.)

"In typical cases [...] the executive always activates the system the way it did under standard conditions, while independent tuning systems modify the response generated by this standard executive signal. This separation of responsibility for activation and tuning, when it works, simplifies the control task [...] *the executive need not be aware of the tuning*" (italics added). This is a remarkable point, in view of the fact that all speech errors obey some of the rules, but are "blind" to other rules. It is most interesting that this blindness can be explained on grounds of general control principles. "The next time the executive tries to use the subsystem, it may be tuned differently [...] This uncertainty introduces ambiguities and errors into an executive system's mem-ory, commands, and communications [...]"

"Once these (descriptions of general "ball-parks") have been translated into a particular mathematical formulation, it becomes possible to prove how (they) mesh, in the sense that any ambiguities and errors to which they give rise [...] will remain confined within (the) ballpark [...] that is, confined to differences that can be corrected at low levels." The ambiguous responses then define an equivalence class. *"The equivalence classes, arising from seemingly trouble-some, proliferating ambiguity, may thus actually be the significant invariant units of information for stating commands* [...] in terms that can be meaningful without explicit knowledge of the changeable details of low-level realization."

The paradox is then that ambiguities are desirable, and indeed, neces-sary, in control systems – and that they sometimes can lead to real problems.

What evidence do we have for such phenomena in the planning and execution of speech? It is very clear that the detailed movement of speech articulators cannot be controlled from the highest level. Indeed, one of the dramatic facts about speaking is how much of it is left to unconscious mechanisms – we are not aware of the syntactic rules we use, of the details of lexical search, or of the detailed movements of the mouth. Moreover, as MacNeilage (1970) points out, such movements have enormous variability and flexibility. So it makes sense to assume that many details of speech are controlled by sub-systems which are not under the immediate control of an executive. The fact that highly rule-governed, involuntary errors are made overtly at all suggests that subsys-tems occasionally espace from executive control.

Can the subsystems be biased? And can such bias lead to internal competition? In our first attempts to elicit experimental spoonerisms, we had people look at rapidly exposed word-pairs such as /GO BACK/ GET BED/GOOD BOY/ followed by the target pair /BAD GOOF/. When the subjects were signalled immediately afterwards to recall the last word pair /BAD GOOF/ as quickly as possible, they often said /GAD BOOF/. Notice that we merely biased their expectations regarding the initial consonants of the word pair and made this induced expectancy *compete* with new input (Baars, 1977). This and other evidence indicates that specialized processors in speech can indeed have "local expectations" that can be independently manipulated, and which can produce actions outside of executive control. Furthermore Baars, Motley & MacKay (1975) and Baars (forthcoming) provide evidence showing that covert lexical and semantic errors, produced by internal competition, can often be edited out before they are made overtly. This implies, incidentally, that the flow of control in speech production can at times go *up into* the structural hierarchy, so that lower-level plans can be checked by higher-level criteria.

Finally, why are biological systems capable of making such errors? Possibly errors reflect an evolutionary dead-end, a non-functional result of adaptation. Much more plausible to me is the idea that there is a design trade-off in complex action systems, which work better if there are intelligent, semi-autonomous subsystems "with a will of their own" so that they can adapt flexibly to local changes. The price we pay for such intelligent decentralized control is an occasionally slip of tongue or lip. The awesome talkativeness of our species suggests that the price has been worth paying.

WOLFGANG WILDGEN

Models of verbal planning in the theory of catastrophes[1]

If one considers formal models in linguistics, one realizes that in spite of many controversies they are all founded on the formalism of elementary algebra and predicate calculus. The reason is that these models are fundamentally classificatory and static. Their view of language is one of levels, hierarchies, structures, sets of rules, mappings from one set of structures into another set of structures etc. Using the new formal language of catastrophe theory, there is the possibility of emerging from this restrictive paradigm – to see language in the light of its dynamics and creativity and in connection with other sorts of dynamics such as the dynamics of the external world with which we are confronted and the dynamics of our cognitive organization of experience and knowledge. The whole field of language research can thus be reorganized under dynamic aspects; it follows that psycholinguistic theory and especially theories of language production and language understanding are privileged domains for the application of dynamic models.

1. Some remarks on the language of catastrophe theory

I should first like to make some introductory remarks giving a rough idea of the theoretical language of Thom's theories, which underlie the application of his mathematical concepts to the human sciences. Catastrophe theory is a section of differential topology, i.e. it relies heavily on differential equations and their properties on one hand and on topological equivalences on the other hand. Key terms are: structural stability, dynamic fields, flows in dynamic fields, stable attractors and sudden jumps of dynamics from the field of one attractor to a dominant neighbouring field (= catastrophe). The central idea is that a set of fundamental equations of the internal variables x, y, ... such as $V = x^2$, $V = x^3$, $V = x^4$, ..., $V = x^2 y$, etc. allows a limited set of *unfoldings* i.e. of deformations by external variables (u, v, w, t, ...). Starting from the notion of topological equivalence of such unfoldings, Thom was able to formulate the classification theorem of elementary catastrophes, which was proved by Mather in 1969. Table 1 summarizes the technical result (Zeeman, 1977: 66).

Table 1

k: number of external variables	1	2	3	4	5	6
c: number of elementary catastrophes found (types)	1	2	5	7	11	(∞)

Intuitively this theorem states that one can only obtain a finite number of stable unfoldings if the space of external variables (= control variables) has less than six relevant dimensions. The elementary catastrophes can be interpreted as basic types of dynamic processes achieving stability.

2. A short outline of a dynamic model of semantics

2.1. A set of basic postulates

Postulate 1: The relation between linguistic sign and extralinguistic referent is not arbitrary, i.e. it is not simply a consequence of social conventions (cf. Lewis, 1969). A mapping from the natural morphology of objects and events into the morphology of language forms can be established. The invariants of this mapping from experience to language can be described within the framework of catastrophe theory.

In this outline we shall consider only the mapping between kernel sentences (clauses with one finite verb and without modifiers) and the states, events and actions they describe.

Postulate 2: Language is considered as an intermediate level of organization between the highly complex world we perceive and the multidimensional activities of the brain, which process perceptual information and store them in memory. The language level accomplishes a drastic reduction of the complexity in these two domains and a filtering of a small set of dominant traits. A model can be set up for this filtering of dominant traits using the concept of catastrophe which was introduced by René Thom.

A *catastrophe* in Thom's usage of the term is a very fast and sudden change in a continuous field of attracting (repelling) forces. While the underlying change effected by the external (control) parameters is smooth, the observable changes of the system are discontinuous. These discontinuous features are selected as the defining characteristics of the process.

Postulate 3: Basic semantic "gestalts" (kernel structures which are not decomposable in a simple way because of the complex dependencies between parts) can be derived from dynamic patterns with a maximum of four control parameters. They are called *semantic archetypes*.

The restriction to dynamic patterns which have a maximum of four control parameters is plausible but not absolutely decisive. Two considerations are important:

a) In the theory of elementary catastrophes, whose domain is determined by Thom's classification theorem (cf. Table 1), the number of control parameters c is not greater than five (if one postulates that the set of semantic archetypes is finite). The unfolding with five control parameters, called "wigwam", does not contain additional structural information.

b) The development of the brain can be understood as an internal reconstruction of the environmental field which the organism tries to control. It is plausible that the cerebral analogue of the four-dimensional environment is also four-dimensional (in an abstract sense, however).

These postulates give only a rough summary of a semantic theory based on recent developments in the mathematics of dynamic systems. For an introduction to this field and a fuller treatment of the theoretical claims and practical accomplishments of a dynamic theory of language the reader should consult Wildgen (forthcoming 1979), or the preliminary reports: Wildgen (1978 ab).

2.2. Two examples of semantic "gestalts" derived from elementary catastrophes

a) The "cusp"

The "cusp" has one internal variable; the starting potential is $V = x^4$. This function is unfolded by two external (control) parameters u and v: the unfolding function is: $V = x^4 + ux^2 + vx$. These functions stand for a huge class of functions which by smooth transformation of the system of coordinates can be reduced to this form. As we want to find the catastrophic lines of this unfolding, we first seek the attracting minima and repelling maxima of the field. This can be done by computing the first partial derivation to x: $\frac{\delta V}{\delta x} = 4x^3 + 2ux + v$. The critical points of V fulfill the equation (1):

(1) $4x^3 + 2ux + v = 0$

For the definition of the catastrophe we need the saddle points where new minima appear (or old minima disappear). We therefore compute the second partial derivation; for the saddle points the first and the second derivation is zero:

(2) $12x^2 + 2u = 0$ $(\delta^2 V/\delta x^2)$

The resolution of the system of equations (1) and (2) isolates the effect of the control parameters u and v, which govern the behaviour of the system. Equation (3) is the function called "cusp"; its graph is shown in figure 1 as a projection from the curved plane of critical points (equation 1) into the "bifurcation" plane of the control parameters (equation 3).

(3) $27v^2 + 4u^3 = 0$

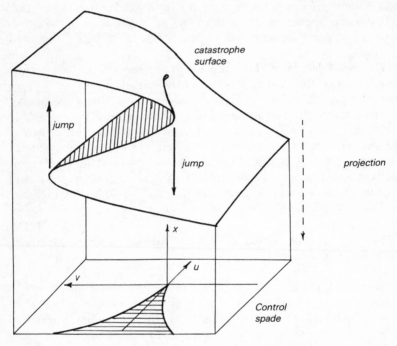

Figure 1

In figure 2 only the bifurcation plane and typical generic sections in it are shown. Processes along these section lines define the semantic "gestalts" or archetypes (in the terminology of R. Thom) of our dynamic theory of language.

The two stable minima in fig. 2, M1 and M2, are interpreted as the dynamic positions of noun phrases. Between the two legs of the cusp there is a conflict of minima which is resolved at the points (1, 2, 3, 4) in which the sections cross the cusp line (cf. ⊙ in fig. 2). The process jumps into the dominant minimum (cf. fig. 1). The type of process occurring in the neighbourhood of point 1 (cyclic section c in fig. 2) is characterized in scheme 1, whereas scheme 2 depicts the corresponding process in the neighbourhood of point 2.

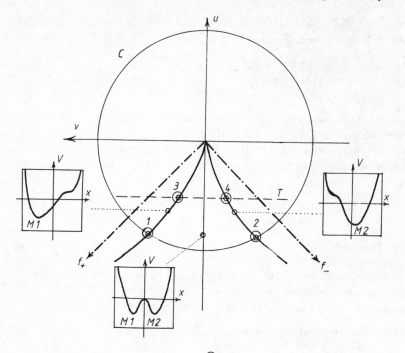

C, T = sections
f₊, f₋ = rotated axes

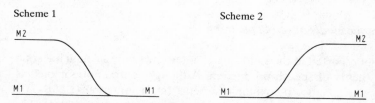

⊚ = bifurcation of the process
M1, M2 = minima of the function V

Figure 2

Scheme 1   Scheme 2

These dynamic structures can be interpreted as the archetypes of transi-
tive sentences, M1 being the subject, M2 the object. In scheme 1 the
object is *affected* or influenced by the subject. It may cease to exist, be
caught or be taken over by the subject which is not so radically affected
by the catastrophe.

Examples: The cat catches the mouse.
          Peter gets money.
          John puts his hat on.

In scheme 2 the object is *effected* (brought to life/existence, created, moved, thrown, ejected, given away).

Examples: John throws the ball.
Bill pays five dollars.
The firm dropped the employee.

Instead of taking directly the control parameters u and v as semantic dimensions, one can define two conflicting factors f_+ and f_- by a 135° rotation of the coordinates (cf. fig. 2). They are interpreted as semantic polarities. A process such as section T in fig. 2 catches the dynamic of a change.

Examples: The student woke up (f_+ = awake) versus
The student fell asleep (f_- = asleep)

b) The "butterfly"
Generic sections in the control space of this unfolding lead to the archetypes of sentences with three obligatory noun phrases. The third noun phrase corresponds to a minimum M3 which by a first bifurcation is separated from M1 and by a second bifurcation is integrated into M2.

Example: Eve gives an apple to Adam
M1   M3   M2

In the present context these derivations should only serve as an evidence of the existence of a semantic theory based on elementary catastrophes. In the following chapter aspects of the model of verbal planning which can be conceived on this basis will be presented.

3. A dynamic model of verbal planning

The model reported in the following chapter gives only a rough idea of a dynamic theory of speech production. Although central notions such as topological resonance of dynamic systems (cf. Thom, 1974: 198–209 and 220–227) and coupling of dynamic systems cannot be explained in the context of this paper, I hope that the informal hypotheses which the model conveys are worth considering when we analyse phenomena of speech production.
The basis of the process of speech production is a coupled dynamic field consisting of:
a) the field of outer and inner perceptions in the time interval $t: E(t)$,
b) the field of psychic excitations in the time interval $t: \varphi(t)$.
The product of these two fields is canonically mapped into the field of

efferent processes in the time interval $t':F(t')$. This mapping can be called *verbal planning*.

But this mapping is not immediate: there exists an intermediate level, which is that of semantic archetypes (or fundamental semantic "gestalts"). Whereas the coupled dynamics of $E(t) \times \varphi(t)$ are high-dimensional (Zeeman speaks of 10 billions of individual activities), the intermediate structure has at most four dimensions (cf. postulate 3). Thom starts from an analyzer A, which by optimizing the resonance of the input dynamics with an inventory of low-dimensional archetypes, selects an archetypal representation G. The archetypal pattern G must now be read, exploited. Thom suggests a sort of circular reading process which after a short time collapses into the attracting origin of the circle (cf. for example the circular section C in fig. 2). The characteristic catastrophes encountered specify the verbal nucleus of the sentence and in a secondary wave the attractors contained in the archetypal map are exploited, such that a first classificatory pattern is derived from the topological archetype.

These semantic archetypes are projected along different dimensions, which roughly correspond to word-classes, into a serial pattern. The serial pattern can now be used as input for the efferent mechanism. Considering the context in which the utterance would be placed at this moment and the possibilities of turn-taking, the speaker decides to utter the sentence or to keep it in his short-time memory, combining the feedback of this possible utterance with new dynamics coming from perception and memory or imagination. The inner speech is continued until the realization of the product of verbal planning is judged to be appropriate.

In most cases the feedback of preliminary results in verbal planning leads to a secondary wave of elaboration introducing modifiers, adverbials of time and place, sentential modifiers, relative clauses etc.

4. Some remarks relating Thom's model of verbal planning to the phenomenon of hesitancy

One of the merits of the reported model is certainly that it introduces a new formal language for the construction of theories of speech production. One could object however that its consequences for empirical work were trivial, that the model would do no more than translate our intuitive conjectures on the structure of verbal planning into the language of topology. It is true that the empirical consequences of Thom's model are not immediate. But good empirical descriptions must be explanatory and I will try to show that certain descriptions of hesitancy can gain explanatory force if their results are interpreted within the framework of Thom's model. The results of Goldman-Eisler can be taken as an example. She distinguishes between "old, well organized speech" and "new, organizing speech" and states: "The delays in the production of speech might accordingly be recognized as the "now" periods of speech organization" (Goldman-Eisler, 1958b: 67). The source of hesitation is located rather in a component of verbal planning called "mentation" than in the final stage called "action". Using Thom's model we can propose a finer classification of components of verbal planning, and derive more sophisticated hypotheses:

a) The input dynamics of speech production can be of different complexity or opacity. For example, on the very concrete level of the description of simple spatio-temporal processes it is rather easy to find those local accidents which can be mapped on a semantic archetype of the type mentioned above.

b) In the reading of a semantic archetype the speaker can choose different levels of complexity as the simpler catastrophes recur in the form of local structures in the higher catastrophes. This feature is very important if we want to describe reduced performance of learners and pidgin-speakers.

c) The realization of the semantic "gestalts", which are derived by "reading" the archetypal structure, is influenced by the availability of abstract lexical items.

Whereas the first two planning stages select the fundamental dynamics of the sentence (concentrated in the semantic base of the verbal constituent) and the role of nominal constituents, the third stage, at which the lexical fillers are chosen, presupposes a feedback loop comparing possible realizations with the input dynamics.

On the basis of this classification of levels of verbal planning some preliminary hypotheses can be stated:

a) The input dynamics become more complex in proportion to the increasing complexity of the task of perception, the internal structure of long term memory and psychic sensitivity.

b) The reading level seems to be rather stable. This explains the astonishing simplicity of our basic syntactic patterns. This level is only severely affected in situations of linguistic reduction (for example in child language, learner language, the language of aphasics).

c) The realization level increases in complexity with the growth of the lexicon; in this respect the amount of lexical alternatives for a specified situation is more decisive than the overall size of the lexicon. Many results of Goldman-Eisler can be attributed to this level.

It can be conjectured that level b) produces hesitancy only in the special situations mentioned above. Planning difficulties on level a) tend rather to influence turn-taking and initial hesitancy, whereas planning problems on level c) will cause hesitancy inside the realization of an utterance.

Note

1. This paper was written in the course of research supported by the Deutsche Forschungs-gemeinschaft. I would like to thank Prof. Jänich and Dr. Withmüller who introduced me to the mathematical field and Prof. Kramm whose mathematical advice was very valuable. I am especially indebted to Prof. Brekle for the support he gave to my research.

SABINE KOWAL and DANIEL C. O'CONNELL

Pausological research at Saint Louis University

We have referred to the research which we wish to discuss as "Saint Louis University" research because of the many other people who have contributed to the research in very significant ways. It is not our research, but the research of a team which we represent.

In our keynote address, we have already acknowledged our debt to Professor Goldman-Eisler (1968), and it is appropriate to repeat it here. The basic hypothesis of our research – a lawful relationship between temporal phenomena in human speech and concurrent cognitive processes – was taken from her, as well as a basic methodology, conventions such as a minimal cut-off point for silent pauses, and an assumption that variation of articulation rate accounts for relatively little temporal variance. She has also given us personal encouragement to pursue a program of carefully controlled experimental research. We have retained this tradition by and large, except that we have found articulation rate to be more variable than we at first expected, have extended our research to include more expressive and affective variables in addition to the cognitive ones, and are moving steadily toward more spontaneous and naturalistic speech genre.

In two specific matters, we have followed the lead of Maclay & Osgood (1959). We adopted their nomenclature of filled and unfilled pauses, repeats, and false starts, and originally at least, we shared their interest in localizing pauses relative to content and function words. But our findings were just the opposite of Maclay and Osgood's: Silent pauses precede function words disproportionately more often than content words in all of the various speech genre studied. From the very beginning of our research, we had opted for Goldman-Eisler's use of physical measurement for the identification of silent pauses. Maclay and Osgood's use of unaided listener judgment to localize pauses undoubtedly accounts for some of their idiosyncratic findings – and our disconfirmation thereof.

In general, our research has been concerned with several principal genre of speech: reading of prose and poetry, public speaking, retelling of stories after reading them, and narrations based on visual and/or auditory input. We have only recently begun to study more spontaneous dialogue. The principal themes of our studies have concerned unexpected semantic contents of readings and retellings, development over age and educational level, cross-linguistic comparisons and contrasts with German, English, and Spanish, a number of pathological groups: stutterers, aphasics, and schizophrenics, and finally expressive or rhetorical speech situations. Apart from the use of a Physioscript in our first experiment, we have produced level recordings of acoustic energy over time by means of a Brüel & Kjær audio frequency spectrometer (Type 2112) and level recorder (Type 2305). The principal response measures have been length, location, and frequency of silent pauses. We have accepted as a convention the minimal cut-off point of 270 milliseconds for silent pauses. Other response measures which have proved to be useful include frequency and location of filled pauses, number of false starts, repeats, and parenthetical remarks, speech rate and articulation rate in syllables per second, and a number of combinatorial measures derived from these. Words per second was considered too variable a measure from one speech genre or sample to another to be used reliably.

Our first study with Professor Hans Hörmann (O'Connell, Kowal & Hörmann, 1969) on the semantic determination of pauses convinced us of both the reliability of temporal measures and their sensitivity to experimental variation, and confirmed us in our suspicion that syntactic variables were being overemphasized in current psycholinguistic research to the neglect of semantic ones. An unusual turn of events literally gave readers and retellers of the story pause. The fact that the semantic influence extended into story retelling and altered its temporal pattern manifests both the retrospective function of pausing and the inadequacy of Markovian or probabilistic models of speech production.

Moreover, the pauses of adult native German speakers and native American speakers were later found to be more alike than those of either group were to adolescents in their own respective languages (O'Connell & Kowal, 1972b). In other words, to oversimplify a bit, foreigners don't speak faster; adults do.

This was the cue to look into developmental variables. Despite the failure of a number of other researchers to find developmental differences on temporal measures (Levin, Silverman & Ford, 1967), we now have overwhelming evidence from more than a thousand experimental subjects with a range of three to eighty years, and for native speakers of German, English, and Spanish, of consistent developmental shifts in the use of pauses and other temporal components of speech (Kowal, O'Connell & Sabin, 1975; Sabin, Clemmer, O'Connell & Kowal, forthcoming; Bassett, forthcoming).

Up to adulthood, speech rate increases and the frequency and length of silent pauses decrease accordingly as age or educational level increase. The gradual decrease in frequency of silent pauses seems to be a more sensitive indicator of development of speech skills than length of silent pauses. In our current research thinking, we have tentatively associated the length of silent pauses with the generation of meaning or a more cognitive aspect of processing, whereas we feel that frequency of silent pauses reflects structural aspects or linguistic execution of semantic planning. In any event, younger children are unable to think and talk at the same time.

Another finding is that parenthetical remarks are almost completely absent in younger children and do not become prominent until the teen-age years. Simply put, teenagers seem to be less tolerant of longer silences in their speech than younger children are. On the one hand, they have learned a new social orientation which makes silence increasingly intolerable; and on the other hand, they have developed the skills required to insert parenthetical remarks into their speech. In terms of temporal dimensions, therefore, speech development "seems to consist of learning to produce overt speech without the necessity of deliberate control" (Kowal, O'Connell & Sabin, 1975: 206).

In adulthood, we find, contrary to Mysak & Hanley (1958), a remarkable stability in speech rate and silent pause usage in particular, even beyond the age of seventy years.

Adults, however, at various stages in their learning of a foreign language, manifest a certain analogy to the speech production of younger children. With increasing proficiency in a foreign language, a corresponding decrease in both number and length of silent pauses in reading occurs (Kowal, O'Connell, O'Brien & Bryant, 1975).

Our cross-linguistic studies have by and large confirmed similarities in temporal phenomena across German, English, and Spanish. These results, along with a number of findings in the literature reviewed by O'Connell & Kowal (1972b), for English and Dutch, Hindi, Japanese, Spanish, and English, and Japanese and English comparisons respectively, suggest, as we stated there, "the possibility that further cross-linguistic comparisons may prove speech rate within a certain range to be another language universal" (p. 163). An exception to the similarities across languages is the finding that Spanish speakers use more silent and vocal hesitations (repeats, false starts, and parenthetical remarks) than an American control group, with the exception of filled pauses (Johnson, O'Connell & Sabin, 1979). The high incidence of Spanish words ending in an unaccented vowel precludes extensive use of the conventional filled pause "uh". Without a knowledge of Spanish phonology in this instance, an analysis of the pausological variables would be quite misleading.

Interestingly enough, our study of a bilingual little girl at the age of five years indicates that she already uses a considerable number of filled pauses in English, but replaces filled pauses with the parenthetical remark "este" when she speaks in Spanish (Johnson, forthcoming b).

To date, we have pursued two projects in sociolinguistics. Low-socioeconomic urban kindergarten children used much longer, but fewer silent pauses than middle- or high-socioeconomic urban children in telling a story. Remarkably, by second grade, school socialization processes eliminate all such differences; the lower-socioeconomic level has caught up with the others in these respects (Bassett, O'Connell & Monahan, 1977). A similar study in Spanish investigated rural lower class children and urban upper and lower class children in the second grade in Guatemala. The urban poor were strikingly different from the other two groups: Although they articulated faster, their silent pauses were twice as long (4.5 seconds on the average), though of the same frequency, as those of the other groups (Bassett & O'Connell, 1978). In general, low-socioeconomic urban children need more time to produce less speech than other groups in comparable situations.

The differences we have noted thus far in our developmental, cross-linguistic, and socioeconomic studies could hardly be termed deficiencies in any pathological sense. We turn now to several groups whose speech is clearly pathological: stutterers, aphasics, and schizophrenics. In engaging research with these groups, we have started from the general tenet that pathological speech production will be reflected in temporal measurements, since their sensitivity and reliability for revealing cognitive planning and execution processes is empirically beyond doubt. In short, the question is how do pathological speakers make use of their available time?

Preliminary results from fourth grade stutterers compared to their peers indicate that the stutterers need more time for narrations told about cartoon pictures. Even though their stories are themselves shorter, their silent pauses are both more frequent and longer. We are continuing investigation of stutterers of both younger and older age levels (Baranowski, forthcoming).

Our aphasic patients show a decrease in speech rate across all speech genre (reading, retelling, and narration) in proportion to the severity and location of cortical damage and inversely to the length of remission time after stroke (Sabin, forthcoming). For example, across all patients and speech tasks, the speech rate two weeks after stroke is 2.20 syllables per second. After four weeks it is 2.45 syllables per second, and after eight weeks, it is 2.65 syllables per second. The comparable figure for a non-aphasic adult is 3.50 syllables per second. Once again, the extraordinary sensitivity of temporal measurements is manifest. We are continuing analyses of the patterning of silent pauses in these patients at the present time.

A group of adult schizophrenics was compared to a matched group of normals in a reading and retelling task. The schizophrenics required an unusual amount of time to read the passage, largely because of a great number of extra erroneous syllables – a finding quite in accord with the traditional concept of the schizophrenic as deficient in reality orientation (Brown, 1973). Or to put it another way: The real world, as portrayed in words, must somehow be transduced cognitively into the schizophrenic's unreal world – and that takes time (Clemmer, forthcoming).

There is another shift in adulthood which involves a decrease in speech rate and a corresponding increase in number and length of silent pauses. However, this shift is not in any sense a function of some deficiency such as pathology or lack of experience. Rather, it characterizes speech situations, which could be called expressive or rhetorical. In our own research, we have studied the following: dramatic readings, public speaking, poetry, and glossolalia.

In such speech production in particular, we have found that the assumption of a relatively invariant articulation rate is not tenable. A good part of the variance of temporal measurement is accounted for in such speech by syllabic prolongation.

In a study in which church lectors, beginning drama students, and advanced drama students read a passage from St. Paul's "First Letter to the Corinthians", we found that skilled dramatic artists use both a faster articulation rate and speech rate than ordinary church lectors (Clemmer, O'Connell & Loui, forthcoming). The dramatic artists also used fewer, but longer silent pauses, a pattern which both expert and ordinary listeners judge to be optimal.

In a study of two levels of spontaneity, a group of radio homilists was compared to a group addressing a live audience. As expected, the group addressing a live audience spoke at a slower speech rate, made use of longer silent pauses, and could accordingly be characterized as the more spontaneous of the two groups. More importantly, however, the rhetorical function of both situations distinguished them from the much faster speech rate of ordinary adult readings (Szawara & O'Connell, 1977).

An even more dramatic departure from ordinary adult reading rate is to be found in the expressive reading of poetry. Relative to ordinary rates for prose readings, the speech rate for poetry reading was found to be considerably slower (Kowal, O'Connell, O'Brien & Bryant, 1975). When recordings by authors of modern poetry were in turn compared with such poetic readings, the authors' readings were extraordinarily slow in speech rate and made use of longer and more frequent pauses. In fact, these are the slowest reading rates in adults we have found to date:

E. E. Cummings reads "Buffalo Bill" at 2.27 syllables per second; Randall Jarrell reads "The Death of the Ball Turret Gunner" at 2.06 syllables per second; Robert Frost reads "Dust of Snow" at 2.65 syllables per second (Funkhouser & O'Connell, 1978).

A by-product of our findings regarding expressive speech has been a thoroughly interdisciplinary application of our methodology to literary criticism. It is fairly safe to assume that an author who publishes a recording of his own reading of his poem considers the recording to be an optimal rendition. The availability of pausological analytic methods now makes it possible for literary critics to base their commentaries on empirical evidence from such readings compared to readings of the same poem by literary scholars or other control groups. The critics need no longer rely solely on their own literary intuitions (Funkhouser, 1978).

An entirely different shift in adult speech rate can be noted in glossolalia, a rather extraordinary situation in which speech rate increases and silent pauses accordingly decrease. It is by definition a state of great excitement and enthusiasm in a religious social setting. The speech sounds and intonational patterns are those of the native language, but words are replaced by meaningless syllables (Bryant & O'Connell, 1971; O'Connell & Bryant, 1972).

Although we have not endeavored to interpret sex differences in temporal measurements at a theoretical level, we have found such differences consistently in a number of developmental research projects. In general, girls are more fluent than boys. In narratives told about cartoon pictures, boys produced longer silent pauses than girls (Kowal, O'Connell & Sabin, 1975). In a reading experiment, boys read at a slower speech rate than girls in both the second and fourth grades, because they used more silent pauses within major syntactic units than did the girls (Kowal, O'Connell, O'Brien & Bryant, 1975). Finally, in a replication of the narrative experiment with Mexican adolescents, speech rates of girls were faster and their narratives longer (Johnson, forthcoming a).

The remainder of our current research has consisted of several critical studies: one on methodology (O'Connell & Kowal, 1972c); a historical review of the literature (O'Connell & Kowal, forthcoming); and a critique of the sentence as the unit of analysis (O'Connell, 1977). We have meticulously analyzed a five-minute dialogue in an idiographic fashion (Grundhauser, forthcoming).

One final aspect should be mentioned. We have ourselves written only one popularized article (O'Connell & Kowal, 1972a), but the press (*New York Times, Saint Louis Post Dispatch,* United Press International) and numerous radio stations have requested interviews. Apparently, pausology touches something of universal human interest and importance. Let us hope so.

Syntactic and structural aspects

Chairman   WALLACE L. CHAFE

JAMES DEESE

Pauses, prosody, and the demands of production in language[1]

For the past several years I have been reporting in various places (e. g., Deese, 1978) some of the preliminary results of a large scale project designed to investigate, in natural settings, the results of thought transformed into speech. I have avoided studying conversation and idle chitchat, because I have been interested in what people do when they must transform difficult and sometimes abstract ideas into speech. I have limited my sampling to the speech of adult, educated users of American English because my interests are more cognitive than sociolinguistic. Using speakers of the "standard dialect" – whatever that may be – minimizes questions arising from such vexatious problems as those of grammaticality or performance versus competence.

The project began when I asked myself: "How do we remember what we have said as we talk sufficiently well to know what to say next?" In short, I was interested in the role of memory in the production of speech. That interest has long since been swallowed up by the varieties of data I have gathered, but it is a convenient point of departure. It is, however, only a point of departure, for clearly much of what I have reported elsewhere and what is reported here is not even tangentially related to memory. Nevertheless, it does serve to focus upon the two levels of structure in the production of discourse that make demands upon memory: (1) the short range grammatical relations within sentences, and (2) the long range relations that constitute the structure of discourse itself. The psychological problems generated by efforts to make discourse coherent at these two levels are considerable, and they are related, as the long history of research on hesitation pauses and other temporal phenomena in speech show, to what speakers actually do.

Because this book is devoted to the temporal characteristics of speech production, I shall use most of this Chapter to discuss those aspects of the data thus far analyzed that bear upon temporal properties. But because the tempo of speech is sometimes connected with other problems, I shall range over other aspects of the data, avoiding as much as possible duplication with material presented in other published sources.

A brief word needs to be said about our samples and our methods. We have recorded speech in situations in which the intrusion of a tape recorder is of very little significance. We have mainly made use of public hearings and committee meetings, though we have also used graduate seminars and discussions intended for presentation on radio or television. In presenting some of our findings, I shall briefly characterize the samples upon which each particular finding is based.

We have limited our participants to mature, native, educated speakers of the standard American dialect. Thus far, we have extensive data from only one person with less than a four year college education and who might be characterized as the speaker of a nonstandard dialect. We have restricted our sample to persons between the ages of 22 and 60. We have recorded and transcribed speech that is completely spontaneous (e.g., answers to unexpected questions) and speech that has been preplanned, perhaps even outlined, though we have from our main analyses excluded speech read from manuscript or memorized.

Our transcription process is a laborious one. We know that it is very hard to be aware of and record all of the disfluencies and other characteristics of speech that are not part of the speaker's intended message, but we believe that the method we have devised captures all of the information in speech we wish to catch.

The main feature of our method is that the transcriber writes down only one feature at a time. This means a very large number of passes through a given segment of tape. Where very many features are transcribed or where the tapes are low in fidelity, there may be as many as 100 passes through a single section of tape. On the initial pass, the transcriber types the words, using Roman characters and standard spelling, except where some interest may attach to phonetic features, such as in elisions, incomplete syllables, etc. On later passes, prosodic features are added, usually one at a time, in an adaptation of the Smith-Trager system. Disfluencies (including filled and unfilled pauses), nonstandard pronunciations, etc., are all added on later transcriptions. Finally, the transcript is divided into well formed sentences and nonsentential segments. Despite the difficulties other investigators have faced in making such segmentation, we have had little trouble. We find, once false starts and internal corrections are taken into account, that most of our sentences are grammatical, within the limits of the dialect assumed. With a little practice it is almost as easy to read these transcripts as, say, the typescript of a written document. Where appropriate, segments of the tapes were subjected to physical measurements.

Without further introduction, I turn to some of the data. Given the theme of this volume, it might be worthwhile to mention the length of sentences, though I have discussed this matter elsewhere. In the main, most of the sentences are short. We have no sample thus far for which the median sentence length exceeds four seconds. Incidentally, we define sentences here as all complete subject-verb clauses together with whatever dependent clauses attached to them. We treat sentences joined by coordinating conjunctions as separate, and we so treat many other sentences joined by other kinds of conjunctions.

We had supposed that very long sentences would exceed the memory span and that they would not parse grammatically. In fact, most deviant sentences, like normal sentences, are short. There are proportionately more long deviant sentences than short deviant sentences, but, in the main, sentences that fail to parse reflect a change of plans rather than a failure of memory. We defined failure to parse generally by syntax. Violation of selectional rules, certain deviations from accepted conjugations, and other matters that might, strictly speaking, be regarded as grammatical lapses seem to be an accepted part of the dialect.[2] Most often, deviant sentences appear to be blends of two syntactic structures (e.g.. "They were monaural tasks are easy to do." "How do the costs of the off grounds programs can students relate to the costs of on grounds programs?"). Because, however, these deviant sentences are very rare, we must conclude that, despite the demands of spontaneous production, speakers exert great effort to produce well formed syntactic structures. As we shall see, it is very possible that they do so at the expense of producing a high density of filled and unfilled pauses. It is also probably the case that, to a certain extent, speakers sacrifice the coherence of larger segments of discourse in order to produce greater coherence at the local level. Our main purpose, however, is to discuss temporal factors in speech, and I mention these results as background mainly for what follows.

I should like to argue for a different approach to defining the difference between hesitation pauses (or, more generally, pauses that are an interruption in the fluent stream of speech) and pauses that appear to serve grammatical and rhetorical purposes. Traditionally, this has been defined temporally. Thus, Lounsbury (1954), who in a sense discovered the significance of hesitation pauses, argued that juncture pauses would be less than 100 msec. in duration and that anything longer than that would be a hesitation. Boomer (1965) argues for 200 msec. as the dividing time, while other investigators have used times as long as 300 msec. to make the distinction. It could be argued, of course, that such variation simply reflects the degree of certainty with which one is excluding from the category of hesitations, pauses that might have grammatical significance. However, I should like to argue that no arbitrary time serves to delimit hesitation pauses from intentional pauses. While it could be argued that strictly grammatical pauses (juncture) may be

limited to very short intervals, anyone who has ever listened with an ear
to the style of a skilled speaker will know that very long pauses sometimes serve rhetorical purposes. The distinction between rhetoric and
grammar, as we shall point out below, is often difficult to draw, so that it
may even be possible that very long pauses serve functions that are at
least related to grammatical usage. However, it is certain that some very
long pauses – up to five seconds in some speech recorded by us – are not
hesitations but serve intentional, communicative functions. Furthermore, these very long intentional pauses do not necessarily occur at
phrase boundaries, though more often than not they occur where a
comma or some other graphemic device might be placed in written discourse. For example, a polished speaker reading from text might say:
"Now (pause of three seconds) let us consider ..."

I believe that hesitation pauses can be separated from linguistically
intentional pauses only by an examination of speech in its complete
context. In fact, though rarely in the kind of speech we have been sampling, video tapes or some other record of nonverbal interactions may be
necessary to distinguish pauses in the flow of speech that are intentional
from those that are genuine hesitations. It is also possible that people use
some rhetorical pauses for the same purpose for which they use hesitation pauses – namely to plan what is coming ahead, but this is not to say
that rhetorical and hesitation pauses are the same thing. Grammatically
and rhetorically relevant pauses are often signalled by other prosodic
features which reveal that the speaker has anticipated them and assimilated them to the flow of speech. But it is only possible to tell which is
which from the total context of speech. Our determination of functional
pauses is based upon three criteria: (1) Does the pause have an interpretation? (2) Does it serve some grammatical function, such as marking the
end of a sentence or phrase? (3) Does it make for ease of interpretation?

Before saying something about our data on pauses, however, we
should turn to some of the ways in which grammatical segments of
speech are marked. In one of our samples, a graduate seminar devoted
to aphasia, about 24% of all sentence boundaries in a randomly selected
sample of 1043 sentences were not marked in any of the traditional
ways. That is to say, the termination of one sentence and the beginning
of another was not marked either by a falling (or rising) contour or by a
perceptible or physically measurable juncture. We have reason to
believe that this percentage is higher in the seminar than in our other
samples, but in every sample we find sentence boundaries that are not
marked prosodically. A large number of these transitions are marked by
coordinating conjunctions. But there are always some that appear not to
be marked at all. The listener must tell when one sentence has left off
and another begun by the sense and the syntax of the sentences them-

selves. Figure 1 compares the recording of instantaneous power envelope of speech for a sentence boundary having no pause or juncture with two sentences that show a pause, one long and one short. It is very clear that there are some sentence boundaries that are not represented by any break in the flow of speech energy.

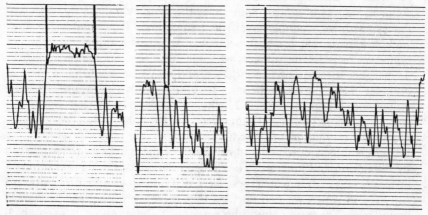

Figure 1. *Sentence boundaries of three different durations measured by the power envelope. The left most boundary, between the words "right" and "now" is not greater than that between those words if they had been in the same sentence, the middle boundary is approximately 200 msec., and the right most boundary is approximately 2500 msec.*

We cannot exhibit a comparable physical measurement for contours, because the conditions under which most of our recordings have been made preclude determining the shape of the F_0 contour with any accuracy. We have, however, checked our intuitive judgments about terminal intonation contours with a psychophysical experiment. We selected 50 sentence boundaries marked by a falling contour. These were also marked by a clear juncture or pause, since a readily detectable pause always seems to follow a terminal intonation contour, though not all pauses are preceded by a change in intonation. We also selected 50 sentence boundaries unmarked by either a falling contour or a detectable juncture. We made a new tape which contained only the last two words of the sentence before the boundary and the last two words of the sentence after the boundaries for all of these boundaries. We also placed on the same tape 50 segments of four words *within* a phrase. These matched for form class, number of syllables and lexical stress the four words for each of the sentence boundaries unmarked by intonation contour or juncture. For example, one unmarked boundary was bridged by the following two sentences: "It would be six months from initiation before we could bring this work to completion. With good luck we might make it within four." The words presented on the new tape would be "to completion with good." That sequence was matched with "by arrangement to new." These three kinds of sequences were randomly mixed on the tapes.

Five naive subjects were tested after having been told in detail the purpose of the experiment. They were told that they would listen to some sequences of words. Sometimes the words would bridge two sentences (with an example given) and sometimes they would not. They were asked to tell, for each sequence, whether it bridged a sentence boundary or not. The subjects were all told about intonation and stress as markers for sentence boundaries, and they were told that some real boundaries presented on the tape were, so far as we knew, unmarked by either intonation or stress. Finally, they were told that $2/3$ of the sequences actually bridged sentences and that half of these were clearly marked by intonation and stress.

These subjects detected 234 or 93.6% of the 250 boundaries marked by intonation and juncture. They judged boundaries to be present in 68 instances (27.2%) in which there were no boundaries and in 77 instances (30.8%) in which we had decided that there were no prosodic cues to boundaries. There was almost no agreement among subjects as to which sequences were sentence boundaries in the cases in which there were no cues to boundaries. It seems reasonable to conclude that, in fact, some sentence boundaries are without any traditionally defined prosodic cues.

We performed a somewhat different experiment on pauses. We had two observers judge the relative duration of pauses for an extended sample of tape from the graduate seminar. The judgments were on a four point scale: No pause, short pause, intermediate pause, and long pause. From these judgments we selected 100 boundaries with no pause and 100 boundaries at each of the three subjective durations of pause. We did the same for a series of four hundred sequences of words within phrases. That is to say, we found 100 sequences within which there was no pause, 100 within which our observers agreed very short pauses occurred, etc. We then measured the physical duration of the pauses. There is a high correlation between perceived and physical length of pause (.85), but there is also an interaction that depends upon whether the pause terminates a sentence or occurs in the middle of a clause. The mean duration of pauses for each category of rating is given in Table 1. In agreement with a similar finding by Boomer (1965), pauses of a given length within clauses are apt to be subjectively perceived as being longer by a listener than pauses between sentences. We checked the times between words very carefully for an extended sample of speech, and our observers appear not to be overlooking anything that could conceivably be a pause (to our measured accuracy of something less than 50 msec.).

Table 1. *The duration in milliseconds of clause-terminal and within clause pauses rated as short, medium, or long.*

Pause Coding	Clause Terminal	Within Clause
Short	400	368
Medium	1,763	1,388
Long	3,856	3,331

Martin (1970) reports that observers sometimes hear pauses where there are none – presumably as the result of the lengthening of the preceding syllable – though we could detect no instances of such. Incidentally, we should remind ourselves that not all within phrase pauses are hesitation pauses.

Despite the fact that sentences can apparently be unmarked by any of the traditional prosodic devices, it is unlikely that there are many sentence boundaries that must be detected by the listener only through a semantic and/or grammatical analysis. We discovered, largely by chance, that syllable rate serves as a clue to sentence boundaries, though variations in rate seem to serve other purposes as well.

We have measured syllable rate for speakers from two of our samples. We measured syllable rate for male speakers from our graduate seminar sample and syllable rate for female speakers from a radio discussion program sponsored by a women's organization (FOCUS), designed to help women who wish to return to professional and occupational activities. The means and standard deviations for these two samples are contained in Table 2. The figures in Table 2 are well within the range of those reported by Goldman-Eisler (1968) and others. The standard deviations are not large, and, pauses aside, the subjective impression one gets in listening to the speech is that there is a remarkable degree of stability to the syllable rate for a given speaker. Despite this fact, however, we noticed that there were occasional sequences of words in which the syllable rate appeared to be remarkably high. In short, there were occasional deviations from this subjective impression of a constant syllable rate. We went through the transcripts and marked, by underlining, the sequences of words that appeared to be a faster than normal rate. We measured the syllable rate for fifty such sequences from each sample. The means and standard deviations for these accelerated passages are also given in Table 2. They are extraordinarily high. The means lie at or beyond 3 standard deviations from the means for all words. They are, then, statistically rare.

But that is not what is important about them. They also have nonrandom locations in speech. Two-thirds of them occur either in (1) the last

Table 2. *Syllables per second in two samples of spontaneous speech, one of male speakers and the other of female*

	All Words Male Sample	All Words Female Sample
Mean	5.48	5.82
S.D.	1.86	1.59

	Accelerated Passages* Male Sample	Accelerated Passages* Female Sample
Mean	9.64	11.25
S.D.	2.90	3.20
Mean Length in Syllables	7.93	8.37

* N = 50

few syllables of a sentence and the first few of the next sentence, or in (2) parenthetical expressions – repetitions in different words of what has just been said, things that are explanatory but unimportant to the main idea in the sentence, etc. In threee samples – hearings before the Charlottesville City Council, the graduate seminar, and the FOCUS discussions – a total of 41% of the accelerated passages consisted of de-emphasized clauses or sentences, generally spoken with reduced voice and a flattening of stress and intonation. The 27% that consisted of bridges between sentences were generally spoken at full voice and with no flattening of stress, though always without a falling contour at the end of the first sentence. The remaining 31% were largely sequences of words that were spoken at reduced intensity, but not always. Occasionally a sequence of words is spoken at an extremely rapid rate by way of emphasis. In such sequences, exaggerated stress also occurs.

The point is that prosody of spontaneous speech is probably very much more complicated than we have hitherto supposed. Syllable rate carries communicative information. Generally, when it is used to bridge the end of one sentence and the beginning of another, it is used to signal that the speaker has come to the end of a sentence but not the end of his discourse. He still wants to hold the floor. The use of acceleration and reduced intonation and stress to signal de-emphasis is obvious.

Is syllable rate prosodic? That is a difficult question to answer, but it clearly works hand in hand with stress, juncture, and intonation to signal intentions. Those intentions are sometimes expressible in grammatical forms and sometimes purely in pragmatic or rhetorical forms. To make matters worse, stress, juncture, and intonation, as well as, we must admit, syllabic rate all function at a lexical level also. Furthermore, they all do so with multiple meaning and with considerable variation in execution. They are usually redundant with one another and with other aspects of the message being communicated by speech. They may be distorted or absent and still the basic message may be communicated. Like the surface forms of grammatical structure and like the total style of discourse, they serve to communicate messages not evident in the actual propositions spelled out in the discourse. Rarely do we say in words "this is unimportant", and only slightly more often do we say, "now listen to this", but these and other commentaries on what is being said are continuously being said by the way in which we say things – the grammatical structures we choose and the prosody of our speech.

As we surely know by now, some pauses are not an intentional part of the message. Less often and less obviously do we have stress and intonation patterns that are the equivalent of a hesitation pause in the sense that they are not intended or represent a mistaken choice. The easiest way to detect such stress and intonation "errors" at the phrase or sentential level as opposed to the lexical level is to task a moderately skilled reader to read something aloud with which he is not familiar. He will govern his stress and intonation pattern (and pauses) by the grammatical structure he perceives in a sentence up to the point at which he is speaking. His guess as to the complete grammatical structure is occasionally wrong, and he will use the wrong stress or intonation accordingly. We can only assume from the patterns we detect in spontaneous speech that the same thing, or something like it occurs. Speakers often change their sentence structures in mid-stream. This pattern is sometimes detectable from the fact that the grammatical structures do not match. An occasional puzzling prosodic pattern may have the same cause. These, however, are minor compared with the obvious and ubiquitous hesitation pauses, both filled and unfilled.

Hesitation pauses, however, need to be considered within the framework of the total pattern of disfluent interruptions to the flow of speech. They have, I believe, a special significance. They result, I shall try to argue, from the need to plan at the local or grammatical level rather than the need to plan larger segments of discourse. Other kinds of disfluencies are more likely to reflect planning at the level of discourse.

Evidence for such a distinction is to be found in Table 3. Table 3 presents rates per 100 words for two types of disfluencies, hesitation pauses and what might be called errors of production. These include false starts on sentences, corrections internal to sentences, and repetition

Table 3. *Disfluencies per 100 words*

Preplanned	Filled Pauses	Unfilled Pauses	Total Type I	False Starts	Correc- tions	Repeti- tions	Total Type II	Total Disfluencies
S_1CC	2.18	6.29	8.48	0.10	0.10	0.41	0.61	9.09
S_2CC	2.35	7.70	10.05	0.36	0.46	1.33	2.14	12.19
S_3CC	2.20	5.85	8.05	0.24	0.49	1.41	2.14	10.19
S_4CC	2.98	4.47	7.45	0.50	0.37	1.24	2.11	9.56
S_5CC	3.88	8.22	12.10	0.00	0.91	1.60	2.51	14.61
S_1GS	4.31	11.04	15.35	1.74	1.32	2.57	5.63	20.97
S_2GS	4.87	5.73	10.60	1.53	1.93	1.47	4.93	15.53
S_3GS	3.25	8.55	11.80	1.97	1.88	2.99	6.84	18.63
S_4GS	2.95	9.07	12.02	0.71	1.31	3.44	5.46	17.49
S_5GS	3.73	2.89	6.63	1.39	1.87	2.65	5.90	12.53
$\bar{x}$	3.82	7.46	11.28	1.47	1.66	2.62	5.75	17.03
Unplanned								
S_1CC	1.61	4.90	6.51	0.39	0.45	1.10	1.94	8.45
S_2CC	1.68	9.06	10.74	0.00	0.34	1.68	2.02	12.76
S_3CC	1.89	4.40	6.29	0.75	0.63	2.01	3.39	9.68
S_4CC	1.44	5.83	7.27	0.43	0.65	0.86	1.94	9.21
S_5CC	3.24	4.85	8.09	0.44	0.59	1.91	2.94	11.03
S_1GS	2.75	7.16	9.90	3.14	1.67	3.63	8.43	18.33
S_2GS	3.28	6.15	9.43	1.56	1.23	2.54	5.33	14.75
S_3GS	2.14	6.18	8.32	2.21	1.53	2.67	6.41	14.73
S_4GS	3.33	7.53	10.87	1.73	2.27	4.80	8.80	19.67
S_5GS	1.23	9.08	10.31	2.54	1.54	4.69	8.77	19.08
$\bar{x}$	2.55	7.22	9.77	2.24	1.65	3.67	7.55	17.31

of words, syllables and sometimes even phrases. We have labeled these Type I and Type II disfluencies respectively.

The data from which the figures in Table 3 are taken are from two samples of five speakers each. One sample was the graduate seminar, and the other was taken from hearings before the Charlottesville City Council. There are, as it turns out, large differences in fluency between the speakers from these samples, and we shall return to this matter shortly. The matter of interest now, however, is that rates were obtained for both samples under two different conditions. In one condition, labeled preplanned in the table, the speaker was presenting something that he had thought about, planned for and, in some instances, produced notes for. In the other condition, labeled unplanned, the speaker was responding to questions or otherwise engaged in discourse that he had not planned before the meeting.

A mixed design analysis of variance applied to the rates for individual speakers shows all main effects to be significant. Type, measure within type, subjects, and type of discourse all result in significant effects. There is a highly consistent pattern of individual differences. There are also large sample differences. The disfluencies of both kinds are more common in the graduate seminar than in the City Council hearings. This may be a kind of audience effect, and we will return to it later.

Our major interest at the moment centers on the differences between planned and unplanned discourse. There is both a significant main effect for planned and unplanned discourse and an interaction between discourse type and type of disfluency. In brief, Type I disfluencies (pauses) are more common in planned than in unplanned speech, while Type II disfluencies are very much more common in unplanned than in planned speech.

This interaction appears to be a result of where the creative process is focussed during the actual production of speech. In preplanned discourse, the general thread of the argument (the plan as defined below) has already been determined, and the main creative activity during production centers on the formation of sentences, the surface form in which the preplanned ideas are to be presented. The result is a greater variety and elegance to the surface sentences (mentioned below) but also a very large reduction in the density of false starts, the need to correct something said and the almost stuttering-like repetitions that plague the speech of most speakers when they are being completely spontaneous. When the speaker is more carefully planning discourse at the local or grammatical level, which he can do when the thread of the argument is preplanned, there will be more pauses to allow for a more deliberate choice of words. Though the data in Table 3 are based upon hesitation pauses only, the total frequency of pauses increases. There are more rhetorical as well as hesitation pauses.

When one considers the disorganization evident in the execution of plans (below), it is evident that the total pattern is for much less fluent production in the absence of planning despite the reduction in filled and unfilled pauses. It is interesting to note that, while we can direct our attention to pauses produced by a speaker, we ordinarily do not. In an earlier study (see Deese, 1978) we compared the ability of subjects to remember and to comprehend sentences extracted from spontaneous discourse when the sentences were presented in their original form and when they were rerecorded by a fluent speaker. The very small difference between the two conditions for both memory and comprehensibility came nowhere near statistical significance. These kinds of disfluencies do not interfere with the hearer's processing of speech (unless they are unusually dense) and they are usually ignored in the conscious monitoring of what we hear. False starts and corrections, on the other hand, are confusing to the hearer. In *his* planning of the discourse, he must go back and correct patterns already initiated. We have evidence to show that hearers find speech dense with false starts, repetitions, and corrections to be difficult and unpleasant to listen to.

Before turning to the question of discourse itself, I shall say just a word about the audience effect referred to above. We have tabulated the disfluency rates for extended segments of four samples, the graduate seminar, the City Council hearings, and for a University of Virginia committee meeting in executive session and a radio-TV discussion (FOCUS). These are presented in Table 4. The main matter of interest is that the Type II disfluencies are reduced when the speech has an audience beyond the targeted hearer. The greatest density of Type II disfluencies occurs in the graduate seminar, whose participants knew one another very well and who were not self conscious in one another's presence. The lowest rate of such disfluencies occurs in the discussion intended for the presumably wide audience made available by broadcasting. The University committee, meeting without an audience, produced the second greatest number of Type II disfluencies and a larger number than the City Council hearings, which were open and which always had a few listeners beyond the Council itself. The Type I disfluencies show no such pattern. They are all about the same, except for the

Table 4. *Disfluency rates for four samples differing in the extent to which an audience other than targeted listener is present (see text).*

Sample	Words per Sentence	Filled Pauses	Unfilled Pauses	Total Type I	False Starts	Correc- tions	Stutter	Total Type II
Graduate Seminar	16.5	2.45	5.79	8.24	1.40	1.37	2.73	6.50
Committee Executive Session	14.5	4.00	11.33	15.33	0.28	0.96	1.24	2.48
Open City Council	15.8	2.29	6.85	9.14	0.17	0.44	1.40	2.01
Discussion for TV	17.4	1.95	5.80	7.75	0.11	0.28	0.34	0.73

University committee sample, the data for which are heavily influenced by a single individual who produced a very large number of pauses.

This brings us to the matter of discourse itself. Discourse may be said to have two kinds of organization, though such a characterization is a bit of an oversimplification. There is, however, an organization of the content, and there is an organization of the way in which that content is put, the style. The organization in content consists, in its most reduced form, to the relations among the concepts in discourse. Most discourse analysis (e.g., Frederiksen, 1975; Kintsch, 1974) is directed to the organization of content. Rhetoricians and literary critics have been the principal students of the way in which content is expressed (but see Hirsch, 1979). I have also been concerned with the way the content is expressed, but in a manner that parallels the interests of the discourse grammarians. Rather than being interested in the meaningful relations among the concepts, however, I have been concerned with the dependency relations among propositions – which statements are presupposed by other statements. These relations are important because, I believe, they reveal something of the plans employed by speakers when they set about putting some particular discourse – or content – into a particular form.

Dependency occurs among propositions whenever one proposition requires the presence of another in order to be interpreted within context. Dependent propositions amplify, explain, modify, or presuppose the existence of propositions dominating them. The basic relation among propositions, then, is one of subordination and coordination. This results in a scheme for analyzing discourse very similar to that proposed by Christensen (1967) for rhetorical analysis. The principal difference between the notions proposed here and those proposed by Christensen is that Christensen uses as the ideational unit the surface sentence, while the analysis proposed here uses as ideational units, propositions the form of which is defined by base phrase structures in the context free portion of a transformational grammar (Chomsky, 1965).

I have assumed that all coherent discourse tends toward a strong hierarchy. A strong hierarchy provides the least burden on memory. A strong hierarchy is a classification system in which a given – here a proposition – never appears in more than one place. If discourse were to tend towards some more complex structure – a weak hierarchy or a generalized network – the dependency relations would become so complex that neither the speaker nor the hearer could follow. Not all discourse is coherent of course. In differing ways, the discourse of schizophrenics and that of very young children departs from a well-formed hierarchy.

Table 5 shows the hierarchical structure for a paragraph from Willa Cather's novel, *A Lost Lady*.[3] This structure is exhibited because it is

Table 5. *Hierarchy for paragraph from Willa Cather's* **Lost Lady**

---

1. The Forrester place was not at all remarkable.
    1.1 As everyone called it (the Forrester place).
    1.2 The people who lived there [PEOPLE LIVED IN THE FORRESTER PLACE].
    1.3 (People) made it seem larger than it was.
    1.4 (People who lived there made it seem) and finer than it was.
    1.5 The house stood on a hill.
        1.5.1 Low (hill).
        1.5.2 Round (hill).
    1.6 (The house was) nearly a mile east of town.
    1.7 A white house.
    1.8 (A house) with a wing.
    1.9 It was encircled by porches.
        1.9.1 (Porches) too narrow for notions.
        1.9.1.1 (Modern) notions.
        1.9.1.2 (Notions of) comfort.
    1.10 (Porches) supported by pillars.
        1.10.1 Fussy (pillars)
        1.10.2 Fragile (pillars)
        1.10.3 (Pillars) of the time.
        1.10.3.1 [THE TIME IS NOW]
        1.10.3.2 [THE TIME WAS] when stick of lumber was tortured.
            1.10.3.2.1 Every (stick of lumber).
            1.10.3.2.2 Honest (stick of lumber).
            1.10.3.2.3 (tortured) into something hideous.
            1.10.3.2.4 (tortured) by the turning lathe.

---

typical. In particular, one second level proposition dominates all of the deep paths in the structure (in this case, 1.10). All discourse implies propositions not explicit in the text, of course. But in most discourse some of the implied propositions are necessary to complete the structure. There is one such example here, proposition 1.10.3.1.

The dominant proposition is not the topical sentence in traditional rhetorical analysis. In traditional rhetoric, the topical sentence tells what the discourse is all about. The speaker or writer may, however, start with an example and then go to a general principle, stating the general principle in the context of the example. Certain genres – fables, parables, jokes – depend for their literary effect upon burying the main idea in the body of the structure. This does not necessarily make for difficulty of comprehension.

We have performed some experiments on the ability of people to recall the content of short discourses presented to them (mainly paragraphs from textbooks, newspapers, advertising copy, etc.). We presented the paragraphs in pairs and then asked for recall in pairs to break up any tendency the listeners might have to recall the passages by rote. One of these discourses was the opening paragraph from the 2nd edition of B.J. Underwood's *Experimental Psychology* (1966). The paragraph explains that human behavior is consistent. It does so by what might be called the parable of the two business men, one of whom always pays his debts on time, etc., and the other of whom reaps poor credit ratings by failing to pay his debts. But, the paragraph is dominated by a statement that explains the nature of organizations that establish credit ratings. The real message is buried well into the paragraph and is well down the structure of propositions. But, all but one of the listeners who heard this passage, perceived the message correctly (one remembered it as having been about how to get credit), and three of the listeners, in their recall, reorganized the content so as to make the statement that behavior is consistent the dominant proposition.

Discourse, then, has two structures: one the semantic relations among propositions and the other the form in which those relations are presented. One might be called the deep structure of discourse and the other the surface structure, though I do not wish to push the analogy too far. The semantic relations, of course, are not dependent upon language. A text grammar, such as that provided by Frederiksen (1975) could just as easily describe a pantomime or motion picture as it could a story embodied in language. The hierarchical structure of discourse, however, may well be peculiar to language, a result of the necessary linearity of language.

Plans in both written and oral discourse are, of course, subject to change as the plan unfolds. But because of the different temporal constraints and because oral discourse does not provide an auxiliary external memory of how the plan has been unfolded thus far, we might expect oral discourse to be much less orderly than written discourse, and that certainly seems to be the case (see Deese, 1978). Also, Type II disfluencies in the flow of speech are much greater when discourse must be planned, not only at the grammatical level but at the level of discourse itself.

At the outset of his discourse the speaker must have some general notion of what he wants to say (something close to the main idea in the surface discourse) and how to say it (at least where to start in the dependency tree, though I think it more plausible that the speaker has in mind, when he begins, certain critical nodes in the hierarchical structure of his discourse). The main idea itself may not be fully specified at the outset, at least in the form in which it eventually appears. It will consist of only certain features, which need additional features in order to be converted to a proposition that can be expressed with the lexical and grammatical tools of language. The very fact that alternative lexical and grammatical expressions are available at this stage testifies to the fact that not all features are specified by the general plans. These general plans, unless the speaker starts over or aborts the discourse, remain. We know, however, that all aspects subordinate to or coordinate with already expressed propositions are subject to change. This may happen even after the last moment, for, deviant sentences show that speakers change plans for a given proposition even after they have begun to utter it. It is even conceivable that certain blends of semantically related words occurring as speech errors may represent such corrections in midstream. One of our speakers uttered the neologism, "stries", in a context in which either tries or strives would have been appropriate. We must not suppose, however, that the process which initiates the change in plan is set off by the beginning of the old plan. In fact, temporal relations involved in at least some instances suggest that the old intrudes after it has already been rejected. One of our speakers uttered the following sequence: "The tax would bring in approx – somewhere in the neighborhood of ninety thousand dollars." There was no juncture between the last syllable of the aborted "approximately" and the beginning of "somewhere." The bridging phonemes, of course, are identical. The whole sequence was uttered at an accelerated pace so that only 200 milliseconds elapsed between the beginning of "approximately" and "somewhere." When the new structure was actually initiated is as mysterious as the reason motivating it, but it must have been earlier than 200 milliseconds.

I suspect that the reason hesitation pauses are to be more characteristically implicated in the lower level choices of plans – in lexical choices pre-eminently, as Goldman-Eisler's (1958a) classical work demonstrates (though see Goldman-Eisler, 1972) – is because uncertainty at higher levels is assimilated to rhetorical pauses. It is closer to the level at which the speaker must collect his wits. In short, it is easy to pause at the level of transition from one node to another in a hierarchy. This, I suspect is mainly a matter of skill. Skilled readers in reading unfamiliar text manage to make pauses serve rhetorical functions.

Notes

1. The research reported here was largely supported by NSF grant No. BNS77-02084. The author is indebted to many people, but principally to Allyssa McCabe and Cassandra Wright, who have carried the main burden of data analysis.
2. Keith Brown reports that in Scottish English speech at all levels of education, distinctions among relative pronouns appear to be disappearing. The relative pronoun *that* is used rather than *who* or *which* in the subject position. (Brown, personal communication.)
3. Cather, Willa, *A Lost Lady*. New York. Vintage Books, 1972, p. 10.

ANDREW BUTCHER

Pause and syntactic structure[1]

Some recent studies have focussed attention on the relationship between the speaker's location and timing of pauses and the syntactic structure of his utterances. It is suggested that more attention might be paid (1) to the perception of pauses in relation to syntax and (2) to the role of other prosodic variables. Data from earlier experiments on the production and perception of pauses by German speakers are re-examined in the light of preliminary results from experiments currently under analysis and it is found that there is a tendency for pause duration to be logarithmically proportional to the syntactic complexity index of the pause position. Under most conditions, however, some additional variable has to be postulated, if only to account for the absence of pauses at certain points of high complexity. This could well be a positional variable (proximity of pause position to midpoint of constituent) as proposed in Grosjean's model, but the possibility is raised that it might be the position in the prosodic structure rather than in the syntactic structure which is relevant and that the former might take precedence over the latter on the rare occasions when the two are not coterminous.

An ever-increasing volume of research into pausing has, if nothing else, left no doubt as to the multiplicity and complexity of the variables which contribute to the speaker's production of silences and hesitations (for comparatively recent reviews of the literature cf. Rochester, 1973 and Drommel, 1974c). Rather less attention has been paid, however, to the parameters underlying the listener's detection of pauses, although the fact that the presence of a measurable period of silence is neither a necessary nor a sufficient condition for the perception of a speech pause was clear from the earliest instrumental studies (cf. Zwirner & Zwirner, 1937; Cowan & Bloch, 1948). The chief interest of the speech researcher is directed toward the communicative function of pauses, one important aspect of wich is the relationship between measurable phonetic parameters such as length and location of silent interval and linguistic variables such as syntactic and semantic complexity. While it should be possible to investigate these functions of the speech pause by eliminating or controlling other independent variables, it would seem, on the other hand, neither feasible nor desirable to investigate pausing separately from certain other dependent variables, in particular prosodic phenomena such as intonation, rhythm and tempo.

In one of the rare systematic studies of pause perception, Boomer & Dittmann (1962) investigated two degrees of variation in the syntactic parameter, which they defined according to intonational criteria: pauses were either between or within phonemic clauses. The experiment showed that, whereas within-clause pauses were detected by 75% of listeners at durations above 200 ms, between-clause breaks were not heard until they were between 500 and 1000 ms in length. Butcher (1973 b) replicated this experiment using German material and extending the range of syntactic variation to four degrees of complexity. The measure of complexity employed was that proposed by Miller & Chomsky (1963), which involved calculating a node-to-terminal-node ratio for that part of the phrase structure tree immediately dominating the pause position. This experiment showed that the perceptual threshold for pauses increased as a function of syntactic complexity. In fact, although there are only four different x-values over which to regress, the best fit for these data (r = 0.995) seems to be a function of the type described by the lower curve in Figure 1, whereby $y = e^{(4.52x - 12.56)} + 50$ (where y = threshold duration, x = syntactic com-

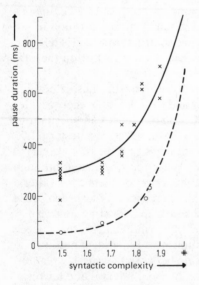

Figure 1: *Pause perception and production in read sentences as a function of syntactic complexity.*

———x mean durations of 'produced' pauses

– –o threshold durations for 'perceived' pauses

plexity index). In other words, the natural logarithm of the perceptual threshold duration of the pause increases in direct proportion to the syntactic complexity at the pause location. Boomer & Dittmann (1962) interpret their results as support for the hypothesis that "the juncture pause, occurring as expected between phonemic clauses, might have a higher perceptual threshold than the hesitation pause, occurring unexpectedly within a phonemic clause." If this 'what is expected is not noticed' interpretation is extended to the data of Butcher (1973b), it would seem to imply that the subject expects to hear longer pauses at points of higher structural complexity in natural speech.

Experimental evidence for such a conclusion is provided by several recent studies. Ruder & Jensen (1972), for example, investigated five levels of syntactic complexity by means of their pause adjustment system, whereby subjects varied pause times in recorded utterances by altering the distance between the playback heads of a twin-track taperecorder. When asked to adjust for 'hesitation' pauses, subjects came up with thresholds which increased as a function of the syntactic complexity. In order to test the pause duration norms in the production of the original stimulus material, Butcher (1975) asked naive subjects to repeat the sentences used in the perception experiments, with 'normal' intonation but leaving a pause after every word. Only the data for the four original pause points were analysed and these were shown to bear a strong resemblance to the perceptual data, in that mean pause duration was longer, the greater the structural complexity at the pause point. An analysis of all the data, however, (19 types, 950 tokens) reveals that, once again, the relationship between pause length and syntactic complexity can be stated in the form of a logarithmic function. In this case $y = e^{(5.49x - 4.50)} + 250$, as represented by the upper curve of Figure 1, obtained by regressing log mean durations of pauses over syntactic complexity indices at pause positions, giving a correlation coefficient of $r = 0.877$.

Thus a fairly simple relationship can be shown when pauses are induced at all possible points in the utterance. Under this condition with recited material, the syntactic structure of the sentence seems to be the main variable affecting pause duration. The question which then posed itself was whether similar results would be obtained with a wider range of sentences, read normally in the form of a connected text and, even more importantly, under the relatively free conditions of unscripted monologue. There was evidence that the first kind of condition might produce broadly comparable results to the single-sentence experiments. Brown & Miron (1971), for instance, found that in a professionally read text, 61% of variance in pause time could be accounted for by measures based on simple immediate constituent *and* deep structure analyses.

In order to carry out a similar analysis for German, 10 subjects read aloud the 'Berlin Butter Story' (cf. Gnutzmann, 1975), 5 at 'normal' speed and 5 both at 'very fast' and 'very slow' speeds, giving 15 versions of the text in all. Sound pressure level was recorded on a Revox A77 taperecorder and played back on to an ink-jet oscillograph (Siemens Oszillimink E) at a paper speed of 100 cm/s. All silences of over 100 ms duration were marked and measured. Unfortunately, although the text provides 234 potential pause points, the nature of the task was such that pauses were made only at points of highest syntactic complexity. Thus if only those 20 points are considered where 7 or more pauses were made, mean pause duration is related to the syntactic complexity index at these points by a function similar to that found previously. In this case $y = e^{(14.54x - 22.40)} + 100$ (lower curve of Figure 2, r = 0.854). However, this excludes all pause points whose complexity index is below 1.8. If all potential pause positions are included in the analysis, then nearly all points below 1.8 are at zero on the y-axis (as well as many above) and there is no longer any correlation between pause time and syntactic complexity (r = 0.434).

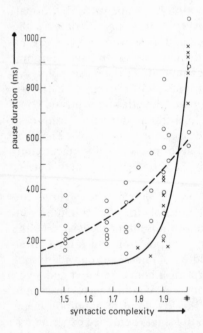

—× mean durations of pauses in read text

– –○ durations of random sample of pauses
      from 'retold' texts

Figure 2: *Pause production in read and retold stories as a function of syntactic complexity*

The ten subjects were also required to retell the story in their own words, which resulted in ten completely different texts of varying length. These have yet to be fully analysed but a random sample of 50 pauses (5 from each text) shows a slightly different relationship between pause duration and syntactic structure. The curve which best fits the data ($r = 0.731$) is shown in Figure 2 and, although it describes a logarithmic function ($y = e^{(2.21x + 1.97)}$, a straight line ($y = 951x - 1273$) would be almost as good a fit ($r = 0.713$). It does, on the other hand, seem clear that there is a great difference between the nature of this task and that in the previous three experiments, all of which involved non-spontaneous speech. It also seems fairly certain, however, that, in common with the story-reading experiment, any apparent correlation between pause time and syntactic complexity will disappear when all (2000 +) potential pause points are analysed.

In this last experiment there is, as might be expected, the problem with many tests of accounting for a certain number of long 'hesitation' pauses. These can, however, be ignored when investigating pause as a syntactic cue as long as a satisfactory criterion for their exclusion from the data can be found. In fact, for the purposes of this experiment, it was found that five naive listeners can agree very consistently on those pauses which may be regarded as "interrupting the speech flow [...] hindering rather than facilitating comprehension of the utterance" (cf. Butcher, 1975). Pauses thus classified were excluded from the study. In fact the major problem in both experiments on connected speech is that of accounting for the absence of pauses at points of high syntactic complexity, and it is these data points which are responsible for the poor correlations obtained when all potential pause positions are taken into consideration. No one, for example, pauses between a short subject and a very long predicate – e.g.:

'Jeder // wußte, daß die Butter schnell ausverkauft sein würde und [...]'

where the complexity index is nevertheless 1.950. There are no pauses after co-ordinating conjunctions or subordinating conjunctions – e.g.:

'[...] daß // man ganz früh kommen müsse, um noch etwas zu erhalten'. (complexity index 1.909).

Grosjean, Grosjean & Lane (in press) and Grosjean (this volume) have suggested that, as well as the need to respect the linguistic structure, the speaker may face a second (sometimes conflicting) demand – the need to equalize the length of constituents in the output. In other words, the further away a pause position is from the middle of a constituent, the less likely it is that a pause will be made at that point. They propose a model which predicts percentage pause time at a given position by combining the complexity index with a measure of relative proximity of that position to the midpoint of the constituent. This model seems to fit the German data well also, giving correlations as high as $r = 0.930$ between predicted pause durations and actual mean pause duration in sentences in the read text.

In those cases where striking disagreements occur between measured pause time and predicted pause time, the pause pattern is invariably in accord with the intonation pattern. In other words, pause times longer than predicted tend to occur at tone group boundaries and pause times shorter than predicted within tone groups, at points where pause would be prosodically inappropriate. There is already some evidence to suggest that variation in pause perception is dependent on the intonation contour rather than on the syntactic structure itself (cf. Butcher, 1975), and it would seem to be by no means impossible that the relationship between syntax and pause production should also be an indirect one. In other words, rather than all prosodic variation, including pausing, being determined by the syntactic structure, pausing is determined by the intonation pattern, which in turn is normally coterminous with the syntactic pattern. This must, however, remain largely a matter for conjecture until further work has been carried out.

Note

1. The work reported here was carried out as part of a research project in the Phonetics Department of the University of Kiel, under the direction of Professor K. Kohler and with financial support of the Deutsche Forschungsgemeinschaft.

FRANÇOIS GROSJEAN

Linguistic structures and performance structures: Studies in pause distribution[1]

Considerable research in the 1960s and early 70s was aimed at demonstrating the psychological reality of surface structures of sentences as they are defined by transformational-generative grammar. Experiments in recall, perception, direct scaling of relatedness and pausing, among others, were used to authenticate the role of syntactic units in processing spoken languages. Some studies were more interested, on the one hand, in showing that clauses are functional units in speech processing. For example, Jarvella (1971) found that words from immediate clauses and sentences were recalled better than corresponding words from previous clauses and sentences, and in the numerous click studies, researchers found that clicks were displaced perceptually toward clause boundaries (Fodor & Bever, 1965; Holmes & Forster, 1970). Other studies were more interested, on the other hand, in showing that lower order surface constituents are also functional units in speech processing. Levelt (1969), for example, used a method of direct scaling of relatedness, and found that the degree of relatedness between words are inversely related to the number of phrase boundaries separating one word from the other. Johnson (1965, 1968), using a recall task to study the psychological reality of phrase structure rules, found high rank-order correlations between the rank of the constituent break and the transitional error probability of that break. He concluded that the surface constituents of sentences are functional units.

Studies of pausing in reading and spontaneous speech have also shown that sentences are made up of functional units: to a hierarchy of pause frequency and duration corresponds a hierarchy of constituents. There will be, at any given rate of speech, more and longer (unfilled) pauses at the ends of sentences than within them, and more and longer pauses at the breaks between major constituents than within them. Goldman-Eisler (1972), in an analysis of nine samples of spontaneous speech, noted that 78% of sentences were divided from each other by pauses longer than 50 csec and that 66% of transitions between clauses and almost all transitions between words (93%) had a pause duration less than 50 csec. In their analysis of English and French interviews, Grosjean & Deschamps (1975) obtained quite similar results. Both languages present more pauses at the end of sentences than within them and these pauses are systematically shorter within clauses and sentences. They noted however that the most important break within the clause is not between the NP and the VP but inside the VP for both English and French. We will come back to this point later on in the paper.

Grosjean & Collins (1979) have shown that linguistic categories are also quite good predictors of the frequency and length of breathing and non breathing pauses in an oral reading task. Figure 1, taken from their study, shows the percentage of pause slots filled by breathing pauses (BPs) and non breathing pauses (NBPs) at each of seven linguistic locations at five reading rates. We can see that the number of pauses (Ps) is a function of both rate and the linguistic status of the pause location. Breathing pauses occur mainly at major constituent breaks and as rate is increased they quickly disappear from minor constituent breaks, so that at rates equal to or superior to normal reading rate, they are confined to the two major breaks (End S and End S Conj) and finally only to the

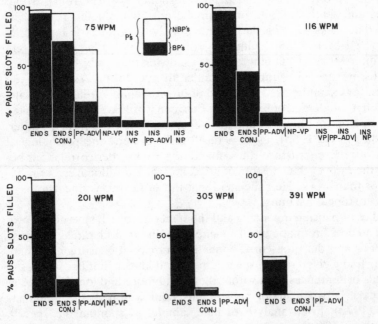

Figure 1. *The percentage of pause slots filled by breathing pauses (BPs) and non breathing pauses (NBPs) at each of seven linguistic locations at five different rates. (After Grosjean & Collins, 1979.)*

End of Sentence location. It is also at these very high rates that Ss no longer take a breath at every sentence break. The frequency of non breathing pauses at a particular pause slot is also determined by rate and the linguistic status of the pause location. However, very few non breathing pauses ever occur at the End of Sentence break and most are inserted at less important breaks. When rate is increased, the minor breaks no longer receive a pause, and consequently non breathing pauses are the first to disappear. Figure 2, also taken from Grosjean & Collins (1979), presents the mean pause duration of breathing pauses (BPs), pauses (Ps; i.e. breathing and non breathing pauses) and non breathing pauses (NBPs) at each of the seven linguistic locations at five rates. As for pause frequency, the mean duration of breathing pauses and non breathing pauses is not only a function of speaking rate but also of syntax. Both types of pauses are longer at the End of Sentence location than at any other location and as the linguistic importance of the breaks diminishes, so does the duration of the two types of pause. Also, breathing pauses are systematically longer than non breathing pauses. Thus, pause fre-

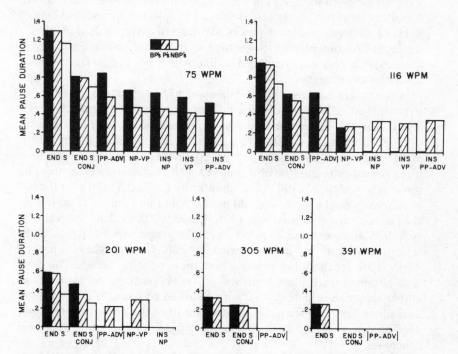

Figure 2. *The mean duration of breathing pauses (BPs), non breathing pauses (NBPs) and all pauses (Ps) at each of seven linguistic locations at five different rates. (After Grosjean & Collins, 1979.)*

quency and duration can also be used to reflect the importance of the syntactic breaks in sentences.

In sum, all these psycholinguistic studies, involving such diverse tasks as recall, perception, direct scaling of relatedness and pausing have shown that a relation exists between the listener's and speaker's segmentation of the stream of speech and a structural description of the sentences comprising that stream and that it is possible, to some extent at least, to delineate processing units from the behavioral data that correspond to structural units – sentences and constituents within sentences.

However, there are ripples on this calm surface that reflect underlying currents. First of all, the studies have not always found a perfect correspondence between the experimental data and the formal linguistic structure. Levelt (1970) reports that the minor constituents were not always reflected in the hierarchical structures obtained from errors made in a perception in noise study; Johnson (1965) found that TEPs were not always predicted by the linguistic structure, and as we reported above, Grosjean & Deschamps (1975) found more and longer pauses inside the VP than between the NP and VP. Second, most studies concerned with constituents within sentences used very simple structures, providing a weak or at least restricted test of the general hypothesis that phrase structure constituents are processing units. Third, most sentences in these experiments were balanced in that their major constituents were of about the same length.

In fact, there is a growing literature which shows that the performance structure of sentences (obtained from experimental data) does not always correspond to the formally motivated phrase markers. Martin (1970), for example, asked Ss to parse sentences by arranging the words of the sentences into 'natural groups'. The data thus obtained were then hierarchically structured with Johnson's (1967) clustering program. The results showed that Ss did not automatically group the verb with the NP object, as linguistic models would predict, but that in many cases (SV)O clusterings were obtained. Suci (1967) assessed the validity of pause in speech as an index of unit boundaries in language. Stories learned by Ss were fractured in two different ways: at points where speakers paused during their recall and at points where there were no pauses. The parts thus obtained were placed in random order, forming two new sets of verbal materials which the Ss were required to learn. It proved more difficult to learn the material constructed from the non-pause fracture. This outcome applied both to narrative passages and word lists. Suci concludes,

> These experiments suggest that organisation of verbal material is not necessarily based on grammatical structure in the traditional linguistic sense [...] This, of course, does not mean that syntax is not an organizational base in everyday

communication. It indicates only that other structural bases may be operative and that pause may serve to identify the units of these other structures.

In a recent study Grosjean, Grosjean & Lane (1979) set out to find out something about these 'other structures.' From the Martin (1970) and Suci (1967) studies, it appeared that sentences may have performance structures quite different from their linguistic surface structures. Therefore, the experimental question was the following: Will the sentence structures obtained from pausing at reduced reading rate reflect these performance structures, and if so, what will be the relation between the linguistic surface structure and these performance structures? Grosjean, Grosjean & Lane (1979) wanted to arrive at a simple model, presumably taking into account the surface structure of the sentence and certain performance variables that would account for most of the variance in the pause durations when reading sentences.

In a first experiment, they asked 6 Ss to read 14 sentences embedded in three paragraphs. These sentences were taken from the Bever, Lackner & Kirk (1969) click study. The method of magnitude production was used to obtain the readings (Grosjean, 1977). Oscillographic tracings of readings were obtained and were then used to measure the silent pauses produced by the Ss. The minimum duration for a silence to be counted as a pause was set at 25 csec. The pauses at each word boundary, in each of the 14 experimental sentences, were then pooled and the mean duration computed and expressed as a percent of the total pause duration in that sentence. These pause durations were then used to make hierarchical clusters of the words within the sentences, according to the following iterative procedure (Grosjean & Lane, 1977): First, find the shortest pause in the sentence. Second, cluster the two elements (words or clusters) separated by that pause by linking them to a common node and delete the pause. (If three or more adjacent words are separated from each other by the same pause duration, make one cluster of these words: trinary, quaternary, etc.). Finally, repeat the process until all pauses have been deleted.

In Figure 3 we present two of the 14 hierarchical pause structures obtained by Grosjean, Grosjean & Lane (1979). An examination of these structures showed that sentences were broken up into groups of words of more or less equal length. For example, in sentence 1, the following groups were separated by pauses longer or equal to 10%: *The expert/who couldn't see/what to criticize/sat back in despair.* A second experiment was conducted to examine whether breathing might be responsible for his tendency. At very slow rate, the "breath group" might be reduced in size, and, instead of comprising the whole sentence, it might extend over only three or four words.

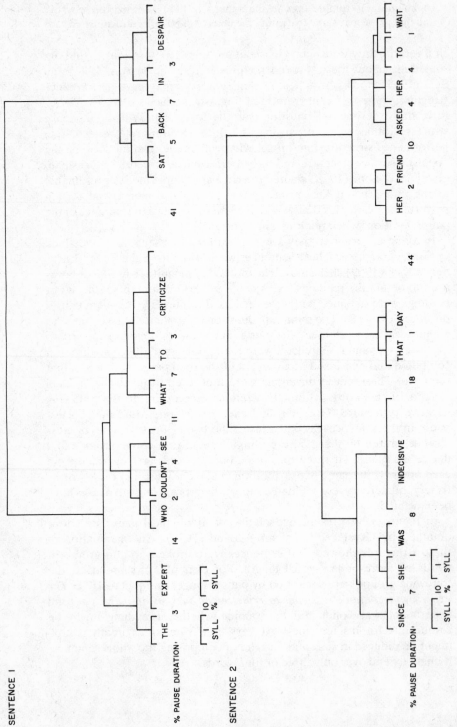

Figure 3. *Hierarchical performance structures of two sentences obtained from pause data. The height of each node is twice the distance between words which in turn is determined by the length of the pauses. (After Grosjean, Grosjean & Lane, 1979.)*

In this second experiment, 5 different Ss read the 14 experimental sentences in isolation. The method of magnitude production was used again but only low values were presented. Ss were told not to inhale during their production of the sentences; if a breath was detected during a sentence, the S was asked to read that sentence again. The pauses produced in this second experiment were analyzed as in Experiment 1. It was found that the two conditions produced structures that were practically identical. For all 14 sentences, the mean coefficient of correlation between the two sets of % pause duration was 0.87. Thus identical pause structures will be obtained from readings of sentences whether embracing one or several breath groups. As there were no systematic differences between the breathing and no-breathing conditions, the data from the two experiments were combined.

From the preceding it would appear that pause duration is determined in part by linguistic structure and in part by performance variables, but that breathing is not one of these. The possibility arose, then, that the relevant performance variables are not peculiar to production but come into play at higher levels of sentence processing. To explore this possibility, before proceeding with the analysis of pause duration, Grosjean, Grosjean & Lane (1979) conducted a third experiment with a very different variable – parsing. 15 Ss were asked to parse the 14 sentences. They were told to find the main break in each sentence and put a slash with a number 1 on top, then to consider the two parts independently and divide them up in turn with slash 2, and to continue dividing each part until all words were separated from one another with a numbered slash. The parsing values given by each S to every sentence were used to obtain a hierarchical structure following the iterative procedure described earlier. A complexity index reflecting the hierarchical relations between words as perceived by the parser was then computed for every word boundary. To do this, Grosjean, Grosjean & Lane counted the number of nodes dominated by the word boundary node, including in the count the word boundary node itself. The complexity indices associated with the parsing of each sentence were pooled across Ss and means were computed for each word boundary.

As can be seen in Figure 4, the hierarchies obtained from pausing and parsing are practically identical; the first main break is after *optimism,* the second after *woman,* the third after *prospects* etc. and the correlation between % pause duration and parsing complexity indices is 0.96. For all 14 sentences, the mean coefficient of correlation was 0.92.

Thus pause durations produced reliable performance sentence structures which are not paradigm specific. Similar structures were obtained in the parsing task and in experiments on short term memory by Dommergues & Grosjean (1978) using transitional error probability (John-

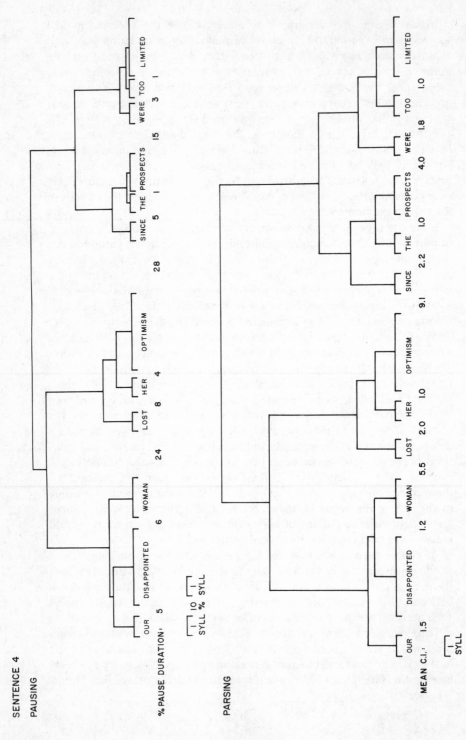

Figure 4. *Hierarchical structures for a sentence obtained from pausing and parsing. Each parsing value at a word boundary is the mean of 15 complexity indices derived from the Ss' hierarchical parsing structures. (After Grosjean, Grosjean & Lane, 1979.)*

son, 1965). The question now became: What variables determine the performance structure of a sentence?

The predictor variable that should account for the greater part of the total variance in % pause duration, if we base ourselves on preceding studies of pausing, is the surface structure of the sentences. Grosjean, Grosjean & Lane (1979) therefore drew a surface structure tree of each experimental sentence, using as a guide the bracketings assigned by Bever, Lackner & Kirk (1969). The next step was to give every word boundary an index of the complexity of the syntactic relations between words in the sentence. They adopted the same measure as in Experiment 3: The complexity index at a particular boundary is the number of nodes dominated by the boundary node, including the boundary node itself.

The 14 linguistic trees were indexed in this way and the complexity values were correlated with the percent pause duration. The mean coefficient of correlation was 0.76. Thus the surface structure of a sentence was found to be a good predictor of the percent pause duration, not only at major constituent breaks, as shown by previous studies, but at all' breaks in the sentence. In Figure 5 we illustrate how surface structure and the corresponding pause structure can be quite congruent (the correlation between the two is 0.92). Most linguistic breaks are reflected in the pause structure (after *book,* after *expert*, etc.), although some slight variation exists at lower levels (for instance, inside *Closing his client's book* and *the young expert*).

Although the complexity index was on the whole a good predictor of percent pause duration, it failed at times to account for the pause structure of entire sentences or constituents. Figure 6 presents such a case. The main surface structure break is after the NP *(John)* whereas the longest pause is situated after the NP object *(the strange young man)* – the NP-VP break receives only the 4th longest pause: 10% – and the third linguistic break is after *quick* but it is given the second longest pause: 19%. These differences are reflected in the correlation coefficient which is 0.60.

It would seem from these results that pausing is affected both by the relative importance of constituent breaks, reflected by the complexity indices, and the relative length of the constituents. When these are of unequal length, as in this case – the NP contains 1 word and the VP 11 – Ss will attempt to displace the pause to a point midway between the beginning of the first constituent (for example, a NP) and the end of the second constituent (for example, a VP), if at that point there occurs a syntactic boundary important enough. It would seem that a compromise takes place between this bisection tendency and the linguistic structure of the sentence. Performance pause structures can therefore be characterized as the product of two (sometimes conflicting) demands on the

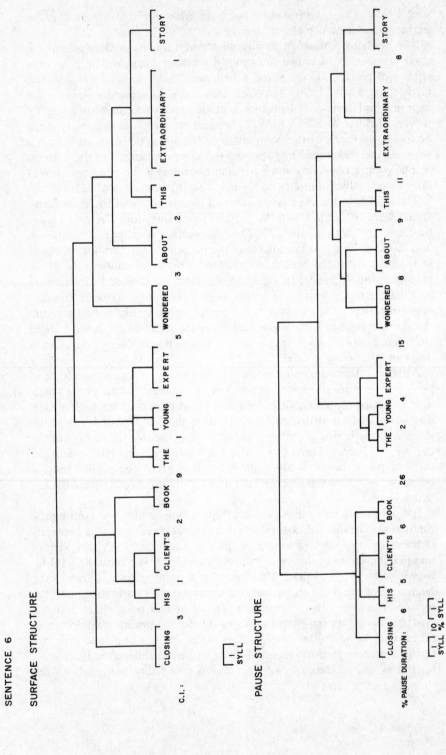

Figure 5. *The surface structure and pause structure of sentence 6. (After Grosjean, Grosjean & Lane, 1979.)*

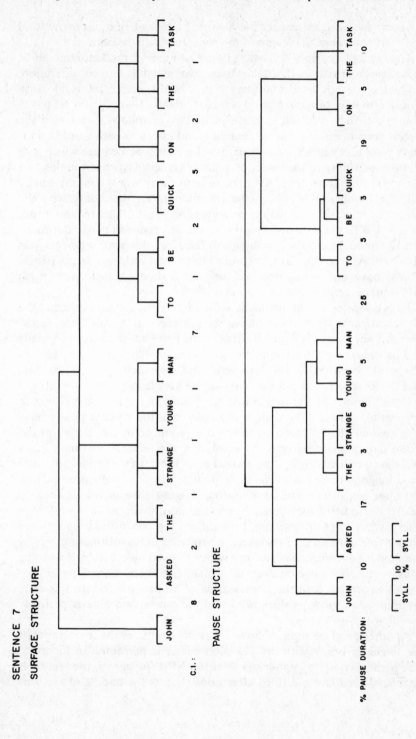

Figure 6. *The surface structure and pause structure of sentence 7. (After Grosjean, Grosjean & Lane, 1979.)*

speaker: the need to respect the linguistic structure of the sentence and the need to balance the length of the constituents in the output.

Grosjean, Grosjean & Lane (1979) propose a predictor model of these pause structures that takes these two demands into consideration. To assign to each word boundary a predicted share of the total pause duration in light of its structural complexity and distance from the bisection point, they used an iterative procedure as follows. Start with the largest constituent, the entire sentence, and assign to each word boundary a complexity index, as described earlier, and a percentage which is its relative proximity to the bisection point: number of words from the start (or end) of the constituent to the boundary (whichever is less) divided by half the number of words in the constituent. The boundary with the largest product is the major performance break. The second order breaks and (a linear transformation of) their predicted pause durations are obtained by repeating the procedure on the two segments just obtained. And so on, iteratively, until the lowest order segments (single words) have been delimited and assigned a (linear transformation of) predicted percent of pause duration.

Figure 7 presents the linguistic structure, the pause structure and the predicted pause structure of one of the sentences in the Grosjean, Grosjean & Lane study. The match between the first two structures (linguistic and pausing) is relatively good but several mismatches do occur: the NP-VP break (between *he* and *brought*) is not respected by the pause data and the prepositional phrase *(By making his plan known)* is organized quite differently in the two structures. Consequently, the coefficient of correlation between the complexity index and the percent pause duration was only 0.75. The structure that is produced by the model fits the pause data almost perfectly: by combining the relative proximity index and the complexity index, the second main break in the model structure is no longer situated after *he,* as is predicted by the linguistic structure, but after *out* (this is still an important linguistic break that is situated near the middle of the sentence) and the third main break is no longer after *by* but after *By making.* In addition, the NP in the prepositional phrase *(the objections of everyone)* is produced in two distinct clusters by the model *(the objections* and *of everyone)* in complete accord with the pause data. The only difference, a small one, between the pause and model structures is in the organization of *he brought out.* In this case, therefore, the model values predicted the pause data almost perfectly (r = 0.96).

Another good example of how the model combines the importance of the linguistic break with the bisection parser is presented in Figure 8. The highest complexity index is after the NP *(The agent),* the second is after *consulted* and the third after *book,* but as the middle of the sen-

NTENCE 8

RFACE STRUCTURE

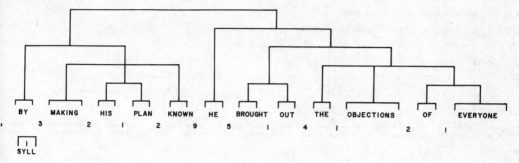

USE STRUCTURE

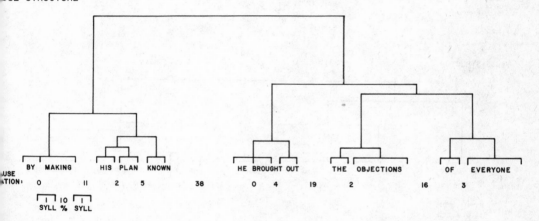

DICTED PAUSE STRUCTURE

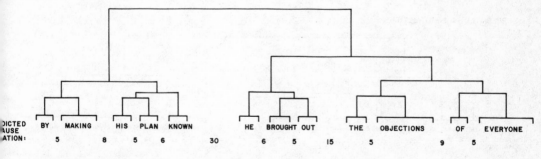

Figure 7. *The surface structure, pause structure and predicted pause structure of sentence 8.*
(After Grosjean, Grosjean & Lane, 1979.)

SENTENCE II
SURFACE STRUCTURE

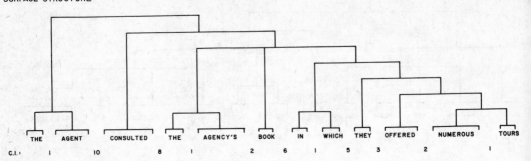

PAUSE STRUCTURE

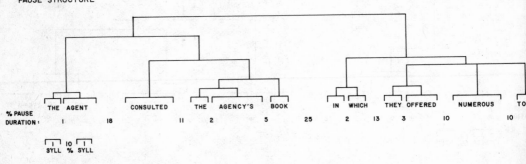

PREDICTED PAUSE STRUCTURE

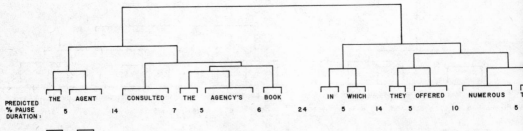

Figure 8. *The surface structure, pause structure and predicted pause structure of sentence 11. (After Grosjean, Grosjean & Lane, 1979.)*

tence is also after *book,* the highest product of the complexity index and the proximity index occurs after *book* (and not after the first two breaks) in accord with the longest pause in the reading data (25%). Each subpart is now reassigned complexity and proximity values by the model and the two highest products again correspond to the next two highest pauses (after *agent* and after *which*). In this way, the 0.72 correlation between linguistic structure and pause structure was increased to 0.92 when pause data were correlated with model values.

The mean correlation between the percent pause duration and the model percent pause duration for all 14 sentences was 0.87. This was significantly different from the mean correlation between the complexity index and the percent pause duration (0.76) at the 0.01 level. Thus the model accounted for 72% of the total variance in pause time as compared to 56% accounted for by the complexity index alone.

The variance that the model did not account for could be due to such factors as the linguistic model itself, the impact that the length of the word has on the preceding and following pause, the stress pattern of the sentence and semantic variables. It was found, for example, that the % pause duration of the break preceding a 1, 2 or 3 syllable word (at a constant complexity index of 1) remains constant (about 4%) but then rises to 9% before a 4 syllable word and to 11% before a 5 syllable word. Nevertheless, the present model not only accounted for most of the variance of the 14 experimental sentences but was also a good predictor of the pause data obtained in other experiments on English and American Sign Language. From these studies, Grosjean, Grosjean & Lane (1979) concluded tentatively that performance structures – the product of linguistic and performance variables – are not language or modality specific.

Further research is now underway to gain a better understanding of these performance structures. We are working to:
– replicate and extend for American Sign Language the Grosjean, Grosjean & Lane (1979) study conducted with English;
– examine more systematically the effect on pause duration of the linear position of the major surface structure break of the sentence;
– isolate other performance variables that play a role in the determination of performance structures;
– determine whether performance structures assist the listener (or observer for sign language) in language decoding. The existence of these structures has become apparent mainly from experimental tasks involving speech production such as pausing and recall. The question now is: Do these structures also play a role in language decoding?

Do they enhance perception and comprehension of speech and sign? Is this indeed why the speaker's and signer's prosody reflect the operation of linguistic and bisection parsers? If performance structures do help the listener, we will conclude that their origin lies in a general language mechanism that is common to both production and perception.

Results from all these studies will then be used to re-examine and improve the iterative model proposed by Grosjean, Grosjean & Lane (1979): We will add to it other performance variables as their importance becomes evident and also explore a variety of linguistic complexity indices. Our ultimate aim is to obtain a model that predicts as accurately as possible the performance structures involved in the perception and production of language, be it spoken or signed.

Note

1. The writing of this paper was supported in part by grant numbers 768 2530, National Science Foundation, and RR 07143, Department of Health, Education and Welfare. The author would like to thank the following publishers for permission to reproduce figures that appeared in journals they publish: S. Karger SA (Figures 1 and 2), Academic Press (Figures 3, 4, 5, 6, 7 and 8).

BOGUSŁAW MAREK

Phonological status of the pause

In this paper I would like to show that the pause should be given its own place in the phonological component of the language, in the sense that the position it can take in the sentence is predictable, rule-governed and derivable in a way similar to that in which the surface, segmental representation is derived.

The claim that the pause is predictable can be supported by a rather trivial observation that native speakers of a language know exactly where to place it. Had the position of the pause been unpredictable, it would have to be true that all instances of correct pause assignment have to be memorized. That this is not the case, can be illustrated by the following sentences, in which / / stands for the pause and ++ marks its absence:

1. a. John++ and Mary++ are a happy couple.
   b. *John / / and Mary / / are a happy couple.
2. You need one cup of milk / / one cup of sugar / / four eggs / / ...
3. a. John++ and Mary++ left for Paris.
   b. John / / and Mary / / left for Paris.
4. a. Betty sleeps in the garden++ because she hates stuffy rooms.
   b. Betty sleeps in the garden / / because she hates stuffy rooms.
   c. *Because she hates stuffy rooms++ Betty sleeps in the garden.
   d. Because she hates stuffy rooms / / Betty sleeps in the garden.
5. a. The boy / / who broke the window / / will be punished.
   b. The boy++ who broke the window++ will be punished.

Looking at the sentences above, we can make the following observations:
- there are sentences, in which the pause is intuitively not allowed to appear (e.g. 1.b. and 4.c.)
- there are sentences in which the pause is felt to be necessary (e.g. 2. and 4.d.)
- there are sentences in which the pause seems to be optional (e.g. 3.a., 3.b., 4.a. and 4.b.)

– there are sentences which can be disambiguated by means of the pause (e.g. 5.a. and 5.b.).

Finally, all native speakers will recognize cases of totally incorrect uses of the pause:

6. Mrs. ... Piglet ... bought ... a ... pound ... of sugar and a ... pound of ... bananas.

There have not been many serious attempts to account for the presence or absence of the pause in sentences like the ones above. It seems, however, that although it may not be possible to provide a complete list of rules for pause assignment, some such rules, or at least some of the principles governing the occurrence of the pause can be determined. In this paper we shall deal with the pause in sentences involving conjunctions and relative clauses.

Without neglecting the well known observation that the presence or absence of the pause may depend on the structure of the sentence (as in nonrestrictive relative clauses, counting etc.), we shall try to show that sentence structure alone is not a sufficient principle governing the assignment of the pause.

(1b) is a case of incorrectly used pauses. On the other hand, both (3a) and (3b) sound correct. This can be accounted for with the aid of the distinction made by Lakoff & Peters (1969), between phrasal and derived conjunctions. (1a) involves a phrasal, underlying conjunction and receives no pause. On the other hand, (3b) can be treated as a sentence transformationally conjoined by a derived conjunction. We could suggest here a first approximation rule for pause assignment:

PA rule $1 : S_1$ and $S_2 \rightarrow S_1 / / S_2$

Thus, having two underlying sentences, e.g.:

7. a. John walked to his office.
   b. Mary drove to the market.

we can conjoin them into:

7. c. John walked to his office and Mary drove to the market.

and apply PA rule 1 to derive:

7. d. John walked to his office / / and Mary drove to the market.

It seems that sentences like (7c) present no difficulties as far as the assignment of the pause is concerned. In fact, PA rule 1 seems to be obligatory in cases where identical conjunct reduction does not apply.

Sentences in (3) present a problem, however, for two reasons. First, identical conjunct reduction transformation does apply if we derive (3 a) or (3 b) from (3 c–d):

3. c. John left for Paris.
   d. Mary left for Paris.

Secondly, (3 a) is ambiguous. It can either be derived from (3 c–d), or it can be an instance of a phrasal, underlying conjunction, just as (1 a) was. To resolve this ambiguity we can apply a test suggested by Lakoff & Peters (1969) who say that sentences with an underlying, phrasal conjunction are sensitive to an optional T-with transformation, which is inapplicable to sentences conjoined transformationally. That is, (3 a) can be derived from a structure transferable to "John left for Paris *with Mary*", or, similarly to (3 b) from sentences (3 c) and (3 d). Does this mean that the pause is optional in sentences like (3)? In some sense the pause is optional, but in no way are the two sentences (3 a) and (3 b) equivalent in meaning. (3 a) can either mean that John and Mary left for Paris together, or simply that they are both away. (3 b), however, carries different information. It can be paraphrased in a way in which (3 a) could not, namely with a sentence like:

John left for Paris *and also* Mary left for Paris.

or,

Not only John but also Mary left for Paris.

The amount of information that (3) can carry and consequently the presence or absence of the pause depends, however, entirely on the context and presuppositions made by the speaker.

There are many instances in which context is important in assigning or not assigning the pause. This seems to be the case with "Because-sentences". If one of the conjuncts carries "given" information, the pause is not assigned. It is obligatory, however, if both conjuncts carry "new" information.

Notice, that (4 a) is a correct response to a "Why-question" like:

Why does Betty sleep in the garden?

(4 a) would be an incorrect reply to a question like "Where does Betty sleep?" or "What can you say about Betty?" (4 b) on the other hand, could function as a response to such questions and the second conjunct, following the pause, introduces new, additional information.

The distinction between "given" and "new" information seems to be important for a disscussion of the pause in restrictive and nonrestrictive clauses.

L. Martin (1968) has made an observation that "if there exists a sentence containing a relative clause, there exists a corresponding conjoined sentence" (Martin, 1968:64). On this basis, he proposes to derive relative clauses from conjoined sentences. It remains unknown, however, how the restrictive clauses are to be distinguished from nonrestrictive relative clauses. L. Martin limits himself to a remark known from other sources that a nonrestrictive relative clause will have "a comma intonation". (Martin 1968:65)

This problem is more clearly presented by S. Thompson (1971) who claims that there is, in many cases, no difference in the underlying structures of restrictive and nonrestrictive relative clauses. The "restricting" nature of relative clauses is described as "a function of the presuppositions which the speaker has about the extent of his hearer's knowledge". (Thompson, 1971:82)

Thompson illustrates her argument with the following two sentences:

Th-48 The boy, who works at the library, is majoring in philosophy.
Th-49 The boy who works at the library is majoring in philosophy.

and suggests that they both have the following underlying representation:

Th-50 /Boy works in library/   /boy is majoring in philosophy/.

The difference between the two sentences is described as resulting from the fact that in Th-48 "the speaker has decided that the boy is already known to the hearer, the speaker is adding two pieces of information about the boy. For (49) the speaker assumes that the hearer knows about the boy who works at the library; [...] and the information which the speaker assumes to be new appears as the main predicate". (Thompson 1971:87)

If Thompson's argument is correct then it seems to support our observations concerning the assignment of the pause in conjoined sentences. Let us recall that the PA rule assigns the pause unless one of the conjuncts carries given information. If the contents of the whole of the first conjunct of Th-50 is "assumed by the speaker to be known to the hearer", or in other words, if the first conjunct is "given", the pause is not assigned. This might be an explanation of the fact that restrictive relative clauses do not (normally) have the pause, or the "comma intonation". They do not, because only the main predicate introduces "new" information; the relativised conjunct carries "given" information and so, the pause is not inserted.

Thompson claims that "the boy" in Th-48 is already known to the hearer. It seems, however, that this "givenness" is irrelevant, and that the first conjunct introduces "new" information about the subject which can be either "given" or "new". This suggestion seems to be confirmed by the fact that if we replace "the boy" with "my wife", (8) below can be followed by the hearer's remark: "Oh, I didn't know you had a wife."

8. My wife, who works at the library, is majoring in philosophy.

We can say then, that the pause is assigned in Th-48, and in other sentences with nonrestrictive clauses in agreement with the PA rule for conjoined sentences because both conjuncts carry "new" information.

It has to be remembered, however, that the pause is not always a reliable criterion for the decision that a given sentence contains a non-restrictive relative clause. It seems that for the sake of clarity and preci-sion, restrictive relative clauses also can be given the pause.

Consider the following sentences:

9. Men / / my dear / / who don't wear ties / / will not attract ladies'
   attention.
10. Men / / who don't wear ties / / will not attract ladies' attention.

It seems that (10) and other restrictive relative clauses which can only be interpreted as restrictive relative clauses will remain such even if the pauses are assigned to them. The only question which remains to be answered is whether they are acceptable. I believe that no native speaker of English will question the acceptability of (9) with parenthesis, or (10), without the parenthetically introduced phrase.

Thus, it is probably the case that the pause signals not only "new" information, but has other functions as well.

Summing up our observations, we can say that:
1. Sentences with phrasal conjunctions receive no pause.
2. The pause is assigned to sentences with a transformationally derived conjunction:
   a) obligatorily – if the identical conjunct reduction is inapplicable,
   b) optionally – if the identical conjunct reduction applies.
   The application or non-application of the PA rule seems to depend in such sentences on the context and the speaker's intentions as to the organization of the information.
3. The pause is assigned to conjoined sentences if both conjuncts intro-duce "new" information.
4. If one of the conjuncts carries "given" information – the pause is not assigned.
5. Points 3 and 4 hold true for restrictive and nonrestrictive relative clauses. However, restrictive relative clauses can also be assigned pauses which means that the so called "comma intonation" or its absence is not always a reliable information about the restrictiveness or non-restrictiveness of a relative clause.

HEINZ KLATT

Pauses as indicators of cognitive functioning in aphasia

In the short history of the investigation of temporal variables in speech, juncture pauses have been the Cinderella of research. This study is concerned with those phenomena of "silence" in speech that according to Maclay & Osgood (1959) "serve to identify linguistically relevant units, such as junctures located at the boundaries of phonemes, morphemes, words, phrases, and sentences". The research of juncture pauses and especially that of internal-open-juncture pauses which break the flow of speech on the syllable and word levels, has been so thoroughly neglected because the latencies in question are very short in duration and difficult to measure. It was hoped that in experimenting with aphasic subjects these pause phenomena would become observable and measurable.

On the evidence of previous research (Klatt, forthcoming b) it was hypothesised in the investigation reported here that a model of dependency grammar, with the concept of valence as its central notion, would predict the frequency of extended pauses at different junctures within a sentence. By adopting the basic model of sentence analysis as developed by Tesnière (1953, 1959), the hypothesis was formulated that the syntactic complexity of different parts of speech would be reflected in the distributional pattern of pauses.

According to Tesnière the verb is the central node which governs the sentence. The predicate is the pivotal point, where the structural analysis must begin. The segments immediately subordinate to the verb are so-called "actants" and "circonstants", all represented on the same level in the hierarchy. These are the subject, the direct and indirect objects, as well as all "circumstances" of the action, such as manner, place, time and so on. Finally, on a level subordinate to the "actants" and "circonstants" are the adjectives, pronouns, and other grammatical categories.

Tesnière compares the function of the verb in governing a certain number of what in phrase-structure grammar would be called noun and prepositional phrases, with the valence of an atom. By logically extending this central argument to nouns, as Admoni (1966) has already suggested, it can be concluded that within the model of a dependency grammar the verb has most valences or "Leerstellen" in the sentence. The verb can be compared with a central switchboard, where all further connections are coordinated. Therefore it was predicted that verbs would be the linguistic segment most difficult to process since, it was assumed, in articulating the verb the entire sentence frame would have to be provided cognitively. As a consequence, we predicted that the greatest number of pauses would occur before the verb.

With respect to the nouns it was hypothesised that they would be the second most difficult category and that they would be preceded by the second greatest number of pauses since their system of valences is less elaborate. They are already determined by the verb and they themselves open up linguistic frames of valences only for subordinate adjectives and pronouns.

For adjectives, finally, it was predicted that they would be preceded by the fewest pauses since they have the least elaborate system of valences of the three parts of speech that we decided to investigate.

Underlying all theoretical expectations was the notion that grammatical categories by virtue of their complexity, expressed in terms of valences, would require different amounts of time to be processed, this latter to be measured in terms of number of pauses, preceding the part of speech in question.

Previous research has shown the validity of the dependency grammatical concept of valence to predict the error rate in the reading of sentences as well as lists of words by aphasic patients (Klatt, 1978 ab). It was therefore decided to use reading as the behaviour to be investigated.

Although this research was designed to investigate questions of primarily theoretical nature, we formulated two hypotheses which are more clinically oriented:

1. Considering the fact that brain injured patients are easily fatigued, and taking into account that reading requires considerable efforts of aphasics we predicted that our subjects would make progressively more pauses towards the end of the sentences. If indeed aphasics show measurable fatigue towards the end of the reading of sentences seven words long, then this information might be helpful for the construction of sentences that are used for therapeutic purposes.

2. The second hypothesis that was formulated from a more practical, clinical standpoint is that the pause pattern would change if patients read the stimulus sentences repeatedly. Since an aphasic's first reading is in general very haphazard and "accident prone", and requires a lot of planning, it was predicted that aphasics would not rely so heavily on pauses as a strategy in the articulation of repeated readings. We predicted fewer pauses in repeated readings as long as fatigue did not have a reverse effect.

Method

The subjects were 15 male, mildly aphasic patients of different etiologies, between 21 and 81 years of age.

The stimulus material consisted of 21 sentences with an identical sentence structure:

Article – Adjective – Noun – Verb – Article – Adjective – Noun
Example: The strong lion seized the tiny sheep.

To test the hypothesis whether or not aphasic patients show fatigue towards the end of the sentences, all stimulus sentences were constructed symmetrically, i.e., with two modified noun phrases. The sentences were presented one at a time, in random order, typed in capital letters. (cf. Klatt, forthcoming a)

To obtain more reliable data and to explore the therapeutic effects of the explanation of word meanings by the patient, we had the subjects explain the meanings of the content words in their own formulations, without any assistance, after having read the sentence twice. After this exercise the subjects read the sentence twice again. Thus, we obtained from every patient 4 readings of each sentence. The readings were tape-recorded.

Verbatim typewritten transcripts were made by an American speech pathologist. The tape-recordings were transferred to an audio frequency spectrometer and level recorder, yielding a graphic record of acoustic energy in terms of amplitude over time. This transformation provided a rather unproblematic, although extremely tedious, measuring of the lengths of pauses.

Lacking a well-founded theoretical rationale for what length should constitute a minimum pause, we accepted the practice of O'Connell and associates (1972 b) and identified lack of verbalization of 270 msec or longer as a pause. There was no attempt made in this research to distinguish between qualitatively different pauses. Occasional filled pauses were considered as part of the ambient silent pause. Whenever a patient spontaneously, and against the instruction, repeated a word or a phrase, and hesitated before both realizations then 2 pauses were recorded. There were altogether 15 × 21 × 4 = 1260 readings of entire sentences.

Results

The major hypothesis was that the cognitive processing of linguistic segments will require time before articulation. The amount of time would be in proportion to the complexity as defined by our competence grammatical model. This hypothesis was confirmed: There are significantly more pauses before *verbs* (73%) than before *nouns* (67%) (p <.05) and significantly more pauses before *nouns* than before *adjectives* (39%) (p <.005).

There were 2 significant differences between *'frequent'* and *'infrequent'* categories. 'Infrequent' nouns were preceded by pauses in 81.5% of all possibilities, 'frequent' nouns only in 52% (p <.0005); infrequent adjectives were preceded by pauses in 45% and frequent adjectives in 33.9% (p <.025). The difference between frequent (69%) and infrequent verbs (76%) was not significant.

With respect to the *length of the words* there were 2 significant differences. There were significantly more pauses before long nouns (75%) than before short nouns (53%): p <.0005, and significantly more pauses before long adjectives (50%) than before short adjectives (29%): p <.005. The difference between long (73%) and short (72%) verbs was not significant. Surprisingly, the category of long nouns was most often preceded by pauses.

To test a possible fatigue effect that might manifest itself within the reading of seven-word-long sentences, we compared the *first noun* in the sentence with the *second,* and the *first adjective* with the *second.* Both analyses yielded significant differences: Of all pauses before nouns, 53% were before the second and 47% before the first: p <.05; with respect to

Table 1. *Average number of pauses before word categories in the four readings per subject.*

Verbs	1	16.73	ns	t = 0.54	df = 14	s = 3.38
	2	16.27	p <0.0005	t = 4.28	df = 14	s = 2.41
	3	13.6	ns	t = 0.65	df = 14	s = 1.99
	4	13.93				
	Max	21				
Nouns	1	31.93	p <0.01	t = 2.91	df = 14	s = 5.14
	2	28.07	p <0.005	t = 3.05	df = 14	s = 6.61
	3	22.87	ns	t = 1.37	df = 14	s = 3.96
	4	21.47				
	Max	42				
Adj.s	1	20.8	p <0.01	t = 2.62	df = 14	s = 4.27
	2	17.93	p <0.025	t = 2.14	df = 14	s = 5.42
	3	14.93	ns	t = 0.39	df = 14	s = 4.61
	4	14.47				
	Max	42				

adjectives 57% were before the second and 43% before the first: p <.005.

To see whether *repetitions* of readings would have any effect on the pause structure we compared the number of hesitations before nouns, adjectives, and verbs per reading. There was a significant decrease in the number of pauses between the first (66%) and second (59%) reading: p <.005, and another highly significant decrease between the second and third (49%) reading: p <.005. The decrease from third to fourth (47%) reading was not significant.

Table 1 shows how consistently the 3 parts of speech contributed to the overall change in pause frequency. The drastic decrease in the number of hesitations from the 2nd to 3rd reading is evidently due to the interpolated explanation of the content words.

Finally, we correlated the number of *pauses* before content words with the number of *errors* subjects made in reading the following word. This correlation is r_s = .32 (p <.0005). It explains only 10.24% of the variance. This result shows that mistakes are preceded by pauses only occasionally. It could well mean that pauses are used effectively to eliminate errors.

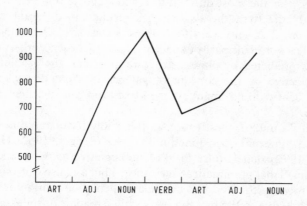

Figure 1. *Number of pauses – 15 subjects, 21 sentences,*
4 readings (max: 1260).

Discussion

The research presented in this report originated in a study that demonstrated dramatic differences in the reading of different parts of speech by aphasics. In this earlier investigation (Klatt, 1978 b; forthcoming b) aphasic patients read nouns, adjectives, and verbs in the form of a list, in which the order of words of different grammatical categories was randomized, as well as in the form of meaningful sentences. In both conditions it was found that the part of speech had a highly significant effect on the error rate of reading. These results raised the question of how it is to be explained that a noun which is short and frequent (girl) induces so many fewer mistakes than a verb which is short and frequent (met). What is it about a verb that makes it difficult to read? Why should a noun that is as short and frequent as an adjective be more difficult to read than the latter? Sequential or positional factors were demonstrated to be as irrelevant as were length and frequency of occurrence.

Measuring the number of pauses rather than errors, we again obtained a highly significant rank order. Although it was not our intention to revitalize grammatical theories and explain aspects of performance with these models of syntax alone, the results of our investigations require an analysis in terms of linguistic categories.

In comparing the rank orders of difficulty obtained in counting errors in reading and measuring number of pauses before words, our studies yielded, however, a remarkable inconsistency. In both investigations the verb was by far the most difficult to read category. But with respect to nouns and adjectives the two studies resulted in different rankings. Counting errors, nouns were the easiest; measuring pauses, adjectives were the least difficult part of speech. The rank order Verb-Adjective-Noun was predicted by phrase structure grammar, the gradient Verb-Noun-Adjective by the concept of valence of dependency grammar. Errors evidently do not manifest the same problems in articulation that pauses do.

The pauses under investigation in this study have traditionally been considered "internal-open-juncture" pauses (Trager, 1962; Hartmann & Stork, 1972) that require little or no cognitive activity, since it had been assumed that grammatical decisions within a clause were such over-learned processes that they did not delay articulation. This interpretation was evidently due to the fact that very skilled readers or speakers always served as subjects in experimentation. It is therefore not surprising to find that authors who consider all pauses as "errors" or "dysfluencies" do not account at all for juncture pauses (Maclay & Osgood, 1959; cf. Clark & Clark, 1977).

There were three major contentions that provided the rationale for our experiment:

1. Syntactic decisions take time. The choice of a specific part of speech implies a grammatical decision.
2. Pauses are not necessarily errors or dysfluencies; they can be part of a strategy to cope with greater complexities; they reflect planning.

3. The reading of aphasics provides a sufficient differentiation of pauses as to make the complexities of syntactic decisions and the strategies of subjects to cope with them observable.

The articulation of words in reading requires the retrieval of words that correspond to the written sign with respect to semantic content, grammatical form and phonology. The fact that the decisions required are indeed separate is indicated by errors of reading such as "animal" for "lion" (semantic confusion; sentence 1), "politician" for "political" (grammatical confusion; sentence 6) or "rion" for "lion" (phonological confusion, sentence 1). (cf. Klatt, forthcoming a). Since semantically and phonologically the words of our sentences can be regarded as random samples, it seems reasonable to interpret the differences in the pause pattern in terms of the only systematically modified parameter: part of speech and number of valences.

Closely linked to this consideration was our second premise. That pauses are not errors per se, as Clark & Clark (1977) suggested, is altogether obvious in the function of delays in dramatic readings. Only a very narrow concept of what constitutes an "ideal delivery" would interpret all kinds of pauses as "dysfluencies".

Whether this reflection applies, however, to the structure of our sentences is not entirely clear. Although it appears evident that different complexities of different parts of speech require different amounts of time to be processed by every normal reader, there seems to be a complementary process in effect in the aphasic reader. Wherever there is a specific difficulty, due to the complexity of the word an aphasic might deliberately lengthen a pause as part of a strategy to avoid any possibility of making a mistake. In this model a pause results because time is required for the retrieval of the word and because the patient needs time to assure and reassure himself of the correctness of the word to be articulated. This is what the low correlation of $r_s = .32$ between the number of pauses before words and the number of errors in the reading of the following word seems to indicate. Mistakes are generally not preceded by pauses. Delays appear to reduce the error rate; they function as part of a strategy to "go safe".

Our third contention, finally, was that the reading of sentences by aphasics would allow us to look at highly automatic cognitive decision making as through a microscope. Due to the breakdown and "stretching-out" of processes that in normal readers do not seem to take any time, these cognitive functions manifest themselves in observable and measurable pauses.

Thus, the third premise as well supports the objective of our research, i.e., to demonstrate that at least in aphasia the number of pauses before words reflects the syntactic-cognitive complexity of the linguistic unit to be processed. Verbs having least valences induce the smallest number of pauses.

With respect to the minor hypotheses of our investigation space does not allow for elaboration. It can, however, be concluded that the length of the following word as well as its frequency of occurrence have in general a significant effect on the number of the preceding pause. Greater length and less familiarity with the word to be read seem to require more time for preformulation or rehearsal.

For clinical application it is useful to note that the nature and length of our sentences might cause fatigue in the second half of the sentence reading, resulting in more pauses. Furthermore, it seems advisable to have the patient repeat the sentence twice and to have him explain the meaning of the content words. A third repetition, however, results in an increase in number of pauses as well as in the error rate (cf. Klatt, forthcoming b) and should therefore not be carried out.

Further research will have to investigate whether or not pauses *following* certain linguistic segments are required to analyse the correctness of the preceding articulation. The relatively high number of pauses before the second article, or rather *after* the verb (Figure 1), seems to indicate an assessment of the reader after the event. But even that might prove to be insufficient. There are some reasons to believe that the "ambient pause" with a word in the centre should be the smallest unit to be studied.

ELISABETH HOFMANN

Speech control and paraphasia in fluent and nonfluent aphasics[1]

Introduction

Following Lecours (1975), we define 'paraphasia' as the inappropriate substitution of a linguistic unit at the phoneme, morpheme or lexeme level. Substitutions of phonemes or groups of phonemes below lexeme level are classified as phonemic paraphasias (example: "Birsen" – "Linsen"), substitutions of lexemes as verbal paraphasia (example: "Bohnen" – "Linsen"). Neologisms, paraphasias with an unidentifiable referent were categorized as extreme phonemic errors (Goodglass & Kaplan, 1972).

The aphasia literature is very contradictory as to the relation of paraphasia to aphasic syndromes and fragmentary as to the explanation of paraphasia within theories of aphasic disturbances. Nevertheless, two main groups of assumptions about a possible explanation of paraphasic errors may be distinguished: some authors understand paraphasia as conscious verbal substitutions, for example Luria (1970) or Bay (1960), others as uncontrolled misproduction for example Freud (1891), Wernicke (1874), Pick (1931) or Alajouanine et al. (1964).

In our study we attempted to investigate the possible relationship of the two explanations of paraphasia to

a) the usual classification of verbal and phonemic paraphasia,

b) different types of aphasia and

c) the severity of the aphasic disturbance.

Because not only hesitations *before* paraphasic errors (cf. Goldman-Eisler, 1968; Butterworth, 1972, 1976, 1977), but also corrections and comments *after* paraphasias might provide clues to the kind of processes underlying the production of paraphasias, the immediate context of paraphasic errors was examined in relation to the kind and severity of the paraphasias and to the kind and severity of the aphasic syndrome.

We used for our investigation a classification of aphasia according to the fluency of speech, because this classification is based on the analysis of spontaneous speech production, which is relevant for this study, as well.

Material and method
(cf. Cohen et al., 1975; Hofmann, 1977)

Subjects were matched subgroups of 19 fluent and 21 nonfluent aphasics. Fluency of speech was determined by the average rate of speech in the immediate reproduction of short stories. A score of 50 words per minute was used as a cut-off point to separate fluent and nonfluent aphasics.

The patients were asked to reproduce four short stories about events of everyday life. Reproductions were chosen as a basis for determining the relation between substituted and substituting linguistic unit.

The following data were determined for each patient:
(1) number and kind of verbal and phonemic paraphasias,
(2) the magnitude of the semantic deviation of the verbal paraphasias and the phonetic similarity of the phonemic paraphasias, as rated independently by judges unaware of the purpose of the investigation, and
(3) the immediate context of paraphasias, including
     a) hesitation incidents preceding paraphasic errors (filled and unfilled pauses and comments referring to the following paraphasia) and
     b) control incidents after paraphasias consisting of corrections and comments referring to the preceding paraphasia.

Groups of aphasics and kinds of paraphasia were compared as to deviation scores and context variables. Comparisons of the two different types of context variables and their correlation with deviation scores and with severity of aphasia were the additional major analyses.

Results

Only the most interesting results will be summarized here. (For the complete presentation of results see the Tables and Figure 1.)
(1) Percentage of paraphasias
     Both groups had significantly more verbal than phonemic paraphasias (cf. Table 1; Figure 1).
(2) Magnitude of deviation of paraphasias
     Whereas semantic deviation of verbal paraphasias and phonetic deviation of phonemic paraphasias correlated with each other in the fluent group, no correlation of the two deviation scores was found in the nonfluent group (cf. Table 2).
(3) Context variables
     a) Nonfluent aphasics showed significantly more hesitations before

both kinds of paraphasia than the fluent – a nontrivial result, as we had rated only pauses discernibly longer than usual in the course of average speech of the patients. As to control incidents, the nonfluent aphasics revealed a significantly higher percentage only after verbal paraphasias; there was no significant difference between the groups as to the amount of control after phonemic paraphasias. (cf. Table 1)

Table 1. *Comparisons between nonfluent (A(NF)) and fluent aphasics (A(F)) by means of MANN-WHITNEY-U-Tests.*

	VERBAL PARAPHASIAS		PHONEMIC PARAPHASIAS	
	A(NF)	A(F)	A(NF)	A(F)
percentage of par. of the total verbal production				
median	1.89	1.22	1.42	0.7
range	0.77–3.17	1.11–3.74	0.31–3.25	0.2–1.5
U-tests (z-values)		2.03		2.09
		<.05		<.05
average scores of deviation of par.				
median	2.94	2.45	2.73	2.95
range	1.76–3.30	1.53–3.22	1.68–3.85	1.6–3.9
U-tests (z-values)		3.00		0.58
		<.01		>.10
percentage of par. with hesitation incidents				
median	52	40	64	40
range	20–100	20–80	0–100	0–100
U-tests (z-values)		2.67		2.11
		<.01		<.05
percentage of par. with control incidents following				
median	48.5	25	50	47
range	0–67	0–67	0–50	0–71
U-tests (z-values)		2.66		0.17
		<.01		>.10

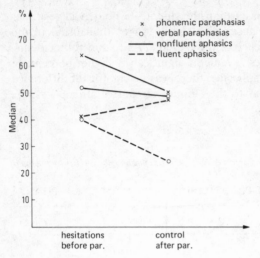

Figure 1. *Hesitation and control in the context of verbal and phonemic paraphasias.*

b) Both nonfluent and fluent aphasics showed significantly more hesitations before verbal paraphasias than control incidents following them; there was no significant difference between percentage of hesitations and percentage of control incidents for phonemic paraphasias. (cf. Figure 1)

(4) Context variables and deviation scores (cf. Table 2)

Table 2. *Rank correlations between deviation scores and context variables.*

	A (NF)					A (F)				
	semantic devia-tion	hesita-tion before PHON. PAR.	hesita-tion before VERB. PAR.	control after PHON. PAR.	control after VERB. PAR.	semantic devia-tion	hesita-tion before PHON. PAR.	hesita-tion before VERB. PAR.	control after PHON. PAR.	control after VERB. PAR.
phonetic similarity	.12	.32	–	–.40	–	–.52*	–.68**	–	–.07	–
semantic deviation	–	–	.19	–	.44*	–	–	.42*	–	.06
hesitation before PHON. PAR.	–	–	.73**	.22	–	–	–	.11	–.34	–
hesitation before VERB. PAR.	–	–	–	–	.41	–	–	–	–	.203
control after PHON. PAR.	–	–	–	–	–.04	–	–	–	–	.06

* significant at 5% level
** significant at 1% level

a) Rank correlations across patients between the number of hesitation incidents per patient on the one hand, and the magnitude of semantic and phonetic deviation of paraphasias on the other hand, were both highly significant for the fluents, but failed to reveal critical values for the nonfluent group.

b) Rank correlations across patients, between the percentage of paraphasias followed by control incidents and deviation scores, were significant only for the correlation between control after verbal paraphasias and semantic deviation for the nonfluent group.

(5) Relationship to token-test scores as measure of the severity of the aphasic disturbance (cf. Table 3)

Table 3. *Rank correlations between Token-Test and other variables investigated.*
Token-Test

	PHON. PAR. %	VERB. PAR. %	phon. simi- larity	seman- tic devia- tion	hesi- tation before PHON. PAR.	hesi- tation before VERB. PAR.	control after PHON. PAR.	control after VERB. PAR.
A (NF)	.68**	−.14	.28	.52*	.27	.45*	.12	.47*
A (F)	.08	.45**	−.25	−.28	−.43	.20	−.15	.27

 * significant at 5% level
** significant at 1% level

a) For the nonfluents the correlation between token-test score and percentage of phonemic paraphasias was highly significant, whereas for the fluents a significant correlation was obtained between token-test score and percentage of verbal paraphasia.

b) Rank correlations of token-test and deviation scores were significant only for the correlation between semantic deviation and token-test score in the nonfluent group.

c) The correlation between context variables and token-test score correlations were significant only for the nonfluent aphasics between hesitation before verbal paraphasias and control after them on the one hand and token-test score on the other hand.

Discussion

The present results indicate that the two explanations of paraphasia may correspond to two different kinds of paraphasic behavior, which are symptomatic of two different kinds of aphasia, fluent and nonfluent.

Let us first consider the outcome for the nonfluent aphasics. They show a relatively high percentage of hesitation incidents before both kinds of paraphasia. This may be interpreted either as a symptom of difficulties in relating semantic and phonetic structure or as a sign of control if we assume a recycling of the word selection process until the speaker has reached the best result within the range of his possibilities. (cf. Rosenberg & Cohen, 1964, 1966) The second interpretation must at least be considered in addition to the first one:

48% of verbal and 50% of phonemic paraphasias were overtly corrected or commented. That the frequencies of hesitation incidents are comparable before verbal and phonemic paraphasias suggests that both kinds of paraphasia might be preceded by editing processes, which at least result in only slightly deviating semantic paraphasia, if no severe semantic and phonemic paraphasias are present. This interpretation is supported by the following results:

(1) The percentage of hesitation preceding verbal paraphasias is higher than is the percentage of control incidents following them; with phonemic paraphasias, however, hesitation phenomena equal control incidents. This may indicate that after verbal paraphasias editing seems less urgent to the patient than after phonemic paraphasias.

(2) With verbal paraphasias control correlates both with semantic deviation and severity of aphasia; this means that the more severe the aphasia and the semantic deviation of paraphasias (cf. the correlation between token-test score and semantic deviation scores), the more urgent the necessity for the patient to edit verbal paraphasias.

(3) The correlation of percentage of phonemic paraphasia and token-test score (Rho = 0.68; p <.05) and the lack of a correlation between verbal paraphasias and token-test scores seem to indicate that phonetic distortion may be more easily avoided with less severe aphasic disturbances, while verbal paraphasias are equally frequent with different degrees of severity of aphasia.

This interpretation of paraphasia for nonfluent aphasics corresponds rather well to an explanation of paraphasias in terms of conscious substitutions. It is also consistent with David Howes' assumption that for the nonfluent aphasics a disturbance of word selection is characteristic, while the patients know what they want to verbalize and thus are able to control word selection by higher functions (Howes, 1967).

In contrast to that, the errors of the fluent aphasics seem to be better explained in terms of uncontrolled misproductions: with the fluent group, hesitation incidents preceding both verbal and phonemic paraphasias are significantly less frequent than with the nonfluent.

Hesitation correlates with both semantic and phonetic deviation. This might indicate that hesitation phenomena are rather more symptomatic of difficulties in performing word selection processes than as expressions of conscious control.

The following results may point towards a deficit mainly of semantic control with fluent aphasics:

(1) Contrary to phonemic paraphasias control incidents are less frequent than hesitations in verbal paraphasias. For both hesitation before and control after verbal paraphasias the fluent group scores significantly lower than the nonfluent.

(2) Token-test scores correlate with the percentage of verbal, but not with the percentage of phonemic paraphasias.

(3) The percentage of verbal paraphasias is higher than that of phonemic paraphasias.

(4) The correlation between semantic and phonetic deviation scores may not only be interpreted as an indication of a relationship between these two symptoms. It may show that difficulties of fluent aphasics leading to phonemic paraphasias may be caused by conceptual disturbances which comprise the loosening of the determination of sound structure by semantic structure.

This interpretation of the results for the fluent aphasics again corresponds to Howes' (1967) assumptions. He suggested that with this group, it is mainly the conceptual processes preceding word selection and thus semantic control that are disturbed.

Note

1. The research reported here was supported by the Deutsche Forschungsgemeinschaft, Sonderforschungsbereich 99 (Linguistik). We are indebted to the following institutions which assisted us in collecting our data:

Abteilung Neurologie der Medizinischen Fakultät an der Rhein.-Westf.-Technischen Hochschule Aachen;

Neurologische Klinik und Institut für Rehabilitation, Bad Homburg;

Rheinische Landesklinik für Sprachgestörte, Bonn;

Neurologische Klinik der Universität Freiburg;

Neurologische Kliniken, Dr. Schmieder, Gailingen;

Neurologische Universitätsklinik, Heidelberg;

Südwestdeutsches Rehabilitationskrankenhaus, Abt. Neurologie, Karlsbad-Langensteinbach;

Neurologische Klinik und Hirnverletztenheim, München;

Max-Planck-Institut für Psychiatrie, München;

Neurologische Klinik des Bürgerhospitals, Stuttgart;

Neurologische Klinik und Hirnverletztenversorgungskrankenhaus, Tübingen.

Conversational aspects

Chairman FRANÇOIS GROSJEAN

GEOFFREY W. BEATTIE

Encoding units in spontaneous speech: Some implications for the dynamics of conversation[1]

Introduction

This paper attempts to elucidate the nature of the units of encoding involved in the generation of spontaneous speech, by analysing two distinct kinds of speaker activity which may provide some clue as to the existence and nature of cognitive activity in speech – one is an integral part of the speech, namely the hesitation structure, the other is extrinsic to the speech, namely speaker gaze direction in conversation. Evidence suggests that both these activities may reflect the cognitive processes underlying the generation of speech (see Goldman-Eisler, 1968; Weiner & Ehrlichman, 1976). Some implications of the presence of planning units in spontaneous speech for the regulation of conversation are also explored.

Hesitations and models of language production

The search for encoding units in spontaneous speech on the basis of the location of hesitations in speech, is based on an hypothesis formulated by Lounsbury (1954: 100) that "Hesitation pauses and points of high statistical uncertainty correspond to the beginnings of units of encoding". The early studies based on the Markov model of language demonstrated a relationship between the occurrence of certain unfilled pauses (silences ≥ 250 msec.) in speech and the transitional probability of the succeeding lexical items, Goldman-Eisler (1958 ac).

However, data reported by Maclay and Osgood suggested that a unit of speech encoding longer than a word is typically involved in the production of spontaneous speech. Maclay and Osgood observed that false starts typically involved not just correction of the unintended word but also correction of the closely associated function words:

> This would suggest that at some level of organisation, the encoding unit is phrase-like, a lexical core with its tightly bound grammatical context (Maclay & Osgood, 1959: 41).

Subsequent analysis of the distributions of hesitations in spontaneous speech also suggested that encoding units are larger than individual words. Boomer (1965) analysed the distribution of hesitations with respect to phonemic clauses (phonologically marked macrosegments containing one und only one primary stress and ending in one of the terminal junctures /I, II, III/, Trager & Smith, 1951). He observed that both unfilled and filled pauses ('ah', 'er', 'um' etc.) tended to occur towards the beginnings of such clauses. Boomer's conclusions were thus that: "planning ranges forward to encompass a structured 'chunk' of syntax and meaning" (1965: 91). One problem with the results of this study is that the modal position for hesitations was found to be between the first and second word of the clause and not before the first word as Lounsbury's hypothesis would predict. There have been a number of explanations offered for this. Barik (1968) suggested that Boomer's decision to regard all UPs at clause junctures (unless accompanied by a filled pause or word fragment) as purely linguistically determined would have meant that a number of real cognitive hesitations were excluded. Barik argued that juncture pauses, longer than say 500 msec, probably had a cognitive as well as purely lingustic function. Fodor, Bever & Garrett (1974) offered a different explanation. They suggested that the modal position of hesitations is after the first word of the phonemic clause because a new syntactic clause is introduced at this point. Choice between these alternative interpretations is not possible unless we have some means of deciding whether pauses at syntactic junctures have an encoding function, in addition to the non-cognitive function of segment-ing the utterance for the listener, as in reading (Goldman-Eisler, 1972). The fact that previous research has not involved consideration of other behaviours which might provide a clue to encoding activity has meant that the question of possible cognitive functions of juncture pauses has either been ignored or received a rather arbitrary answer (cf. Barik, 1968).

Evidence from a different source

However, analysis of patterns of speaker eye-gaze may provide a partial answer. Speaker gaze at the facial region of the listener is mainly used to monitor information from the listener to ascertain how the speech is being received, and do determine if any of the anticipatory movements which precede listener interruption are occurring (Kendon, 1967, 1972). Speaker-gaze also has a number of social functions: the regulation of the interaction, the maintenance of a social bond and the signalling of atten-tion and interest, (see Argyle & Cook, 1976). Since eye-gaze does open a potential channel for transmission of information about the state of the listener, and the immediate context, it has been hypothesised that gaze aversion will occur during planning periods in speech to reduce potential interference between such cognitive planning and the interpretation of incoming visual information. This has been demonstrated in a number of studies. Nielsen (1962) observed that subjects averted gaze when preparing arguments in conversation. Kendon (1967) found that gaze aversion was more likely during slow hesitant speech than during fluent speech. Exline & Winters (1965b) found that the overall amount of gaze in conversation was inversely related to the cognitive difficulty of the topic of conversation. Weiner & Ehrlichman (1976), in a reanalysis of some data collected by Ehrlichman, Weiner & Baker (1974), found significantly more instances of eye closings when subjects were answering spatial rather than verbal questions (presumably because more interference is likely between the incoming visual information and the imagery processes required in answering spatial questions). Analysis of speaker gaze should therefore provide valuable information about the occurrence and possibly even the nature (Weiner & Ehrlichman, 1976) of cognitive processing in speech; it may even shed some light on the question of the cognitive or non-cognitive origin of juncture pauses – a problem which has dogged research in this area.

Returning to the literature on encoding units in speech, there is evidence, in addition to that which suggests that clausal and lexical units are the primary encoding units, that supraclausal units are also involved. This evidence was obtained in studies of spontaneous speech which plotted measures of individual pauses and phonations across time and fitted lines to represent changes in relative fluency. When this was done for samples of spontaneous speech, cyclic patterns of relatively steep slopes (high pause/phonation ratio) alternating with relatively shallow slopes (low pause/phonation ratio) were found. This does not occur however in more fluent prose readings. It has also been observed that the fluent phases of these cycles are characterised by fewer filled hesitations (FPs, repetitions and false starts), and by a higher proportion of pauses at grammatical junctures. The amount of pausing in the hesitant phases of these cycles has also been found to be directly related to the amount of phonation in the succeeding fluent phase. It has been hypothesised that the fluent pauses are planned (or partially planned) in the preceding phases (Henderson, Goldman-Eisler & Skarbek, 1966; Goldman-Eisler, 1967). Cycle times have been found in one study to range between 10.6 and 39.2 secs. with a mean of 18.0 secs. (Butterworth, 1975), which suggests that such units are substantially larger than individual clauses. The evidence for these cycles has, however, been called into question by Jaffe, Breskin & Gerstman (1972) who demonstrated that cycles could be discerned in randomly generated pause-phonation series. It was also found in the simulated speech, as well as in real spontaneous speech, that the longer the pause time in the steep (hesitant) slope, the longer the phonation time in the succeeding shallow (fluent) slope. Some additional evidence for the psychological reality of the cycles, however, comes from a study by Butterworth (1975) who found a significant relationship between cycle boundaries in speech and the boundaries of 'ideas', as judged by subjects in a transcript of speech. However in this study a rather arbitrary criterion of more than 50% of the judges' agreement on an 'idea' boundary had to be employed.

Aims of the present research

The aim of the present research is to test the various models of language production and to determine to what extent they are compatible. The models based on continuous samples of spontaneous speech (the clausal, Boomer, 1965, and supraclausal models, Goldman-Eisler, 1967) have left a considerable amount of the data unaccounted for. In the Boomer (1965) study only 54.3% of hesitations could be accounted for by holistic planning of the clause, since 45.7% of hesitations occurred later than the second word of the clause. Similarly, in the Henderson et al. (1966) study, 45.7% of all UPs at nongrammatical junctures occurred in the fluent phases of cycles and therefore could not be accounted for by distal semantic planning. Thus, these models may, to some extent, be mutually compatible.

The first specific aim of this research is to investigate any cycles which may emerge in pause/phonation series and to investigate the psycholinguistic reality, if any, of these cycles. One way of doing this is to test the cohesion of sentences falling within temporal cycles by assessing a judge's ability to place a random series of sentences taken from within a cycle in the order in which they were originally spoken. There are two possible sources of information which judges can use in the reordering – the first is the semantic nature of the underlying propositions. Thus in the example below:

(1) Jack stood up
(2) Jack walked out of the room

one can state with some assurance that sentence (2) followed sentence (1) since 'standing up' is (usually) temporally antecedent to walking out of the room. However in the example below:

(1) Jill stood up
(2) She sat down

the underlying semantics does not help since 'standing up' and 'sitting down' can occur in either order. In this case, it is the presence of a linguistic tying device – the anaphoric reference "she" which provides the clue (see Halliday & Hasan, 1976). The prediction is thus that if temporal cycles do constitute some kind of semantic units, as Butterworth's study suggests, judges should be able to reorder sentences falling within these cycles with more accuracy than adjacent sentences which cross cycle boundaries. This prediction is tested in this study.

This study also tests the clausal model by investigating whether there is a tendency for hesitations to occur towards the beginnings of such clauses. Speaker eye gaze is analysed to provide further information about a possible cognitive origin for specific problematic pauses (e.g. juncture pauses) and the relationship between any cycles in the hesitation data and patterns of eye gaze are also explored. The implications of any such patterns for the regulation of conversation constitutes the final investigation.

Procedure

Speech corpus

The speech samples analysed were randomly selected from 4 video-recorded dyadic interactions (supervisions, involving a tutor and an undergraduate), with the constraint that the speaker's turn in conversation had to be at least 30 secs in length, so that temporal cycles could be identified. The present corpus consists of 202 syntactic clauses, 1433 words and 137 hesitations.

Hesitation analysis

Two types of hesitations were examined – unfilled pauses (UPs) and filled pauses (FPs). UPs were defined as periods of silence $\geq$ 200 msec (cf. Boomer, 1965); these were identified and measured using an Ediswan pen oscillograph and pause detector. FPs consist of 'ah', 'er', 'um', etc.

The location of each hesitation was marked on the speech transcript. A distributional analysis of UPs and FPs with respect to syntactic (surface structure) clauses was carried out. Hesitations occurring in the juncture between 2 clauses were classified as occupying the clause-initial position of the succeeding clause (see Boomer, 1965: 34).

A visual analogue of the speech, identifying periods of pausing and phonation, was prepared in the manner described by Henderson et al., 1966. Each individual pause and period of phonation was plotted on a graph. Lines were fitted to represent changes in the pause/phonation ratio across time, in such a way as to minimise the deviation of local changes in these 2 variables from the lines (see Henderson et al., 1966:208). This procedure was checked by 2 independent judges. Some minor adjustments were necessary before perfect agreement was reached.

Analysis of gaze

Subjects were filmed with Sony cameras, fitted with zoom lenses, and a split-screen video circuit was employed for the judgement of gaze. The occurrence of speaker gaze at the listener was noted at each word boundary in his speech. The inter-observer reliability for two independent judges in the scoring of gaze was 94.6% (scoring gaze at each word boundary location).

Results

(1) Hesitation analysis
(a) Temporal cycles:
    When individual pause and phonation periods were graphically represented, and lines fitted to represent changes in relative fluency across

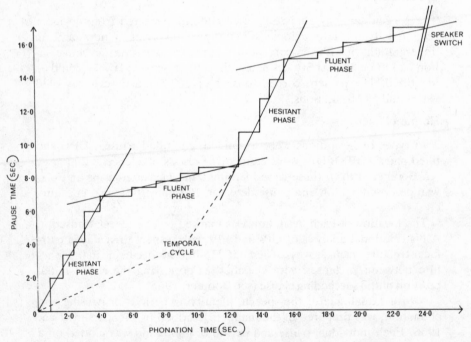

Figure 1. *Cyclic patterning in pausing in the speech of one subject in conversation.*

time, cyclic patterns could be discerned in all of the samples, except one,[2] with hesitant phases (high pause/phonation ratio) alternating with fluent phases (low pause/phonation ratio) (see Fig. 1). In all, 20 complete cycles (both phases present) were observed, as well as 6 incomplete cycles, bounded by speaker switches. The mean cycle time was found to be 21.88 sec. The cycles contained a mean of 8.80 clauses, hesitant phases a mean of 3.57 clauses, and fluent phases a mean of 5.23 clauses.

To test the psycholinguistic reality of these cycles, 5 sets of sentences (each set consisting of either 3 or 5 sentences, with each sentence written separately on a plain card) were presented to each of 6 judges, who were asked to place the sentences in the order in which they were originally spoken. A reordering accuracy score was computed, by counting the number of sentences which followed each successive sentence in the reconstructed order, which had also be done so in the original order.

To make this clearer consider the following examples: if 5 sentences were originally spoken in the order: ABCDE and a subject judged the order to be BCDAE, the reordering score would be 7 calculated in the following manner.

If a subject judged the order to be ABCDE i.e., placed the sentences in the correct order, the reordering score would be 10.

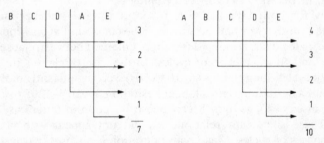

The reordering score for each set of sentences from within a temporal cycle was compared with the score for a matched set, consisting of the same number of sentences, spoken by the same individual but crossing a cycle boundary. The difference between the reordering scores can be seen in Table 1; "−" represents a difference in the predicted direction, that is, the reordering score for the set of sentences from within a cycle was greater (i.e. more accurate) than for its matched control.

The probabilities from the different sets of sentences were combined using the Jones & Fiske (1953) procedure. This test revealed that judges were significantly better at reordering sentences that occurred within a cycle than successively occurring sentences which transcended a cycle boundary.

$$\chi^2 = 29.941 \ (df = 10), \quad p < 0.001.$$

Table 1. *Difference between computed reordering scores for sentences falling within or across temporal cycles.*
(−: *reflects difference in predicted direction*)

SPEECH COMPARISONS

SUBJECT	SET 1 (3-sentence)	SET 2 (3-sentence)	SET 3 (5-sentence)	SET 4 (5-sentence)	SET 5 (3-sentence)
S_1	−1	0	−6	−4	−2
S_2	−1	+1	−2	−2	−2
S_3	−2	−1	−3	−4	−1
S_4	+1	−2	−1	−5	−3
S_5	−1	−2	−1	−2	−2
S_6	−3	−2	−3	0	0
PROBABILITIES Sign-test (1-tail)	≤0.109	≤0.188	≤0.016	≤0.031	≤0.031

b) Hesitations and syntactic clauses

The relationship between hesitations and syntactic clauses is described in detail in Beattie (1978b; forthcoming b, c). There was a significant tendency for both UPs and FPs to occur towards the beginnings of syntactic clauses, over half occurring in the clause-initial position (clause juncture). However, striking differences emerged between clauses in the hesitant and fluent phases of cycles. In the case of clauses in hesitant phases of cycles, long clauses (6–10 words) were significantly more likely to contain a hesitation (and a longer hesitation, mean = 1205 msec) than short clauses (2–5 words). Mean pause duration in latter case = 669 msec. These significant relationships did not appear with clauses in fluent phases of cycles. Mean pause duration for pauses in clause-initial position of long and short clauses in fluent phases of cycles: 657 and 682 msec respectively.

(2) Analysis of gaze

Analysis of speaker-gaze revealed that gaze aversion was significantly more probable at nonjuncture pauses, and juncture pauses in the hesitant phases of cycles, than at fluent transitions, but no significant difference emerged in the case of juncture pauses in fluent phases of cycles.[3] 40% of juncture pauses in fluent phases of cycles were accompanied by gaze aversion compared with 34% of fluent transitions in both phases.

These results thus suggest that some, but not all, juncture pauses (i.e. those in hesitant phases of cycles) probably serve a language encoding function whereas these juncture pauses in fluent phases of cycles accompanied by speaker gaze at the listener are presumably used to segment the speech for the decoder, and to allow the speaker to receive feedback from the listener.

Analysis of gaze with respect to the temporal cycles (see Beattie, 1978b) revealed that fluent phases of cycles were approximately $2^{1}/_{2}$ times as likely to be dominated by gaze (i.e. 50% or more of the total duration of the phase occupied by gaze) than gaze aversion, as were hesitant phases. Furthermore, those fluent phases dominated by gaze were significantly more fluent than those phases dominated by gaze aversion. Nevertheless, the sequential organisation of speaker-gaze diverged from the pattern predicted on purely cognitive grounds, in a number of ways. The most striking was that a number of hesitant phases of cycles (13) were dominated by speaker-gaze. It was subsequently observed however that there were significantly more filled hesitations, particularly false starts (incomplete or self-interrupted utterances) in temporal cycles whose planning phases were dominated by gaze than by gaze aversion. This suggests that a number of presumably social constraints on speaker-gaze can interfere with this behaviours' reciprocal relationship with cognitive processing and that such interference can result in a higher incidence of certain types of speech error.

The significance of cognitively based patterns in speaker-gaze for the regulation of conversation

This paper has explored the patterning of speaker-gaze with respect to the units of encoding in spontaneous speech. It now investigates the effects of this basic patterning on one specific social function of this phenomenon – that of regulating the flow of conversation, of informing the listener when it is his turn to speak (Kendon, 1967).

Recent investigations of the floor-apportionment function of gaze in conversation have succeeded in clarifying its interactional role. It has become clear that speaker gaze is not an indispensable cue in the regulation of turn-taking. A substantial proportion of speaker switches occur in the absence of speaker gaze (30% observed by Kendon, 1967; 34.4% by Rutter, Stephenson, Ayling & White, 1978).

The fact that one can hold conversations by telephone allows similar conclusions. However there is some support for the view that gaze may facilitate speaker switching. Kendon (1967) observed that gaze at the ends of utterances is more likely to result in an immediate speaker switch than is gaze aversion at the ends of utterances. A recent study which concentrated on the magnitudes of speaker switches, however, failed to corroborate this result (Beattie, 1978a). Such a discrepancy suggests that there may be contextual constraints which affect the facilitatory floor-apportionment function of speaker gaze. One possibly important contextual difference is the overall amount and distribution of gaze between, and within, conversations. In the Kendon study, the mean percentage of gaze while speaking was in the range 28.7% to 71.2% with a mean probably around 49.4% (calculated by the present author), as compared with a mean of 66.8% in the supervisions studied by Beattie (Beattie, 1978b). It may be hypothesised that gaze becomes more significant and effective as a turn-taking cue in a context of general gaze aversion.

The aim of the present study therefore is to test the hypothesis that the efficacy of gaze as a facilitatory floor-apportionment cue is affected by psycholinguistic context (position in the encoding cycles), which itself partially determines background level and patterning of gaze (for more detail see Beattie, forthcoming a).

Procedure

The analysis focussed on long speaker turns, i.e. ≥ 30 secs in length, which ended in a speaker-switch. Only "complete" utterances were considered (i.e. those not involving simultaneous speech and accompanied by one or more of Duncan's (1972) turn-yielding cues).[4] The relative fluency of the speech immediately preceding a speaker-switch was determined and phases were classified as either hesitant or fluent. In all, 110 speaker-switches (and 110 speaker turns) were considered. The category of gaze accompanying the end of the utterance preceding each switch was noted, as was the duration of the succeeding speaker-switching pause. The switching pause was measured using an Ediswan pen oscillograph and pause detector. Inter-observer reliability in the categorization of gaze at the ends of utterances was 90.9%.

Results

It was discovered that the longest switching pauses tended to follow "complete" utterances occurring at the ends of hesitant phases in speech and accompanied by gaze aversion ($\bar{t} = 1.918$ sec; range 0–5.60 sec). The shortest switching pauses tended to follow utterances at the ends of hesitant phases of speech terminating with speaker gaze ($\bar{t} = 378$ msec; range 0–3.20 sec). In the former case 23.5% of speaker-switches were immediate (i.e. latency ≤ 200 msec) compared with 50.0% in the latter case.

An ANOVA revealed a non-significant effect for phase type preceding the speaker-switch and for occurrence/nonoccurrence of gaze at the ends of utterances, but a significant phase type/gaze occurrence interaction effect ($p < 0.001$). This result suggests that the facilitatory floor-apportionment function of speaker gaze is context-specific; gaze resulted in a significant decrease in speaker-switch latencies only in those contexts in which hesitant phases of speech associated with a lower overall level of speaker-gaze immediately preceded the speaker-switches.

Discussion

This paper began by attempting to test several different models of language production by examining the location of hesitations within samples of spontaneous speech occurring within the context of conversation. It introduced additional evidence in the form of an analysis of patterns of change in speaker gaze direction. None of the models reviewed could account for all the observations made. The clausal model of language production (Boomer, 1965; Fodor et al., 1974) could not explain the cyclic patterns of unfilled pauses which emerged, with a mean cycle time of 21.9 secs. These temporal cycles had been observed in the past (Henderson et al., 1966; Goldman-Eisler, 1967; Butterworth, 1975), but had been dismissed as being nothing more than an artefact of random variations in pausing and phonation across time (Jaffe et al., 1972). However in this paper, evidence is presented that there are more ties (presumably of both a semantic and linguistic kind)[5] between sentences within a temporal cycle, than between sentences which cross cycle boundaries. The evidence for this is that judges can reorder sentences from within cycles with more accuracy than they can other sentences. This is at least tentative evidence that these cycles do have some linguistic reality.

The supraclausal model proposed by Goldman-Eisler was supported by the emergence of cycles in the pause/phonation data but it could not explain the tendency of hesitations to occur towards the beginnings of syntactic clauses, especially in the hesitant phases of the cycles. Evidence was obtained of clausal planning in these hesitant phases – long clauses were more likely to contain a hesitation (and a longer hesitation) than short clauses, and analysis of speaker gaze direction revealed that gaze aversion was more likely at clausal juncture hesitations in such phases than at fluent transitions, suggesting that these juncture hesitations were not merely serving either a linguistic or social function. No evidence was obtained for clausal planning in the fluent phases of cycles. The evidence obtained thus suggests that a hybrid model is most appropriate. Some form of planning in speech does seem to transcend individual clauses, but whilst this planning is occurring, speech is nevertheless being produced (there were a mean of 3.57 clauses in the hesitant phases of the cycles). This speech appears to be planned on a clausal basis. The evidence obtained thus suggests that there is not a single fundamental unit of encoding in speech, as many researchers in this area seem to have assumed, but there is evidence of forward-planning in speech of varying degrees. Both clausal and supraclausal planning does appear to occur and hesitations do appear to serve both proximal and distal planning functions.

Some evidence was also presented that the structure of at least one form of nonverbal behaviour (speaker gaze) does bear some relationship to the temporal structure (see Butterworth & Beattie, 1978 for a description of the relationship between speaker gesture and hand movement and these cycles). The implications of this crude patterning for conversation was explored by comparing the effectiveness of speaker-gaze as a turn-yielding cue in different psycholinguistic contexts. Some interesting and striking results emerged which suggested that temporal structure is an important variable in the processes of conversation. Studies of conversation will ignore psycholinguistic units at their peril! It may also be suggested that conversational context is an important variable with respect to these basic speech patterns. Unfilled pauses in conversation are interactionally significant – they can easily lead to interruption (Maclay & Osgood, 1959; Beattie, 1977). In monologue conditions five or six second pauses may be acceptable – in conversation they are not. Therefore, it can be predicted that any cycles which emerge in monologue conditions will display steeper hesitant phases (a higher proportion of long UPs) than cycles recorded in the context of conversation. Thus the hybrid model of language production which found support in the present study may be peculiar to conversation; in monologue, speakers may not produce speech (or as much speech) during periods of forward planning. Thus, there may be no need for clausal planning in the long-term planning phases.

The final suggestion is thus that not only does there appear to be no single fundamental unit of encoding, but further, the amount and nature of forward planning in speech will probably be a function of the social context in which the speech occurs. The effects of social context on the temporal structure of speech must be a prime target for further research.

Notes

1. This research forms part of a Ph.D. thesis passed by the University of Cambridge (Trinity College), 1978. It was financed by a Northern Ireland Research Studentship, 1974–77.
2. The sample in which cycles could not be identified had a mean pause rate of about 10%. Suspicions were raised however about the spontaneity of this tutor's supervisions.

3. These statistical calculations were based entirely upon those instances in which the hesitation phenomenon was accompanied by gaze or gaze aversion, and not by both for fractions of the time. Clauses longer than 10 words in length were excluded.
4. Floor-switches preceded by "incomplete" utterances can be regarded as interruptions by the listener (see Beattie, 1978 a).
5. Further research is currently being carried out into the kinds of linguistic devices binding these sentences together (following Halliday & Hasan, 1976).

DAVID A. GOOD and BRIAN L. BUTTERWORTH

Hesitancy as a conversational resource: some methodological implications

Introduction

In a previous paper (Good, 1978) it was argued that the levels of hesitancy in the speech of an individual form an important prosodic cue, for
the participants in a conversation, as to the relationship between the
speaker and his utterance. This claim was made principally in the context
of hesitancy as an indicator of cognitive load for the speaker, it being
proposed that, whilst speakers may well need to hesitate more when
faced with a heavy task demand, they may also increase the relative
amounts of hesitation in their speech to achieve some interactional goal,
even though the difficulty of the particular utterance would not directly
necessitate the change.

However no direct empirical evidence was offered to support this
position, nor were any claims made as to whether speakers who were
hesitating more than they needed to, would produce patterns of speech
and silence that corresponded to those found in spontaneous speech or
not. The purpose of this paper is to report an investigation of speaker
behaviour when producing material that was already well known, whilst
under the constraint of attempting to generate the impression that the
converse was true. Thus the hypothesis offered by Good (1978), would
be directly tested, and samples of 'simulated', and genuinely hesitant
speech would be provided for a comparative analysis.

Method

For this investigation to be successfully undertaken, it must first be
clearly demonstrated that the subject is indeed well acquainted with the
verbal material that he will subsequently utter in the simulation exercise,
which forms the focus of this study. One solution to this problem would
be to have subjects read aloud a specially prepared passage whilst
attempting to generate the desired impression. This method of con-

straining the verbal content has been used elsewhere (Fairbanks & Hoaglin, 1941; O'Connell, Kowal & Hörmann, 1969), but was seen to be unsuitable for two reasons. First the strategy employed in reading the passage could well affect the resulting pattern of hesitancy. This could be overcome by having the subjects commit the passage to memory, but again the strategies employed in doing this may produce patterns at variance with what might normally occur. Second it would not result in a natural spontaneous form of the utterance, composed of the same content material, with which to compare the simulation.

Another solution would be to have the subject talk about something with which he is already familiar, repeat it once to increase the degree of familiarisation, and then repeat it again, but in this final instance as the content for the simulation exercise. The rationale for this procedure comes from Goldman-Eisler (1961) who reported that pause time per word fell sharply on the first repetition of an utterance, with the value tending towards an asymptote on subsequent repeats. This was taken to indicate that after the first repeat the material was relatively well-learnt. Thus any increase in hesitancy on a second repeat could not be attributed to the demands of producing the utterance.

We therefore needed to find a topic that subjects would be relatively familiar with anyway, but not necessarily so since we did not wish to present the subjects with a totally improbable task in the simulation exercise; and that was relatively low in emotional content, for all speakers, since many researchers have found significant correlations between anxiety and rates of verbal productivity as indicated by the speech/ silence ratio (Murray, 1971). Furthermore we also wished to elicit an utterance which was genuinely difficult, so as to provide a standard against which to contrast the simulation, and it was seen as desirable to have this as being of the same character.

The topic which most easily met these criteria was that of giving directions to a stranger about, (a) a route that was well known to the speaker, and (b) one which was not. The task chosen for (a) was the subject's daily route to work, which we assumed most individuals would be relatively familiar with; and that for (b) by having subjects complete a questionnaire about their knowledge of different parts of Cambridge. From this a location was selected on the basis of three criteria; first, it was among the least known to the subject; second, no substantial part of the route liable to be offered corresponded to the "work-route"; third, it demanded a similar level of description in terms of distance and number of decision points as the "work-route".

The subject was then asked to do the following, in each case from the perspective of being with the experimenter, whom the subject was told was a relative stranger to Cambridge, at the subject's home. *A,* give directions on how to get to the subject's place of work. *B,* repeat the directions given in *A* (the subject was told that it was not expected that he would be able to offer an exact replication, but that he should try and keep the overall content of his directions the same). *C,* give directions on how to get to the place selected from the questionnaire. *D,* again repeat the directions given in *A,* as in *B,* but with a difference. In this instance he was instructed to do so under the following constraint, "I want you to imagine that for some, perhaps Machiavellian, purpose of your own, you want to generate the impression in the listener, that in fact you don't know this route well at all, in fact that it is one you may have only travelled on once or twice a long time ago". He was then asked if he understood the instructions. If he claimed that he did not, he was then presented with a scenario in which he was talking to someone whom he had told that he had been out of the district for a considerable time and that to appear to know this route well would undermine his previous lie.

It was also recognised that in this experiment the subject would, as is normal in any interaction, be monitoring the listener, i.e. the experimenter in this instance, for the various kinds of "back-channel communication" that pass from listener to speaker, and that this could have a differential effect on the levels of hesitancy, depending upon the response the speaker received. Since it was not a practicable proposition to give each subject identical feedback it was decided to try and reduce this factor to a minimum. Consequently, the seating arrangements were structured as in Figure 1 so that the subject could not visually scan the experimenter, and while the subject was performing the four tasks, the

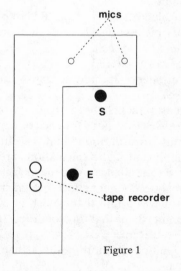

Figure 1

experimenter remained silent (this was checked by having the whole experiment recorded via a hidden microphone).

Since it was essential that tasks *A, B* and *D* were presented in that order, and that *B* should directly follow *A,* only three orders of presentation were possible (ABCD; ABDC; CABD). Subjects were randomly assigned to one of these three.

Twelve subjects (5 female and 7 male) were used, all of whom had lived in Cambridge and travelled the same "work-route" for the last six months.

Their utterances were recorded, via stereophonic microphones on an Akai GX 360-D tape recorder. These were subsequently transcribed and the transcriptions matched against the visual record of the same from an Ediswan pen oscillograph. In common with other studies (see Rochester, 1973) all pauses of less that 250 msec were ignored.

Results

Of the protocols of the twelve subjects, those of five had to be rejected for the following reasons. Two of them offered a route that was inaccurate, that is to say a stranger following the directions would not have arrived at the intended destination. Two gave directions in *D* that were substantially different to those given in *A.* One did not complete task *D.*

The utterances of the remaining seven subjects in each of the four conditions were analysed using the visual records from the pen oscillograph, and measurements were made of the following quantities for each subject in each condition.

1. Total amount of silence between first and last phonation.
2. Total amount of time occupied by, and number of, filled pauses.
3. Total time occupied by speech.
4. Total number of words uttered.
5. Total amount of silence located at clause boundaries and the total number of clauses.

From these measurements the percentage of total utterance time occupied by silence was calculated for each of the subjects in each condition. At this point it is worth noting that the differences to be reported below are also significant if the calculations are based on the ratio of number of words to total silence. Also the inclusion or exclusion of filled pauses from the analysis does not effect the statistical argument.

On comparison it was found that speech in condition *A* was significantly more hesitant than that in condition *B* using the Wilcoxon Matched Pairs Signed Ranks Test (T = 0, p < .01). *C* produced utterances that were significantly more hesitant than *A* (T = 2, p < .025).

Table 1. *Silence expressed as percentage of total utterance time.*

Subject	A	B	C	D
Ch	19.4	13.9	22.3	26.9
Ni	27.2	25.7	34.1	32.8
Ba	23.5	16.9	28.4	31.4
So	33.0	28.8	40.0	47.4
Pe	49.0	44.4	49.8	57.2
St	36.8	29.9	35.1	45.0
Pa	40.3	31.0	46.6	57.4
Mean	32.74	27.23	36.61	42.59

Table 2. *Percentage of total hesitancy at clause boundaries.*

Subject	A	B	C	D
Ch	47.9%	76.0%	54.2%	62.4%
Ni	50.7%	61.3%	29.1%	62.5%
Ba	56.4%	78.7%	55.2%	45.0%
So	87.9%	85.9%	91.6%	69.3%
Pe	58.2%	54.9%	57.5%	56.2%
St	54.3%	76.1%	66.3%	52.8%
Pa	55.8%	73.2%	41.4%	61.2%
Mean	58.74%	72.3%	56.47%	58.49%

Similarly D produced utterances more hesitant than those in A (T = 0, p < .01). However D was also more hesitant than C (T = 1, p < .05 – for a two-tailed test).

The percentage of the total pause time at clause boundaries was also computed.

Clearly from these figures there is no difference between conditions A, C and D (for example A compared with D gives a T value of 14). However those utterances in condition B had a significantly higher percentage of the total pause time located at the clause boundaries than those in any of the other three conditions; A/B (T = 3, p < .05), C/B (T = 3, p < .05), D/B (T = 3, p < .05).

Discussion and conclusion

Obviously then these results support the position that speakers will mark an utterance as being concomitant with a degree of thoughtfulness on their part, by increasing the ratio of silence to speech, even though the strict demands of the verbal production do not warrant such an increase. The expected decrease in hesitancy on the repeat of the "work-route" was observed, and if this factor resulted solely as a consequence of the cognitive demands of the verbal production, then a further decrease should be observed on the second repeat i.e. under condition *D*, as the material becomes even more well learnt. This, however, was not the case, and the observed proportion of hesitancy was in fact significantly higher than that found in the original spontaneous utterance. Thus this increase must be due to other elements in the task, of which we would argue the intention to generate the impression of not knowing the route well, being the most critical.

Furthermore it would appear from these results that not only do speakers use hesitancy in this way, but also that when they do so, they accurately reflect the relative distribution, with regard to major syntactic boundaries, of silence in normal spontaneous speech. The expected increase in percentage of total silence located at clause boundaries on the first repeat was found, and normally this is a trend that would be expected to continue on subsequent repeats. However we have found that contrary to this expectation subjects return to a pattern which parallels that found in spontaneous speech.

The results from condition *C*, which it had been hoped would provide a truly difficult task against which to compare with results from *D*, are harder to interpret. Now the task in *C* did indeed result in utterances that were significantly more hesitant than those in *A*. However whilst producing this contrast these utterances were nevertheless significantly less hesitant than those in *D*. This may be interpreted in one of two possible ways. First that *C* does represent a truly difficult task and that the behaviour elicited in *D* is peculiar to the constraints of this experiment and is not representative of a behaviour the subject may normally produce. Alternatively it may be the case that *C* wasn't that difficult for subjects and that consequently it does not provide an adequate standard against which to contrast *D*. Two factors speak in favour of the latter explanation. First, most subjects in the post-experiment debriefing suggested that *C* wasn't in fact that hard and that in a small place like Cambridge one would simply either know or not know how to get to a particular place. Secondly the rates at which subjects spoke in condition *D* do not fall outside the range reported by others. Goldman-Eisler (1968: 56) reports a mean pause to speech ratio for within utterance hesitancy of 1.07, S.D. = 0.4, and the figures from condition *D* are 0.90, S.D. = 0.5. Thus by this standard the productions in condition *D* do not appear to be abnormal.

Now given these findings certain implications follow. Much research has been undertaken into the social psychology of the psychological experiment, and some would claim that it provides a singularly unique form of social interaction (Orne, 1973). Without wishing to enter into an extended discussion of the overall merits and demerits of this work certain of its findings do seem to be relatively clear. In particular that subjects will seek to perform in most cases in a way which will influence the results in the direction of what they perceive to be the experimenter's hypothesis. Typically they will seek to be the 'good subject'. Also it has been shown (Orne, 1973) that the aims of the experimenter may be communicated to the subject in a variety of ways, all be it unintentional and unconscious, by the total experimental situation and the experimenter's actions within it. Thus it has been argued that the variance achieved in the results of a particular study may be more a function of the 'experimenter demand characteristics' than the task the experimenter believes he is studying.

Therefore, since it has been demonstrated here that the levels of hesitancy in an individual's speech are something which he may successfully manipulate, in order to generate an impression of "thoughtfulness", when explicitly requested to do so then there is a clear case that he may also do this when there is a strong implicit request offered by an experimenter and the context of his experiment. There is not room here to investigate all instances of research, that has used hesitancy as a critical measure, that may be confronted with this problem. However the point will be illustrated by reference to one example.

In a study by Goldman-Eisler (1961) the utterances of subjects, first describing and then interpreting, sets of cartoons, without captions, were compared for amounts of hesitancy. It was found that interpretations were significantly more hesitant than descriptions. This difference was ascribed to the postulated greater difficulty of processing that interpreting would offer when compared to describing. Two factors in the experimental procedure, however, suggest that the case may not be so simple. The first is the description of the task to the subject, the relevant of which is reproduced in (i).

(i) [...] proceed to describe the content of the story as depicted in the pictures before you; conclude by formulating the general point, meaning or moral of the story in as concise a form as you can.

Clearly a constraint is offered here to the subject by the ways in which the two tasks are described. The first is simply to "describe", the other is to "conclude by formulating the general point meaning or moral ... in as concise a form as you can". This contrast, we would argue, constrains the subject to appear as if he is putting more effort into the interpretations even though he may find them relatively easy. This point is accentuated when we consider the second factor, which is that subjects always performed the two tasks in the same order. Thus, they come to the second task realizing that they must differentiate their performance on it from that on the first, they have already been constrained to appear thoughtful, and will thus increase their hesitancy relative to that in the production of the description. Both these factors combined will strongly bias the results in favour of the hypothesis under test.

Now this specific example obviously requires direct empirical investigation to ascertain its validity, but this does not detract from the force of the argument. This study has demonstrated that an individual's hesitancy may be as much a function of some interactional goal as some cognitive processing demand. This finding renders problematic the necessary assumptions of some workers in this field that hesitancy is directly, and only, consequent upon some underlying process that they are investigating. Furthermore, those instances, where subjects are simulating thoughtfulness, may not be simply distinguished from those, where the behaviour is more genuine, by reference to the distribution of the silence. It is possible that some other metric or level of descriptions may distinguish the two. One such possibility is a comparison of the apparent rhythms (Henderson et al., 1966; Butterworth, 1975) in the two cases, others also exist. Nevertheless these findings point to real problems of both experimental control and subsequent inference from the data obtained.

MARK COOK

The relationship between gaze and speech examined afresh with a Mackworth eye-mark camera

Introduction

The length, distribution and possible meanings of pauses in speech have been extensively studied, by Goldman-Eisler (1968) among others. Similarly the length, distribution and possible meanings of glances at the other person during conversation have been extensively studied, in research reviewed by Argyle & Cook (1976).

Kendon (1967) first studied the relationship between speech and gaze. He found that speakers tended to look up when they had finished and to look away at the beginnings of utterances, and suggested that these looks were used by speaker and listener as signals to each other. He also showed that speakers tended to look away during hesitation pauses within an utterance, but tended to be looking up during phrase boundary pauses. It has been suggested (Argyle & Cook, 1976) that speakers look at phrase boundary pauses both to see how the listener is reacting to what is being said, and to mark off for him the sections of the utterance. Kendon (1967) suggested that speakers look away during a hesitation pause to avoid giving the appearance of having finished the utterance (or presumably the sentence). By contrast Exline & Winters (1965a) argued that people look away when uncertain what to say, because the sight of the other person makes it hard to gather their thoughts.

Kendon's account of the link between gaze and speech at the beginning and end of utterances has been questioned by Beattie (1978a) and by Rutter et al. (1978); no further work has been published on the relationship between pausing and gaze within an utterance. Kendon's data were relatively crude, being taken from cine film shot at two frames per second. Many hesitation pauses are shorter than $1/2$ second, as are some looks or looks away. It is also difficult to determine whether the subject looks away before pausing or vice versa. More precise data would confirm or reject Kendon's account of gaze and pausing within utterances and might strengthen one of the several competing hypotheses.

Method

Subjects were four psychology students, one female and three male. Speech sample consisted of extracts from ten-minute conversations between S and the experimenter, in which the experimenter asked some difficult questions, e.g. do you approve of experiments on animals. All answers lasting 10 seconds or more were analysed. A total of 6 min. 31 secs. speech was analysed.

Apparatus. Subjects' speech was recorded. Additionally a throat microphone operated a voice relay which lit a small light bulb.

The Ss' eye-movements were recorded by a NAC eye-mark camera. This shines a small light on to the right eye, and records the differing angles at which it is reflected as the eye moves. The reflected image of the light is superimposed on an image of the Ss' field of view (containing on this occasion the experimenter sitting against a white background). Both images were recorded by a TV camera, a videotimer, which numbers the successive scans (50 per second) of the TV camera, and a video tape recorder. The light operated by the Ss' throat microphone appears in the lower left hand corner of the video film.

The Ss' eye movements are recorded to the nearest 1 degree of visual field and to the nearest $^1/_{50}$ second. Speech and pausing are also timed to the nearest $^1/_{50}$ second. Breaks in speech of less than $^1/_{10}$ second were not counted as pauses.

The apparatus allows a record of the type illustrated in Figure 1 to be constructed. The record shows the start and finish of each speech burst, and what is said in it, the start and finish of each fixation, its target, and the occurrence and duration of blinks. (When the subject closes his eyes the reflected image of the light is extinguished.) Gaze directed anywhere within the experimenter's face was counted as looking at him. Pauses were categorised as hesitation or phrase boundary pauses.

Results and discussion

General characteristics of the sample. The data are comparable with those of Goldman-Eisler (1968) and Kendon (1967); the Ss pause 33–43% of their speaking time, and look at E 33–48% of speaking time. 135 hesitation pauses are recorded and 107 phrase boundary pauses. The Ss' modal length of gaze at E was only .30 seconds, with a considerable skew towards longer glances. A gaze pattern as fragmented as this could not possibly be coded accurately by human observers. Gazes away from E are generally either rapid glances to one or other side of E or an upward glance frequently merging into a blink. All glances away from E were directed at a featureless white wall.

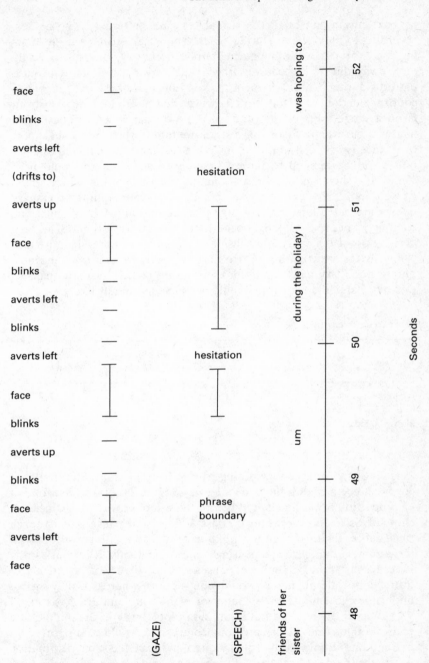

Figure 1. *Illustrative sample of the record of speech and gaze.*

Gaze during pauses. Table 1 analyses gaze patterns during pauses, according to pause type. During hesitation pauses Ss are typically looking away throughout, while during phrase boundary pauses Ss typically look away during the pause. Otherwise the two distributions of gaze patterns during pauses are the same. At first sight these data appear to confirm Kendon's account. Note however that Ss are looking away from E on average 60% of the time, so the fact that 71 of 135 hesitation pauses occur when S is looking away is not far off what one would expect by chance ($\chi^2 = 3.08$, d.f. $= 2$, n.s.). If the same argument and calculation could be applied to phrase boundary pauses, there would be a significant shortage of phrase boundary pauses during which the S doesn't look. However they do not apply because phrase boundary pauses are much longer on average than hesitation pauses – quite long enough to allow S to look up or look away during them. The only definite proof that gaze and pausing are linked, and not randomly coinciding, is the fact that Ss are five times as likely to look away during a phrase boundary pause as to look up during one. If gaze and pausing were unrelated the two events would of course be equally likely.

Table 1. *Gaze patterns during two types of pauses.*

	Looks throughout	Looks away throughout	Looks, then looks away	Looks away, then looks
Hesitation pauses	30 (22%)	71 (53%)	21 (15%)	13 (10%)
Phrase boundary pauses	20 (19%)	23 (21%)	53 (50%)	11 (10%)

Timing of gaze aversions during pauses. Table 1 shows that a silence appears to be a cue for the S to look away. Figure 2 plots the distribution of proportion of pause elapsed before the S looks away. A slight tendency for Ss to look away in the last 10% of the pause fails to reach significance. Figure 2 therefore, like most of Table 1, is consistent with the argument that gaze and pausing coincide randomly. If Ss consistently looked away at the beginning of pauses, Exline's theory of "avoidance of distraction while planning" would gain support, whereas if they waited until near the end Argyle's theory of monitoring and emphasis might gain support. If they did both, but didn't look away in the middle of a pause, both theories, which are not incompatible, would be supported.

Blink rate. Blinks occur equally often and have the same distribution of lengths (mode .15 seconds) during speech and silence, but occur more frequently – 64 against 25 – at the ends of silences than at their begin-

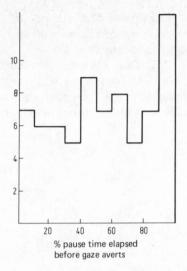

% pause time elapsed
before gaze averts

Figure 2. *Distribution of proportion of pauses –
hesitation and phrase boundary – elapsed before
speaker averts gaze.*

ning. These data appear at first to offer strong confirmation of the avoidance of distraction hypothesis; shutting the eyes altogether is an even
better way of avoiding the sight of the experimenter than looking away
from him (and is very unlikely to be a signal of any sort). However, the
timing of these blinks at the beginning of utterances presents problems
for the distraction hypothesis. They occur most frequently – 49% of
them – less than $^1/_{10}$ second before the utterance starts. Little if any
planning or thinking could be done in such a brief interval.

If blinks are not signals, and if they occur too soon before speech starts
to be periods of planning, why do they occur? The hypothesis that fits
the blink data best is that they are 'adaptors' (Ekman & Friesen, 1969).
Ekman argues that some gestures may be made because they once had a
use or purpose, which no longer applies. The behaviour has become
habitual and is evoked by something associated with the no-longer-rele-
vant purpose. Thus if speakers had found it useful in the past to close
their eyes while thinking, eye-closing before speaking may have become
habitual; the cue for eye-closing is now "I am about to start speaking"
rather than "I can't think what to say", so the interval between speaking
and eye-closing has become compressed. Other hesitations may be
'adaptors' also. Very many speakers say "Er, John Smith" when asked
their name; anxiety, uncertainty or fear of interruption seem very
unlikely causes of this but perhaps it is a habit carried over from starting
to speak when one of these does apply.

To conclude, the present data find only one point at which the gaze
looking and pausing seem significantly linked. A phrase boundary pause
is often the occasion for the speaker to look away but only rarely the

occasion for him to look up. The present data do not demonstrate any link between looking and hesitation pauses, being consistent with the parsimonious explanation that the two merely randomly coincide.

A significant tendency for subjects to close their eyes in extended blinks at the beginning speech bursts would be consistent with the hypothesis that they are avoiding distraction while planning their remarks, if the interval between closing the eyes and starting speaking were not typically extremely short.

WOLFGANG KLEIN

Verbal planning in route directions

This study is part of a larger project that is undertaken at the Max-Planck Projektgruppe "Psycholinguistics" at Nijmegen. It deals with the role of situational and verbal context, on the one hand, and with complex language production on the other. More specifically, I am interested in the use of deictical expressions, as a particularly important type of context-dependent expressions, and in the way people perform complex verbal tasks. In the present context, I shall only be concerned with the second aspect, namely with complex verbal actions in which certain tasks are solved.[1]

By complex verbal action, I understand activities like giving a talk, telling a narrative, explaining a game, describing an apartment, arguing together, etc. In general, several participants, at least two, are engaged in such an action, but their roles may be different. According to that, I classify them into basically monological and basically non-monological ones (giving a talk is basically monological, arguing together is basically non-monological); a complex verbal action might indeed be composed of several passages, some of them being monological, some not. A second subdivision follows the type of information to be presented or elaborated: it may prestructure the verbal planning to a high or a low degree. Narratives are strongly prestructured by the temporal order of events, explaining games is weakly prestructured; that's why most people soon get confused when they try to explain a complex game. In the weakly prestructured case, people typically try to introduce some temporal ordering, for example by following the running of the game, by imagining a tour through an apartment (Linde & Labov, 1975), and so on.

In the following, the planning of such an action is considered in more detail. In English, there seems to be no standard term for the complex cooperative verbal action that consists of asking for route directions and giving them, as for instance "Wegauskunft" in German; in the following, I will call this action "route communication." One of its characteristics is the clearly asymmetric role of its participants that is reflected in the verbal tasks they have to carry out: the person who asks for directions (henceforth F), wants to know something, and he tries to get that information from somebody that he thinks to be competent and willing to do so (= A).

F's initial tasks are:

(a) getting into contact with A
(b) making clear what he wants
(c) effecting that A takes over the task of giving his directions.

If he succeeds, it is up to A to make clear to F how to reach his destination; he has the task of

(d) describing the way (route directions proper)
(e) seeing that F understands.

It is then up to F, who gave the task, to take it back and to conclude this interaction;

F has the task of

(f) attesting to A that his job is done
(g) acknowledging
(h) ending the contact.

As a rule, these three groups of tasks correspond to a clear interaction scheme of successful route communications. In the first part ("introduction"), F is dominant from an interactive point of view: (a)–(c) are carried out. In the second part ("central sequence"), A takes over and becomes dominant: (d) and (e) are solved. In the third part ("conclusion"), F is dominant again: (f)–(h) are carried out. There may be some kinds of deviations. If F is not successful with (a), the whole action fails; if F is successful with (a), but not with (b), everything drops until (h). There may also be some overlaps or repetitions, but typically, a route communication follows this scheme.

Route communications are interesting from an interactive, a cognitive, and a linguistic point of view. They all are closely linked, of course; but in the following, I shall concentrate on the third aspect, with some remarks on the second one, when it seems necessary; nearly nothing will be said about the interactive aspect. Only point (d), the route directions proper, are dealt with here, because it is most yielding in the present context.

The study is based on 40 route communications in natural context. They were gathered in May 1977 in the inner city of Frankfurt/Main by students (cf. map below).[2] At the upper Zeil, the main shopping street of Frankfurt or at the Hauptwache (a small historical building from the early 18th century), people were asked either for the "Alte Oper" or the "Goethehaus", both well-known landmarks in Frankfurt. The whole action was candidly recorded by a Nagra SNN audio tape machine. Approximately 100 route communications were recorded, some of them very noisy because of the traffic. The first 20 ones from each group (Alte

Oper, Goethehaus), if fully understandable, were selected and transcribed for further analysis; they are labelled as O1–O20 and G1–G20;
a selection is given in the appendix. The transcription is in usual ortho-
graphy, with some slight touches of dialectal pronunciation for some
speakers. Pauses and parallel speaking is transcribed as accurately as
possible. Sometimes, more than one person was answering; in this case,
indices are used: A_1, A_2, etc.

In order to describe how to go from the actual point to the destination,
A must have some cognitive representation of the area in question. In
general, he owes his knowledge to his own previous experiences: he
remembers what he has seen and heard and how he moved, or how the
streetcar moved, and this remembrance must be structured into a cognitive map:[3] he knows that at a certain place, there is such and such a
building where he can turn left, that he can't cross the street there, etc.
Two people may have different favorite routes, and their attention may
be focused on different objects. They are surely objects which might be
salient landmarks for nearly everybody (cf. Lynch, 1960), but whether
the image somebody has of an area is marked by book stores or by
fashion shops is individually different. Thus, cognitive maps may be

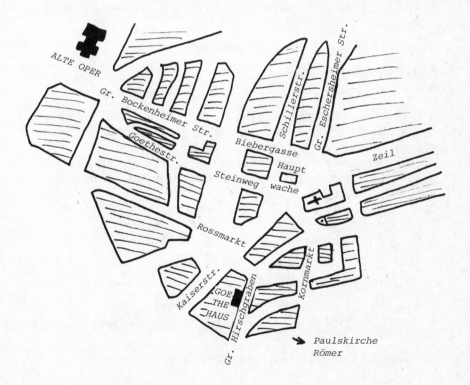

differently structured to a large extent. Moreover, they can be vague, incomplete, or even wrong in some respects. This can, but need not be relevant for route directions.

A's cognitive map is activated, at least to some extent, by F's initial request. What A has to do then is localize position and destination on his map. Such a segment of a cognitive map with position and destination localized will be called "primary plan" of the route direction. Localizing the destination is sometimes not easy, and it might involve complex strategies (cf. text G2 or the fantastically complex G1). The position in general raises no problems because it is in the domain of visual perception, whereas a great deal of what else is represented in the primary plan, for example, the destination in most cases, is not in the domain of visual perception; indeed, it sometimes happened that A looked or even went around to find out where he was, to localize his position. Building up the primary plan may be done in advance, or step by step. Consider G11:

F   Entschuldigung, können Sie mir bitte sagen, wo's zum Goethehaus
A

F   geht?   Ja
A   [3 sec] Goethehaus? ja, gehn Se da rauf, immer gerade

F   erste links, erste
A   aus, erste Straße links, erste Straße rechts

F   rechts dankeschön
A   ja

A makes a planning pause after the question; then he reaffirms himself that he correctly understood the question, indicates that he is able and willing to answer; and then, he carries out his description in one stroke. When speaking, he apparently has a sufficiently clear primary plan; he is an "advance planner". His counterpart may be called "stepwise planner". A clear example is in G15:

F
A   Ja; [10 sec] hier die Zeil runter, auf der andern Seite,

F
A   ja [14 sec] praktisch gehn Se jetzt hier an [3 sec] eh [3 sec]

F
A   Sie müssen wohl von hinten rüber, weil da ne Ampel is, ja; da

F
A   hinter der Kirche lang; dann gehn Se rechts die Straße wieder

F
A   grad runter und dann müssen Se bis zur [2 sec] wie heiß'n das?

F
A   auf der linken Ecke [4 sec] bis die ne Rolltreppe kommt, da is

F
A   Möbel Mann, diese Straße müssen Sie links rein; und die erste

F   gut, dankeschön
A   wieder rechts;   also, auf der einen Seite ist, eh

F
A   Neckermann, Reisebüro, und auf der andern Straßenecke ist Möbel

F
A   Mann; *die* Straße links rein und dann die erste rechts.

Though reflecting at the beginning, A has no clear plan when he starts speaking. He soon comes to a point that proves to be problematical; he then reflects on the situation – he tries to elaborate his primary plan there –, restarts at the beginning, reaches again that confusing place, reflects again (two times three seconds), and then, he advances a little bit, until the next unclear position is reached; he tries to picture the situation there to himself, and then, he is able to go until the end. Thereafter, he has no problem of recapitulating a part of his description: the plan being there, he is able to repeat, to vary or to extend his description. He doesn't work out a complete plan in advance, but he starts speaking as soon as the beginning is clear, and he goes on step by step. Planning in advance and planning stepwise are complementary techniques, and it is open whether they represent individual styles or whether their use simply depends on the particular task. Having a hole in the conversation, and a long planning pause is such a hole, is awkward, and it may well be that A in G15 starts speaking simply because he doesn't like that hole.

The primary plan, whether built up in advance or step by step, is a first condition for a successful description. But not the whole primary plan is reported, of course; it contains a lot of information that is superfluous for the purpose of the required route directions. The speaker must select from it and arrange those pieces of information he thinks to be relevant for the listener. He has to form a "secondary plan" which immediately underlies the linearized sequence of verbal expressions, by which A describes the route. The organizing principle of this secondary plan is that of an "imaginary wandering" from position to destination through the primary plan. During this wandering, certain points of the primary plan are selected and marked; this series of "fixed points" forms the skeleton of his description. His directions have three components: fixed points are introduced, directions relative to the fixed points are marked, and actions (or events) are indicated. Consider the following passage from O4:

F   [...]   ja
A   Ja, [5 sec] jetzt gehn Sie vor, bis ganz vorn hin   bis Sie

F   ja
A   an den Kaufhof stoßen   dann gehn Sie links rein, die Biebergas-

F   ja
A   se   also Sie gehen hier vor und halten sich dann ganz links,

F   mhm
A   dann kommt erst die Schillerstraße, die überqueren Sie   da is

F
A   vorn an der Ecke is ein Herrenboutique, da gehn Sie dran vorbei.

The first fixed point after the starting position is the Kaufhof (a big department store); here, the wanderer has several possibilities; one of them is marked: "links rein". In other cases, alternatives are explicitly excluded, e.g. in O2: "oben drüber, nicht unten durch". This is not done here; only the correct direction is indicated; it is indeed given twice: by the deictic statement "links rein", and by the additional information "die Biebergasse"; A has taken over a unit of his primary plan that is not absolutely necessary but that is an additional help. Then, the route is repeated until a new fixed point is reached: Schillerstraße. In this way, point after point is selected, verbally introduced, and this skeleton is completed by some commentaries or some additional information that help make sure that F gets the message. And he got it if he has succeeded in building up a rudimentary image of the area, that essentially consists of a series of selected points, and if he knows what he has to do at these points.

This information is given by three types of descriptive expressions[4] the speaker uses: expressions that introduce fixed points, deictic expressions that link certain actions to certain fixed points, and expressions for what F has to do there or what happens there; in a sequence like: "... to a small house with green shutters; there, turn left", a fixed point ("a small house with green shutters") is introduced; the local deictic "there" refers to that fixed point, or rather to a locality close to that fixed point, and then, it is said what has to be done at the denotatum of "there".

This is an invented example. How the information is really encoded in route directions, is much more complex, but highly informative for an understanding of language as it is actually used. This is indeed not my topic here.[5]

Appendix

Selected route communications

O1:

F   Können Sie mir bitte sagen, wie ich zum alten Opernhaus komme?
A

F   zum alten Opernhaus
A   wie?   zum alten Opernhaus; gradaus, net;

F   ja ja
A   kommen Sie, ich zeig's Ihnen grad   [10 sec] hier vor bis zum

F   jaa
A   Kaufhof; rechts is der Kaufhof, ja?   un da halten Sie sich rechts,

F   ja, die eh   eh
A   gradeaus durch die Fressgasse   die wird neu   also is

F   mhm
A   ganz neu gestaltet, die Fressgasse, ja   da kommen Sie direkt

F   dankeschön, vielen Dank
A   auf den Opernplatz, also zur Opernhausruine

O2:

F   Zum alten Opernhaus?
A   Ja?   jaaa [10 sec] da gehen Sie jetzt

F   ja   oben drüber,
A   bis zur Zeil,   oben drüber, nicht unten durch

F   ja
A   oben drüber, gehen durch die Goethestraße durch, und dann

F   dankeschön
A   kommen Sie direkt an die alte Oper   bitte, Wieder-

F
A   sehen.

O10:

F   Wir suchen's alte Opernhaus
A   oh [5 sec] ja, am Opernplatz, und

F   nein
A   zwar, eh, kennt ihr euch hier einigermaßen aus?   also, durch

F   mhm
A   die Hauptwache durch, da wenn ihr jetzt links geht, ja   jetzt

F   mhm
A   nicht hier, sondern die nächste, ja   müßt ihr ne Unterführung

F
A   durch, ehm [5 sec], eh, bißchen kompliziert; also dann geht ihr

F
A   ganz die Unterführung durch; dann macht ihr mal'n Bogen

F
A   und da fahrt ihr ne Rolltreppe wieder hoch; dann lauft ihr gerade-

F   ja   okay
A   aus, aber am besten, ihr fragt dann nach'm Opernplatz   da

F
A   kennen sich die meisten aus.

G1:

F   Können Sie mir sagen, wie wir zur alten Oper – eh zum Goethehaus
A_1
A_2

F   kommen?
A_1 Goethehaus, Goethehaus, eh *Goethehaus;* kennen Sie
A_2

F
A_1 das Goethehaus [zu A_2]
A_2 Goethehaus, ja, hinten, da hinten irgendwo,

F   ja
A_1 aah, Goethehaus
A_2 wo die Kirche is, da hinten   die Paulskirche   gell

F   ja   ne, ne
A_1 [2 sec] wo
A_2 da is's Goethehaus   wissen Se wo die Paulskirche is?

F
A₁ die Paulskirche is   *da* is das Goethehaus; is das
A₂   wo die Paulskirche is jaa

F
A₁ da wo? da is doch der Römer
A₂   ja is der Römer, ja da müssen Se hin

F   ne, ne, zum Goethehaus
A₁ *da* is das Goethe-   wollen Sie zum Römer
A₂   ja

F   jaa
A₁ Goethehaus
A₂   Goethehaus, des is in der Nähe vom Römer   da müsse,

F
A₁   is das auf dem Platz?
A₂ Sie müsse da hin   auf dem Platz, ja, nein, in

F
A₁   sehn Se, ich weiß das auch nicht
A₂ eine Seitegass rein, eine Seitegass

F
A₁ ganz   also, kommen Se, kommen Se   ich geh sowieso
A₂   also, ich kann,   doch ich weiß   also, auf'n

F   nee, wir
A₁ runter
A₂ Römer müssen Se; Sie müsse da rüber   wo die Paulskirche is

F wir wollten erst nochmal woanders hin wir wollten nur schon mal
A₁
A₂

F wissen, wo's is, ja'
A₁   so ich will mal so sagen, ich glaube Sie
A₂   ach so

F   ja   ja
A₁ müssen hier durch, dann   da kommen Sie durch, ja?
A₂   hier da durch

F
A₁ wenn Sie da runterkommen da kommen Se ungefähr doch ganz be-
A₂

F   ja   ja
A_1 stimmt hin   am Römer, da is die Paulskirche
A_2 jaa, und da is ne,

F   ja
A_1
A_2 eine Seitenstraße geht da rein, gell   ich mein vielleicht Sand-

F   ja   ja, dankeschön.
A_1 also ich bin ja überfragt
A_2 gasse, ja   ja, also da isses

G2:

F   Können Sie mir sagen, wie man zum Goethehaus kommt?
A   Goethehaus?

F   zum Goethehaus   wissen wir eben nicht genau
A   Goethehaus? wo?

F   nee, Großer Hirschgraben war das, glaub ich
A   Goethehaus? keine Adresse?

F   Großer Hirschgraben, die Straße   Wissen Se nicht,
A   bitte?   [5 sec]

F   fragen wir nochmal.
A

Notes

1. For a detailed analysis of the former aspect, see Klein (1978, forthcoming).
2. This work has been done by Elke Habicht, Michael Kahn and Christa Reinhardt. I am very grateful to them.
3. No attempt is made here to define this concept; see for example Downs & Stea (1973) or recently Kuipers (1977).
4. The expressions used in the route directions may be subdivided into three classes, according to their function: descriptive expressions, commenting expressions and interactive expressions. The speaker may comment upon what he says, or on the difficulty of the task, or the way; typical are expressions like "oh, that's quite near" or "well, it's complicated", etc. With interactive expressions, A checks whether F got the message or simply whether F is still following his explanations, and F signalises that he is still "receiving" and that A can and should continue; a standard means is "mhm" with question intonation on A's side and with affirmative intonation on F's side. For some details cf. Klein (forthcoming).
5. I wish to thank Veronika Ehrich, Angelika Kratzer, Pim Levelt, Max Miller, Brigitte Schlieben-Lange, Jürgen Weissenborn and Dieter Wunderlich for helpful comments.

WALLACE L. CHAFE

Some reasons for hesitating

There is a natural tendency, when some interesting phenomenon is being explored, to want to treat it as something which can be studied in and of itself, without regard for its interrelationships with other phenomena. The entire field of linguistics has to some extent suffered from this tendency, in that a great deal of research has attempted to deal with language apart from its psychological, social, and cultural settings. It is a healthy development that fields like psycholinguistics, sociolinguistics, and ethnolinguistics have begun to bring a broader perspective to linguistic studies. On a different level it has seemed to me that there has been the same tendency in research on hesitations, or pausology, or whatever it may be called, to look at the phenomenon in isolation. But in the long run I am sure we are going to find that such a specialization of effort is futile; that hesitational phenomena can be understood only as natural consequences of the processes which occur during the production of speech. Viewed in that way, they can be seen as contributing important clues to the nature of these processes.

Perhaps the only time that hesitations have been thoroughly integrated into a theory of speech production was in Lounsbury's brief discussion (1954). There, the production of speech was seen to be governed by habits associating each linguistic unit in turn with the unit next to be uttered. It was thought that these units were associated by habits having varying degrees of strength, so that there were varying transitional probabilities from one unit to the next. "Hesitation pauses correspond to the points of highest statistical uncertainty in the sequencing of units of any given order." Transitional probabilities were making a splash in linguistics at the time (cf. Harris, 1955), and it was natural to combine them with the behaviorist notion of habit strength to produce such a model of speech production. Nowadays, for a variety of reasons, few would believe that speech is well explained as the implementation of association habits between linguistic units. But there has never since then been a theory that accounted for hesitations as an aspect of speech production in as straightforward a way.

In fact, the dominant linguistic theory in the meantime has been content to focus most of its attention on an ideal condition of language production, thereby sweeping hesitations under the rug. "A record of natural speech will show numerous false starts, deviations from rules, changes of plan in mid-course, and so on. The problem for the linguist [...] is to determine from the data of performance the underlying system of rules that has been mastered by the speaker-hearer and that he puts to use in actual performance." (Chomsky, 1965:4). This view is, I think, misleading to the extent that it suggests that the speaker has some grammatical ideal toward which he is striving, and which he is often prevented from attaining because of various imperfections in the psychological processes involved in "performance".

I would like to suggest on the contrary that the speaker's chief goal is to get across what he has in mind, and that he is not likely to be interested in grammaticality unless there is some special reason to think of it, as there usually is not. The speaker is interested in the adequate verbalization of his thoughts. Pauses, false starts, afterthoughts, and repetitions do not hinder that goal, but are steps on the way to achieving it. After some one has said something, it would not be a damaging criticism to tell him, "You spoke ungrammatically (or disfluently)." I doubt if the average person would care. But it would be damaging to say, "You didn't get across what you had in mind." For that, I suggest, the speaker might have genuine regrets. We may even find, when we study comprehension in relation to these phenomena which we are too prone to regard as infelicities, that they not only enable the speaker to express his ideas more effectively, but also enable the hearer to assimilate them more effectively too.

The more specific, if only partially developed suggestions I will put forward here come from a concern with the ongoing, real-time production of speech as a reflection of the ongoing sequencing of the speaker's thoughts. In this kind of investigation "ungrammatical", "disfluent" speech constitutes the primary data, and hesitation phenomena are welcome as overt, measurable indications of processing activity which requires a certain amount of time. They provide good evidence that speaking is not a matter of regurgitating material already stored in the mind in linguistic form, but that it is a creative act, relating two media, thought and language, which are not isomorphic but require adjustments and readjustments to each other. A speaker does not follow a clear, well traveled path, but must find his way through territory not traversed before, where pauses, changes of direction, and retracing of steps are quite to be expected. The fundamental reason for hesitating is that speech production is an act of creation.

I have been particularly interested in how people talk about things

they have recalled from memory (cf. Chafe, 1977 and 1979, which explain some of the assumptions underlying the present discussion). Let us
regard memory as a vast store of information, somehow established by
previous experience but also creative in itself, which is potentially ready
to be activated by a process which may be called "bringing into consciousness". Such activation takes place as a series of brief resting places.
William James suggested a similar metaphor when he wrote of the
stream of consciousness: "Like a bird's life, it seems to be made of an
alternation of flights and perchings. The rhythm of language expresses
this, where every thought is expressed in a sentence, and every sentence
closed by a period." (James, 1890:243). Introspection, I believe, supports this notion. We recall the past more as a series of salient snapshots
than as a continuous movie film. Eye movements lend support to the
idea too, by showing that the focusing of consciousness on visual
phenomena follows discrete, discontinuous "centers of interest" (Buswell, 1935). The work of Newtson (1976) also shows that we break up
continuous experience into a sequence of discrete actions. And as James
suggested, language lends support to the perching metaphor. Numerous
recent observers of spontaneous speech have noticed that it is produced
in well defined spurts (see, for example, the "information units" of
Halliday, 1967c). In the data available to me at the moment these spurts
are slightly less than 2 seconds in mean duration, and contain a mean of
about 5 words. They tend to be single clauses syntactically, but under
certain conditions may be more or less than a clause. They usually
exhibit a "clause-final" intonation contour. I hypothesize that these
spurts of language are expressions of underlying perchings of consciousness. If so, they provide us with excellent evidence of how consciousness
successively activates small chunks of information: the kinds of information it lights on, how long and for what purpose it dwells there, and the
patterns it follows in moving from one perching to the next. Hesitations
are especially useful in showing us where it is easy to move on, and
where it is difficult.

In what follows I will refer to each separate perching as a "focus of
consciousness", or simply as a "focus". Many hesitations, I will suggest,
are attributable to the kind of process just described: to the speaker's
need to find the next focus. Others, as we will see at the end of this
discussion, stem from the need to find the best way to verbalize a focus,
once found. In other words, sometimes speakers hesitate while they are
deciding *what* to talk about next, and sometimes they hesitate while they
are deciding *how* to talk about what they have chosen. Most of the
hesitations in the data I will be discussing stem from one or the other of
these two main types of reasons.

The data in question come from a situation in which 20 adult female speakers of American English were asked to "tell what happened" in a movie they had seen shortly before. It was a 7-minute color and sound film produced as a means of eliciting speech about the same subject matter from speakers of various languages at various times. All the subjects were quite willing to tell what they remembered of the film, and most of them probably regarded the exercise as a memory task. Although the situation was an unusual one, the language was in all cases natural and spontaneous. Preliminary comparisons with narratives embedded in more typical conversations suggest that the findings from these film narratives are generalizable to less artificial speech situations, but more systematic comparisons of this sort have yet to be made.

The basic method I will follow here is to note correspondences between hesitational phenomena and other phenomena available in the linguistic record, including the content of what was said. I realize that there is a research tradition which regards the interpretation of content as too subjective of intuitive to allow any reliable conclusions, I would urge on the contrary that it is only by looking in detail at what a speaker is talking about at each point in a discourse that we can come significantly closer to an understanding of speech production processes. What follows is, among other things, an attempt to illustrate this point.

Most of the 20 speakers began their narratives by expressing acquiescence in the interviewer's request that they "tell what happened in the movie". Twelve said "OK", two said "all right", one each said "sure", "certainly", and "I'll try", and only three plunged in without any acknowledgment of the request. For most speakers there then followed a considerable period of floundering, filled with pauses, pause fillers, lengthened syllables, false starts, and repetitions. The following is an example:

1. OK.
2. (.3) Um–– (1.0) let's see.
3. (1.1) Uh–– the first part of the .. m (.45) movie,
4. (.4) uh well,
5. the .. the–– .. the basic action,
6. (.5) i––s that there's–– (.2) a man (.4) uh .. on a ladder,
7. (.55) uh picking pears from a pear tree.

Clearly this speaker was having trouble getting started. The content of her floundering provides some evidence as to what her mind was doing. After the initial "OK", it is evident that she was buying time as she searched for a satisfactory initial focus to verbalize. The phrase "let's see" in line 2 is a commonly used way of communicating such a state. By line 3 she had apparently gotten no further than to decide she was going to talk about the first part of the movie. She bought more time in lines 4 and 5 with "well" (another commonly used word in this situation) and the thrice repeated "the". At this point she had at least settled on "the basic action", though still without a clear focus on what that action involved. There is a familiar narrative pattern in which a speaker introduces first a character and then an ongoing background activity in which that character is engaged. Apparently guided finally by that pattern, this speaker got around to introducing the pear picker by the middle of line 6, and his activity in line 7. Everything prior to line 6 is a gradual zeroing in and clarifying of these first substantive foci of her story.

It is interesting to compare another subject who seems to have avoided this need to search and clarify:

8. Sure.
9. There was a man――,
10. picking――,
11. (.9) um―― (.1) a Latin looking man,
12. and he was picking pears,

This speaker moved directly from acquiescence in the interviewer's request to the introduction of a character and his activity. In spite of this efficiency, however, she showed signs that she had moved too precipitously, first through her lengthening of the words "man" and "picking", then through her significant hesitating at the beginning of line 11, where she evidently felt the need to bring the man into clearer focus and describe his most salient property. In summary, when one begins a narrative, some time-consuming mental processing usually needs to be devoted to the finding and clarification of an initial focus. Even when this processing is accomplished with ease, as in the last example, there is still a need to allow enough time to establish the essentials of this starting point.

The majority of foci of consciousness are expressed in linguistic phrases or clauses which end in a rising pitch contour (marked here with a comma), but approximately one-third of those in our data end instead with the kind of falling pitch contour interpreted as "sentence-final intonation" (marked here with a period). This conspicuous sentence-final contour, as well as various other criteria including the syntactic properties associated with a "grammatical sentence", define what I will call a "focus cluster". In other words, foci of consciousness appear to cluster together to form larger units which are verbalized as sentences. There are various kinds of coherence that bind the foci within such clusters together. Here I will point out only two patterns which occur with considerable frequency. One involves focusing on various simultaneous facets of a single image, much as the eye scans a scene to acquire various kinds of information from it. In the following excerpt the separate foci achieve an overall coherence through the unity of the scene being described:

13. OK,
14. .. uh–– (.3) there's a–– .. man,
15. (.45) picking pears,
16. in a pear tree,
17. out .. somewhere in the country,
18. (1.1) uh–– he looks (.95) like your uh (.2) typical .. farmer,
19. or (.3) whatever,
20. kind of plump,
21. and (.7) moustache,
22. and he wears a white apron,
23. (1.3) to .. hold the pears in.

Another common pattern is one in which a series of foci are unified by their contribution toward a single goal, the fulfillment of an intention of one of the characters. In the following excerpt everything is aimed toward the theft of the pears, and coherence is provided by this single aim:

24. (.95) Then um–– (1.5) a little boy on a bicycle,
25. (1.15) comes riding past the tree,
26. (.75) a––nd (.2) sort of goes past the pears (.3) the (.2) pears in the baskets
27. and then stops,
28. (1.0) and looks up at the guy in the tree,
29. he's still on the ladder,
30. and he's not .. watching him,
31. so he (1.0) st .. puts his bike (.6) down,
32. (.85) he walks over,
33. a––nd he picks up a (.2) the whole basket of pears,
34. (.9) and puts it on the handle (.2) no, on the (.4) front (.15) fender of his bike.

In general there is more hesitating between focus clusters – that is, between sentences – than there is between foci within a cluster, as the following table shows:

	Within Cluster	Across Clusters
No Hesitation	42%	26%
Hesitation	58%	74%
Mean Length of Hesitation when Present	.84 sec.	1.18 sec.

In other words, the breaks in coherence which are found at sentence boundaries, whether they result from a shift to a new image, to a new goal, or whatever, require more time-consuming mental processing than does the moving from focus to focus within a cluster.

However, if we look at all the cases of hesitating between sentences, we find a range all the way from no hesitating at all up to 7 seconds or more (including pauses, pause fillers, and false starts). Notice the great variety in hesitation lengths between the sentences in the following excerpt:

35. .. And he pulls the (.8) tsk goat by the guy who's up in the tree,
36. (.9) and disappears.
37. (.9) A––nd (2.9) the next people .. who come by,
38. (.9) and there's a little boy on a bicycle
39. .. who comes by from the other direction,
40. .. he's riding a bike,
41. .. it's a little too big for him.
42. (1.15) A––nd (.4) he rides by,
43. .. and then he stops,
44. (2.2) tries to .. take a pear,
45. .. a––nd then he (.35) he can't reach it.
46. .. So he puts down his bike,
47. (.9) he sort of takes a pear,
48. and then he decides he wants the whole basket.
49. .. So he takes the whole basket,
50. .. and puts it near his bike,
51. .. lifts up the bike,
52. .. puts the basket on .. the front part of his bicycle,
53. (.5) and rides off.
54. And all this time the guy's up in the (.6) tree,
55. .. and he doesn't notice it.
56. (.9) However the sounds are extremely loud.
57. (1.95 including cough) So .. it's kind of funny.

The sentence beginning in line 54 is preceded by no hesitation at all. The sentences beginning in 35, 46, and 49 are preceded by less than 50 milliseconds of pausing. On the other hand, the total hesitating at the beginning of 37 adds up to 4.35 seconds, and at the beginning of 42 to 2.5 seconds. Significant hesitating occurs also at the beginning of 56 and 57. It thus does not go very far to say that the mean length of hesitating between sentences is 1.18 seconds. We would like to be able to explain why the individual lengths vary as much as they do.

Again, observation of the content of what is being said can lead us

toward some answers. The simplest hypothesis would be that focus clusters themselves cluster into larger conceptual units, call them
"episodes", which correspond in written language to paragraphs. Thus
we could explain the very brief hesitation at the beginning of line 35 by
saying that the sentence in 35–36 expresses a focus cluster that belongs
to the same episode as the cluster immediately preceding (not shown
here), whereas the long hesitation at the beginning of 37 reflects the
beginning of a new episode. This interpretation is supported by the fact
that 35 begins with a pronoun, and in fact maintains the same grammatical subject as the preceding focus, whereas 37 begins with a full noun
phrase which represents a change of subject. Differences like these can
be interpreted as additional evidence for same-episode vs. different-
episode transitions.

Closer examination of the variability of hesitations between sentences
suggests that the episode explanation, while on the right track, is something of an over-simplification. The factors which lead to such hesitating
are in fact several, and while they sometimes coincide to produce what
appears to be a clear-cut episode boundary, they may also occur independently and in various combinations to produce hesitations of various
lengths at various places in a narrative. Rather than to think of "episode
boundary" as a monolithic notion, therefore, it is preferable to think of
several kinds of transitions which are likely to require extra processing
time.

Looking again at the long excerpt in lines 35–57 above, we can see
some of these factors illustrated. The importance of the factors I will
mention is confirmed in other narratives, but there is not space here to
present the range of evidence available. The factors which seem to be
important in triggering significant hesitations between sentences are the
following:
(a) Introduction of a new character or set of characters
(b) Change of location
(c) Change of time period
(d) Change of event schema
(e) Change of world
In other words, speakers seem to require some time to recall or clarify in
their minds any changes of these types. When several occur together, as
they often do, the processing time required generally increases.

Such a combination is illustrated in lines 37–38. A new character
enters the narrative at this point, there is a minor spatial change (he
"comes by from the other direction"), and there is the beginning of a
new event schema in that it is here that the events culminating in the
theft of the pears begin. It took the speaker more than 4 seconds to cope
with this combination of changes. In fact, line 37 is actually a false start,

and the speaker did not really settle on a clear focus until she was one second into line 38.

The foci within the rest of this cluster (37–41) were settled on without much further interruption. It is interesting, however, to observe that 38–39 make use of a highly familiar syntactic pattern, "there is a ... who ...", which is commonly used for introducing a new character and involving him in some kind of background activity, in this case his "coming by". By the end of 39 the speaker had used up this syntactic pattern. She had not, however, said everything she wanted to say about the image she had activated; specifically, she needed two more clauses to communicate the inappropriate size of the bicycle. Hence 40 and 41 were tacked on, syntactically as afterthoughts, to complete the cluster. It is often the case that a syntactic pattern will prove inadequate to what a speaker has in mind, and be supplemented by independent clause increments like 40 and 41.

Once the boy had been introduced in 37–41, the speaker used up again a considerable amount of time getting started on a description of his actions. Although the section beginning with line 42 would probably be regarded as belonging to the same episode or paragraph as the preceding sentence, it nevertheless represents the beginning of a coherent event schema which the speaker evidently needed more time to pull together. Introducing a new character thus does not necessarily bring automatically into focus the actions of that character. Getting the character involved in his actions may be another reason for hesitating.

The 2.2 second hesitation at the beginning of line 44 has a special kind of interest. Lines 44–45 are in a sense false; they describe an event which did not happen in the film. The boy did not try to take a pear while he was still on his bicycle. An interesting possibility is that the construction and verbalization of a nonveridical piece of information is also likely to be a cause for hesitating. Constructive recall takes time.

From here on speech moves fairly fluently through four sentences, up to the end of 55. Lines 42–53 present three basic actions involved in the theft of pears: trying to take one pear while still on the bicycle, taking one while on foot, and taking the whole basket. Three separate sentences are used to express this sequence here. However, six weeks later the same speaker, asked to tell about the film again, coalesced the three into a single sentence, giving evidence of a conceptual unity in 42–53 which helps to account for the easy transitions at the beginnings of 46 and 49.

But why should there be no hesitation at the beginning of 54, where a different character is reintroduced and there is a clear change of both grammatical subject and subject matter? The six-weeks-later version may shed some light here too. In that version the speaker began to make this comment about the man in the tree just after she had begun the theft sequence, but she then immediately abandoned it, uncompleted, as inappropriate at that point:

58. And he stops,
59. (4.45) bu––t (.25) the man who's in the tree.
60. .. And he um

It seems that the unwatchfulness of the pear picker in the tree was something the speaker had "in the back of her mind", or was peripherally conscious of, simultaneously with the events of the theft, so that this idea was ready to be brought forward without hesitation in 54–55. This example suggests both (1) that it may sometimes be instructive, in explaining hesitations, to see how a speaker would verbalize the same material on another occasion, and (2) that it is also of some interest to see where people do *not* hesitate, especially under conditions where a hesitation might normally be expected.

Lines 56 and 57, which end this excerpt, exhibit the effect of a change in worlds. The longest hesitation by this speaker, 7.05 seconds long, came at a point earlier in her narrative where she inserted a comment on the sound track:

61. (2.55) Um (4.05) the thing I noticed all the way through is that ..
    there's (.5) there's no–– .. dialogue in the film,
62. but there .. is (1.0) a lot of sound effects. etc.

Here, at the beginning of 61, there was a clear shift from the world inside the film to the world outside it, where one could take a critical stance and talk about properties of the film as a film. In 61 this shift was a highly time-consuming process. A recurrence of the shift in 56 required only .9 seconds of extra time, suggesting that once a transition between different worlds has been established in the speaker's mind, it subsequently becomes easier to move back and forth between them.

Finally, line 57 provides an evaluative comment (cf. the discussion of evaluative devices in Labov, 1972). Such a comment is in a sense a shift to still another world: the world of the speaker's attitudes. It is clearly another reason for hesitating. Of additional interest is the fact that evaluative material is often accompanied by some audible expression of affect: often a laugh––sometimes, as here, a cough.

My discussion up to this point has dealt with hesitations caused by the speaker's need to decide what to talk about next. Such hesitations typically occur between the phrases and clauses which express the foci of consciousness. But many hesitations occur within these phrases and clauses as well. One may also hesitate *during* the verbalization of a focus. Such hesitations are usually attributable to difficulty the speaker is having in deciding, not what to verbalize, but how to verbalize something he already has in mind. The basic problem for the speaker here is one of categorization, more or less in the sense of Rosch (1973) and others. Some concepts that a speaker may have in mind are easy to categorize, are "highly codable", while others may be more or less difficult, may be low in codability. In the seminal study of Brown & Lenneberg (1954), "reaction time" was one of the indices of codability investigated. The implication of that study for the explanation of hesitations is that it takes time to verbalize a referent which has low codability. Put simply, some referents are harder to find words to communicate than others, and the degree of hesitating is correlated with the degree of difficulty.

We deliberately included in our film both objects that we expected to be high in codability and objects with which we expected speakers to have difficulty. In the former class, for example, was the boy's bicycle. Although people called it either a "bicyle" or a "bike", no one hesitated even briefly before such a word. No one said anything like:

*there's a boy on a ... uh ... bicycle,

The object at the other extreme, the one which was most successful in causing difficulty for speakers, was something we have come to call the "paddleball". Only one of the sixteen subjects who mentioned this object failed to hesitate in referring to it:

63. (1.6) um one's playing with a paddleball.

Others said things like:

64. one of them has a .. what do you call those little .. um (.85) paddleball?

or:

65. one was (.25) had a little (.55) paddle with a ball−−,

but the prize for the best attempt to communicate the idea of this object went to the speaker who said:

66. (.4) I don't remember,
67. I used to play with it when I was a kid,
68. but (.75) it's like a .. wooden paddle
69. (.3) that (.15) there's an elastic string attached to
70. and there's a ball,
71. (.3) you know that that kind of thing that you (.4) you
72. (.15) I .. don't remember the name of them,
73. (.35) but I played with them for hours.

Although this excerpt may seem ungrammatical or "disfluent", I suggest that the speaker was quite successful in conveying what she had in mind, and that this kind of hesitation-ridden speech should actually be highly valued as an accurate expression of a speaker's thoughts.

In summary, I have tried with a few examples, which are representative of numerous others in our material, to show some of the factors which produce hesitations as the speaker's consciousness moves from focus to focus. Such factors include finding and clarifying an initial focus, moving to the next focus within a cluster, and moving across a cluster boundary. There may be more or less difficulty in the transition, depending on such factors as change of characters, of scene, of time period, of event structure, of world. Evaluative comments function as world changes, but may be accompanied by audible expressions of affect. Other factors may enter the picture sporadically, such as the construction of nonveridical material. Having something in one's peripheral consciousness may inhibit hesitating where it would otherwise occur. Finally, a considerable proportion of hesitating stems from the need to verbalize something that is low in codability. I expect that this procedure of carefully examining the content factors which are present at the points where hesitations occur is going to be an important and necessary aspect of hesitation research.

Prosodic aspects

Chairman   JOHN LAVER

ANNE CUTLER

Syllable omission errors and isochrony

Introduction

English is said to be a stress-timed language. Stress-timing refers to a
supposed tendency for stressed syllables to be produced isochronously,
i.e. at regular intervals. The notion of isochrony has been criticised by
many linguists, since experimental evidence shows that intervals between stressed syllables in English utterances are not, when measured by
any technique whatsoever, physically equal. Nevertheless, the notion
stubbornly persists in the literature and many arguments have been
made in favour of its psychological if not physical reality. (For a review
of the relevant literature see Lehiste, 1977.)

Isochrony has reality, for instance, in perception; listeners asked to
match the rhythm of a sequence of noise bursts to the rhythm of an
utterance will adjust the noises to a more regular rhythm than that of the
utterance (Donovan & Darwin, 1979), indicating that they hear the
utterance as more isochronous than it really is.

The perceptual reality of isochrony naturally leads one to suspect that
there is indeed an underlying regular rhythm in production, and that it is
this underlying rhythm which the listener picks up in spite of the multiple
perturbations resulting from segmental variations which obscure it in the
acoustic signal. In fact Lehiste (1977) has recently argued that the
speaker imposes a rhythm for the purpose of being able to disrupt it to
signal the presence of a syntactic boundary – e.g. in syntactically ambiguous strings such as "old men and women". Cutler and Isard (forthcoming) have examined productions of such syntactically ambiguous sentences and have found that far from an underlying rhythm being disrupted, it is preserved, with the presence of a boundary being signalled
by "skipping a beat".

Furthermore it has often been pointed out that speakers of English
have at their disposal a wide variety of devices by which sentence rhythm
can be adjusted, and that they make considerable use of such options.
For instance, lexical stress in certain words and compounds is variable;

thus we say "I counted fourtéen" but "I've fóurteen books"; "the comment was mispláced" but "a mísplaced comment". Similarly, rhythmic constraints can underlie the choice between synonyms – for instance, "the man was drunk" versus "the drunken man". Redundant elements can be inserted, e.g. "he waited half an hour" rather than "he waited a half hour" (cf. "he waited a good half hour"). Bolinger (1965), in a comprehensive discussion of such phenomena, argues that they can be accounted for simply by the speaker's desire to avoid one stressed syllable immediately following another, without postulating underlying rhythmic tendencies. But this claim confines the adjustments under consideration to the insertion of one or more syllables between stressed syllables and thus implies that rhythmic manipulation does not occur via the omission of syllables. In the following sections some syllable omission errors in spontaneous speech are described. Because these errors have the effect of producing a closer approximation to isochrony, they provide evidence against Bolinger's claim and in favour of the psychological reality of an underlying regular rhythm in production.

Speech errors and rhythm

An error in speech performance can change the rhythmic pattern of an utterance in two obvious ways: either one or more syllables can be added or deleted, or stress can shift from one syllable to another. At times the two occur together (e.g. when *botánical* is pronounced *bótnical,* i.e. the stress is shifted back and the second syllable is deleted). The question of whether such errors have a systematic effect on the regularity of speech rhythms can be investigated by comparing the rhythm of the target utterance and the rhythm of the erroneous utterance and determining which of them provides a closer approximation to isochronous rhythm.

To do this analysis it is of course necessary to have recorded the sentence context in which the error occurred. Since sufficient context is only rarely included with published errors, the majority of examples on which the following discussion will be based come from my own collection. In recording an error I have taken pains to include as much of the phonetic detail as possible, noting, for instance, which syllables were contracted, and which syllables were stressed. But the transcription nevertheless falls far short of the ideal (a tape recording on which exact measurements could be made, for instance), and of course no exactly equivalent data are available for the target utterance. Most of the errors in my corpus were corrected immediately, and it is the speaker's correction which I have taken to be the original target. The analysis which I will present should be regarded as suggestive rather than definitive. It is important to notice, however, that it is an analysis performed on data collected well in advance of the formulation of the present hypothesis.

The analysis consists in segmenting each and each target utterance into feet, where a foot is the interval between stressed syllables. The stressed syllables in question are all those syllables marked for lexical stress in the major lexical items of the sentence (i.e. not only those bearing sentence accent – though if sentence accent occurs on a word not normally marked for stress, such as an article or a conjunction, that word will also count as stressed for the purposes of division into feet). In the absence of any more rigorous measurement of foot length, the error-target pairs will be compared in terms of number of syllables within each foot.

It is not clear what the null hypothesis should be, i.e. what would be the chance effect of a syllable omission on rhythm. To determine this one would need to measure the effect on rhythm of deletion of each syllable of a very large corpus of spontaneous speech. Since this tedious chore is unlikely ever to be performed, I have arbitrarily assumed that 50% of syllable omission errors would result in a more rhythmic utterance by chance alone. This estimate may in fact be conservative, because if speech is more often than not rhythmic, an omitted syllable will more often than not disrupt the rhythm.

Syllable omission errors

Typical syllable omission errors include:

(1) Next we have this bicéntial rug.
    (Target: ... bicenténnial rug)
(2) ... inferences about what the speaker thinks his ínterlocker knows
    (T: ... interlócutor knows)
(3) In his life there seems to be ambíguty.
    (T: ... seems to be ambigúity)
(4) In the metrólitan area
    (T: ... metropólitan area; from Fromkin (1973))
(5) This kind of question can not be appróprally interpreted
    (T: ... apprópriately interpreted)
(6) a tiny mail-order firm ópering out of a front room in Waltham-
    stow (T: ... óperating ...)

It can be seen that some involve a shift of lexical stress, others do not. This kind of error, in which a syllable (occasionally two syllables) is omitted from within a word, appears to differ from errors in which the speaker skips from the middle of one word to the following word (haplologies) or in which whole words are omitted. Haplologies and word omission errors will be discussed separately below.

Meanwhile, let us compare the above error and target pairs. Example (1), for instance – which was uttered fairly rapidly by an amateur auctioneer – is divided into feet as follows (each foot begins with a stressed syllable):

/Next we / have this bi/cential / rug

whereas the target utterance would have been:

/Next we / have this bicen/tennial / rug

In the target utterance the second foot contains four syllables, whereas the error reduces the length of that foot to three syllables, closer to the length of the preceding and following feet. The same tendency to equal-ise number of syllables per foot can be seen in:

(2) E: what the / speaker thinks his / interlocker / knows
    T: what the / speaker thinks his inter/locutor / knows
(3) E: /in his / life there / seems to / be am/biguty
    T: /in his / life there / seems to / be ambi/guity
(4) E: /in the met/rolitan / area
    T: /in the metro/politan / area
(5) E: can / not be app/proprally in/terpreted
    T: can / not be ap/propriately in/terpreted
(6) E: /opering / out of a / front room in / Walthamstow
    T: /Operating / out of a / front room in / Walthamstow

In (2), the error has the same number of syllables in the two marked feet, whereas the target would have had six syllables in the first foot and half as many in the second. In (3), the error has resulted in four successive feet of two syllables each whereas in the target utterance the fourth of these would have had three syllables. In (4), again, the foot length in the error is a constant three syllables, whereas the target would have four syllables in the first marked foot. In (5), the error has led to the second marked foot being reduced from five syllables to four, closer in length to the surrounding three-syllable feet. In (6), finally, the error has reduced the first marked foot from four to three syllables, thus matching the three-syllable length of the following feet. Clearly these errors have resulted in utterances more rhythmical than the intended utterances.

Although errors in which an extra syllable is inserted are rare, they too appear to result in a more regular rhythm:

(7) E: /That's transan/actional an/alysis
    T: /That's trans/actional an/alysis

In (7), the error has extended the first foot to a length more comparable with that of the following feet.

Space does not suffice for a complete listing of my corpus of syllable addition and deletion errors. I have in all 20 errors in which one syllable was deleted (eight of which involve a stress shift as well), three in which two syllables were deleted (all involving a stress shift), and five in which a syllable was added (no stress shift), making a total of 28 errors, in 24 of which the erroneous utterance was more rhythmic than the intended utterance would have been (a difference significant on the binomial test at a level beyond .001).

Other omission errors

In haplologies, words are telescoped – the speaker skips from one point in the sentence to a later point, and the intervening material is omitted. Usually such errors occur when segments are repeated, and the utterance skips from the first occurrence of the repeated element to the second, as in:

(8) It's a pritiotic idea
    (T: it's a pretty idiotic idea; from Fromkin (1973))
(9) a large number of words in the language seem to become
    unique aftoo (T: ... unique after two)

It is probably reasonable to assume that this type of error occurs at a point after the entire utterance has been assembled in a pre-output buffer; the sequential dependencies of individual elements become confused when elements are repeated in fairly close succession, so that, for instance, the [prIdi] of (8) summons up the [atIk] which should actually have awaited the utterance of another [Idi].

Whole words, of any length, may also be omitted, as in (10)–(12):

(10) I hope you mind my – I hope you don't mind my not going
(11) some more alternative ...
    (T: some more efficient alternative strategy)
(12) and most of what you'll doing
    (T: ... what you'll be doing)

Various explanations exist in the speech literature for certain kinds of word omission errors – for example, Freud's (1904) well-known explanation of errors such as (10). Neither haplologies nor whole word omission errors show any tendency to regularise utterance rhythm (in each case about half of my examples result in an error more rhythmic than the target, while half result in a rhythmically indistinguishable or less regular utterance). Although pressure towards isochrony may be operative in a few isolated cases, it is probably true that these two error types, both of which produce a surface structure different from that of the target because substantial material has been omitted, usually arise in a manner different from the genesis of syllable deletion and addition errors, in which the error makes alterations only within a single word.

Lexical stress errors

Some of the syllable omission errors described above also involve a shift of lexical stress within the word. Very often, however, lexical stress errors occur with no syllable omission, as in (13)–(14):

(13) we do think in spécific terms
(14) I think those disambiguáting effects ...

Elsewhere (Cutler, forthcoming) I have given a detailed description of such errors; since the erroneous stress pattern is always that of some related word (in (13) and (14), *specify* and *disambiguation* respectively), I have accounted for them in terms of confusion within the lexicon between differently stressed derivatives of the same morphological base. There is no compelling reason, however, why a tendency to regularise utterance rhythm may not also play a part; a distinction can be drawn between mechanism (in this case confusion between conjointly stored related words) and cause (factors which might precipitate such confusion). Isochrony might act as just such a precipitating factor; when the lexical entry accessed contains, as well as the target, a related word with a stress pattern which would fit better into the overall utterance rhythm than the stress pattern of the target, then that better-fitting stress pattern might be selected by mistake, resulting in a typical lexical stress error. And indeed, almost two-thirds of the lexical stress errors result in an utterance with a rhythm more regular than the target utterance would have shown (a result significant on the binomial test at a level beyond .03). But this difference is also significantly less marked than the difference to be found in the syllable deletion/addition errors (chi square, $p < .02$). (On the other hand, deletion errors which do involve a stress shift, and deletion errors which don't, show no difference in their effects on utterance rhythm.) It is probably fair to conclude that while a tendency towards isochrony may quite often be the underlying cause of a lexical stress error, not all such errors arise in this way.

Conclusion

Certain kinds of speech errors tend to result in a closer approximation to isochronous speech than the target utterance would have achieved. This tendency appears to be most strongly at work in errors of syllable omission and addition. Lexical stress errors also appear to be to a somewhat lesser degree rhythmically determined, whereas errors involving omission of relatively large amounts of material, such as entire words, do not. Independent accounts have been offered for these latter types of error, but no explanation has hitherto been suggested for syllable deletion or addition errors. It is argued here that a sufficient account of their genesis is provided by a tendency to isochronous rhythm in the production of English. Many devices of syntax and vocabulary are available to the English speaker to adjust the rhythm of a target utterance; furthermore, the length of individual syllables can be fairly considerably contracted, or expanded even to the extent of allowing a complex pitch movement to occur on a single syllable. Nevertheless, the pressure to regularise the rhythm of an utterance is sufficiently strong that on occasion an utterance will be forcibly adjusted towards isochrony by the deletion or addition of a syllable. It is not surprising, we can now see, that syllable deletion errors are relatively common while syllable addition errors are rare. There are few constraints on how far a syllable can be stretched to lengthen a foot, but there are limits to the degree to which a syllable can be contracted to shorten a foot – in the extreme case it is contracted out of existence and becomes a syllable omission error.

It is clear that this discussion of omission errors raises many further questions, for instance:

1. To what extent is the effect of rhythmic regularity on speech errors confined to English? Does it show up in other stress-timed languages as well? Meringer & Mayer (1895) – the only extensive collection of speech errors in German and the first ever published collection of errors – contains a section on syllable omission errors of which only one is given with full context:

(15) E: Meine /Vorlesung /sinken /nach und /nach her/ab
       T: Meine /Vorlesungen /sinken /nach und /nach her/ab

In this case it would certainly seem that omission of a syllable has resulted in a more equivalent foot length. German is, like English, a language for which a tendency to isochrony has been claimed; an investigation of German syllable omission errors could well produce results similar to those of the present study of English errors. One would certainly not expect, however, any tendency towards isochrony to be operative in speech errors of nonstress-timed languages such as the Romance languages.

2. Does the nature of the omitted syllable itself play a role in the error? One might hypothesise, for instance, that syllables with fewer consonantal segments might be easier to contract and hence be less likely to be omitted than syllables with a greater number of segments. No evidence in favour of this hypothesis can be found in my present corpus, however; in most of my syllable omission errors the omitted material consisted of only one or two segments and in no case were more than two consonants omitted.

3. Is a tendency to regular rhythm also detectable in other types of speech error? For example, when two words with different numbers of syllables exchange position in the sentence, the sentence rhythm will be affected; do exchange errors show, like errors of omission, a consistent regularising effect on rhythm? Finally, can the pattern of pauses and hesitations in spontaneous speech be similarly correlated with rhythmic factors?

HANS-GEORG BOSSHARDT

Suprasegmental structure and sentence perception[1]

Introduction

In the experiment to be reported here, the intelligibility of different constituents in isolated sentences was investigated. It will be shown that the intelligibility of a certain constituent is determined by the preciseness with which the constituent has been articulated by the speaker and by the suprasegmental variation of sound which enables the *listener* to anticipate the phonetic characteristics of speech.

Before discussing the experiment, it is necessary to outline shortly the theoretical background from which we started. It is assumed that, during speech perception, the phonetic and the semantic/syntactic aspects of speech are the result of two different stages of speech processing. Massaro's distinction (1975) between the prelexical primary and the secondary recognition appropriately characterizes both levels of speech processing. Primary recognition allows the listener, for example, to shadow a sequence of nonsense syllables. Phenomenally, this primary recognition provides the basis for hearing and discriminating speech sounds. Whatever the relevant perceptual unit of this primary recognition may be, it provides the basis for accessing conceptual information and deriving meaning. The secondary recognition transforms the "perceptual information into conceptual information, that is, meaningful units in generated abstract memory" (Massaro, 1975:12). The secondary recognition process is assumed to identify individual words and short phrases. Perceptual responses generally are the joint result of primary as well as of secondary recognition.

At both levels of processing, contextual dependencies exist. The recognition of one unit is not independent from the recognition of another one. At the level of primary recognition the suprasegmental variation of fundamental frequency, intensity, pausing, and duration are preserved. Presumably, this kind of information is the basis for rather long-range expectations in real time. These expectations cover greater segments of speech. These segments may roughly correspond to what Bierwisch (1966) called the 'Phrasierungseinheit' or to the "breath group" of Lieberman (1967) or to the 'phonological unit'. The phonological unit presumably is not only the most comprehensive articulatory but also the most comprehensive perceptual unit. Within this unit the suprasegmental parameters vary predictably. Thus, depending on their position within the phonological unit, the phonetic segments sound different in a regular and predictable way.

Contextual dependencies do not only exist at the prelexical level of primary recognition. There exist also semantic/syntactic constraints of speech which facilitate the secondary recognition by limiting the set of valid alternatives (cf. Bruce, 1958; Miller et al., 1951; Miller & Isard, 1963).

Generally, it is assumed that the redundancies inherent in a sentence can be used to compensate for local degradations of the acoustical stimulus. Pickett & Pollack (1963) and Pollack & Pickett (1963) excised small segments of speech from conversational context. Increasing the length of the segment improved its intelligibility considerably. This experiment demonstrates convincingly the influence of contextual information on speech perception. More specifically, Lieberman (1963) showed that the predictable or redundant parts of the message are articulated in such a way that they cannot be recognized without their appropriate context. On the other side, those parts of the message which are relatively new and difficult to anticipate are articulated more precisely, such that they can be recognized even if presented without context.

From these experiments it can be concluded that the listener compensates for local degradations of the stimulus input. Only poor perceptual evidence is needed for the recognition of those speech stimuli for which strong expectations exist. However, from the experiments of Pollack & Pickett it cannot be determined what kind of redundancy is perceptually relevant. The listener may develop expectations about *the phonetic aspects* of the sign and/or he may anticipate *the meaning* of what will be said. The listener may use the suprasegmental information and/or his semantic/syntactic knowledge to restrict the range of possible alternatives.

At this point two questions arise which we tried to answer experimentally:

1. The first question is whether the listener in fact uses the suprasegmental structure to compensate for local degradations of the speech signal.

2. The second question is whether the speaker does adapt his articulatory behavior perfectly to the requirements of the listener. This question requires some comment. If the speaker's behavior is perfectly adapted to

the requirements of perception he should articulate very carefully those words which are relatively new and difficult to anticipate. On the other hand, he should pronounce those words less accurately for which strong contextual expectations exist. Therefore, the speaker should articulate the beginning of an isolated sentence more precisely than its end. Overall, this will result in an equal intelligibility of all constituents of the sentence.

We designed an experiment the results of which are decisive for answering both questions. I will present those experimental conditions first which are pertinent to the second question: We investigated whether all constituents of a sentence are equally intelligible.

The intelligibility of the constituents within 'normal' sentence versions

The intelligibility of the constituents of a certain sentence was determined in three different versions of the same sentence (cf. Table 1). The sentence version AA can be translated as "The student writes his paper in the cold attic". Without producing ungrammatical sentences, one can set either the subject (version AA), or the adverbial (BB), or the object (CC) in the initial position. We had 36 different sentences of this general frame. Each of these sentences consisted of four constituents (subject, predicate, object, adverbial).

Table 1. *Illustrative example of three different versions of the same stimulus sentence.*

AA Der Student schreibt seine Arbeit in der kalten Dachstube.
BB In der kalten Dachstube schreibt der Student seine Arbeit.
CC Seine Arbeit schreibt der Student in der kalten Dachstube.

A set of 12 different sentences was presented as version AA, or BB, or CC to three independent groups of 10 subjects. This basic experiment was replicated three times with different sets of 12 sentences. Thus, the complete design contains nine independent groups of subjects.

A male speaker produced these three sentence versions with normal intonation and stress. The intelligibility of the sentences was measured by presenting them to the listener under white noise. In addition to the 12 'normal' sentences AA, or BB, or CC, each subject heard 24 'manipulated' sentences. The principles according to which these other sentences were manipulated will be described below. The normal sentences were presented in random alternation with the manipulated sentences. Immediately after each sentence, the listeners were instructed to reproduce the whole sentence or parts thereof.

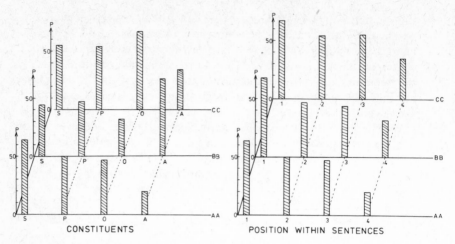

Figure 1. *Perceptual profiles for three different versions of the same sentence.*
Left: The profiles for each are ordered according to the constituents' syntactic function.
Right: The profiles are ordered according to the ordinal position of the constituents within the respective sentence version.

Figure 1 shows the perceptual profile for each of these three sentence versions. For every constituent, these profiles show the probability of being correctly perceived. In the left part of Figure 1, the profiles are ordered with respect to the constituents' syntactic function. It can be clearly seen that the same constituent is perceived with different probability in different sentence versions. These differences disappear when the constituents are ordered with respect to their ordinal position within the sentence. The right part of the figure presents exactly the same data as the left part. In the right part, however, the bars are ordered with respect to the ordinal position of the constituent within the respective sentence version. After this rearrangement, the profiles of different sentence versions are highly similar.

The results of the statistical tests support this intuitive evaluation of the data. Each triple of profiles represents a two-factorial interaction the significance of which was evaluated with a nonparametric analysis of variance (Bredenkamp, 1974). While the interaction corresponding to the left triple is highly significant ($\chi_r^2 = 154.04$; df = 6; p < .001), the interaction represented in the right part of Figure 1 does not reach the criterion of significance ($\chi_r^2 = 2.32$; df = 6; n.s.). This result indicates that the profiles in the left part of Figure 1 have significantly different shapes, whereas in the right part, the shapes differ only within chance limits. From the main effects, only the factor "position within sentence version" is significant ($\chi_r^2 = 172.2$; df = 3; p < .001). The intelligibility of a certain constituent depends almost exclusively on its ordinal position within the sentence. The constituents which are articulated and/or received at the beginning of a sentence are more intelligible than the final ones. The syntactic function of the constituent influences the perceptual profile only within chance limits.

The main question which arises from these results is whether the serial position effect originates in the listener and/or in the speaker. The speaker may articulate the initial parts of the sentence more accurately than the later ones. However, it seems likewise possible that the listener is apt to perceive the first constituent better than the final ones.

To decide among these alternative hypotheses, the results of the following manipulation on the intelligibility of the constituents were studied: The constituents were presented in a sequence which differed from that which the speaker originally produced. After this manipulation, a sentence version was presented to the listener that differed from the version the speaker originally produced. By comparing the perceptual profiles of the 'manipulated' versions with their original or normal counterparts, it can be determined whether the serial position effect is produced by the speaker or by the hearer.

Moreover, the effect of this manipulation on the perceptual profiles provides information about the anticipatory activity of the listener. By combining the constituents in a new sentence version, abrupt changes in pitch, loudness, and timing are introduced at the constituent boundaries. These perturbations of the suprasegmental structure will presumably interfere with the listener's anticipation of sound. Therefore, the effect of this manipulation on the perceptual profiles provides information about the role of suprasegmental structure in sentence perception.

The intelligibility of the constituents within manipulated sentence versions

The production of the stimulus material will be described with reference to the 'student sentence'. We first tape recorded the original or 'normal' sentence version AA as pronounced by the speaker. By cutting the original tape and recombining the constituents in a different order we produced two different 'manipulated' sentence versions: The versions are marked with double letters AB and AC. The first letter refers to the normal sentence version which the speaker originally produced and the second letter indicates the sentence version which was produced out of this phonetic material. Similarly, the manipulated sentence versions BA and BC were produced out of the normal sentence version, BB, and the versions CA and CB out of CC.

Each subject heard a set of 12 'normal' sentences in random alternation with two different sets of 12 manipulated sentences. Thus, each subject heard 36 different sentences. There were three independent groups of 30 subjects, each one receiving three different sets of sentences, i.e. AA, AB, and AC were presented to the first, BB, BA, and BC to the second and CC, CA, and CB to the third group respectively.

The perceptual profiles obtained in these three groups of subjects are shown in Figure 2. The data from each group were combined into one triple of profiles. The stimulus sentences corresponding to each triple originate from the same phonetic material. They differ with respect to the sentence version which is presented to the listener.

The data corresponding to each triple of Figure 2 were subjected to three separate nonparametric analyses of variance (Bredenkamp, 1974).

The data of every triple represent a two-factorial design with "sentence version" and "constituents" as the two factors. The main effects of the factors "sentence version" ($\chi_r^2 = 144.2$; $\chi_r^2 = 170.1$; $\chi_r^2 = 131.1$; df = 2; p < .001), and "constituent" ($\chi_r^2 = 87.9$; $\chi_r^2 = 69.0$; $\chi_r^2 = 66.9$; df = 3; p < .001) are highly significant in every triple. These results indicate that the over-all differences between the constituents are significant and that the manipulated and normal sentence versions differ significantly from one another. The interaction between both factors is comparatively small but significant in the upper and middle triple ($\chi_r^2 = 26.3$; df = 6; p < .001; $\chi_r^2 = 15.8$; df = 6; p < .02). The lower triple reveals no significant interaction between both factors ($\chi_r^2 = 1.9$; df = 6). This comparatively small interaction component indicates that the profiles of one triple are highly similar to one another. Two results deserve a more elaborate discussion:

1. The first result will be referred to as the *articulatory primacy effect*. As can be seen in Figure 2, the constituent which the speaker originally produced first (i.e. the subject in sentence versions AA, AB, and AC, the adverb in versions BB, BA, and BC and the object in versions CC, CA, and CB) is perceived with higher probability than those constituents which were produced thereafter. Thus, the intelligibility decreases with the ordinal position of the constituent in the speaker's sentence version. Contrary to our original hypothesis the speaker does not convey equal amounts of information for all constituents of the sentence. Rather, the speaker produces the initial constituents in a way that makes them easier to perceive behind white noise.

2. The second result which can be seen in Figure 2 is that the manipulated sentence versions generally have a lower intelligibility than their normal counterparts. To be sure, the extent to which the intelligibility is reduced differs somewhat for different constituents. Nevertheless, the manipulation reduces mainly the level of the profiles[2] and has only slight (though sometimes significant) effects on the shape of the profiles. Theoretically, this result can be interpreted as an indication of contex-

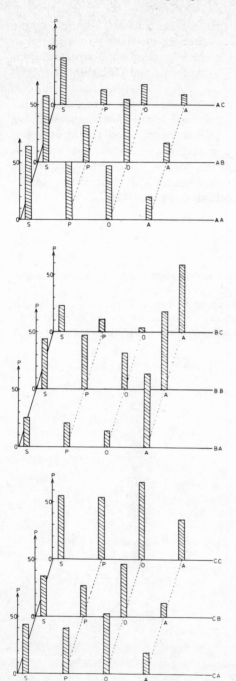

Figure 2. *Perceptual profiles for three different versions of the same sentence. The profiles of the same triple differ only with respect to the sentence version as presented to the listener (details see text).*

tual dependencies at the level of primary recognition. Recombining the constituents of a sentence in a new sequence produces perturbations in the suprasegmental information. If the suprasegmental structure continues in a way the listener cannot anticipate the efficiency of speech recognition is reduced.

It is assumed that the temporal patterning of speech enables the listener to develop expectations about the continuation of sound. Within a phrase unit, the acoustic cues by which elementary speech units (probably syllables) are identified change in a regular and predictable way. This suprasegmental structure enables the listener to develop long-range expectations about the continuation of sound. This anticipatory activity improves the efficiency of prelexical primary recognition.

Notes

1. The data to be reported here come from an experiment which was designed cooperatively by H. Hörmann and the present author.
2. This result cannot be readily interpreted within the frame of Martin's theory of rhythmic expectancy (1972, 1975). From this theory I would derive that the distortion of the temporal structure should reduce the intelligibility primarily of those constituents which carry the sentence's main accent.

ALAN I. HENDERSON

Juncture pause and intonation fall and the perceptual segmentation of speech

In a well known series of studies Bever and his associates have investigated the role that syntax plays in the perceptual segmentation of speech. In their research they have been at pains to either control or eliminate the prosodic features which are normally an integral part of a speech message, e.g. Garrett, Bever & Fodor (1966); Abrams & Bever (1969); Bever & Hurtig (1975). In these experiments the material was explicitly devised so that syntax was the principal source of information available to the Ss. The intended paradox of experimental situations in which the basis of segmentation is not made explicit in the speech signal is that for a listener to detect the end of a unit presupposes knowledge of what the unit is. Normal speech is clearly a redundant multi-cue signalling system and one in which speech is typically syntactically less well formed than in the material devised for experiments. In this situation it seems probably that reliance upon systematic prosodic cues will increase.

Two prosodic cues which have been identified as acoustic correlates of structure by Garrett, Bever & Fodor (1966) are intonation and pause. One of the effects of eliminating these potential cues is to leave us in ignorance of their relative importance in the perceptual segmentation of speech. In situations in which structural knowledge is absent or imperfect prosodic cues may provide the basis for breaking into the speech code. Such situations are illustrated by infants exposed to the speech of adults or adults exposed to an unfamiliar foreign tongue. It is the relative salience of two prosodic cues in the initial perceptual segmentation of unfamiliar foreign speech, which is of interest here. The cues are the final fall in phonation which characterises the end of an unmarked breath group and the so called juncture pause. These normally but not invariably occur together to form a prosodic complex. It is their relative salience in cueing the end of a natural unit of speech that this experiment investigates.

The experimental rationale used here is that used by Abrams & Bever (1969). They used S's reaction time to a click superimposed upon a sentence as an index of the way in which S's structural knowledge modifies attention strategies during speech processing. They found in Experiment I that reaction time was longer to a click placed before a clause break than after a clause break and that reaction time to a click placed in a clause break was faster than the latter but slower than the former. These results were repeated in Experiment II in which they used artificially constructed sentences free from any systematic prosody cues. They interpret these results as indicating that the attentional processes of the listener are modified by his linguistic knowledge. They conclude that the clause is a natural unit for internal perceptual analysis, a view confirmed by Bever & Hurtig (1975) using a technique involving the detection of near threshold tones. Can attention be similarly modified by prosodic features in the absence of syntactic and semantic information? The status of intonation fall and pause as decoder usable cues is unclear. This investigation uses reaction time latencies to a non-speech stimulus as a measure of how attention is modified when it coincides with a final fall in intonation and/or a juncture pause. The assumption is that if the prosodic cues serve as cues to the end of a processable unit of speech then attention to the non-speech stimulus will be modified and the latency of the reaction time will be longer than it would be if the non-speech stimulus does not coincide with a precipitating cue.

Materials and design

The language chosen was Czechoslovakian. The sentences used in the experiment were devised in collaboration with a native Czech speaker who had a good command of English and spoke it fluently. The stimulus materials were 12 word strings. By manipulating prosodic features they were capable of being restructured so as to form two sentences in each of three ways. This produced two 6 word sentences, a 3 word sentence followed by a 9 word sentence and a 9 word sentence followed by a 3 word sentence. Six strings capable of this sort of prosodic restructuring were constructed. Table 1 shows the English translation together with the 6 filler sentences.

There were six conditions. The six 12 word strings appeared in every condition so that the segmental phonemic structure was the same in each condition. The six experimental conditions were designed so that a 30 msec. 1000 Hz tone (approx. as loud as the loudest speech sound) was placed in each 12 word string so that it appeared in one of 4 possible locations.

(1) Over the end of an intonation fall. Conditions B and C (see below).
(2) Towards the end of a pause (i.e. approx. 330 msec. after the offset of speech). Conditions D and E.

(3) Towards the end of a pause where the pause followed a fall in intonation (again approximately 330 msec. from the offset of speech). Condition A.

(4) Between two successive words not separated by either a pause or an intonation fall. Condition F.

Table 1. *Experimental and filler sentences used in the experiment.*

Experimental set

1. He grew up during the war. Many years ago he was wounded.
2. I walked home almost every time. During the summer I played football.
3. She stood still looking at us. Through the mist she became visible.
4. He wandered on kicking the leaves. In front of him he saw flowers.
5. We waited together for many minutes. Outside the house we felt cold.
6. He climbed trees on fine days. In the orchard he felt happy.

Filler set

1. I looked out of the window. I saw a small brown bird.
2. I came into the big hall. I looked up at the ceiling.
3. I opened the flat, white envelope. We all looked frightened and upset.
4. He watched it. The blue hammock was swaying from side to side.
5. The teacher closed the door when he came in. The children stared.
6. The sun rose. The man with the little dog pulled my sleeve.

The sentences were constructed and presented to the subjects in Czech. The English translation above represents the experimental material as 2 six-word sentences.

The six conditions were:

A: The 12 word strings were read as 2 six word sentences with a natural fall in intonation at the end of the first sentence, which after a juncture pause of 385 msec. (see below) was followed by the second 6 word sentence. The stimulus tone was placed in the juncture pause.

B: The 12 word string was read as 2 six word sentences with a natural fall in intonation at the end of the sentence but with no pause separating the two sentences. A pause occurred after the third word of the first sentence. The stimulus tone was placed over the end of the terminal fall of the first six word sentence.

C: This was similar to condition B except that the pause occurred after the third word of the second sentence. The tone again was placed over the end of the terminal fall of the first six word sentence.

D: The 12 word string was read as a 3 word sentence followed by a 9 word sentence, with a natural fall in intonation occurring at the end of the first 3 word sentence but with no separating juncture pause. A pause occurred after the third word of the second sentence. The tone was placed in this pause.

E: The 12 word string was read as a 9 word sentence followed by a 3 word sentence with a natural fall in intonation occurring at the end of the first sentence. No juncture pause separated the two sentences. A pause occurred after the 6th word of the first 9 word sentence. The tone was placed in the pause.

F: The 12 word string was read as a 3 word sentence followed by a 9 word sentence with a natural intonation fall at the end of the first sentence. A pause occurred after the second word of the first 3 word sentence. The tone was placed over the boundary between the third and fourth words of the second sentence, i.e. in a position unassociated with either a terminal fall or a pause.

The tone was always placed over the end of or immediately after word 6 in order to minimise a possible length of sentence effect (Abrams & Bever, 1969; Holmes & Forster, 1970). Each of the six experimental 12 word strings appeared once in each condition. They were read by a female native speaker of Czechoslovakian. She was instructed to read the strings respecting the normal intonation and to pause at the end of each sentence and at other none juncture points if the condition required it (e.g. condition D). When the sentences had been satisfactorily recorded the pauses were either edited out or adjusted in duration as required by the experimental conditions using a technique developed by Henderson & Smith (1972). In editing out pauses a criterion based upon the Czech speaker's normal articulatory shifts was used so that a pause between two sentences which was to be edited out (e.g. conditions B and C) did not exceed a between or within word break. A criterion of 255 msec. met this constraint. A pause intentionally introduced as an independent variable was set at 385 msec. This was a duration consonant with the Czech speaker's naturally occurring juncture pauses.

There were then six basic 12 word strings appearing in each condition. Six subjects were randomly allocated to each condition. Within each condition the order in which the strings were presented to each subject was regulated by a latin square. In this way every subject heard the same basic word strings with only the intonation contour and pause defined grouping distinguishing between the conditions. The six filler sentences appeared in every condition and were alternated with the experimental strings. The tone was randomly placed in the filler sentences with the constraint that it was not to fall between words 6 and 7 of the string. This was done to mask the fact that in the experimental strings the tone always occurred after word 6. There were 36 unpaid volunteer subjects – all undergraduates. They all claimed unfamiliarity with the Czech language and none of them was able to identify the language after the experiments.

The test material was presented to the subject through stereo headphones – the speech to the left ear and the tone to the right ear. The stimulus tone triggered an electronic timer which was stopped by S closing a morse key using his preferred hand (all subjects were right handed). A 15 sec. interval occurred between each trial. During this time S was instructed to mark the location of the tone on a written version of what he had just heard. This second task was merely a ruse to ensure that S attented to the speech message and did not treat the first test as a simple reaction time study. One complete practice trial was allowed on a sentence not subsequently used in the experiment.

Results

No practice effect was found across the six trials on each condition.

Table 2. *Reaction time data (in msec.)*

Condition	x̄	SD
A	349	149.6
B	333	117.7
C	317	77.8
D	265	76.7
E	253	86.0
F	230	54.2

Table 2 shows the means and standard deviations of the untransformed reaction times to a 1000 Hz. tone in the 6 conditions. The tone was placed 1) over the end of a fall in intonation (conditions B & C); 2) towards the end of a pause (conditions D & E); 3) towards the end of a pause following a fall in intonation (condition A); 4) between two words separated neither by a fall in intonation nor by a pause. Each mean is based upon 6RTs from each of 6 subjects.

Table 2 shows the reaction time data in msecs. Because of the skewed nature of the distribution a reciprocal transformation ($\frac{1}{x} \times 1000$) was taken of each reaction time and an analysis of variance was carried out using the average of the transformed latencies for each subject in each condition. A significant treatment effect was found F = 4.02 (with 5 and 30 df, p = 0.01 = 3.70). A Duncan's Multiple Range Test was carried out to inspect the differences between the means of the transformed data used in the analysis of variance. This analysis is shown in Table 3.

No clear a priori hypotheses were formulated although it did seem that pauses would be less reliable cues to structure. At the protection level with α = 0.05 comparisons using condition F (in which the tone was not associated with either a pause or an intonation fall but fell between two words), as a standard show that in the three conditions involving intonation fall, i.e. conditions A, B and C, subjects took a significantly longer

Table 3. *Duncan's Multiple Range Test applied to the differences between the means of the transformed reaction time data.*

x̄	Conditions							Shortest significant ranges	
	B	A	C	D	E	F		0.05	0.01
	3.246	3.268	3.509	4.011	4.201	4.312			
B 3.246		0.022	0.263	0.765*	0.955*	1.066**	R2	0.684	0.922
A 3.268			0.241	0.743*	0.933*	1.044**	R3	0.719	0.961
C 3.509				0.502	0.692	0.803*	R4	0.742	0.988
D 4.011					0.190	0.301	R5	0.758	1.007
E 4.201						0.111	R6	0.770	1.022
F 4.312									

The main body of the table shows the difference between the 6 treatment means. The columns on the right of the table list the shortest ranges which must be exceeded for a difference to be considered statistically significant.

time to respond to the tone. In conditions D and E (in which the tone coincided with a pause) RT was not significantly different from that in condition F. However, whereas RT in conditions A and B was significantly longer than in conditions D and E the RT in condition C was not significantly different from that in either condition D or E. No other comparisons showed a significant difference at this level of protection. At the more stringent protection level with $\alpha = 0.01$ the only significant differences to emerge were comparisons of B and A with F.

Discussion

An inspection of the differences revealed at the lower level of protection suggests where the differences might lie. Conditions in which the tone coincided with a pause, i.e. D and E, modified attention no more than did condition F in which the tone is unassociated with either a pause or a fall in intonation. However, conditions in which a tone coincided with a fall in intonation (B and C) or was adjacent to (A) a fall in intonation did modify attention when compared to condition F. Furthermore conditions B and A modified attention significantly more than did conditions D and E. The fact that condition A also involves a pause and that the tone was not placed in exactly the same place with respect to the intonation fall makes the comparison with conditions B and C less direct. However, it seems likely that the effectiveness of condition A in modifying attention was due primarily to the only feature appearing in all three conditions, i.e. intonation fall. This would be in accord with a model of speech processing in which at the ends of decoding units the listener is actively organising an internal representation of what he has just heard and suggests that the final fall in phonation characteristic of the end of an unmarked break group serves as a cue to the perceptual segmentation of speech.

The lack of a difference between conditions D and E and condition F suggests that by itself a pause does not serve as a cue to the segmentation of speech. What clouds the picture is the absence of a clear difference between conditions C, D and E. A possible explanation for the dis-crepancies between the B vs. D and B vs. E comparisons which are significantly different and the C vs. D and C vs. E comparisons which are not, could be found in the role of the pause in these conditions. It may be that a pause by itself does not serve as a cue to the segmentation of a speech unit but rather signals the lack of completion of a unit. In condi-tion B attention to the speech signal at the end of the unmarked breath group is primed by the prior pause and this results in a longer latency than appears in condition C which in other respects does not differ from B. However, this cannot be regarded as a satisfactory explanation for the absence of a significant difference between conditions C and D and conditions C and E.

A problem associated with the use of reaction time in investigating the role of a pause as a decoder usable cue is the location of the stimulus tone relative to the onset of the pause. This problem reflects the diffi-culty of considering a pause as a cue to the end of a unit. How much silence must elapse before terminal significance is attributed to a pause? The criterion chosen here may not have been long enough (330 msec.) and this may account for the lack of an effect. What is at issue here is the nature of the distribution of pause durations and also a subject's ability to detect breaks in speech signals. Martin (1970) provides some justifi-cation for the criterion used here. In his material he found that 21% of correctly identified pauses were shorter than 200 msec. and that listeners could detect pauses down to 50 msec. In the context of the experimental material used here a pause of 330 msec. may be reasonably considered long enough to be detected as a significant break in the speech energy. Furthermore the data of Boomer & Dittmann (1962) and Ruder & Jen-sen (1969) show that juncture pauses have a higher perceptual threshold than non juncture pauses. Their evidence suggests that a break in signal energy is perceived as it is because of its context rather than being a cue to the structuring of the context.

In an analysis of the hesitation in the speech of mothers to their children Dale (1974) and Broen (1971) show a progressive decline in the occurrence of pauses at sentence boundaries as the age of the addres-see increases. Although the present study cannot comment directly on

Dale's findings it seems probable that the pauses he identifies at the end of sentences also coincide with a terminal fall of intonation and that it is this latter prosodic feature which is a more consistent index of structure. It seems probable that English speakers learn not to place great reliance on hesitation as a cue to the segmentation of speech. Faced with an unfamiliar language he is likely to rely in the first instance upon intonation fall as a cue to the perceptual segmentation of speech. To the extent that the unmarked breath group may be regarded as a universal feature (Lieberman, 1967) it seems safe to do so.

VIVIAN J. COOK

Some neglected aspects of intonation

The majority of the papers presented to this workshop have been within the discipline of psychology. This contribution, however, tries to relate other areas to the study of speech production, namely work on describing and teaching English intonation. The starting point in terms of intonation is the kind of analysis suggested in Halliday (1967 a). Halliday described three systematic choices that confront the speaker. One is how to divide the utterance up into tone-groups; a second is where to put the major change of pitch, the "tone"; the third is which tone to use. This analysis is useful for the study of speech even if it does nothing more than indicate that intonation is a complex of several factors, not just the rise and fall of the voice.

For most of the approaches that have been used to intonation in the literature of speech production have been one-sided. Commonly, in fact, intonation has been ignored. Equally commonly people have relied on the concept of "normal English intonation" as, for instance, in O'Connell, Turner & Onuska (1968). The parallel concept of normal stress has been attacked by Schmerling (1974) and the existence of normal English intonation can also be challenged. One reason is the question of regional variation.

While the neutral intonation for decontextualised declarative sentences in Southern British is usually claimed to be a fall, without leaving the British Isles, in Belfast the neutral intonation is said to be a rise (Jarman & Cruttenden, 1976). Specifying "normal intonation" in an experiment is of no use if we do not know the background of the speaker. A second reason for distrusting "normal intonation" is concerned with the location of the tone. The reason for putting the tone on one syllable rather than another is usually felt to reflect the structure of discourse. Within Halliday's framework, the location of the tone is seen as contributing to the cohesion of the discourse, particularly by drawing attention to new information, though this is queried by Goodenough-Trepagnier & Smith (1977). A similar point is to claim that the location of the tone depends on semantic focus (Cutler & Foss, 1977). The location of the tone then depends upon the context – what the participants already know about the subject and what they have already said. Most psychological work with speech has dealt with sentences and has deliberately ignored the effects of context, including intonation. Perhaps this is the right approach and intonation is psychologically irrelevant.

However, there is a body of evidence from other types of experiments that intonation is far from irrelevant. This starts with Neisser's discussion of rhythmic groups in active verbal memory (Neisser, 1967), and includes Glanzer (1976) who showed that tone-group division was connected with memory for related nouns in word-lists, O'Connell et al. (1968) who found that intonation was more important with structured than with unstructured material, and Bower & Springston (1970) who found that grouping by pauses and "vocal intonation" aided recall. Certainly division into tone-groups, and probably also location of the tone, play an important part in speech processing. Any experiment with speech, whatever it is ostensibly about, needs to control and specify some aspects of intonation.

But intonation also needs investigation in its own right. It may be that intonation is central to the planning of speech production (Laver, 1970); it may also be important to language acquisition (Du Preez, 1974). As the contributions to this workshop show, some aspects of intonation are indeed being studied; but the link between intonation and context is still under-explored. From a linguistic point of view Brazil (1975, 1978) has been looking at the intonation of discourse. One of his ideas is called *key*. This adds another choice to the speaker, whether to use a high key, medium key, or low key. Usually the progression through an utterance is from high to low, each new "paragraph" starting the cycle up again. Thus a switch to high key marks the tone-group as contrastive, a switch to low key as an equivalence between items in successive tone-groups. Each tone-group is measured against the one preceding to see whether it is higher or lower in key. Aspects of intonation and discourse must be taken into consideration in studying speech; the place of the sentence in the utterance may play a crucial part in its production.

The rest of this paper looks at the place of intonation in the structure of one type of discourse, ordinary conversation, particularly in terms of tone. Conversation is a process of give-and-take in which the participants have certain moves that they are allowed to make. In a scientific sense, little is yet known of this. However those who teach foreign languages often have to make leaps beyond our present state of knowledge if they are to do justice to their students' needs. The scheme that is used here is a leap of this kind embodied in a book called *Using Intonation* (Cook, 1979). This is a teaching scheme for intonation that brings out some of the aspects of the intonation of conversation that the psychological experimenter will eventually have to take into account. The system of description employs five tones: high and low rises, high and low falls, and a fall-rise. More sophisticated versions of the same type of analysis can be found in O'Connor & Arnold (1961) and Cook (1968). The structure of conversation is analysed into seven categories and the most common tones for each of these is given. Obviously this scheme covers only certain intonation patterns found in Southern British English but at least it shows what kind of analysis of intonation is going to be necessary.

The first category is *checking* what people say. It is vital in conversation that the participants are talking about the same topic. Checking usually involves a rising tone, either with repetition of part of the other speaker's remark – "I went to Bristol yesterday", "You went to Bristol?" – or with question words or special checking forms – "You went where? Where did you go?", "Sorry?". The second category is *asking for information*. This implies a potential shift of roles in that the listener can take over the active part of the conversation. It is usually believed that tag questions and Yes/No questions have low rises – "Have you been to Germany before?", "It's nice, isn't it?" – while question-word questions have falls – "How much is it?" – except perhaps when introducing a new topic of conversation – "What's the time?" The third category is *answering questions* with short answers. Falls may be used, the low fall suggesting the speaker doesn't want to go on talking about that topic – "Do you like beer?", "Yes." – the high fall sounding more interested in the topic – "Can you speak Spanish?", "Yes." The fall-rise suggests the speaker is doubtful – "Can you dance?", "Well".

The fourth and fifth categories are stating things more or less positively. *Saying something positively* involves a fall – "I think he's wrong" – and a tag question with a fall expects brief agreement from the listener rather than allowing him to take over the active role – "It's hot today, isn't it?" *Saying things less positively* uses either a fall-rise to show doubts or reservations – "I like the breakfasts in the hotel." – or a low fall preceded by low syllables suggesting reluctance to continue speaking – "That's enough." – or a low rise suggesting the speaker is not committing himself – "The food's all right I suppose." Category six is *reacting;* listeners are expected to show that they are paying attention by showing a reaction of one kind or another. Usually this involves falls, the height of the fall showing the degree of enthusiasm or astonishment – "Did you?", "Oh." – or a low rise urging the speaker to continue – "Were you?" Finally category seven is *getting things done*. The different tones appear to relate to the speaker's role. If he is authoritative he may use a low rise – "Put your hands up."; definite, a low fall – "Don't move."; friendly, a high fall – "Give me the money."

This simplified model begs certain questions: whether intonation goes with grammatical structure, which has been queried in Kenworthy (1978); and whether it conveys attitudes. Nevertheless it highlights certain aspects that are relevant to the study of speech. One is simply that it is dangerous not to control intonation in any language experiment; probably most of the classic psycholinguistic experiments would fail to replicate if their intonation patterns were sufficiently distorted. The second aspect is that intonation shows how sentences form part of discourse. There are relationships between sentences in terms of many aspects of cohesion, lexical, grammatical, and intonational. The study of speech will have to take into account higher levels of organisation than the sentence.

Arising from this, perhaps the most important aspect is that speech is a meaningful activity that involves at least two people. Language has a purpose. Except in psychological experiments we are not forced to speak but talk when we want to. If we cut speech off from discourse and from purpose, our experiments tell us as much about speech production as would experiments into breathing which studied the behaviour of subjects in a vacuum. The disciplines of linguistics, applied linguistics, and developmental psycholinguistics have taken this crucial step towards looking at language as a process of interaction between human beings. If it is to progress, the study of speech production and comprehension must follow their lead.

THOMAS T. BALLMER

The role of pauses and suprasegmentals in a grammar

In this short paper I try to present theoretical and empirical evidence for the existence of a whole category of hitherto underrated linguistic entities: punctuation signs. Punctuation signs – not to be confused with punctuation marks, which are (ortho)graphic entities – are signs in the fullfledged linguistic sense, i.e. signs having a phonetico-phonological aspect, a morpho-syntactic aspect and a semantico-pragmatic aspect. Their primordial function is to define linguistic entities such as words, sentences and paragraphs by a demarcation of some sort in the flow of speech. In many languages the predominant means of demarcating linguistic entities is pauses (and suprasegmentals). Thus we could say that the topic of this short paper is to establish theoretically and empirically the existence of the grammatical category of pauses (and suprasegmentals).

We shall pursue this program in three different steps. First we shall give a short *typology* of pauses to which we refer in order to explain what kind of pauses we are interested in. Secondly, we shall sketch a purely theoretical argument to *establish the existence* of a grammatical category of pauses. Thereafter we shall provide, thirdly, a series of different arguments to establish the existence of the grammatical category of pauses *empirically*.

1. A classification of pauses

Before we present theoretical and empirical evidence of the category of pauses we need to know somewhat more specifically what kinds of pauses may exist in a language. Thus we will give a (presystematic) classification of pauses as they occur typically in speech. We are going to consider three different aspects of classification: intensity of airflow, controllability, and interlocutors' concern. We should keep in mind thereby that pauses may serve various functions at the same time as they are used.

(1) A (Tripartite) Classification of Pauses

    A) A Classification of Pauses by the Intensity of Airflow
        I.   *Empty pauses*
        II. *Low voice pauses* (e.g. parenthetical fillers, ...)
        III. *Filled Pauses* (full intensity, cf. hesitation)

    B) A Classification of Pauses by their Controllability
        I.   *Unintentional pauses* (accidental, unconscious)
        II. *Intentional pauses* (controlled, conscious)

    C) A Classification of Pauses by the Concern of the Interlocutors
        I.   *Speaker Relevant Pauses* (Selfpauses)
           a. *unintentional*
              breathing pauses
              planning pauses
              lexical/syntactical search pauses
              hesitation: conflict between contradicting plans
              turnkeeping pauses (in the middle of phrases, sentences)
              time laps pauses
              pauses caused by rhythm
           b. *intentional*
              planning pauses
              time gain pauses
              rhythm stressing pauses

        II. *Communicative Pauses* (Transpauses)
           a. *reifying pauses*
              propositional unit pauses (reification of theory)
              constituent, phrasal, clausal, sentential, textual, ... unit
                pauses
              commitment pauses
              rhythm establishing pauses
           b. *enactive pauses* (answering, communication ...)
              signalling inability
              signalling inattention
              signalling affront ("vom hohen Roß")
              imposing/impressing
              turn offering pauses
              feedback requesting pauses
              allowing for things to happen (: soccer-reports)
           c. *reposing pauses*
              Verschnaufpausen
              prospective pauses
              retrospective pauses

III. *Hearer Relevant Pauses* (Altropauses)
pauses to help parsing
(by gaps and rhythm)

In this paper we shall concentrate on reifying pauses, i.e. pauses establishing linguistic entities such as (words), phrases and sentences in a spoken text.

2. Semantic form and word order

Semantic forms, or logical forms as they are also called, are the representations of what is expressed by utterances made in a context. These representations contain in a standardized way all relevant aspects of what is expressed by the utterance in question. Because there are different ways of expressing the meaning coded by semantic forms, namely different word orders, there must be a contextually controllable mechanism to regulate the way it is expressed. There must be a place in linguistic descriptions to account for just this kind of grammatical and stylistic decision. In the framework of language reconstruction systems, which is a more developed kind of λ-categorial language (cf. Ballmer 1978), it is possible to show that such stylistic decisions have to be made over and over again, after single words, after phrases and predominantly after sentences. There is a purely formal argument leading to this view (cf. Ballmer 1975). Thus at language surface we have the situation that ordinary words are interspersed with other, nonstandard words, which in many languages are realized as pauses. These pauses go together with the speaker's and hearer's task of deciding upon the stylistic and grammatical means which are to be used to compile the phrase or sentence in question. A typical text looks thus as follows, considering the pauses (ₒ) demarcating sentences and clauses:

(1) ANNE WRITES A LETTER ₒ SHE NEEDS MONEY ₒ ...

The squares in (1), with respect to language reconstruction systems, have an internal structure correlating with the complexity of the phrase to be analysed (or generated). This complexity taken to correlate with the duration of mental processing is a basis for empirical consequences of the description by language reconstruction systems. The linguistic entities which show up at language surface as pauses – but also as suprasegmental features like falling or rising intonation – which show that compiling processes of speakers and hearers are going on towards the end of linguistic entities, and which thereby demarcate those linguistic entities naturally we call punctuation signs, by analogy with the (ortho)-graphic marks used in written texts.

For details the reader is referred to Ballmer (1975, 1978). In order to illustrate nonetheless how the semantic form of pauses varies according to the complexity of the preceding constituents, without exceedingly detailed explanations, the following two punctuations are given.

(2a) $\varkappa\Pi_{V1}\varkappa\Pi_{NP}[\Pi_{NP}(\Pi_{V1})]$

(2b) $\varkappa\Pi_{NP}^2\varkappa\Pi_{V2}\varkappa\Pi_{NP}^1[\Pi_{NP}^1((\lambda v\Pi_{NP}^2(\lambda w\,\Pi_{V2}(v,w)))]$

The prefix of the punctuation (outside the square brackets) shows which constituents can be accepted and semantically analysed. In (2a) these are first a NP then an intransitive VP, in (2b) these are first one NP, then a twoplace VP, then a second NP. Selection of the correct grammatical pattern has to be made from n! (n factorial) pause patterns following an occurrence of n constituents. This determines the complexity of processing in a first, rough way, and allows for empirical predictions of a functional type: pause length is functionally correlated to the complexity of linguistic patterns.

3. Existential and functional claims and their validation

Having found strong theoretical arguments for the existence of a grammatical category of pauses, and having illustrated the structural complexity of pauses, and deduced a functional correlation between linguistic patterns and pause length, we may risk going further and looking for empirical validation of these claims. First let us briefly consider the functional correlation mentioned, and then let us examine the more fundamental question of existence.

3a. The functional correlation between complexity and pause length

The prediction made on the basis of language reconstruction systems (see above Chap. 2) is that the length of pauses is, in appropriate speech circumstances, related to the syntactic complexity x according to a factorial. Expressed in a formula, this means that if we set the complexity of a phrase, say, to equal the number n of constituents, the pause length l is proportional to a linear function in the factorial of n. Allowing for non-integer, but continuous arguments we in fact need what is called the Γ-function. This function is the appropriate generalization of the factorial to continuous arguments. Accordingly, the pause length l is then assumed to be $a.\Gamma(b.n+c)+d$.

Under the experimental conditions of Butcher (cf. his article in this volume) a very similar, though differing result is obtained. He proposes a linear function of the exponential, i.e. $a'.e^{bx}+c'$, as the pause length l with respect to the syntactical complexity x. The two proposals are similar enough considering the various approximation formulas of the Γ-funktion like Stirling's formula (for large arguments) or the formula $\Gamma(bn+c) \sim 2\pi\, e^{-bn}(bn)^{bn+c-\frac{1}{2}}$ ($|arg| <\pi$, $b > o$). It is an open question whether it is at all possible to discriminate statistically between these two proposals. The great advantage of the one advocated here is that it has a theoretical derivation.

3 b. The existence of the grammatical category of pauses

Before a detailed study of functional and numerical correlations is undertaken, it should be established that pauses exist in a linguistically relevant way. We shall present three arguments of which each one is already sufficient to confirm the existence of something beyond what Bloomfield calls primary morphemes or words.
The Minimal Pairs Argument:
Because of lack of space, we shall present the first two arguments only very briefly. The first argument rests on minimal pairs (quadrupels). There are sentences which have the same primary morphemes, but differ in pause setting (and intonation). There is a real difference in meaning accompanying this difference in expression in each case. Saying that this is merely a consequence of different syntactic structures will not do as an explanation. What we are after is not a theoretical construct but a linguistic entity showing up at language surface.

(3) *Minimal Pairs* (Quadrupels)
    (a) THE MAN ASKED THE WOMAN WHO WAS NEXT.
        THE MAN ASKED THE WOMAN, WHO WAS NEXT.
        THE MAN ASKED THE WOMAN: "WHO WAS NEXT?"
        "THE MAN ASKED THE WOMAN. WHO WAS NEXT?"
    (b) ARE YOU EATING, SANDRA?
        ARE YOU EATING SANDRA?
    (c) A FISHERMAN SAYS "HELENA" TO ROSA.
        "A FISHERMAN?" SAYS HELENA TO ROSA.
    (d) DEINE ELTERN KOMMEN, NICHT?
        DEINE ELTERN KOMMEN NICHT.
    (e) ICH DENKE, ALSO BIN ICH.
        ICH BIN, ALSO DENKE ICH.
        ICH BIN ALSO, DENK ICH.
        ICH DENKE ALSO, BIN ICH?

The Understandability Argument:
The next argument rests on the notion of understandability. It says that if linguistic entities are necessary to render large classes of texts understandable, and these entities in fact do render those texts understandable, then these entities exist in a linguistically relevant way. According to this statement and the fact that there exist texts like the following we have to conclude that pauses exist as linguistically relevant entities.

(4) *Understandability Tests*
FOR BUSDRIVERS PLEASE ASK
STEVEN SAID NOT TOO LONG
AFTER HIS FRIENDS LIKE ME
GOT THE JOB AT THE NEXT
WINDOW IS IT OPEN THE OTHER
GUY FOR NOBODY ELSE REACTED
IMMEDIATELY RESPONDED THE
OFFICER WHOM THE MAN WHO
ANSWERED WATCHED WENT ON

The Rhythm Argument:
We now turn to the last and in my view most effective argument to establish the reality of the grammatical category of pauses. The argument is roughly like this: Spoken language is, like every other form of overt bodily behaviour (like dancing, eating, walking, thinking), rhythmically structured. Rhythm means some sort of temporal periodicity of intensity patterns. In speech there is, as every musician will agree, a more or less complex beat structure based on these periodical intensity patterns. Roughly, every stress signals the beginning of a new beat. Considering more than one sentence one recognizes that there is, normally, a full beat *between* sentences. Pauses take a whole beat; they are, so to speak, complete stressed words even if no sound is produced normally while uttering them. They may be realized, however, with slight variation in length in different environments. In extreme cases where they are filled by upward beats, fillers etc. they do not even appear as surfacial pauses. The condition for this can be given explicitly in such cases, however. The different realizations of pauses comprise the grammatical category of pauses. This argument is illustrated and elaborated by the following examples which are explained in brief comments. The rhythm and beat structures can be calculated in Language Reconstruction Systems.

(1) *SLOW RHYTHM*

Remark: "Pause Words" (= Punctuation signs) show in Rhythm as full
beats.

(2) *ACCELERATED RHYTHM*

Remark: One-Syllable Words, longer Text.

Remark: More-than-One-Syllable Words.

(3) *WHAT IS THE BEST TIME?*

Remark: Best *overall* Time is ³/₄ but sometimes it is better to have *mixed*
Times:

(4) *MORE COMPLEX RHYTHMS*

Remark: Stresses mark off beats. Pause words are stressed. Unstressed
syllables are "squeezed" in.

(5) *A PROBLEM: "UNDETECTABLE" PAUSES* (an argument
against positivistic – i.e. data inductionist-approaches)

Remark: The pause 𝄽 is very short and not essentially longer than other
intrasentential pauses. The corresponding "pause word" is not
positivistically detectable.

(6) *CUT TRANSFORMS*

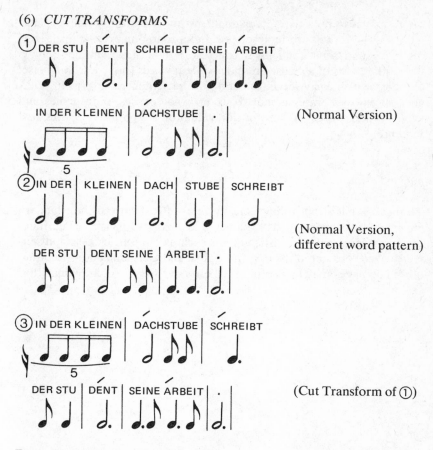

(Normal Version)

(Normal Version,
different word pattern)

(Cut Transform of ①)

Remark: – The Cut-Transform ③ cannot be understood at the beginning (cf. Normal Rhythm Version ②) of the sentence
– Towards the end there is an *off beat* situation
– This proves that rhythm is essential for Speech Production
and Analysis (also automatic Speech Production!)
– cf. Bosshardt (this volume)

4. Generalizations

The function of demarcating linguistic expressions, typically taken care
of by pauses in Indoeuropean languages, may be accomplished by other
means in other languages. Instead of pauses we may have clause final
particles (Cantonese, Lisu, Lahu), or special morphemes at clause final
verbs (Korean) which indicate the end of main and subordinate clauses.

There may also be affixes indicating constituent patterns (Caucasic languages) where the verb indicates the (nonpronominalized) constituents occurring and thus implicitly the clause boundaries. Another way to define the limits of a clause are independent words (modals in Buginese, Celebes) which carry the information of the sentence pattern. In probably all cases suprasegmentals back up what pauses, morphemes and even normal words do for the individuation of phrases, clauses and sentences.

5. Conclusion

We have argued that a linguistically relevant category of nonstandard morphemes (or words) exists, namely a category of pauses. Their function is to demarcate linguistic entities such as phrases, clauses and sentences. We considered the case in English and German and noticed that other languages may have different expressive means to individuate linguistic entities.

JANINA OZGA

A functional analysis of some pause and pitch step-up combinations

This report presents the results of a preliminary investigation of a prosodic complex consisting of a brief pause followed by a slight pitch step-
up. The break in pitch level across the pause, which may be compared to
a geological fault, occurs utterance-internally and marks the introduction of a new topic or resumption of one abandoned earlier (in a speech
or a conversation).

The term "utterance" is used here in the sense of Crystal (1969: 277):

> ... an ad hoc term ... used to refer to stretches of spoken (or written) lan-
> guage, used without a break by a single person, that are capable of being
> formally characterized in some way. It is used as a convenient means of
> breaking down long passages into more readily discussable units.

In this paper utterances are not broken down into tone-units directly:
there is an intermediate level of higher prosodic units which will be
called "thematic units" (units of thought, topics). The hierarchy may be
represented as follows: U $\geq$ Th-U $\geq$ T-U (U – utterance, Th-U –
thematic unit, T-U – tone unit). Utterances consist of integers (1 ... n) of
thematic units, which in turn consist of integers of tone-units (1 ... n). It
may be inferred from the above that an utterance may consist of a single
tone-unit, but in the paragraphs to follow more complex U's will be dealt
with.

While utterances and tone-units are easily delimited prosodically, the
thematic units are not, although they may be clear-cut semantically,
grammatically or pragmatically (or in combination of all three). It is the
purpose of this paper to discuss one type of thematic unit and determine
its prosodic exponents.

The introduction of the intermediate prosodic unit Th-U neccesitates
the postulate that its overall intonation contour differs from the contours
of the other two types of units, and particularly from those of tone-units.
Let us then start by examining the basic prosodic factors in the identification of tone-units. There are two such factors: pitch change and pause
(Crystal, 1969: 205ff.). These two cooperate although pitch change can
signal tone-unit boundary even if the pause is suppressed (O'Connor &

Arnold, 1961:26). The pause which may occur at tone-unit boundary is "never as long as brief (.)" (Crystal, 1969:171); the longer pauses (brief, unit etc.) are reserved for other purposes (e.g. for "effect"). Cutting across and superimposed on this system are pauses for breath and pauses of hesitation (Goldman-Eisler, 1958b), but these constitute a different dimension. However, it is clear that every transition between tone-units has the "fault" configuration, with a pitch step-up or step-down across the pause. If this is so, this "fault" must be different from the configuration marking the introduction of a new topic, if the latter is to be treated as a signal of thematic-unit boundary, in accordance with the postulate above.

The fault transition investigated for the purposes of this paper has the following characteristics:

(1) a brief (.) pause;

(2) normal pitch descent (or, rarely, ascent) in the pre-pausal tone-unit; "normal" in the sense that it does not behave like e.g. a speech paragraph boundary signal, with its typical cadence and tempo (Ozga, 1975);

(3) a higher onset of the post-pausal tone-unit; "higher" in the sense that the tone-unit starts at a pitch level above the expected archetypal constant level (Crystal, 1969:205f, 227) – if the tone-unit starts with a Head, it is a Head with a "booster" (↑) and if it starts with a Pre-head, it is a marked Pre-head (high or medial).

(4) segmental cues, such as speeding up the first part of the post-pausal tone-unit, clipping and glottalization.

The total auditory (and also physiological) effect, in impressionistic terms, is that of a *switch,* a momentary check and shift, which indeed is connected with the transition when one considers the semantic information associated with the adjacent tone-units belonging to different thematic units.

The switch which is effected by the fault transition with the above characteristics cannot be equated with the ordinary tone-unit transition because of (1), (3), and (4). Even if the pause should happen to be shorter or practically non-existent, the difference of onset, together with the segmental cues, is sufficient to set this type of transition apart (Q.E.D.).

Having demonstrated the essential difference, it is now necessary to define more precisely the nature of thematic units which are signalled by the fault and separate them from similar but non-identical prosodic syn-dromes. Thus, the thematic units in question may not be identified with e.g. such high-onset units as (a) paragraphs of news in BBC bulletins or (b) new themes in public speeches (both reported in Crystal, 1969:144). As regards (a), such transitions will also be marked by the paragraph cadence of the pre-pausal units, which is absent in the fault transition (cf. (2) above); and cases in (b) will be characterized by longer pauses between particular themes, since that is a regular feature of scripted or semi-scripted speech as opposed to spontaneous "change of subject" which the fault transition appears to signal.

The situational definition of the fault appears to involve the following factors:

(1) extemporaneous nature of the discourse

(2) a component of simultaneity of thought processes which may but need not be triggered by a novelty component in the pragmatic/situational setting (e.g. the latter will be absent where no external factor introduces the other "track" of thought which runs parallel to the thought currently verbalized for a period of time prior to the occurrence of the switch; in such cases the switch is triggered by sudden mental association);

(3) non-urgent character of the novel information: the speaker retains full control over his verbal planning and there is no interruption or distortion of the message which would take place if the new information was urgent.

As an illustration of the above consider the following passage:

"Please, would you tell me," said Alice timidly, for she was not quite sure whether it was good manners for her to speak first, "why your cat grins like that?"
"It's a Cheshire cat", said the Duchess, "and that's why. Pig!"
She said the last word with such violence that Alice jumped; but she saw in another moment that it was addressed to the baby and not to her ..."

(L. Carroll, *Alice in Wonderland*)

The Duchess must have observed that the baby needed admonishing before she finished the sentence about the cat, but that was not urgent enough for her to break in the middle of the sentence or rush the sentence to its close.

In the reading of the passage native speakers of English and Polish learners of English used a fault transition between *That's why* and *Pig!*, with the few exceptions of readers with poor scanning ability (the reading was not rehearsed), who were at a loss at that point.

The above observations concerning the fault transition are based primarily on an analysis of English. The prosodic complex is not, however, limited to English. In a (rehearsed) rendering of the dialogue presented below and of its Polish translation the fault transition was invariably used by all readers between *rich boy-friends!* and *See you when you come out of the bank!*

Diana and Caroline in town. Outside the bank.
Diana: Let's go and get some money first, shall we?
Caroline: All right. Which bank do you go to?

D: I've got my account at the Midland. Where do you go?
C: I go to Barclays. What did you do at the weekend, by the way?
D: I went to the cinema with Martin.
C: Your new boy-friend?
D: No, just an old friend.
C: *Is* he?
D: His father is a company director.
C: I suppose he paid for you?
D: Of course! I always expect men to pay for *me!*
C: No wonder you can live on your grant! Do introduce me to some of your
    rich boy-friends! See you when you come out of the bank!

                              (Abbs, Cook, Underwood, *Realistic English*)

It is quite possible that the fault transition is a universal feature, though such a statement would naturally have to be corroborated.

Although auditory judgements were used in the analysis of the data, the fault transition appears to be a reality for the speaker rather than the hearer. This is caused by the fact that often semantic and situational factors offset and overshadow the prosodic signal itself to the point of rendering it redundant and merely concomitant with the other clues. If this could be extended to all cases, it might be argued that the prosodic complex has no function and cannot be called a signal at all; it would merely be a speaker-based phonetic norm, the departure from which would be insignificant. Such arguments may, however, be refuted by showing that a departure from the norm *is* significant. The removal of fault transition characteristics (with all other things being equal, except possibly gestures that accompany a "switch") may, in extreme cases, lead to a breakdown in communication. More frequently, however, it is removed on purpose, for special effect or a conversational resource. Consider for example the situation in which people talking about a person just entering the room change the subject smoothly, without overt prosodic signalling which would give them away. Other examples come from those innumerable films in which shady characters glide effortlessly from *What a pleasant evening!* to *Keep moving. I have you covered.* The above examples, trivial as they are, *do* constitute sufficient evidence for the case in point, i.e. the functional aspect of the prosodic complex considered.

It is obvious that the fault transition is only one of the exponents of the "switch" intonation. That there are other factors involved may be shown by comparing a "natural" fault to an "artificial" fault, occurring in edited versions of radio interviews, where the editing causes a break in the prosodic continuity in much the same way as the natural fault does, without, however, breaking text coherence (there is no change of topic). It appears from a preliminary survey that listeners distinguish between the two kinds of fault by reference to the total intonation contour (the influence of semantic factors is removed by using a language unknown to the listeners). It remains to determine the nature of the cues which lead to such distinction to give the thematic unit under consideration its full prosodic shape.

RAIMUND H. DROMMEL

Towards a subcategorization of speech pauses[1]

> The search for language competence
> has to be a search for a multitude of
> psychological variables including com-
> petence in non-verbal communication
> and in the evaluation of the informa-
> tion needs of the receiver. (Moerk,
> 1974)

0. Introduction

Speech pauses have never occupied an important place within the
framework of generative grammar in general and of generative phonology in particular.[2] The reason for this is, without any doubt, the fact
that pauses are, to a large extent, performance and not competence
phenomena: the production of *all* pauses (which corresponds to the non-
productution of speech sounds) is part of *performance,* the position of
certain pauses belongs to the domain of *competence,* i.e. it depends heavily on syntactic structure (syntactic boundaries).

When I started working on speech pauses, there was no satisfactory
bibliography available, so I tried to make one (Drommel, 1974b). Nowadays, there is no lack of bibliographical information, the latest – and
largest – bibliography being compiled by Gabriela Appel et al. on the
occasion of our interdisciplinary workshop at Kassel.

A lot of work has been done on pauses since Oscar Israel Tosi (1965)
furnished, in the course of his psycho-acoustic research, the famous
definition of "pausology".[3]

Nevertheless, it is rather disconcerting, that there is not only general
disagreement on terminology, which seems to be symptomatic of linguistics and psycholinguistics in general (not of phonetics!), but that there
exists no general theory of current pause types, categories or features. I
will, therefore, try to outline very roughly and, of course, tentatively, a

subcategorization or subclassification of speech pauses which might at least stimulate further discussion on pause typology.

I am not, however, going to adapt Tosi's 'narrow' definition but should like to propose, in this study, a synthesis between the generative approach with its cyclical structure, on one hand, and psycholinguistic and empirical data, on the other.

1. A tentative classification of speech pauses

Je pause, donc je suis.
(presque Descartes)

At first glance, there are two main aspects of pause definition: an *acoustic* (or physical) one, and an *auditory* (or perceptive) one. In both cases, pause has to be considered as a context-sensitive variable. Both approaches include a pause threshold.

In acoustic analysis, the threshold is variable, depending at least on voice intensity, which becomes zero (absolute reduction of energy), and on the duration of that voiceless interval, partly on the analyzing system, too, and on the equipment available. A silent interval of a given or adjusted duration fulfilling certain conditions (mainly that of a reduction of the amount of energy to zero for a certain time) can be called *acoustic pause*.

Now, acoustic pauses occur within phoneme realisations (varieties of phonemes) or at the boundaries of such allophones. Pauses within such phoneme realisations which I call *intrasegmental pauses* can be considered as distinctive features of phonemic segments. Intrasegmental pauses, which are relatively short, are important constitutive elements of plosive segments representing plosive phonemes, such as /p, t, k/, for example in intervocalic position. The distinctive value of such "plosive pauses" has been proved since Alvin Liberman and his colleagues from the Haskins Laboratories coined the notion of "categorial perception".[4]

In spite of the distinctive value of such silent intervals, I shall reserve the term "distinctive pause" for *intersegmental pauses*. Intersegmental pauses, normally they have a longer duration than intrasegmental pauses, cut off formant transitions which can be analyzed in sonagramms. In fact, it is only the intersegmental pause which can be perceived as such, which can be heard as a pause (but need not), and not the intrasegmental pause.

Therefore I propose the following tentative classification:

(1) *acoustic pause*

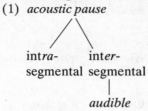

intra-   inter-
segmental segmental

audible

There have been some discussions on the definiton of an *audible pause*. According to Cowan & Bloch (1948:90) a pause can be called "audible" when it is identified by at least 50% of all subjects. In a later study, Boomer & Dittmann (1962) insisted on 75%.

An auditory pause is something above a certain *threshold of perception,* as, for example, Andrew Butcher (1973a) has shown in his interesting studies. There is, or should be, a general agreement on the fact that the *auditory threshold* is an intersubjective variable which is derived from at least (1) the phonetic-phonological, (2) the syntactic, (3) the semantic context, and (4) the objective, i.e. measured pause duration. In my papers, I have always insisted on the importance of the idiosyncratic and sociological features of the subjects listening in a "speech mode" (Lehiste, 1972). But this seems to be a problem of speech perception in general.

Audible pauses are either *syntactic* or *non-syntactic*. Non-syntactic pauses are particular pauses within Noun or Verb Phrases. Syntactic pauses occur at syntactic boundaries or constituent boundaries of the surface structure. A detailed description and a satisfactory definition can only be furnished within an adequate theory of syntax.

Henning Wode (1968) was the first to give a list of syntactic pause types of German on the basis of the normal, i.e. non-emphatic and non-contrastive intonation of Modern Standard German.[5] Antonio Quilis (1964) has determined syntactic groups or speech units of Spanish in which syntactic pauses do not occur, a complementary approach.[6] The relationship between syntactic pause durations and blanks in Old Hindoo has been examined by Klaus Janert (1967/68).

Syntactic pauses are either *final* or *tentative pauses*.[7] These are categories or subtypes which have already been mentioned by the Soviet linguist Peškovskij (1956:455–461), by Kenneth Lee Pike (1945) and, analogously, by Henning Wode (1968).

Therefore I suggest the following system:

(2) *audible pause*

```
          audible pause
             /    \
            /      \
     syntactic    non-syntactic
        /  \
       /    \
    final   tentative
```

The subclassification *syntactic* vs. *non-syntactic* is a categorization *positione*, i.e. on the basis of pause position in text.

Tentative pauses can be *distinctive* or *non distinctive*. These distinctive pauses, which until now have been rather neglected, have a distinctive function or value on sentence level, as, for example, the pause in the minimal pair:

(a) I téll you: / pause / Nóthing!
    vs.
(b) I tell you nóthing
Or:
(c) Der gute Mensch denkt an sich / pause / selbst zuletzt.
    ('The good man always takes care of himself' or 'Good people think of themselves to the end')
    vs.
(d) Der gute Mensch denkt an sich selbst zuletzt.
    ('The good man takes care of himself last' or 'Good people always think of themselves last')
(e) Er kaufte für fünf Mark / pause / zwanzig Blumen.
    ('He bought 20 flowers for 5 DM')
(f) Er kaufte für fünf Mark zwanzig / pause / Blumen.
    ('he bought flowers for 5.20 DM')[8]

Such a systematic binary classification can be useful from various points of view and for a number of approaches, e.g. for a discussion of the phonemic status of pause, which was stimulated by my teacher Harald Weinrich in a 1961 paper.

Now, speakers can consciously and deliberately omit pauses at syntactic boundaries, i.e. mark a syntactic boundary by suprasegmental features only, or they can, on the other hand, make pauses consciously in non-syntactic positions, as the rhetoricians have pointed out, according to their "communicative intention". I have proposed to substitute the notion of communicative intention by "communicative instruction".[9]

The theory of communication can provide an adequate feature of pause subcategorization, when the two notions of *transinformation* and *dissipation* are used.

The Venn diagram shows "transinformation" at the intersection of *input entropy* ($H_{(x)}$) and *output entropy* ($H_{(\lambda)}$), "dissipation" ($H_{x(\lambda)}$), then, can be defined as *output entropy – transinformation* (R). Transinformation is the central, basic or kernel information. Dissipation is the undesired information or noise which is assumed to accompany every act of communication.

Venn diagram (taken from Meyer-Eppler, 1969:159)

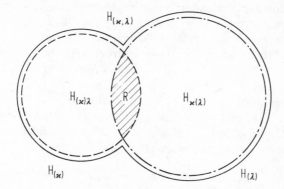

Venn diagram, representing the interdependence of input entropy $H_{(x)}$, output entropy $H_{(\lambda)}$, total entropy $H_{(x,\lambda)}$, dissipation $H_{x(\lambda)}$, equivocation $H_{(x)\lambda}$, and transinformation R.

So pauses which are intended by the speaker in order to give an instruction to the hearer (in this broader sense I even understand emphasis or deliberate suspense as an instruction) are called *pauses of transinformation or T-pauses*. Pauses which are not intended by the speaker are often "cognitive pauses". These "hesitation pauses" may also be the result of psychological stress (see Almeida et al, 1977), of the speaker being emotionally involved[10], of a sudden non-interest in communication etc. As a rule, these pauses do not facilitate speech processing, so I call them *pauses of dissipation or D-pauses*. There are some rare cases, where a speaker, in search of a word or a speech unit makes a hesitation pause, e.g. after a complex syntactic unit, which, though not intended as such, is an aid for the hearer in understanding the verbal information.

Certainly, the 'degree of dissipation' is even greater when a D-pause is filled with a *schwa* or with certain [r]-sounds. Such pauses are commonly called *filled pauses*.[11]

T-pauses and D-pauses can only be defined according to the judgement of competent subjects or hearers. Andrew Butcher (1973a) is right in postulating a *perturbation threshold* for D-pauses, a threshold which can be defined in rather complete analogy to the auditory threshold. A pause is beyond that perturbation threshold if it is considered "longer than normal" in a certain linguistic and extralinguistic context.

The distinction between syntactic and non-syntactic pauses has been called a distinction *positione,* the differentiation between T- and D-pauses is *natura,* i.e. there is a difference in communicative value or quality, in spite of the fact that our empirical criterion is duration as a context-sensitive variable.

Since, in empirical analysis, it seems impossible to grasp directly the degree of a speaker's intention or cognition, particularly when, as is the case with most of the tape recordings, the speaker is not available, it seems appropriate to propose the following substitutions:

intention of the speaker	→	instruction of the hearer
		transinformation
not intention of the speaker	→	*dissipation*
(mainly cognition)		perturbation[12]

It is now evident that the subcategorizations *syntactic* vs. *non-syntactic* and T- vs. D-pause are *completely independent classifications.* So the following feature combinations are possible:

$(3)^{13}$

	1	2	3	4
syntactic	+	+	−	−
T-pause (fluent)	+	−	+	−

1: Syntactic T-Pause
2: Syntactic D-Pause
3: Non-syntactic T-Pause
4: Non-syntactic D-Pause

Nevertheless, the feature combination [+ syntactic, − transinformation] does not occur so often. Hearers may be distracted or bored when a pause at a constituent boundary is too long. They might not even be sure whether, at a final pause, the speaker's contribution is finished or not.

These are certainly not all possible pause types. I have deliberately neglected articulatory pauses and the features of inspiration or expiration, or pauses caused by emotion, obstinacy or verbal deficiency.

I hope that you will now agree with me that a systematic typology of speech pauses is necessary or at least desirable. Such a typology could include:

(1) rewrite rules for the speech pause categories
(2) a satisfactory description of boundaries (or boundary symbols) and their relation to pauses
(3) a list of the speaker's performance variables.

ad 1.): *Generative sketch 1: Rewrite Rules*
The following rewrite rules are possible:

(1) [+ speech pause]
$\rightarrow$ [+ inter] / ... [ ] – [ ] ... $\Leftrightarrow$* ... / / – / / ...,
with [,] = allophone $\Big\}$ boundaries
, = phoneme

(2) [+ speech pause, + inter]
$\rightarrow$ [+ synt] / $\begin{Bmatrix} NP \\ VP \end{Bmatrix} - \begin{Bmatrix} NP \\ VP \end{Bmatrix}^{14}$

(3) [+ speech pause, + inter, + synt]
$\rightarrow \begin{bmatrix} + \text{ final} \\ - \text{ final} \end{bmatrix} / \begin{matrix} \downarrow -, \text{where} \\ \uparrow - \\ \rightarrow \end{matrix}$ $\begin{matrix} \downarrow = \text{falling} \\ \uparrow = \text{rising} \\ \rightarrow = \text{level} \end{matrix} \Big\}$ intonation contour
(with consideration of syntactic context information)

(4) [+ speech pause, + inter, + synt, ± final]
$\rightarrow \begin{bmatrix} + \text{ fluent} \\ - \text{ fluent} \end{bmatrix} /$ 'perceptive value' of the speech pause

$$\begin{bmatrix} < W_2 \\ \geq W_2 \end{bmatrix},^{15}$$

where $W_2 = F(x, y, z, t)$,
with x = phonetic-phonological $\Big\}$
y = syntactic pause context
z = semantic
t = objective (i.e. measured) pause duration

(5) [+ speech pause, + inter, + synt, – final, + fluent]
$\rightarrow$ [+ dist] / $\exists$ SU$_k$,** SU$_j$: (SU$_k$ = SU$_j$ $\cup$ pause) $\wedge$ (meaning of SU$_k$ $\neq$ meaning of SU$_j$)

---

* corresponding or equivalent to.
** A speech unit (SU) is a coherent and meaningful succession of speech signs, which are linked by junctors, "translatives" (in the sense of Lucien Tesnière, e.g. relative pronouns) or tentative pauses, and which are not separated by final pauses (cf. also Peškovskij, 1956 : 8). Speech units have no constant duration. Their duration seems not only to have idiosyncratic character, but to differ according to the test type.

ad 2.): Generative sketch 2: Speech pauses and boundary symbols

Abbreviations:

SU = speech unit
S = sentence
NP/VP = Noun-/Verb Phrase
MO = morpheme
seg = segmental
slb = syllabic

All boundary symbols have a minimal specification $\begin{bmatrix} - \text{seg} \\ - \text{slb} \end{bmatrix}$ in common. A text boundary symbol could be introduced with the features $\begin{bmatrix} + \text{seg} \\ + \text{TEB} \end{bmatrix}$. Differentiation between the various types of boundary symbols is ascertained by further features.

	SU-boundary	S-boundary	NP/VP-boundary	MO-boundary	=
//	+	−	−	−	−
/	+	+	−	−	−
#	+	+	+	−	−
+	+	+	+	+	−

There is:
'//' = boundary of a speech unit ('double boundary symbol')
'/'   = sentence boundary
'#'   = NP-/VP-boundary
'+'   = morpheme boundary

// has four positive specifications because every SU-boundary is sentence boundary and NP-/VP-boundary at the same time. Every NP-/VP-boundary, however, is also a morpheme boundary. Thus, because of the transitivity of this relation, every SU-boundary is also a morpheme boundary. We then obtain the following redundancy-free feature complexes:

SU-boundary   = $\begin{bmatrix} - \text{seg} \\ + \text{SUB} \end{bmatrix}$

S-boundary   = $\begin{bmatrix} - \text{seg} \\ - \text{SUB} \\ + \text{SB} \end{bmatrix}$

NP-/VP-boundary $=$ $\begin{bmatrix} -\text{ seg} \\ -\text{ SUB} \\ -\text{ SB} \\ +\text{ NP/VPB} \end{bmatrix}$

MO-boundary $=$ $\begin{bmatrix} -\text{ seg} \\ -\text{ SUB} \\ -\text{ SB} \\ -\text{ NP/VPB} \\ +\text{ MOB} \end{bmatrix}$[16]

"$=$" $=$ $\begin{bmatrix} -\text{ seg} \\ -\text{ SUB} \\ -\text{ SB} \\ -\text{ NP/VPB} \\ -\text{ MOB} \end{bmatrix}$

According to these feature configurations the SU-boundary and not the formative or morpheme boundary results to be the most elementary boundary symbol. This analysis modifies the proposition of Mayerthaler (1970:167) and contradicts Chomsky & Halle (1968:365).[17]

ad 3.): Generative sketch 3: Performance Parameters

1. [+ speech pause, − inter, + dist] ∈ {phonological features}
2. [+ speech pause, + inter, + dist] ∈ {segmental phonemes}
3. [+ speech pause, + inter, + synt, − final] ∈ {functional morphemes}, more exactly: {functional morphemes m/∃ phoneme p: p∈m}
4. [+ speech pause, + inter, + artic] ∈ {morpheme boundary symbols}
5. [+ speech pause, + inter, + synt, + final] ∈ {sentence boundary symbols}

A speech pause [+ SP] has a perceptual reality and consequently bears, contrary to the proper boundary symbols, the attribute [+ seg]. Since every boundary symbol can have a perceptual value when marked by a speech pause according to performance parameters, one needs a late phonetic rule which, in the cases 4 and 5, as well as for all boundary symbols (as a specification of these boundary symbols see generative sketch 2), transforms [− seg] into [+ seg]:

$$[-\text{ seg}] \rightarrow g\begin{bmatrix} +\text{ seg} \\ +\text{ SP} \end{bmatrix}$$

g = f (performance parameters).

The following speaker variables can be considered as performance parameters which cause speech pauses and pause durations:
- degree of spontaneity (if there is an operative definition which
  is independent from speech pauses)
- emotional disposition
- sociological variables (see Labov, 1969)
- stylistic variables
- idiosyncratic (competence and performance) features

            ⋮

(for further performance variables see Moerk, 1974).

Feature sets and redundancy rules could shed light on the interrelations
of pause subtypes and pause features. Since the criteria of syntactic
distribution and of transinformation are independent, there are no
redundancy rules for these feature sets.

Every final or tentative pause is a syntactic pause. This follows from
the proposed classification. But what about the distinctive pause?

My last proposal in 1974 was the following: On sentence level, even
on the level of complex sentences, all distinctive pauses must be syntactic
pauses:

$$[+ \text{dist}] \rightarrow [+ \text{synt}].$$

As the feature $[\pm \text{dist}]$, which is, of course, a structural one, is independent from the communicative feature $[\pm \text{transinformation}]$, all of the
four combinations are possible.

All this suggests that psycholinguistic evidence is needed in order to
specify those minimal integer units of thinking which are called *encoding
units;* and this is not only a question of pseudo-grammatical norms or of
"bon usage" of a language, but a problem of encoding mechanisms on
one hand and of situation variables on the other. However, it is difficult
to establish an approximation and, perhaps, a synthesis between the
inductive-generative approach and the structuralistic or psycholinguistic
method.

Notes

1. First section of the announced paper "Pauses, suprasegmentals, guessing games". The
   other sections had to be omitted because of time and place constraints.
2. As exceptions should however be quoted: M. Bierwisch (1966); J.W. Harris (1969);
   W. Mayerthaler (1971).

3. "Pausology is a doctrine constructed by integrating studies dealing with pauses and signals from speech, music and similar sounds [...]."

4. Cf. J. Bastian, P. Delattre, A.M. Liberman (1959:1568); J. Bastian, P.D. Eimas, A. Liberman (1961:842); K.S. Harris, J. Bastian, A.M. Liberman (1961:842A); G. Heike (1973:32ff.); Ching Yee Suen, M.P. Beddoes (1974:126ff.).

5. The author tried to give a systematic survey of those syntactic positions ("Pausenstellen"), where pauses are possible or even necessary ("[...] die Stellen, wo im Rahmen der Normalintonation des Hochdeutschen Pausen auftreten können [...]", p. 169):

> "Die Pausenstellen sind festgelegt durch die jeweilige syntaktisch-morphologische Struktur einer Äußerung. Sie lassen sich als inhärente Merkmale dieser Struktur auffassen." (Wode, 1968:169).

6. See particularly pp. 77–78. In his study of the structure of the run-on-movement *(enjambement)* he has furnished a systematic analysis of inseparable or "coherent" syntactic units. There are in Spanish twelve parts of speech, "las únicas partes del discurso que permanecen intimamente unidas, [...] los únicos elementos que salvo alguna circunstancia anormal, no se aislan" (p. 77).

7. It is evident now that a definition of syntactic pauses can only be proposed with respect to a particular language (*langue* in the Saussurian sense) to be analyzed.

8. It must be clearly stated that distinctiveness as the result of an analytical procedure does not fit, traditionally, in the generative frame.

Distinctive pauses on "phrase level" are reduced to what is commonly known as "juncture" or "hard vowel-onset", cf. German

> Weihnachts / pause / mánnerchor ('a chorus of men at Christmas')

vs. Wéihnachtsmänner / pause / chor ('a chorus of Santa Clauses').

These pauses form part of the set of *articulation pauses* which are hardly audible and often correspond to an articulatory necessity, for example, in hiatus-position. Articulation pauses have a real distinctive functuion only in those phrases which are speech units and, at the same time, extremely reduced texts. Otherwise, phrase pairs which are homophonous in their segmental structure are, even without distinctive articulation pauses, always distinguished by the surrounding verbal context of the corresponding speech unit. It seems that native speakers (particularly non-linguists) become conscious of the distinctive value of prosodic features within microsyntactic (phrases) and macrosyntactic units (speech units) through speech pauses. German homonymous morphemes as the prefixes *ver-* in *(jdm. etwas) verspréchen: (sich) vèrspréchen* can be distinguished by articulation pauses (*sich ver* / pause / *sprechen*) (problem of the 'verticality' of the syntagmatic value of distinctive articulation pauses).

9. Drommel (1974:22). See also H. Weinrich (1976). According to Weinrich's "Instruktionslinguistik" every communicated (speech) sign is understood as an "Instruktion des Sprechers an den Hörer [...], sich in einer geeigneten Situation in bestimmter Weise zu verhalten." (p. 11).

10. This research was stimulated by J. Karger (1951, unpublished phil. diss.).

11. I should rather insist on a narrow definition of filled pauses, which are hesitation sounds or sound clusters, which neither are linguistic signs nor form part of a linguistic sign.

12. Therefore I called the sum of all measured T-pauses of a text "time of instruction", the sum of all measured D-pauses of a text "time of perturbation". The "time of (speaker's) cognition" constitutes most of the perturbation time.

13. I shall not insist on my terminology here. Perhaps some colleagues will not like my T-pause and call it *fluent pause*.
14. "Sister rules" could be formulated for [− inter] (within phoneme boundaries) and [− synt] (within NP or VP) and [− dist].
15. Since D-pauses contradict the generative axiom of well-formedness, such performance phenomena as dissipation have to be adapted: The perturbance threshold W_2 can be interpreted as a "restriction".
16. Contrary to R. Lass (1971) [− seg] is introduced for morpheme boundaries. I cannot, however, wholly agree with Mayerthaler's statement (1971: 166, c), but insist on the fact that even morpheme boundaries are primarily marked by suprasegmental features and only secondarily by phonotactic − phonetic and phonological − elements, as are certain consonant clusters and the glottal stop in German.
17. The particular position of the speech unit can be proved by various arguments. Speech units, thus, define the scope of explicit junctors: To a pause which occurs ('elliptically') in the same syntactic relation ('uniting relation') as an explicit junctor is attributed the (same) functional value of that junctor (Drommel, 1974a: 28). When, in spontaneous speech, a final pause immediately precedes a junctor, the syntactic delimitation (disjunctive value) of that pause is stronger than the uniting force of the following junctor.

JENS-PETER KÖSTER

Perception of pauses and automatic speech recognition

1. Principal problems of speech recognition

The natural speech signal which carries the phonetic information needs the enormously high information capacity of about 160,000 bit/sec. In addition, the morphology of natural languages only makes use of a very few of the forms which their phonological systems allow them to produce (with an inventory of about 32 phonemes on the average). Shakespeare's lexicon, for instance, comprises 24,000 different words, and the number of words used by the average European does not exceed 12,000. (This inventory could be created by a phonological system of only six phonemes by systematically using all pronounceable phoneme combinations in diphones, triphones, tetraphones, pentaphones and a limited number of hexaphones.) The human perceptual system can easily manipulate this huge information capacity and doesn't seem to suffer from the fact that linguistic systems waste much of their morpheme construction potential. Moreover, the natural perception mechanism, when decoding the incoming signal, has at its disposal the whole of the individual's linguistic (and non-linguistic) experience which is closely correlated with his general intellectual competence. Under certain conditions, this allows the acoustic signal to serve only as a stimulus for an active creation of a "well" formed counterpart. Thus, in a number of cases, the natural mechanism of speech perception will not reflect a one-to-one correspondence between the acoustic signal and its pseudoform, which will serve as the actual pattern of reference for the higher processes of the mechanism of speech perception.

A machine for speech recognition, however, cannot simulate human intelligence, since, apart from theoretical implications, its application demands a simple and most economically working concept. Here we have the fundamental dilemma of speech recognition: the necessity for simplicity on the one hand and indispensable complexity on the other exclude each other!

2. A compromise: phonocodes

Many ways out of this dilemma have been proposed. They mainly concern a strict limitation of the material to be handled by the machine in respect to the word inventory and the number of speakers. The disadvantages of recognition systems submitted to such restrictions are obvious: they can only offer closed systems, and the smallest alteration, i.e. interchange of words/speakers, extension of vocabulary/speakers, or different conditions of transmission would result in a complete modification of the whole mechanism.

A more practicable idea was proposed by the Swiss engineer Dreyfus-Graf. In order to fit the technical possibilities of simple recognition machines that would draw all their information from the acoustic signal, i.e. without referring to any form of stored information, he attempts to develop artificial languages on the basis of a restricted inventory of phonemes which are combined in an optimal manner. Thus, with his special languages, he approaches a one-to-one correspondence between the speech signal and the signal his recognition machines work on. The adoption of an artificial language (phonocode) frees speech recognition from nearly all impeding restrictions if only the language is well elaborated.

The first and most important step in developing a phonocode is the selection of the phonemes to be used. The criteria for their selection are
– that their acoustic structure guarantees a maximum of distinction
– that they occur in the phonological systems of international languages
– that they are produceable with relatively high speed
– that they can easily be memorized.

The number of phonemes selected is a function of the purpose the code is to serve. By logical rules, the phonemes are combined to form syllables and words and finally entire syntactic patterns.

3. A special phonocode: SOTINAKEMUʃ

In collaboration with Dreyfus-Graf, a group of phoneticians at Trier University has optimized the SOTINAKEMUʃ code with a view to its application to a mathematical language based on the decimal system. The word inventory of such a language is very small since it can be reduced to the ten words for the basic digits (0 to 9) plus a few other words for arithmetical and logical operations and commands.

The SOTINAKEMUʃ code offers 5 vowels (i, e, a, o, u) and 6 consonants (t, k, m, n, s, ʃ), combinations of which produce 121 diphones, 1,331 triphones, 14,641 tetraphones, 161,051 pentaphones, 1,771,561 hexaphones etc. Out of this inventory those words had to be selected that were best suited to recognition by man and machine, and this under various special conditions of transmission (see Fig. 1).

condition	transmission	microphone	filter	noise	S/N ratio
1	direct	dynamic	none	none	
2	direct	dynamic	none	72 dB	−6 dB
3	direct	dynamic	300–3,400 Hz	none	
4	telephone	carbon	300–3,400 Hz	none	
5	telephone	carbon	300–3,400 Hz	60 dB	+6 dB

Figure 1. *Conditions of transmission.*

It was thought that a speculative limitation of the material to mono-, di- and triphones would exclude the difficulties that the use of longer units could entail for memorization and speed of production. This brought the theoretical word material down to $11 + 11^2 + 11^3 = 11 + 121 + 1,331 = 1,463$ words out of which 798 were, in practice, pronounceable.

In order to select the few words necessary for the language envisaged, the 798 words were submitted to subjective and objective (i.e. with recognition machines) tests. The stimuli were spoken by a German male speaker, transmitted under five different conditions (Fig. 1), and recorded on tape in random order. They were presented to eight women and eight men over thirty years of age and two groups of eight women and eight men between twenty and thirty in the subjective tests. During the tests, the subjects wrote down on a prepared sheet what they perceived. The results were analyzed with a TR 440 computer.

A list of words with decreasing rates of intelligibility was obtained. All the words with a recognition score of up to 100% can in theory be selected as elements of the final code. Nevertheless, in additional analyses, it was found that some of them were better suited than others, not only because they allowed a higher speed of production or a better memorization but because they were insensitive to the trends which obviously rule misperception in natural speech. The great variety of mistakes made by the listeners can be classified into three categories:

- substitution of speech sounds (the listener perceives a different speech sound)
- unperceived speech sounds (the listener does not perceive the sound)
- pauses (the listener perceives a sound which does not exist in the acoustic signal).

4. Unperceived speech sounds

When looking at the distribution of the total of the unperceived speech sounds, three groups of sounds can be isolated according to their resistance to the listener's tendency not to perceive certain phonetic information: most resistant are /o, k, ʃ/, less frequently affected are /a, e, i, u, m/, most frequently affected are /s, t, n/.

The question is whether the obvious sound specific or sound-group specific distribution of this category of mistakes is of a general nature, i.e. whether it is valid for all conditions of transmission, or a function of the particular quality of the transmitted signal. The answer to this question can easily be found by a rough examination of the data obtained in our test: the total number of errors as well as their sound specific distribution varies according to the condition of transmission. The unmanipulated (condition 1) as well as the two frequency-manipulated (conditions 3 & 4) signals can be characterized by a relatively low error rate whereas the noise-manipulated signals (conditions 2 & 5) suffer very much from misperception. The fact that frequency manipulation is more likely to affect vowels than consonants and that noise manipulation affects both vowels and consonants (with the exception of /k/ and /m/), however, may be interpreted as a more general tendency.

Finally, our analysis uncovered yet another interdependence: the position of a speech sound in an artificial word and error-rate. In initial position a speech sound will never be affected, in intermediate position only a very few mistakes can be observed, but 95% of the errors caused by failure to perceive sounds occur in final position.

The observations made above admit the formulation of the following general rule: the risk of a speech sound not being perceived depends on the sound itself, its position in the word, and the condition of transmission (i.e. the quality of the signal).

5. Perception of pauses

The mechanism of speech perception may disregard certain phonetic information in the sender's signal, but it may even do the contrary,

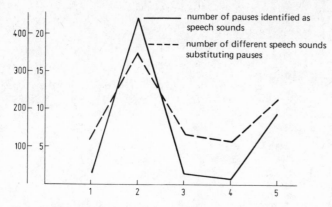

Figure 2. *Pauses identified as speech sounds.*

namely create pseudo-phonetic information without any reference pattern in the acoustic domain. This phenomenon turns out to be extremely dependent on the condition of transmission (see Fig. 2).

The noise-manipulated signals are more frequently perceived with an additional preceding or following speech sound than the frequency-manipulated or "natural" signals and show a larger span of sounds substituting the pauses (i.e. the places preceding and following the artificial words). Figure 3 shows the different speech sounds (with their frequency of occurrence) that were perceived at the places specified above where there was no acoustic information. It can be observed that the conso-

condition	vowels					consonants											
	i	e	a	o	u	t	z	k	n	s	m	l	p	d	r	f	g
1	7	4	1	4		2	1										
2	45	25	3	15	29	120	10	106	32	22	12	4	3	3	2	1	1
3		2	6		1		4		2	5	3						
4	2	2	2		1						1						2
5	2	23	1	2	7	46	1	43	31	6	23						3

Figure 3. *Speech sounds perceived instead of pauses.*

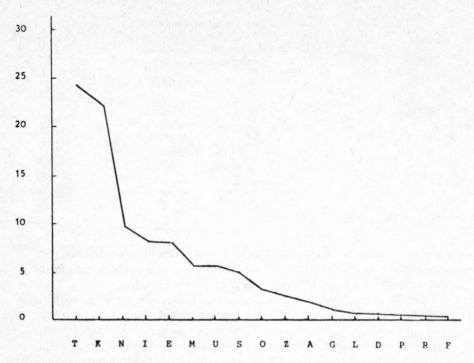

Figure 4. *Speech sound perceived instead of pauses.*

nant/vowel ratio (condition 2 = 316:117; condition 5 = 153:35) is in favour of consonants for the noise-manipulated signals, but in favour of vowels (condition 3 excepted) for the unmanipulated signals (condition 1 = 3:6; condition 3 = 14:9; condition 4 = 3:7). This is in accordance with the tendency isolated when the errors provoked by unconscious obliteration of phonetic information were analyzed.

If one considers the total of occurrences of the different speech sounds in pauses, a grouping seems to be possible. /t/ and /k/ represent the class of highest occurrence, followed by /a, e, i, o, u, m, n, s, ʃ/ as representatives of the class of moderate occurrence. /g, d, p, l, r, f/ finally are very rarely found in place of pauses (see Fig. 4). These are all sounds which do not occur in the SOTINAKEMU ʃ code. Thus, the listener seems to prefer speech sounds which are used in the artificial code rather than new ones for the substitution of the pauses.

The general rule reflected by these findings is as follows: pauses preceding and following the words of a phonocode risk being perceived as speech sounds. It depends on the condition of transmission and the phoneme inventory of the code used how great the risk of substitution is, which class of speech sounds and which speech sound will probably be chosen.

6. Conclusions

The results of our investigation prove that a one-to-one correspondence between acoustic patterns and the perceived speech sounds does not exist since phonetic information may be completely neglected by the listener, who, on the contrary, may "extract" phonetic information where there is no corresponding acoustic correlate. The laws governing these particular forms of misperception depend on
– the sounds themselves
– the conditions of transmission
– the position of the speech sounds in words
– the phoneme inventory of the code.
They allow a fair prediction of the quality of speech sounds for a phonocode from the point of view of natural perception and, together with the results of objective tests, help to establish optimal artificial languages on a mere theoretical basis in future.

HEDE HELFRICH

A digital method of pause extraction

The basic problem of any automatic pause analysis is to define a cut-off point which allows clear separation of non-speech from speech. It must be ensured that even weak speech sounds such as fricatives are classified as speech and that even relatively loud noises are classified as non-speech. A further complication is that, in general, noise is not stable in terms of level of intensity but changes over time. Thus, it is not sufficient to use a cut-off point fixed to one value. Rather the cut-off point has to be adaptive according to the changes of noise level of intensity.

The method to be described here attempts to meet these requirements. It is based on the ideas of Hess (1973). The basic assumption is that acoustic intensity of noise changes more slowly over time than level of intensity in speech. Thus, short time segments of pause resemble each other more with respect to their level of intensity than speech samples resemble each other. Moreover, it is assumed that acoustic intensity of noise is generally lower than that of speech. Fig. 1 gives an example for a digitalized signal containing speech and pause.

The vertical lines mark time segments of a given length (e.g. 40 msec.). A derivative of intensity (aj) is computed by squaring each value of the digitalized signal and integrating resp. summing up all values over each time segment. The values obtained resemble each other, concerning pauses, more than speech. This is to say that time samples like segments 1, 2 and 5 in Figure 1 bear a stronger resemblance to each other than segments 3 and 4. Moreover, the acoustic intensity of segments like 1, 2, 5 is generally lower than that of segments 3 and 4. A histogram (Figure 2) obtained from the values of many adjacent time segments shows the frequency of occurrence for each intensity value. It indicates that values representing low intensity have high frequency of occurrence, whereas values representing higher intensity have lower frequency of occurrence. The transition form high- to low-frequency values provides the criterion for the definition of the cut-off point which separates pauses from speech. Using this procedure, weak fricatives may be misclassified as non-speech, since they differ from pauses not in terms of absolute inten-

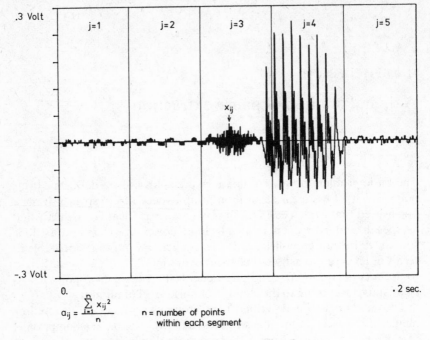

$$a_{ij} = \frac{\sum_{i=1}^{n} x_{ij}^2}{n} \qquad n = \text{number of points within each segment}$$

Figure 1. *Example for a digitalized signal containing speech and pause.*

sity, but only in terms of alteration of intensity. In order to account for this, an additional histogram of the summed up differentiated values (Δa_j) is created. It serves the purpose of establishing a special cut-off point for the weak fricatives. The cut-off points for both absolute and differentiated values are automatically set at that point at which the low-frequency values begin, as indicated by the vertical line in Figure 2.

Since the noise level changes over time, the cut-off points are automatically altered depending on the continuously updated histograms. Additionally, past values are attenuated by weighting them with a factor less than 1. If a given time segment surpasses at least one of the two cut-off points, it is classified as "speech". If it is less than any of the two cut-off points, it is defined as "non-speech". A speech pause is coded if a certain number of adjacent non-speech segments are detected. For example, if a minimum pause duration of 240 msec. is chosen by the user, a pause is counted only if at least 6 adjacent time segments each of 40 msec. have been classified as "non-speech".

The flow chart (Figure 3) gives an impression of the way the computer program works. The program processes tape-recorded speech samples which have been previously A/D converted and stored on digital tape by

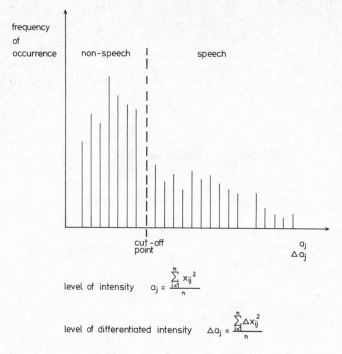

level of intensity $a_j = \dfrac{\sum\limits_{i=1}^{n} x_{ij}^2}{n}$

level of differentiated intensity $\Delta a_j = \dfrac{\sum\limits_{i=1}^{n} \Delta x_{ij}^2}{n}$

Figure 2. *Histogram of level values.*

means of another program developed in our laboratory. The data on digital tape are organized in files, each file usually containing one utter-ance.

The method has been applied in our Giessen laboratory to studies inves-tigating pauses as a function of both personality and emotional states.

In order to test the validity of the method, samples of segments which had been classified either as speech or non-speech were perceptually judged in isolation by means of a digital segmentation program (authors: R. Standke and W. Gohl). This program has been designed to look at and listen to each segment in isolation. Thus, it could be verified that most of the segments can be classified appropriately by the program.

Finally, the advantages and disadvantages of digital pause extraction methods compared with analogue-acoustic and perceptual judgement methods should be discussed. The column on the left hand side in Figure 4 shows some categories which seem important to me for assessing the appropriateness of a method. The cells of the matrix in Figure 4 contain a gross evaluation of the three kinds of methods listed in the top row with respect to each category. The first criterion to be considered is reliability, i.e. the assessment of how, exactly, results can be reproduced

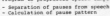
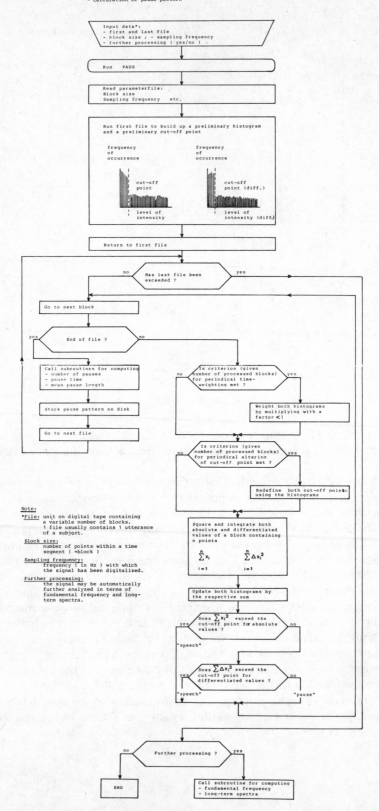

Figure 3. *Flow chart of the program for pause extraction.*

and how independent they are of an individual judge. There is no doubt that both digital and analogue-acoustic are superior to perceptual methods in terms of reliability. It is a well-known phenomenon, that judges often disagree when judging pauses, especially short ones. Even the pause perception of the same judge is not stable over time. As regards the general acoustical validity, i.e. the exact identification of silent pauses in speech, highest precision is attained with digital methods at present. Compared with analogue-acoustic methods the reason for this is the adaptiveness of digital methods (at least the one presented here). Compared with perceptual methods, acoustic methods are superior on account of their independence of linguistic context phenomena, which exert a strong influence on the human judge. However, the human observer has no difficulties in identifying sudden noises, which often cannot be avoided in natural recording settings, as non-speech, whereas all automatic methods fail to do so. Another matter of importance is the flexibility of a method, i.e. how well the method can be adapted to a special research purpose. It seems that digital methods are optimal in this case, since single dimensions such as minimum pause length can easily be varied. When a relationship to spoken words has to be established, as in many psycholinguistic studies, acoustic methods are

	Digital-acoustic	Analogue-acoustic	Perceptual
Reliability	high	high	low
General acoustic validity	high	not as high as in digital methods	low
Identification of sudden noises	not possible	not possible without additional support	easily possible
Flexibility	high	not as high as in digital methods	?
Establishing a relationship to spoken words	not possible without additional support	not possible without additional support	easily possible
Psycholinguistic/ psychological validity	?	?	?

Figure 4. *Evaluation matrix for pause extraction methods.*

inferior to perceptual methods, since time pattern of pauses cannot be assigned to time pattern of the spoken message without additional support. A most intricate problem is the evaluation of the psychological and psycholinguistic validity. On the one hand it might be argued that perceptual methods are in closer relationship to the process of speech production and perception. On the other hand, the impreciseness concerning time resolution and the context-dependability may prevent perceptual judgement from detection of micro-processes which might influence the speech process, although not apparently being perceived.

We may conclude from this evaluation, that a decision on the most appropriate method cannot be made without consideration of the special research purpose.

Crosslinguistic aspects

Chairman ROBERT J. DI PIETRO

ALAIN DESCHAMPS

The syntactical distribution of pauses in English spoken as a second language by French students

Introduction

The present paper is part of a series of studies initiated by François Grosjean concerning temporal variables in spontaneous oral language, both in French and in English. The first study (Grosjean & Deschamps, 1972) dealt with interviews in French, the second (Grosjean & Deschamps, 1973) with descriptions in French, and the third (Grosjean & Deschamps, 1975) with interviews in English, the results being in each case compared with what we had found in our previous studies. Up to now we have considered speakers using their native language, here our viewpoint will be different since this analysis concerns oral productions made in a foreign language. Using the same methods as in the previous studies, we shall analyse the temporal variables of our descriptions in English as a second language and compare them with our study concerning the variables in French as a first language.

The aim of this study was to get indications about the way spontaneous speech is organized when people use a second language, and about the various procedures of hesitation that appear in such a case.

Methodology

Our subjects were students of the University of Paris VIII – Vincennes aged between 20 and 30 and attending the courses of oral English. Among the group of twenty, 10 were in their second semester at the university, 10 in their fourth semester.

Each student was asked to describe orally two series of cartoons of the kind one may find in newspapers (each constituting a logical series of pictures, one with three and one with eight pictures). Before starting, each student had one minute's preparation, then he had to begin recording by himself. The experiment took place in a language laboratory with individual tape-recorders. The descriptions had to be done successively in French and English or in English and French, one group beginning with the French description, the other group with the English one, so as to avoid deviations in the results that might be caused by an influence of the first description over the second. Since each student had two cartoons to describe he was able to start once with the French description and once with the English description.

The recordings were transcribed word by word, with indication of silent and filled pauses, drawls, repetitions and false starts. Then the tape was submitted to an oscillographic analysis which allowed us to determine all silent pauses whose length was over 0.04 sec. As before, we chose to eliminate all pauses under 0.24 sec.

It must be added that those students were not what might be called fluent in English, their knowledge of the language corresponding to seven years in a secondary school plus one or so at the university.

The last remark to be made before going on to the various results is that the average length of the descriptions is not very different in French and in English L 2, the differences were mainly individual, the descriptions being either long or short in both languages. As regards the first cartoon the average length was 83 words in French and 88 in English L 2. This might be explained by the fact that each student had to go through the whole story regardless of his or her encoding difficulties. The length of the texts will therefore be omitted as an element of comparison.

The way of determining the various syntactical categories is the one we had used in our previous studies, with a main division between "end of sentence" and "inside sentence". "Inside sentence", the sub-categories were determined by the following division:

$$S$$

(COMP)   NP   (COMP)   VP   (COMP)

Roughly, the sentence is divided into two major categories, NP and VP with a possibility of inserting complements at various places inside the sentence, (COMP representing various kinds of phrasal adjuncts such as adverbs, prepositional phrases, ...). We added a few more categories i.e. pauses before appositions or coordinated phrases, between prepositions and NP, and pauses that accompany other hesitation phenomena such as filled pauses, drawls, repetitions, false starts.

As regards the main category, end of S (sentence or clause), we used four sub-categories:
– end of S proper,
– end of S before a relative clause,
– end of S before a coordinated clause,
– end of S before a subordinated clause.
(for further details refer to Grosjean & Deschamps, 1972).

Results and discussion

For the comparison of descriptions in the native language with descriptions in a second language, we expected considerable modification of several variables, namely: speech rate, articulation rate, number of silent or filled pauses, length of silent pauses, number of drawls, false starts and repetitions.

The first difference we noticed concerned the speech rate which dropped from 153 syllables per minute to 102 for English as a second language. This drop could be explained by a modification of primary variables:
– articulation rate,
– number of silent pauses,
– length of silent pauses.
What we immediately noticed was that as regards the length of silent pauses, no change had occurred with the passage from L1 to L2, as shown in the following table:

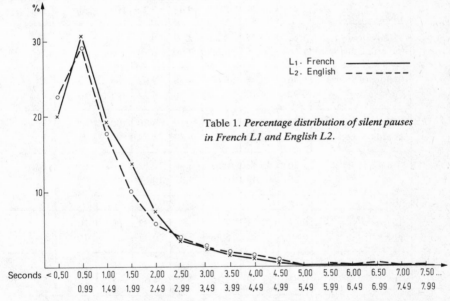

L_1 . French ——————
L_2 . English — — — — —

Table 1. *Percentage distribution of silent pauses in French L1 and English L2.*

That Table gives the percentage distribution of silent pauses in French L1 and English L2. Where we had expected a shift to the right, that is a general increase in the length of pauses, nothing of the sort happened. We found that the length of pauses was not longer in English (L2) than in French (L1), but even a bit shorter. On the contrary when we compared interviews in French (L1) to descriptions in French (L1), we

Table 2. *Percentage distribution and length of silent and filled pauses in descriptions in French L1 and English L2.*

E = English; F = French; Length = median length

		①	②	③	④	⑤	⑥	⑦	
		Silent pauses			Filled pauses		Percentage of subjects pausing in each place		
			Percentage distribution		Percentage distribution				
	Syntactical divisions	Median length	Total	End of S = 100% / Inside S = 100%	Total	End of S = 100% / Inside S = 100%	Silent pauses	Filled pauses	English / French
End of S	End of S or clause	1.36	18.54	40.82	9.90	24.50	100	65	E
		1.43	34.78	55.71	19.48	65.22	100	60	F
	Before or after subordinating word	1.32	3.28	7.22	2.77	6.86	80	25	E
		1.16	3.65	5.85	2.60	8.70	60	15	F
	Before or after relative	0.96	2.75	6.05	1.58	3.92	85	15	E
		0.92	4.70	7.52	1.30	4.34	65	10	F
	Before or after coordinating word	1.12	20.85	45.89	26.19	64.70	100	85	E
		1.08	19.30	30.92	6.49	21.74	90	45	F
	Total end of S	1.20	45.43	100%	40.47	100%	100	95	E
		1.25	62.43	100%	29.87	100%	100	70	F
Inside S	Between NP and VP	0.94	7.71	14.14	14.28	15.33	100	50	E
		0.84	5.75	15.28	9.12	20.37	65	40	F
	Inside NP	0.44	0.97	1.78	1.58	2.66	40	20	E
		0.86	1.39	3.70	3.25	4.60	35	10	F
	Inside VP	0.60	20.67	37.88	26.19	44.00	100	85	E
		0.62	8.00	21.31	25.97	37.04	80	70	F
	Between complement and NP or VP	0.80	3.54	6.50	3.57	6.00	65	35	E
		0.86	4.17	11.11	3.90	5.56	65	25	F

Table 2 contd.

Syntactical divisions	① Median length	② Silent pauses — Percentage distribution — Total	③ End of S = 100% / Inside S = 100%	④ Filled pauses — Percentage distribution — Total	⑤ End of S = 100% / Inside S = 100%	⑥ Silent pauses	⑦ Filled pauses	English French
Between NP or VP and complement	0.70	5.32	9.75	3.57	6.00	100	25	E
	0.79	7.30	19.44	4.55	6.48	80	20	F
Before coordination or apposition	1.08	0.26	0.48	0.	0.	15	0.	E
	1.06	1.91	5.09	0.	0.	40	0.	F
Between preposition and NP	0.60	0.53	0.97	1.58	1.58	30	10	E
	0.64	1.39	3.70	5.84	8.33	25	20	F
After repetition or after false start	0.80	15.52	28.45	13.88	23.33	95	70	E
	0.76	7.66	20.37	12.34	17.59	85	35	F
Total inside S	0.73	54.56	100%	59.52	100%	100	90	E
	0.77	37.57	100%	70.13	100%	100	80	F

E = English
F = French
Length = median length

Silent pauses — Percentage distribution; Filled pauses — Percentage distribution; Percentage of subjects pausing in each place.

(Left margin: Inside S)

noticed that the median length of pauses more than doubled. Thus, when using a foreign language our students did not use lengthened pauses as an extra hesitation procedure.

The global results of Table 1 are supported by the figures given in Table 2, col. 1. That Table gives the median length of the pauses at the different syntactical places that we had selected.

Once more we noticed a perfect similarity of distribution, except in the case of pauses inside the NP subject, but this may be due to an insufficient number of items (under 1%), as we shall see when considering the percentage distribution. If we consider the total results for two main categories "end of S" and "inside S", we find:

1.20 sec for English L 2 and 1.25 for French L 1 at end of S.

0.73 sec for English L 2 and 0.77 for French L 1 inside S.

When we had compared interviews and descriptions in French L1 we had gone

from 0.50 sec (int.) to 1.25 (desc.) at end of S, and

from 0.40 sec (int.) to 0.77 (desc.) inside S.

So the difference that we had noticed when we changed the cognitive task was not reproduced when we went from native to second language, the cognitive task remaining the same.

Nevertheless, the fact that the length did not change does not imply that the number of silent pauses remains constant. This is confirmed by an analysis of the length of runs, since the number of syllables between two pauses drops from 7.4 to 4.2. The reasons for that drop might be looked for in two directions, either an increase in the percentage of pauses at various places or a decrease in the length of the sentences. Both of these possibilities were observed.

The same decrease in the length of runs will be noticed as regards filled pauses proper: in French L1 one for every 40 syllables, in English L2 one for every 31 syllables. This also means that the number of filled pauses will be greater.

Finally, another element that we studied was the distribution between the different types of pauses including drawls:

	French L1	English L2
silent pauses	67.8	74
filled pauses	18.2	16.5
drawls	13.9	9.4
TOTAL	100%	100%

On this particular point, the proportion between filled pauses and drawls which was between 4:3 and 5:4 in French L1 (whether we consider interviews or descriptions) and 3:1 in English L1 (interviews), becomes 7:4 when our students speak English. They seem to be adopting some of the characteristics of the English language with its closed syllables, namely less use of drawls.

As regards drawls, we noticed too that the repartition in English L2 is not far different from what it was for interviews in English L1. Grammatical items appear in 98% of cases (91,68% in English L1). The words that appear most frequently in the drawls used by our students are: "the" 29% (22,5%), "and" 14,5% (13,3%), "a" 7% (10%), "to" 13,5% (4%), "he" 19% ("it" was not recorded in the figures given for drawls in interviews in English L1). It must be noticed that most sentences in the descriptions made by our students begin by "he". We have found only three examples of drawls corresponding to words stressed on the last syllable when the stress should have fallen elsewhere.

The syntactical distribution of pauses

Table 2, col. 2 gives the percentage distribution of silent pauses in the different categories which we have selected. A comparison between French L1 and English L2 shows an important decrease in the number of pauses at "end of S" for English L2, and a corresponding increase "inside S". It does not mean that the number of pauses is less important at "end of S", but that there are more pauses inside the sentences. The main differences appear where we had predicted: inside VP and after false starts and repetitions account for an increase in the number of hesitations proper inside the sentence (the NP being most of the time "he", no difference is found "inside NP"). As regards the differences at "end of S", they will be illustrated more clearly in Table 2, col. 3.

In this Table we distinguished pauses at the end of S (total 100%) from pauses inside S (total 100%), so as to be able to compare the results in the main categories separately. For "end of S" we have found an inversion in the order of the two main categories, "end of S proper" and "end of S before a coordinated sentence". This difference is explained by the tendency shown by the students to link their sentences by a coordinating word (mostly "and"), very frequently accompanied by some kind of hesitation procedure, a drawl or a silent pause in most cases.

This will lead us to another remark concerning what we call pauses at grammatical junctures (that is: end of S, between NP and VP, between NP or VP and complement, between complements and NP or VP); the percentage of such pauses becomes higher in proportion as the cognitive task becomes easier (reading or interviews of people talking about their job), and decreases as we go towards spontaneous speech. In our experiments, the percentage of pauses at grammatical junctures goes down from 79.6 for French L1 to 58 for English L2. So hesitation phenomena are marked by an increase in the number of pauses at non-grammatical junctures.

Col. 4 of Table 2 gives the percentage distribution of filled pauses. We notice an increase in the number of filled pauses in English L2 at "end of S" (from 30% in French to 40% in English), which emphasizes the phenomenon of hesitation in a foreign language.

In col. 5, which gives separate results for the two main categories, "end of S" and "inside S", a considerable inversion is found in the category "end of S before or after coordinating word". Once more that inversion is due to a systematic use of linking words (mostly "and"), allowing the speaker to gain time before beginning the next sentence.

In col. 6 and 7 we give the percentage of subjects using silent and filled pauses in the different syntactical categories that we had selected. The results indicate a general increase in the figures when we go from French L1 to English L2, with the exception of two categories that have practically never been used in English.

Conclusion

The present study was intended to give indications about hesitation phenomena when speakers are asked to perform the same cognitive task in their own language and in a foreign language.

The first result was that these speakers, confronted with a task which is much more demanding for them, tend to modify a certain number of variables, such as articulation rate, length of runs, but do not use the length of silent pauses as a means of slowing down their speech. Instead of lengthening the pauses, they will generally increase the number of pauses, so as to avoid the long pauses that speakers naturally try to eliminate.

French students making descriptions in English L2 will tend to reproduce in this L2 the organization of hesitation processes that exists in their own native language, with an inevitable slow-down of speech rate and an increase of all types of hesitation phenomena due to a lack of fluency.

A detailed study remains to be done with English students submitted to the same experiment, using the same cartoons, and having to do the same description both in French L2 and English L1, so as to give comparable results. In addition to this, a further study would consist in a comparison of the types of syntax and vocabulary used when the students shift from their own to a foreign language.

MANFRED RAUPACH

Temporal variables in first and second language speech production

Introduction

The cross-linguistic aspect of temporal patterning seems to have been of little interest up to now. In view of the paucity of work in the field, it is not surprising that descriptions of temporal variables in first and second language (L1 and L2) speech performance, which might profit from comparative studies, are almost non-existent. Apart from the project presented by Deschamps, only a few theoretical remarks by Leeson (1970), especially in his book *Fluency and Language Teaching* (1975), have come to our attention.

Under the circumstances it would seem to be premature to expect recommendations for the development of teaching programs or testing materials, though both are pedagogical implications of the study of temporal variables. Instead it will be our primary concern to examine in a preliminary fashion the validity of some proposed variables and give an interpretation of their distribution in L1 and L2 speech performance.

With respect to the analysis of speech, we feel that the most important findings are not necessarily to be derived from the use of descriptive statistics such as the mean or the median, but rather from a more detailed examination of those texts which turn out to be unusual or exceptional cases. In consequence, our contribution is oriented toward "making a case for case studies". In our opinion the descriptions of individual "pause profiles" in L1 and L2 performance may contribute to confirmation of the hypothesis of individual "interlanguages" built up gradually in the process of L2 acquisition.

Method

French and German undergraduate students were asked to give a description in their native language of a cartoon which was presented to them without an accompanying text. After the text had been added, the students had to give an explication of the same cartoon. Immediately afterwards they repeated the performance in L2, i.e. in German or French respectively. Several interesting questions arise from this experimental design, namely: how restricted competence in L2 alters the structure of student's performance as compared to their L1 performance, and to what extent students give a literal translation in L2 of what they have just said in L1.

We will limit ourselves to some temporal variables in these data by adopting, for the most part, the categories used by Grosjean & Deschamps (1972). Our use of these categories implies that we are not interested in studying pauses in isolation, but that we wish to integrate them into the network of various hesitation phenomena. Moreover, we will investigate intonational patterns and textual idiosyncrasies characteristic of individual speaking style. The evaluation of our corpus recorded by 5 German and 5 French students was based on a combined instrumental and "pencil and paper" analysis and was carried out with the help of research students in the Department of Language and Literature of the University of Kassel.

Results

The results are presented in the form of three comparisons:

(1) between the German and French *native* language performance,

(2) between L1 and L2 performance, and

(3) between the pause profiles of two individual speakers.

(1) Table 1 shows the mean results obtained by speakers in both native language groups. The distinctions between primary and secondary variables and between complex and simple variables are based on the suggestions made by Grosjean & Deschamps (1972). Comparisons of native-language performance are shown in the first two columns of Table 1.

The *speech rate* (number of syllables spoken per minute), which includes the pause time (in contrast to the *articulation rate*), indicates that, on the average, the German students produced notably more syllables in one minute (154.4) than the French did (116.4). Only if compared to the results obtained by Grosjean & Deschamps (153.05) there would be no appreciable difference. It should be noticed, however, that our cut-off point for silent pauses is 0.3 sec. against 0.25 sec. in the study of Grosjean & Deschamps. Since we are not primarily concerned with the comparison of German and French as native languages, we shall not go into a detailed interpretation.

Table 1. Temporal variables *(means based on data of German and French native speakers)*.
The figures added in parentheses represent the results which Grosjean & Deschamps
(1973) found in descriptions given by French speakers.
The figures for A and B refer to the means based on data of a German (A) and a French
(B) speaker, whose performance will be discussed in some detail under section (3). Their
means are computed into the total mean.

PRIMARY VARIABLES

	1 German L 1	2 French L 1	3 German L 2	4 French L 2
COMPLEX VARIABLES				
SPEECH RATE (syl./min.)				
Total:	154.4	116.4 (153.05)	95.4	99.7
A:	83.0			60.8
B:		134.6	127.0	
SILENT PAUSES (%)				
Total:	37.9	44.6 (41.29)	38.0	44.4
A:	63.1			63.7
B:		25.7	19.4	
SIMPLE VARIABLES				
ARTICULATION RATE (syl./sec.)				
Total:	4.09	3.69 (4.45)	2.26	2.98
A:	4.05			2.78
B:		3.01	2.62	
LENGTH OF RUNS (syl.)				
Total:	10.25	7.0 (7.42)	4.63	5.94
A:	6.64			2.68
B:		7.50	7.40	
LENGTH OF SILENT PAUSES				
Total:	1.61	1.71 (1.32)	1.10	1.50
A:	2.71			1.73
B:		0.87	0.68	

SECONDARY VARIABLES (%)

	1 German L 1	2 French L 1	3 German L 2	4 French L 2
SILENT PAUSES				
Total:	64.6	53.6 (56.26)	55.6	74.8
A:	80.7			71.4
B:		48.4	49.7	
FILLED PAUSES				
Total:	23.0	16.9 (15.75)	19.5	14.6
A:	16.1			21.8
B:		23.2	19.2	

SECONDARY VARIABLES (%)

	1 German L 1	2 French L 1	3 German L 2	4 French L 2
DRAWLS				
Total:	5.6	15.4 (13.09)	11.3	4.2
A:	–			–
B:		21.2	21.2	
REPETITIONS (of syllables, words or phrases)				
Total:	1.9	6.9 (7.97)	6.1	2.3
A:	3.2			3.0
B:		2.6	5.3	
FALSE STARTS				
Total:	4.9	7.2 (6.93)	7.5	4.1
A:	–			3.8
B:		4.6	4.6	

Percentage of *silent pause* time over total time is greater in the French performance (44.6 > 37.9), *articulation rate,* excluding pause time, is slower in the French productions (3.69 < 4.09); this, incidentally, is partly responsible for the relatively low speech rate.

Length of runs indicates the average number of syllables between two pauses; the French speakers' sequences are in general shorter (7.0 < 10.25 syl.). In other words, the French speakers paused more often than the German speakers did. In addition to this, the *length of their pauses* was slightly greater in comparison with those of the German speakers (1.71 > 1.61 syl./sec.).

As to the secondary variables, which reflect the percentage of the hesitation phenomena including silent pauses as an undifferentiated category, further differences between the German and French recordings become obvious. *Drawls,* i.e. the nonphonemic lengthening of syllables, deserve special attention: the percentage is remarkably high in the French performance (15.4 > 5.6), probably as a result of the specific syllabic structure of French, as Grosjean & Deschamps and others have suggested.

Generalization of the results of this first set of comparisons would be quite premature. They are based on a relatively small sample: total speaking time was 77 min. (8,250 syllables). They reflect to a high degree the pecularities of individual speakers and are primarily useful as evidence in combination with the results of our second series of comparisons.

(2) Columns 3 and 4 of Table 1 show the results obtained in L2 performance. Compared to the data for L1 performance, they reveal some predictable general tendencies, explicable from the design of the

experiment. Since semantic planning had already been taken care of by the students in their native language performance, we should expect them not to have extremely long pauses in their L2 performance, in spite of the difficulties imposed by the use of the second language. There should be, instead, *more* pauses as evidence of uncertainties on the syntactic and lexical levels. This is exactly what we find: a reduction in the length of silent pauses in L2 (1.50 < 1.61 for the German, 1.10 < 1.71 for the French speakers). In the French students' L2 performance the percentage of pause time over total time is even less than in their native language (38% < 44.6%). But the length of runs has considerably diminished in L2 performance of both groups (5.94 < 10.25 and 4.63 < 7.0), which means that pauses appear much more frequently. In addition, articulation and speech rates have decreased. So, even under the conditions peculiar to our experiment, it is noteworthy that pauses occur more often in L2 than in L1 performance.

Our hypothesis that hesitancy in L2 would take place especially on the syntactic and lexical levels is confirmed by the distribution of the silent pauses (see Table 2):

Table 2. *Position of silent pauses* (cf. Grosjean & Deschamps, 1973)

	1	2	3	4
	German L1	French L1	German L2	French L2
Sentence-final position (%)				
Total: 61.2		59.8 (62.43)	37.1	48.5
Sentence-internal position (%)				
Total: 38.8		40.2 (37.57)	62.9	51.5

The data concerning the position of silent pauses indicate that in L2 performance there has been a shift toward a preference for pauses *within* sentences.

If we turn to the secondary variables for the comparison of L1 and L2 performance (Table 1), the findings in the *drawls* category may give a good illustration of another lawful relationship: the data in the two inner columns (2 and 3), which represent the percentage of drawls found in L1 and L2 performance of the French speakers, are notably greater than those in the marginal columns (1 and 4). The French speakers tend to transfer their preference for drawls to their L2 performance. On the other hand, the German speakers make as little use of this device in their French performance as they do in their native language. The hypothesis that speakers are likely to transfer idiosyncratic performance from L1 to L2 finds support in the results of most of the other secondary variables also: except in the use of filled pauses, the inner columns represent approximately the same percentages, clearly distinct from those of the marginal columns.

The hypothesis is also generally confirmed by the distribution of the primary variables, though this cannot be immediately deduced from the composite data of Table 1. One finds a remarkable regularity in that nearly all speakers maintain their L1 pause profile in their L2 performance. Those speakers whose speech or articulation rates in L1 deviate considerably from the statistical mean show similar deviation in L2. This also holds true for the percentage of pause time, the length of runs and the length of silent pauses.

(3) To illustrate this regularity, we have included in Table 1 data from a German (A) and a French (B) speaker who differ markedly from each other in their temporal patterns. We will briefly summarize the German speaker's data in order to exemplify this regularity, and then go on to a more detailed analysis of the French speaker's performance.

Speaker A's performance is characterized by sizeable deviations from the mean of his experimental group. This is especially true for the extremely low speech rate ($83.0 < 154.4$ and $60.8 < 99.7$), the large percentage of silent pauses ($63.1\% > 37.9\%$ and $63.7\% > 44.4\%$) and the extremely short runs ($6.64 < 10.25$ and $2.68 < 5.94$), in both L1 and L2 performance. Consequently, it is precisely nonconformity with the expected statistical values which enables us to describe his special type of speech as nonfluent. Our understanding of the term fluency is not as a facet of ideal speech behavior uninterrupted by hesitancy. It is rather a relative measure of a speaker's ability to avoid numerous very long pauses. In the last analysis, this concept of fluency should also be related to the speaker's ability to plan and arrange his speech performance.

A closer examination including the secondary variables and what has been called "parenthetic remarks" and "fillers" would reveal that speaker A has no particular strategy at his disposal to overcome difficulties in his speech: the only devices he makes use of are silent and filled pauses.

Speaker B, on the other hand, conveys the impression of great fluency in L1 as well as in L2. While for speaker A the transfer of his L1 fluency – or, in this case, his nonfluency – is not particularly of advantage, the transfer of L1 strategies is undoubtedly of great help for speaker B in improving fluency in L2 performance. There is only a slight decrease in speech and articulation rates, whereas the values of the other primary variables partly suggest an improvement relative to L1 performance: pause time is less and pauses are also somewhat shorter; the length of runs is similar to that found in L1 performance.

The distribution of the secondary variables is a good indicator of individual command of hesitation phenomena. In this case it shows that speaker B succeeds in maintaining to a high degree the L1 pause profile. This becomes obvious when we note the percentage of drawls: this variable is of considerable importance in French as well as in German performance of this speaker. The fact that it notably exceeds the average percentage of the experimental group enables us to interpret some idiosyncrasies of speaking mentioned above: the small percentage of pause time as well as the relatively low articulation rate correlate with the high frequency of drawls. This result supports our view that there is not much evidence for treating pauses separately. A speaker's performance is determined by a number of different hesitation phenomena operating in consort.

The only variable that increases in speaker B's L2 performance is *repetition;* the other variables have been maintained at the same frequencies as in L1; the percentage of pauses has even been reduced. Speaker B thus behaves in L2 performance as she would have been expected to do if she had had to repeat the task in French rather than in German.

To refine the analysis, other factors have to be taken into account. In combination with pause distribution, *intonation* may reflect the structure a speaker has assigned to performance. If we accept the tripartite distinction of "rise, fall and sustain", we find that a falling intonation contour followed by a pause indicates in most cases the end of a particular unit. The control of this device may be taken as proof of a mastery of the task; it may reflect a certain ease on the part of the speaker and an excellent capacity for planning his speech performance. Speaker B confirms this impression by continuing with summary fillers after falling intonations. Thus, in L1 performance, every final intonation is followed by one of the expressions: *bon, bon alors, et alors, oui, donc, voilà.* In accord with our prediction, she uses the same device in her German performance, where we find after almost every falling intonation fillers like *so, ja, ah ja, und.*

In order to determine the degree of fluency, the analysis of speaker B's performance must be extended to those fillers and parenthetic remarks which are not necessarily associated with final pauses. Here we come across a series of expressions like *enfin, c'est-à-dire,* and so on. Accordingly the fillers in L2 are also quite numerous: *also, und dann,* and above all *wie sagt man.* The use of these expressions is responsible for the low percentage of pause time in German, which is even less than that in the L1 performance of the German students.

Speaker A, to conclude this brief description, has hardly any of these expressions at his disposal. In his native language performance they are completely absent, in his French version there is a single *ah oui.*

The most general implication of these findings is that the temporal variables considered above obviously allow us to determine different degrees of fluency. A further analysis would have to focus additionally on textual structure, i.e. the cognitive units of speech performance.

Conclusion

Our line of argument may be summarized in the following three statements:

1. The study of pause distribution must include all available hesitation phenomena that work directly on the percentage of pause time in speech performance; note, for example, the compensatory effect of drawls in the performance of speaker B. Parenthetic remarks deserve special attention; this category should even be expanded to include those expressions which are not wholly without semantic content, but which serve primarily to help the speaker in constructing his sentences, allowing him to gain time for working out what he will finally articulate. In French, examples of this type would be *au niveau de, sur le plan de, en ce qui concerne, quant à* ... These expressions are highly idiomatic and should not be neglected in L2 teaching.

2. The compensatory effect of different temporal variables is likely to be effaced in a purely statistical approach which primarily takes into account only general distributions, but not the individual characteristics.

3. A consideration of pause profiles leads to the formulation of two generalizations. First of all, there is normally a loss of fluency in L2 performance. In itself this appears rather trivial, but we were also able to specify the different ways in which loss of fluency was reflected in speech performance. The second generalization is that speakers have a strong inclination to transfer their pause profile from L1 to L2 performance. This implies that a speaker can hardly be expected to be more fluent in L2 than in L1. It might also be taken as an invitation not only to aim at the improvement of a learner's L2 performance, but to work simultaneously on the development of fluency in L1.

HANS W. DECHERT

Pauses and intonation as indicators of verbal planning in second-language speech productions: Two examples from a case study

Problem

Since the onset of Psycholinguistics in the 1950s, the questions of how messages are transformed into speech and what its constituting units are have been of central concern.

For years the perceptional side of this problem has been almost entirely the focus of attention, and has perhaps been overemphasized.

Different descriptions of the sequence of steps in the production of speech (e.g. Fry, 1969; Taylor, 1969; Fromkin, 1973; Garrett, 1976) have been based on rather controversial concepts, especially as to the initial function of syntax vs. semantics.

In the course of time, sequential probability models of speech production (e.g. from Lounsbury, 1954 down to Jaffe & Feldstein, 1970) have been replaced by more complex hierarchical ones (e.g. Miller, Galanter & Pribram, 1960; Osgood, 1954; Lenneberg, 1967).

Various attempts have been made to assess and describe relevant units of speech: *word* (e.g. Lounsbury, 1954; Levelt, 1969), *phonemic clause* (e.g. Trager & Smith, 1951; Boomer, 1965; Crystal & Davy, 1975), *agent-action-effect unit* or *predicate-argument structure* (Fillmore, 1968; Grimes, 1975; Engelkamp, 1973, 1974), *sentence* (e.g. Yngve, 1960; Johnson, 1965, 1968; Goldman-Eisler, 1972; cf. O'Connell's summary 1977), *paragraph* (e.g. Koen, Becker & Young, 1969), *idea unit* (e.g. Meyer, 1971, 1975; Butterworth, 1975), *information* or *thematic unit* (e.g. Halliday, 1967bc, 1968), *vectorial unit* (e.g. Labov & Waletzky, 1967; Linde & Labov, 1975), *speech act* (e.g. Austin, 1962; Searle, 1969), etc.

None of these attempts has led to a psycholinguistic unit generally considered as the unit of speech production. Most likely it does not exist.

Throughout these attempts there has been an astonishing neglect of natural oral material, and little attention has been paid to the obvious fact that individual speakers under natural conditions might come to very individual procedures of production of speech, which may not be governed so much by the ideal rules of the linguistic system used as by a lot of other factors such as the context of the situation to be verbalized, the individual speaker's history and capability, the particular genre of speech, and so forth.

There seems to be a demand for an assessment of such corpora of natural speech, taking into consideration the multidetermination of particular speech events of individual speakers. The results of such an endeavour will certainly lack generality, but may eventually provide some deeper insight into the problems individual speakers have while planning, monitoring and executing speech in particular contexts.

The crosslinguistic approach working with L 1 – as well as L 2 – corpora may not only contribute to a more adequate understanding of the problems one has learning and speaking a second language, but also to the more general problem of competing speech plans within speakers.

Subject

The two reproductions of George (a 23-year-old undergraduate English major) dealt with in this paper are examples taken from a larger corpus. They were recorded on January 12 and April 4, 1978, immediately before and immediately after a visit to the United States.

At the time he had been at Kassel University for one year, after nine years of English in High School (Gymnasium), with average grades in German and English, but practically no experience in a native English-speaking environment.

George had not done any oral reproductions of the type mentioned below. He did not have any training in text linguistics.

Method of elicitation

The text of "The War of the Ghosts"[1] was presented to George in printed form with its original paragraph structure. Both times he was given the same instructions; we wanted to find out how well this story could be retold by a German adult speaker of English. No questions concerning unknown words or structures or the elicitation task itself were allowed.

George was exposed to the text as long as he thought it necessary to understand and then reproduce it. This took him exactly 5 minutes the first time (Jan. 12), and 4 minutes and 20 seconds the second time (Apr. 4). During the reproductions he had no access to the text. No notes were taken during reading.

Transcription and analysis

The recordings were transcribed by two graduate student assistants and myself, independently. Special care was taken to register and identify all speech "errors" (including filled pauses, slips of the tongue, false starts, repeats, prolongations, etc.) and their "corrections" as well as unfilled pauses and intonation contours.

The resulting transcripts were compared with each other; obvious listening and transcription mistakes were discussed and omitted. A few cases of remaining uncertainty or disagreement were left undecided.

The recordings were then analysed with a Frøkjær-Jensen Fundamental-Frequency-Meter Type FFM 650 and a 4-channel Siemens Oscillomink L^2, showing the inherent speech-pause-patterns as well as the intonation contours of the recordings.

The graphic displays of the instrumental analysis were then compared with the transcripts. The remaining uncertainties and disagreements among the transcribers as well as those resulting from the comparison between the results of the aural and instrumental analysis were discussed and decided upon (cf. Pike, 1972: 18).

Results

A comparison of the two versions of George's reproduction before (Version A) (App. 4) and after (Version B) (App. 5) his three-months' visit to an English-speaking country reveals remarkable differences; undoubtedly he has become less hesitant and more fluent.[3] On the other hand, interferences and fossilizations are found in both versions without any noticeable progress whatsoever in the second one.

What is striking in the context of this paragraph is the fact that both versions, as the transcripts clearly demonstrate, are highly structured. In each case they reflect the internal "grammar" of the story. With few exceptions only, the structures of both reproductions are practically identical with the story "grammar" of "The War of the Ghosts", delineated from an entirely different point of view by Mandler & Johnson (1977), although Bartlett's text is extremely incoherent and thus offers tremendous problems of perception and production not only for second-language speakers of English, but for native speakers of English as well.[4] Nevertheless, due to an overall formal schema which George uses as a frame of reference, he manages to organize his material into astonishingly coherent stories, in spite of a large number of special planning problems he has on the way. In doing so, he applies certain strategies that have been described by Bartlett (1932) and others (e.g. Kintsch,

1977: 362ff; Clark & Clark, 1977: 167f) and which need not be repeated here. What mainly enables him to solve the elicitation tasks is his creative construction of an overall structure during perception and/or production, and his following its patterns while working on subordinate problems in particular slots, such as searching for words.

The sequence of utterances which are the constituting components within the framework of the total structure does not follow the paragraph structure of the original. It is George's own invention.

In our analysis, these story constituents, in the tradition of Daneš (1960), Halliday (1967/68), Crystal (1969) and Pike (1972), are characterized by pause and intonation features marking their boundary lines. Intonation contours falling to pitch level 4 in connection with final pauses are considered as the decisive unit criteria in our assessment of a sequential order of utterances.

The tone units thus found are additionally delimited by the fact that all repairing corrections of speech "errors", if they do occur, take place within their boundary lines.[5]

These units are identical neither with *propositions,* as a comparison of our transcripts (App. 4, 5) with Mandler & Johnson's analysis of the propositional structure of the original text shows (App. 3), nor with *phonemic clauses, predicate-argument structures, sentences* or the original *paragraphs.*

These units obviously represent a particular type of utterance which has its own status. Since they are closely linked with the episodic structure of the story in question, I have called them Episodic Units.[6]

Episodic Units of speech are furthermore characterized by verbal opening and closing signals.[7]

Episodic Units have narrative functions such as describing setting, location, vector, beginning, reaction, attempt, outcome etc. In some cases they are identical with narrative episodes, in other cases they represent functionally different smaller constituents of narrative episodes, as shown in our transcripts.

Above all they seem to provide a schematic procedural device that enables a speaker to construct things with words.

As the comparison of George's less "fluent" first production (Version A) with his more "fluent" second production (Version B) reveals,

(a) the context-constructing story schema in both cases is responsible for the more or less "fluent" solution of the elicitation task;

(b) the particular ability to handle lower-level problems in slots with high processing load makes certain passages of the second production sound more "fluent".

Episode VI in Version B is such a passage. A comparison of this Episode (B 26–28) with Episode VI of Version A (A 30–34) clearly demonstrates that George, in producing the second version, needs less effort (25 words: 4.0 sec pausing time vs. 37 words: 13.3 sec pausing time) and has only little trouble finishing the story in case of Version B. Quite obvious are the enormous processing problems occurring during the planning, correcting, and editing of this Episode in Version A.

A thorough comparison of Episode VI in the original text (App. 3; 37–42) with lines A 30–34 (App. 4) can give a good example of the underlying processes (cf. App. 6).

As our synoptic transcripts show, both texts, though different in detail, naturally follow the same order of events with a number of common phrases, centred around the pronominalized main character in this Episode HE:

HE → HE → HIS → HIS → HE

HE BECAME QUIET → ROSE → HE → SOMETHING → CAME OUT OF HIS MOUTH → UP AND CRIED → HE WAS DEAD

These phrases are common in both versions; they indicate the existence of sort of a semantic network. This goes so far that the past of " to rise" in the original text serves as a noun in George's reproduction

THE SUN *ROSE* → THE *ROSE* OF THE MORNING

which one might consider rather poetic if he disregards the tremendous speech-planning problems causing this kind of creative but odd construction. They are clearly shown by the preceding filled and unfilled pauses

"AND (.) (hm) (in) (–) IN ..."

What seems to be the cause for the main disruption in lines A 32–33, initiated and accompanied by long pauses and the false start "(he suddenly)" are at least two – possibly more – problems;

(a) the breaking into parts of the phrase "His face *became* contorted" which has not been fully understood[8] and therefore only partly or fragmentarily stored and retrieved through the wrong slot of the established network (cf. App. 6);

(b) the interference of a monitoring system trying to control the fields Germ. *kam* – *bekam* vs. Engl. "came" – "became"[9] putting an unusually high processing load on this slot.

The total confusion at this slot seems to show that George's planning is out of step with the chosen network, as BECAME, referring to the phrase HE BECAME QUIET (line A 30) and probably still mentally present, competes with parts of the phrase "His face *became* contorted", referring too early to the original at the wrong place, and finally blends with the intended expression "black". These overlapping plans cause the following sequence of the subphonemic slip, the blended form, the following attempts at dissolution and the final solution with the help of the cue OUT.

In this process, finally, the cue OUT connects this passage with the restated network; the phrase OUT OF HIS MOUTH becomes the connecting link.

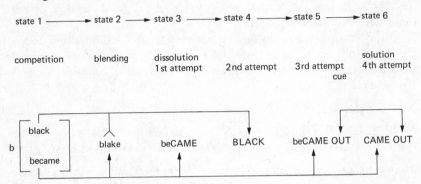

Three months later the possibility of another occurrence of such a confusion resulting from competition among plans and blending, over-monitoring and a lack of the decisive cue still seems to exist. All three elements BECAME – BLACK – CAME are present. But this time, with the "help" of pauses and prolongations and following the framework set by the original text, George smoothly gets over his internal planning problems. He seems to have become a more competent editor of his speech.

Notes

1. Bartlett, 1932: 65; cf. App. 1.
   It must be emphasized that this task was not aiming at an immediate free recall, although, as is the case with all primary and secondary speech productions, the organization of memory and thus the retrieval of linguistic information from memory seems to have been unduly neglected in crosslinguistic speech research up to now.

2. A more detailed description of the functions of this kind of system is given in Helfrich, 1973: 71–73.

3. In Version A pauses take 45%, in Version B 33% of the total time for speech-plus-pauses. An example of this increase in fluency is discussed in detail below.

4. This was exactly the reason for Bartlett's choosing this kind of text for his experiments, since he "wished particularly to see how [...] subjects would deal with this lack of obvious rational order" (Bartlett, 1932: 64).

5. This delimiting feature of Episodic Unit, also mentioned by Boomer (Boomer, 1965) with reference to the phonemic-clause, taken from Trager and Smith (Trager & Smith, 1951) is verified by all the material we have looked into so far, including Crystal and

Davy's corpus (Crystal & Davy, 1975). It does not mean, however, that Episodic Units themselves cannot be corrected or repaired by additions etc., as lines A 08 and B 29–32 clearly demonstrate.

6. Dechert, forthcoming. The term "Episodic Unit" is intended to allude also to Tulving's concept of "Episodic Memory" (Tulving, 1972) and to suggest a research problem. One of the tasks of this research is to relate the notion of Episodic Unit of processing to the notion of pragmatic context-dependent verbal behavior, as delineated by Karl Pribram in this volume.

7. In both transcripts (cf. App. 4 and 5), opening and closing signals are marked by italics.

8. Among the words and expressions that proved to be unknown or not clearly known in a free inverview some time after the second recording was "contorted".

9. This is a well-known learning problem for German speakers of English and often dealt with in the teaching of English, mostly on an elementary level. However, as in many other cases of fossilization, it may be the particular "stress" of the competition of speech plans here that is responsible for the surfacing of this additional problem. Two similar cases of fossilization are found in B 25 ("fell" for "feel" in connection with "didn't") and in B 31 ("he didn't have felt" for "he hadn't felt").

Appendix 1

The War of the Ghosts

(Original Version)

One night two young men from Egulac went down to the river to hunt seals, and while they were there it became foggy and calm. Then they heard war-cries, and they thought: "Maybe this is a war-party". They escaped to the shore, and hid behind a log. Now canoes came up, and they heard the noise of paddles, and saw one canoe coming up to them. There were five men in the canoe, and they said:

"What do you think? We wish to take you along. We are going up the river to make war on the people".

One of the young men said: "I have no arrows".

"Arrows are in the canoe", they said.

"I will not go along. I might be killed. My relatives do not know where I have gone. But you", he said, turning to the other, "may go with them."

So one of the young men went, but the other returned home.

And the warriors went on up the river to a town on the other side of Kalama. The people came down to the water, and they began to fight, and many were killed. But presently the young man heard one of the warriors say: "Quick, let us go home: that Indian has been hit". Now he thought: "Oh, they are ghosts". He did not feel sick, but they said he had been shot.

So the canoes went back to Egulac, and the young man went ashore to his house, and made a fire. And he told everybody and said: "Behold I accompanied the ghosts, and we went to fight. Many of our fellows were killed, and many of those who attacked us were killed. They said I was hit, and I did not feel sick".

He told it all, and then he became quiet. When the sun rose he fell down. Something black came out of his mouth. His face became contorted. The people jumped up and cried.

He was dead.

Appendix 2

Key to Symbols

Pauses:

( )	−0.2 sec
(.)	0.2–0.5 sec
(–)	0.6–1.0 sec
(––)	1.1–1.5 sec
(–––)	1.6–2.0 sec
(––––)	2.1–2.5 sec
(–––––)	2.6–3.0 sec
(––––––)	3.1 sec and longer

(e), (hm)	Filled pauses
AND	Prolongations
/ /	Falling intonation preceded by pause: unit boundaries
(and)	"Errors": small letters, in parentheses
[and]	Additions by the author, in brackets
AND ...	
... OF THEM DIED	Opening and closing signals, in italics
E	Episodes
EU	Episodic units

Appendix 3

The War of the Ghosts

(Propositional Structure according to Mandler & Johnson)

	E	
01		One night two young men from Egulac went down to the river to hunt seals,
02		and while they were there it became foggy and calm.
03		Then they heard war cries,
04		and they thought, "Maybe this is a war party."
05	I	They escaped to the shore
06		and hid behind a log.
07		Now canoes came up,
08		and they heard the noise of paddles
09		and saw one canoe coming up to them.
10		There were five men in the canoe,

11		and they said, "What do you think? We wish to take you along.
12		We are going up the river to make war on the people."
13		One of the young men said, "I have no arrows."
14		"Arrows are in the canoe", they said.
15	II	"I will not go along.
16		I might be killed.
17		My relatives do not know where I have gone.
18		But you," he said, turning to the other, "may go with them."
19		So one of the young men went,
20		but the other returned home.

21		And the warriors went on up the river to a town on the other side of Kalama.
22	III	The people came down to the water,
23		and they began to fight,
24		and many were killed.

25		But presently the young man heard one of the warriors say, "Quick, let us go home; that Indian has been hit."
26		Now he thought, "Oh, they are ghosts."
27	IV	He did not feel sick,
28		but they said he had been shot.
29		So the canoes went back to Egulac,

30		and the young man went ashore to his house and made a fire.
31		And he told everybody and said, "Behold, I accompanied the ghosts, and we went to a fight.
32		Many of our fellows were killed,
33	V	and many of those who attacked us were killed.
34		And they said I was hit
35		and I did not feel sick."
36		He told it all,
37		and then he became quiet.

38		When the sun rose he fell down.
39		Something black came out of his mouth.
40	VI	His face became contorted.
41		The people jumped up and cried.
42		He was dead.

Appendix 4

The War of the Ghosts

(Version A)

	E	EU	
01		1	(e) *ONCE A DAY* (.) TWO YOUNG MEN (.) FROM EGULAC (––) WENT
02			DOWN TO THE RIVER (–) (to go) (e) TO (c) CATCH SEALS (––) //
03	I	2	**(e)** *AFTER A WHILE* IT BECAME (.) FOGGY AND CALM (––) (an) (.)
04			BUT SUDDENLY (e) (they heard s) (.) THEY HEARD A NOISE (–––) //
05			**(e)** THEY HID (–) (e) (behind) (––) BEHIND A STONE (–)
06		3	SUDDENLY **(e)** THEY SAW (.) A CANOE (––) **(e)** (coming) (.)
07			(a along) (.) *COMING UP THE RIVER* (.) //
08		4	(e) WHERE FIVE MEN WERE SITTING IN (––––––) //
09			(e) THEY (.) SAW (e) TWO MEN (.) AND ASK THEM (e) (––)
10		1	WHETHER (e) THEY WANT TO COME WITH THEM **(hm)** TO MAKE
11			WAR ON THE PEOPLE (–) IN THE OTHER (–) TOWN *UP THE RIVER* (––) //
12			(the one said) **(e)** (that he that) THEY SAID THAT THEY HAD
13		2	**(e) (e)** (no) (–) NO ARMS (and) **(e)** BUT THE OTHERS IN THE
14	II		BOAT REPLIED (.) THAT THERE ARE SOME **(e)** IN THE BOAT (–) //
15			*THE ONE SAID* THAT HE (e) WON'T COME (e) WITH THEM BECAUSE
16			HIS RELATIVES **(e)** DO NOT KNOW WHERE HE IS (––) SO
17		3	ONLY ONE OF THEM (e) WENT ALONG WITH THEM AND **THEY (e)**
18			PADDLED UP THE RIVER (hm) *TO THE OTHER SIDE OF THE TOWN*
19			*KALAMA* (–––) //
20	III	1	*THERE* THEY (e) MADE WAR ON THE (.) PEOPLE (–) AND *MANY OF*
21			*THEM DIED* (––) //

22		1	(e) *SUDDENLY* IN THE WAR (e) ONE OF THEM SAID **(e)** LET'S
23			STOP NOW COME ALONG (e) THE INDIAN IS HIT (–) //
24	IV	2	BUT (e) HE NEVER FELT(t) (–) SICK (–) BUT THEY **(e)** WENT *OFF*
25			*WITH THE CANOE* (–––) //
26			*BEING AT HOME AGAIN* (––) (e) HE SAID (–) TO THE OTHERS (.)
27			THAT **THEY (e)** MADE WAR ON THE OTHERS IN THE CITY (–) AND
28	V	1	(e) (that) (.) THAT (e) THE OTHERS (said) SAID THAT HE WAS HIT
29			BUT HE NEVER FELT SICK (––) //
30			*AFTER THAT HE BECAME QUIET* (.)
31			AND (.) (hm) (in) (–) *IN THE ROSE OF THE MORNING* (–––) (e) (he suddenly) (–––) (e) (––) SUDDENLY (.)
32			(b) SOMETHING (blake became) BLACK (became out)
33	VI	1	(.) CAME OUT OF HIS MOUTH (–) THE OTHERS **(e)** STOOD UP AND
34			CRIED (–) AND (.) *HE WAS DEAD* //

Appendix 5

The War of the Ghosts

(Version B)

	E	EU	
01 02		1	*TWO MEN FROM EGULAC* WERE ON A RIVER (.) SOME NIGHT **AND (e)** *WENT ALONG THERE* ( ) //
03 04	I	2	*SUDDENLY* (.) IT BECAME FOGGY (–) **AND** THEY HEARD (a noi) (.) A NOISE (– –) //
05 06		3	*SUDDENLY* (.) THEY SAW SOME CANOES COMING UP (and) **(e)** WHERE SEVERAL MEN WERE IN (–) //
07 08 09		1	THEY ASKED **IF (e)** THEY WANTED TO COME WITH THEM **TO (e)** KALAMA (–) A TOWN UP THE RIVER (–) WHERE THEY WANTED **TO** FIGHT *A WAR AGAINST SOME* (– – – –) //
10 11 12 13 14 15	II	2	**(e)** *THEY FIRST SAID* THAT THEY HAD NO ARMS AND THAT THEY **COULDN'T** JOIN THEM AND **SO (e)** ONE OF THEM (–) (said or) SAID THAT HE (–) DIDN'T WANT TO COME WITH THEM AND SO **(h)** WE WENT HOME BUT THE OTHER ONE (–) JOINED THE OTHER MEN (.) IN THE CANOES AND (.) THEY MADE *WAR ON THE PEOPLE IN* (.) *KALAMA* (– – – – – –) //
16 17	III	1	THE WAR (.) WENT **ON** AND SEVERAL MEN (were f) FOUGHT (.) AGAINST EACH OTHER AND (e) *SOME WERE BEATEN* (–)
18 19 20	IV	1	*AND SUDDENLY* **(e)** SOME OF THE MEN SAID (– –) COME ON LET'S GO (–) **(e)** *THE INDIAN IS HURT* (– – –) BUT **(e)** THE MAN DIDN'T FEEL SICK AND (.) ALTHOUGH *THEY WENT HOME* (and e) ( ) //

21			(when they) *AFTER THEY WENT ASHORE* (−−) THE MEN WENT BACK
22	V	1	AND SAID (at home and) AFTER ARRIVING AT HOME (−−) THAT THEY
23			HAD FOUGHT (−) *AGAINST SOME IN* **(e)** *KALAMA* (−−) //
24		2	(and he) (.) (had) AND HE HAD BEEN HURT (.) BUT *HE DIDN'T*
25			(fell s) *FELL SICK* (−−−) //
26			*BUT IN THE MORNIN* WHEN THE SUN (−) AROSE (−) SUDDENLY (.)
27	VI	1	THE MAN BECAME SICK (−) **AND (e)** SOMETHING BLACK CAME
28			OUT OF HIS MOUTH **AND** *HE SUDDENLY DIED* (−−−−) //
29			BEFORE HE HAD SAID THAT **(e)** THEY HAD FOUGHT AND THAT
30	V	3	HE HAD BEEN HURT BUT (e) (that he didn't) (.) THAT HE
31			*DIDN'T* HAVE *FELT* (e) *SICK* (−−) //
32			*BUT ALTHOUGH NOW HE WAS DEAD* //

Appendix 6

Original version	Version A, 30–34
AND THEN HE BECAME QUIET	AFTER THAT HE BECAME QUIET AND . hm . in
WHEN THE SUN ROSE	IN THE ROSE OF THE MORNING
	e
HE FELL DOWN	he suddenly
	e

processing

[black]

| SOMETHING BLACK | SUDDENLY b   SOMETHING blake |

his face   became   contorted

became   BLACK   became out

CAME OUT OF HIS MOUTH	CAME OUT OF HIS MOUTH
HIS FACE BECAME CONTORTED	
THE PEOPLE	THE OTHERS
	e
JUMPED UP AND CRIED	STOOD UP AND CRIED AND
HE WAS DEAD	HE WAS DEAD

⟶ _____ processing _____ ⟶

MARC FAURE

Results of a contrastive study of hesitation phenomena in French and German

1. Introduction

The following contribution is a report of research into the occurrence of hesitation phenomena and their syntactic distribution in spontaneously spoken French and German. Because of the numerous varieties of spontaneous language, however, this empirical study was restricted to three forms of spontaneous speech – narrative, discussion and conversation recorded from television and radio transmissions. In addition, recordings were analysed from one French-speaking and two German-speaking motor aphasics, in order to compare their hesitations with those of non-aphasic speakers.

2. Method

2.1. Categories of hesitation phenomena
Since the investigation of Maclay & Osgood (1959) served as a basis for our study, the same principal categories were used:

2.1.1. All silences (PV/S), breath intakes which interrupt the fluency of speech (PV/r) and omissions of words or parts of words (PV/O), were counted as unfilled pauses (PV = French abbreviation for 'pause vide').

2.1.2. All interruptions filled by non-language sounds, as well as lengthened syllables (PP/ph), non-identifiable sound combinations (PP/SI), filler words (PP/L) and phrases (PP/T), are counted as filled pauses (PP = Fr. abbr. for 'pause pleine').

2.1.3. False starts may be corrected (FD/RS) or the sentence or structure may remain incomplete (FD/inc). The speaker may interrupt himself, to progress to another, for him more important idea (FD/SC). In this case, the interruption manifests itself in a sudden change in sentence prosody. Finally, the speaker may be interrupted by the listener (FD/int).

2.1.4. Repetitions may involve one or more sounds (R/ph), a word (R/L), morpheme (R/M) or phrase (R/T).

2.2. Syntactic categories

The terms 'function words' and 'lexical words' were retained, without however implying the same categories as Fries. Following Zemb (1968, 1970, and 1972 ab) we consider as function words deictic elements, coordinators, prepositions and subordinators. Content words include adjectives, adverbs (A), proper names and nouns (N), pronouns (Fr) and verbforms (V). It will be clear that these categories differ from those of Fries: possessive pronouns and auxiliary verbs, for example, are classified as content words.

3. Evaluation of recorded material

For each type of hesitation phenomenon, conventions were set up for the identification of their syntactic location. For the variables (FD/RS) and (FD/SC) the syntactic category of the immediately preceding lexeme was considered. For (PV/O) the word directly affected by the hesitation was noted. For the remaining types (PV/S), (PV/r), (PP/ph), (PP/SI), (PP/L), (PP/T), (FD/inc), (FD/int), (R/ph), (R/L), (R/M) and (R/T) we considered the syntactic category of the word immediately following the hesitation.

It might be objected that for each variable we considered only the adjacent words, whereas it would have been more advisable to have taken account of the whole context, in order to study better the role of verbal planning. In answer to this we would point out that verbal planning, which may be both progressive and retrogressive, may progress from the word level to the phrase and to the text. Which level we consider is a matter of convention, although the results obtained must remain speculative. Ideally, all levels of verbal planning should be considered. In a quantitative empirical investigation, however, this would be impracticable.

4. Results

4.1. To compute the length of the text of each speaker, the unit of the spoken syllable was used. The results show 15.9 occurrences of hesitation phenomena to each 100 syllables in French, compared to 13.9 in

German. This corresponds to one hesitation for 6.29 (6.3) spoken syllables in French and 7.19 (7.2) in German. These results suggest that rather more than one hesitation phenomenon occurs each second (cf. Goldman-Eisler, 1968 and Grosjean & Deschamps, 1972). This is the only instance where we have considered the temporal aspect of pausing.

4.2. Aphasic vs. non-aphasic
Like Quinting (1971), we failed to find qualitative differences between the two groups of speakers, only quantitative differences. Since, however, our material was limited, no further generalizations can be made.

4.3. Syntactic categories
Quinting (1971), who investigated two types of hesitation phenomenon in English, considered it impossible to support the hypothesis of a non-random distribution of PV and PP in respect to syntactic categories. Although in the present work four hesitation categories were studied, the results do not point to differences between the categories, either in French ($P < 0.01$) or in German ($P < 0.001$). Hesitation phenomena affect grammatical and lexical words equally. It could, however, be shown that in the case of a choice between a grammatical and a lexical word, hesitation will predominantly affect the lexical word.

4.3.1. Grammatical categories
In French, the deictic elements are particularly affected by filled pauses ($P < 0.01$) and false starts ($P < 0.01$), whereas in German, all the hesitation categories are involved ($P < 0.01$). In both languages, the distribution of hesitation phenomena before coordinators, prepositions and subordinators was statistically insignificant. This could indicate that during verbal planning, in particular when the choice of a word is involved, hesitation phenomena will occur before the first element of the phrase, and not before the initial coordinator, preposition or subordinator.

4.3.2. Lexical categories
The distribution of the different types of hesitation phenomena is significant in both languages ($P < 0.01$). In connection with lexical categories, however, it was only in relation to verbs ($P \simeq 0.025$) that the distribution of hesitation phenomena was significant in French, whereas in German, all lexical categories were significant ($P < 0.01$), hesitation phenomena being most frequent in connection with pronouns, followed by nouns, verb forms, and finally adjectives/adverbs. This ordering corresponds closely with German syntax (cf. Zemb, 1968). The subordinate

clause – the most frequently occurring clause-type in German – places pronouns first, e.g.:

$$\overbrace{\Rightarrow \text{Fr} \quad \text{Fr} \quad \text{F} \quad \text{F} \quad \text{V}}^{\text{Fq}}$$

,weil er ihm sein Geheimnis zu spät preisgab

In English, Boomer (1965) and Cook (1971) have shown that pauses at the beginning of a phrase occur either before the first or the second element. This also seems to be true for German, whereby the hesitation phenomena before pronouns (Fr) are rather an indication of sequential planning, and those before nouns and verbs a sign of the planning of words and word groups.

Furthermore, the results seem to suggest that in spontaneous speech, Fq sequences do not function as in a), but as in b):

a) $[\Rightarrow \text{Fr} \quad \text{Fr} \quad \text{F} \quad \text{F} \quad \text{V}]$
b) $\Rightarrow \underbrace{[\text{Fr} \quad \text{Fr} \quad \text{F} \quad \text{F} \quad \text{V}]}_{\text{Fq}}$

5. Non-syntactic characteristics of hesitation phenomena

No relationship was found between hesitation phenomena and the speech situation. On the other hand, it could be shown that several hesitation variables were related to the emotional state of the speaker. Under normal, that is familiar circumstances, the speaker will tend to use unfilled pauses, and, according to his personality, unfilled and filled pauses. In agreement with Helfrich (1973), it was found that in French and German, filled pauses are rather an idiosyncratic feature of the individual's manner of verbal expression. However, when a speaker is under stress, his speech is characterized in addition by false starts, accompanied by repeats when the stress is greatest.

In order to determine whether the occurrence of hesitations is significant on a metalinguistic level, they were analysed from the point of view of theme-rheme structure (cf. Zemb 1968, 1972a and 1972b). No relationship could be found. This is indirect evidence that hesitation phenomena are directly implicated in the act of speaking.

BARRY MCLAUGHLIN

Towards a theory of speech processing:
Some methodological considerations

One of the major problems in the study of speech processing is the lack of a coherent theory. There is, however, a coherent theory of speech processing in the literature on second-language (L2) learning. While specifically developed for L2, the theory has some implications for first language (L1) as well.

The Monitor Model

The theory is known as the Monitor Model and was proposed by Stephen Krashen (1975, 1977a, 1977c). Krashen argues that an adult L2 performer can "internalize" the rules of a target language via one of two separate systems: (a) an implicit way, called subconscious language *acquisition,* and (b) an explicit way, conscious language *learning.* Language acquisition is similar (if not identical) to the process by which children acquire L1. It comes about through meaningful interaction in a natural communication setting. Speakers are not concerned with form, but with meaning; nor is there explicit concern with error detection and correction. This contrasts with the language learning situation in which error detection and correction are central. Formal rules and feedback provide the basis for language instruction in typical classroom settings. Nonetheless, it is not the setting *per se* but the conscious attention to rules that distinguishes language acquisition from language learning. In the natural setting an adult can receive formal instruction by asking informants about grammar and by receiving feedback from friends. Similarly, language can be acquired in the classroom when the focus is on communication—— e.g., through dialogues, role-playing, and other forms of meaningful interaction.

Table 1 outlines the acquisition-learning distinction. Acquisition is said to correspond to the tacit knowledge of a native speaker in Chomsky's sense (Krashen, 1977a). In the acquisition process, input stimulates the operation of a Language Acquisition Device. The process is governed by

Table 1. *The Monitor Model*

Adult second language performance is a function of:
  (a) Acquisition: subconscious, implicit rule internalization, attention to meaning not form, typical of "naturalistic" settings.
  (b) Learning: conscious, explicit rule internalization, attention to rules of grammar, typical of formal classroom instruction.

Thesis:
  (1) Adult second language performance initiated by acquisition.
  (2) Learned component serves only as a Monitor, which alters the form of the output when
       i) enough time
       ii) concern with form and correctness

Thus:

                                    Learning
Acquisition ——→ Output
(Creative Construction Process)

universal strategies available to all acquirers (Krashen, 1978b). Krashen describes this as a "creative construction process", whereby the native speaker acquires the structures of the language in a fairly stable order.

Learning is the conscious internalization of the rules of a language. One of the uses of learning is to monitor one's own performance and to correct that performance so that it corresponds with what has been learned. The Monitor, however, is not available to all performers, it tends to be limited to the simpler parts of language, and can best be applied only when time is available and when focus is not on communication but on form and correctness (Krashen, Butler, Birnbaum & Robertson, forthcoming).

The central claim of the Monitor Model is that conscious learning is available to the performer only as a Monitor. Utterances are initiated by the acquired system with conscious learning used to alter the output of the acquired system, sometimes before and sometimes after the utterance is produced. In other words, production is based on what is "picked up" through communication, with the Monitor altering production to improve accuracy toward target language norms (Krashen, no date a).

It should be noted that self-correction does not come only from what has been "learned". The acquisition process also monitors performance–– e.g., when native speakers self-correct in their first language. Krashen seems to distinguish monitoring with a small "m" (which occurs in both acquisition and learning) and the use of the Monitor (which occurs only in learning). His statements on this point, however, are contradictory (Krashen, 1977b, 1977c, 1978a, 1978b; Krashen, Butler, Birnbaum & Robertson, forthcoming).

To summarize, Krashen argues that two processes are involved in L2 performance. The first, acquisition, accounts for the subjective "feel" that one has that something is right or wrong; the second, learning, accounts for the fact that we can consciously call to mind rules that we use in monitoring our speech production. The utility of the model, Krashen maintains, is that it provides a non-*ad hoc* account of a variety of phenomena in L2 performance.

The problem of falsifiability

Table 2 lists the areas that Krashen has identified as providing support for the Monitor Model. Extensive discussions of the evidence can be found in Krashen (1977b, 1977c, no date a). Elsewhere I have presented a detailed critique of this research as well as the outline of an

Table 2. *Evidence Supporting the Monitor Model*

1. Morpheme Studies:
   "Natural order" of difficulty in Monitor-free conditions (acquisition)
   "Natural order" disrupted by the Monitor (learning)

2. Aptitude and Attitude Tests:
   Aptitude and attitude tests statistically independent
   Aptitude shows strong relationship to L2 proficiency in "monitored" test situations
   Attitude shows strong relationship to L2 proficiency when sufficient intake and when Monitor-free measures are used

3. A "Feel" for Grammaticality:
   Adult judgments of grammaticality show more "rule" judgments for "easier" items
   More "feel" judgments for "harder" items

4. Individual Differences:
   Evidence of different users of the Monitor: optimal, over-users, under-users

5. Interference Phenomena:
   Structures acquired earliest also show L1 influence
   Interference less common in naturalistic--acquisition-rich--settings
   More interference in classroom--acquisition-poor--settings

6. Adult-Child Differences:
   Conscious learning not a strong predictor of L2 success in children
   Attitudinal factors predict children's success

7. Other Forms of Post-Critical Period Learning:
   Tennis is acquired, not learned

alternate approach that I believe will be more open to empirical scrutiny (McLaughlin, forthcoming).

It is my conviction that the Monitor Model, for all its intuitive appeal, fails as a theory because it is not empirically falsifiable. The acquisition-learning distinction rests, ultimately, on whether the processes involved are "conscious" (as in learning) or "subconscious" (as in acquisition). Krashen does not attempt to define conscious or subconscious. He does, however, operationally identify conscious learning with judgments of grammaticality based on "rule" and subconscious acquisition with judgments based on "feel" (Krashen, Butler, Birnbaum & Robertson, forthcoming). The difficulty with such an approach is that it is impossible to know whether subjects are actually operating on the basis of "rule" or "feel". Krashen and his associates had subjects state the rule when they made judgments on the basis of "rule", but the subjects may have done so because the demand characteristics of the situation stressed rule articulation. Moreover, subjects may have given "feel" answers because they were not sure as to how to articulate the rule on the basis of which they had operated.

Introspectively at least, it seems that we initially approach a task such as learning a second language, deliberately and consciously. Krashen (1977c) argues that this is not the case. Since there are a limited number of grammatical rules, he believes adults must acquire some items (without rules) right from the start. It may be, however, that they initially work with L1 and the rules of L2, as Krashen elsewhere (1977a, no date b) seems to imply.

The question of which comes first, learning or acquisition, like the question of the use of "rule" or "feel" in judgments of grammaticality, cannot be resolved in these terms. Arguments on either side depend on subjective, introspective, and anecdotal evidence. I would suggest another distinction––one that is more empirically based and ties into a general theory of human information processing. This is the distinction between "controlled" and "automatic" processing (Schneider & Shiffrin, 1977; Shiffrin & Schneider, 1977). The advantage of this distinction is that it enables one to avoid disputes about "conscious" or "subconscious" experience, since the controlled-automatic distinction is based on behavioral acts, not on inner states of consciousness.

If memory is viewed as a large and permanent collection of nodes that becomes increasingly interassociated through learning, we may think of two different types of storage: (a) the long-term store where most of the nodes are passive and inactive, and (b) the short-term store of currently activated nodes. A *controlled process* is a temporary sequence of nodes activated by the individual utilizing short-term store. Because active attention is required, only one such sequence may be controlled at a time without interference. Controlled processes are therefore tightly capacity-limited, but capacity limitiations are balanced by the ease with which such processes can be set up, modified, and applied to new situations.

Two features of controlled processes are especially relevant to our discussion. First, not all controlled processes are available to conscious perception. Many are not because they take place so quickly. Second, controlled processes regulate the flow of information between short-term and long-term store. Since learning is the transfer of information to long-term store, controlled processes are seen to underlie learning.

An *automatic process* is defined as a sequence of nodes that nearly always becomes active in response to a particular input configuration and that is activated without the necessity of active control or attention by the individual. Since automatic processes utilize a relatively permanent set of associative connections in long-term store, most automatic processes require an appreciable amount of time to develop fully. Once learned, an automatic process is difficult to suppress or alter.

Automatic processes are learned following the earlier use of controlled processes. Once established, they allow controlled processes to be allocated to higher levels of processing. In L2 learning, for example, the initial stage will require moment-to-moment decisions, and controlled processes will be adopted and used to perform accurately, though slowly. As the situation becomes more familiar, always requiring the same sequence of processing operations, automatic processes will develop, attention demands will be eased, and other controlled operations can be carried out in parallel with the automatic processes as performance improves. In other words, controlled processes lay down the "stepping stones" for automatic processing as the learner moves from simple to more and more difficult levels (Shiffrin & Schneider, 1977).

At this point I would like to return to the evidence listed on Table 2 as supporting the Monitor Model. I contend that much of the evidence Krashen has presented is not evidence at all in any formal sense. What Krashen has done is simply to show that one can talk about certain phenomena in terms of the acquisition-learning distinction. There may, however, be other ways of talking about these phenomena that are equally valid and more parsimonious.

For example, the argument that adults experience a "feel" for grammaticality (Table 2, number 3) rests on rather questionable empirical grounds. The data rely on introspective reports that are contaminated by instructions that require subjects who said they were operating by "rule" to specify the rule they used (Krashen et al., forthcoming). It is not too surprising that there were fewer "rule" judgments and more "feel" judgments for the "harder" items under these conditions. What the study indicates is that it is possible to induce subjects to say they operate on the basis of "feel," especially with more complex items where the rules are more difficult to articulate.

A more objective approach to the question of grammatical judgments is possible using the automatic-controlled processing distinction. Some grammatical judgments—presumably those that are not yet mastered—involve controlled processes, whereas others are so well established that they involve automatic processes. Operationally, this could be tested by using reaction time measures, for example, since controlled processes require more time than automatic processes.

The argument regarding individual differences (Table 2, number 4) can be viewed in the same terms. Rather than saying that some individuals are optimal, some under-, and some over-users of the Monitor, one could say that people vary in the extent to which they use controlled processes in L2 learning. Other sources of individual differences are the different strategies language learners employ in their L2 performance. Thus, adult-child differences (Table 2, number 6) can be accounted for in terms of the strategies adults employ (focus on vocabulary and the use of formal rules), and personality and social factors (inhibition, ties to reference groups, motivation, etc.).

Krashen also argues that other forms of post-critical period learning can be accounted for on the basis of the Monitor Model (Table 2, number 7). In tennis, for example, performance is seen to reach the point where subconscious acquisition becomes more important than consciously learned rules. But again, there is no way of knowing when such a point is reached without appeal to subjective experience. It seems better to me to speak of controlled processes becoming automatic as they are practiced and committed to long-term store. As I argued earlier, the advantage of this approach is that the focus is on the behavioral processes themselves and not on conscious or subconscious experience.

There are three areas that Krashen has given special attention to in building a case for the Monitor Model. The first of these is research on morpheme accuracy (Table 2, number 1). Krashen claims that under "Monitor-free" conditions a "natural order" of difficulty is obtained in L2 performance. This he regards as the product of acquisition. When conditions are such that the Monitor operates, the natural order is disrupted. This Krashen sees to be the product of learning.

Aside from the circularity of this argument, there is the question of what conditions lead to Monitor use. Apparently, in order to bring out conscious grammar, one needs to give subjects time, inform them that a potential error exists, and indicate where the error may be (Krashen, 1977c). Yet even when these conditions appear to be present, inconsistent results are obtained (Fuller, forthcoming; Krashen, Sferlazza, Feldman & Fathman, 1976).

What the research indicates is that adult L2 learners generally produce a definite order of morpheme difficulty. It has been suggested that this order relates to the frequency of the morphemes in the speech heard by L2 learners (Larsen-Freeman, 1976). It may be that this order is disrupted under conditions that focus the subject's attention on rules of grammar, but we are not sure precisely what these conditions are and, in any event, it does not seem necessary to invoke a Monitor to account for this finding. It is enough to say that the task demands may be such as to alter "normal" response tendencies. It could be that most conditions tap learning, but that individual differences in performance become more prominent when the task requires grammatical accuracy of a particular sort.

A second area given special attention is the distinction between aptitude and attitude. Krashen argues that the statistical independence of aptitude and attitude tests indicates that two different processes are involved in performance in L2 (Table 2, number 2). Aptitude is seen to be related to learning and the conscious use of the Monitor. Attitude is seen to be related to acquisition and "Monitor-free" performance.

The distinction is no doubt an important one. Krashen (no date a) has argued that the classroom should mimic as much as possible the "natural" setting so that learners are exposed to meaningful input. I have also advocated more emphasis upon a communication model in classroom teaching and less emphasis on formal rules and error correction (McLaughlin, 1978a). Too often classroom instruction is oriented toward reading skills and linguistic manipulation, in spite of the fact that many learners want to be able to communicate in the language. I think it suffices to say that there are two different tasks involved, one oriented toward formal rules and the other oriented toward meaningful communication. Since the tasks are different, it is not surprising that different tests correlate with the different tasks.

Finally, Krashen cites certain findings concerning interference as "evidence" for the Monitor Model (Table 2, number 5). Since the model postulates that utterances are initiated through the acquired system, Krashen sees L1 as providing a substitute utterance initiator when competence in L2 is lacking. This is the case early in the learning process, and so more transfer errors occur in the initial stages (Krashen, 1977c). It seems, however, that early sentences can also be produced, by using the Monitor to alter the surface structure and word order of L2 vocabulary (Krashen, 1977b). It is not clear what the consequences for interference are in this case. Nor is it clear whether the model is meant to be applied to early sentences (Krashen, 1975).

Researchers have indeed found more interference in classroom than in naturalistic settings (McLaughlin, 1978b). It is not clear to me why the

Monitor Model predicts this. Why is it that the use of the Monitor leads to interference? Cannot interference occur in the acquisition process as well? The theory says nothing about this and consequently all attempts to explain interference phenomena in these terms are *ad hoc.*

Conclusion

I believe that the Monitor Model does have a basis in subjective experience, but I do not believe that subjective experience should be the testing ground for a theory of language processing. Krashen has called our attention to certain interesting phenomena––especially to the finding that the same order of difficulty is found for certain English morphemes in L2 learners regardless of age, primary language, or experience with English. His pedagogical advice––that classroom instruction should be oriented more toward communication and less toward formal rules and error correction––is doubtless well taken.

Yet his model fails, I believe, because its empirical underpinnings are weak. The evidence he cites is often not evidence at all or can be explained more parsimoniously in other terms. I am particularly uncomfortable with the learning-acquisition distinction, since this distinction rests ultimately on whether the processes involved are conscious or subconscious. Furthermore, Krashen does not provide any evidence at all for the main hypothesis of the model––that what is learned is not available for initiating utterances, but that only what is acquired can be used for this purpose.

I believe that a more successful model is one that avoids recourse to conscious or subconscious experience and that ties into human information processing generally and the literature on language development. Elsewhere (McLaughlin, forthcoming) I have proposed such a theory, arguing that its advantage over the Monitor Model is that it is empirically falsifiable. Whether the theory will succeed in generating fruitful hypotheses and research on speech processing operations remains to be seen. At present, unfortunately, there is no adequate theory to guide research on processing language. We remain in a night in which all cows are black. The effort to develop an empirically grounded theory would seem to be one of the most important tasks facing investigators concerned with speech processing.

PAUL MEARA

Probe latencies, foreign languages and foreign language learners

This paper describes some work that makes use of an experimental technique which is not directly relevant to pausing or hesitation phenomena. It does, however, relate temporal and syntactic variables, and the work I shall describe raises some important questions for Pausology. The paper first describes the technique, then discusses the results of some experiments in which I attempted to use the technique with speakers of Spanish. Finally I shall discuss some of the implications of these results for Pausology.

The probe latency technique was first used by Suci, Ammon & Gamlin (1967). They presented their subjects with a series of simple English sentences, and after each sentence a single probe word was presented. The probe word was always one which had occurred in the preceding sentence, and the subject's task was to respond as quickly as possible with the word in the sentence that immediately followed the probe word. Given for example a sentence such as (1)

(1) The traffic was very noisy.

followed by a probe word *traffic,* the subject's task is to respond by supplying the word *was.* The main variable of interest is the latency of this response, that is how long it takes the subject to produce the right answer. S, A & G's experiment compared the latency patterns produced to two types of sentence, matched for length, but differing in their syn-

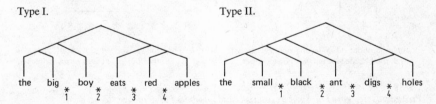

Figure 1. *Syntactic structures of the two sentence types used by S, A & G.*
Probed positions are indicated by asterisks and numbered in sequence.

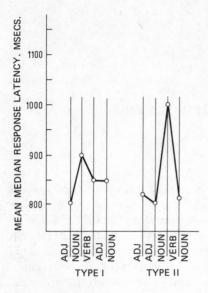

Figure 2. *Mean median latencies for two sentence types.*

tactic structure. The sentences were six words long, and for each sentence type, four probe positions were tested, each position being probed four times in the two sentence types. (The experiment also tested latencies produced by other materials, but these are not relevant to this discussion.) The two sentence types used in the experiment, and the syntactic structures ascribed to them by S, A & G are shown in Figure 1.

The details of S, A & G's syntactic analysis are not important. The main point to note is that the two sentence types differ in the position of their major constituent boundary (MCB). In type I sentences the MCB occurs

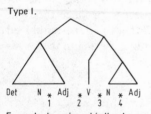

Type I.

Example: la mujer rubia llevaba zapatos negros.
i.e. the blonde woman wore black shoes.

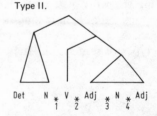

Type II.

Example: el turista dejó dos maletas pesadas.
i.e. the tourist left two heavy suitcases.

Figure 3. *Sentences used in Experiment 1:*
Probed positions are indicated by asterisks and numbered in sequence.

Det = Determiner   *N* = Noun
Adj = Adjective   *V* = Verb

in probe position 2, while in type II sentences the MCB falls at the third probe position. The results of the experiment are shown in Figure 2.

The results show clearly that the latency patterns produced by the two sentence types are not identical, and that the difference can be explained in terms of the syntactic structure of the sentences. The longest latencies are found in the probe position that corresponds to the major constituent boundary, position 2 for the type I sentences, and position 3 for the type II sentences.

My own interest in the probe latency technique arose out of some work I had been doing with foreign language learners. This work had led me to investigate the idea that learners might be responding to stimuli in the foreign language as if they were composed of unstructured lists of words rather than syntactically structured sequences, and that inappropriate processing strategies of this sort could account for a large part of learners' difficulties in handling material in the foreign language. The relevance of the probe latency technique to this question will be obvious: if learners respond to sentences as if they were unstructured lists, then the latency patterns they produce to sentences of differing syntactic structure should be identical, and learners should fail to distinguish be-

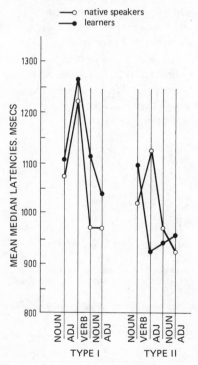

Figure 4. *Mean median latencies for two sentence types. Experiment 1.*

tween sentence types that are readily distinguished in this way by native speakers.

The first experiment I did to test this idea used a group of native Spanish speaking subjects and a group of native English speakers learning Spanish. The material consisted of two sentence types (in Spanish) which corresponded as closely as possible to the original sentences used by S, A & G. These sentence types are illustrated in Figure 3. In these sentences the MCB lies at probe position 2 for type I and in probe position 1 for the type II sentences.

The main differences between theses sentences and S, A & G's stimuli are the position of the Adjectives. In Spanish, Adjectives usually follow the Noun they modify, and this rules out the Adjective Adjective Noun sequences used by S, A & G in their type II sentences. Instead, my type II sentences contained Object Noun Phrases consisting of an Adjective Noun Adjective sequence. All other Adjectives followed their Nouns. The other main difference lies in the use of polysyllabic words in place of the monosyllables used by S, A & G. Monosyllables are relatively rare in Spanish. The sentences were presented auditorily, and the probes were presented visually. (This cross-modal form of presentation is a standard variation which is claimed to produce slightly larger effects than when the sentences and probes are both presented in the same medium.) The results of this experiment, shown in Figure 4, were surprising.

The native speaker group failed to discriminate between the two sentence types, and showed instead a marked serial position effect. The learners on the other hand, showed a significant interaction between probe position and sentence type which corresponded exactly with what had been expected of the native speakers. Their latencies were long at the MCB and shorter at the within constituent probe positions.

Type I.

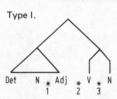

Det   N $_*$ Adj $_*$ V $_*$ N
         1   2   3

Example: el obrero cansado bebía cerveza.
     i.e. the tired workman was drinking beer.

Type II.

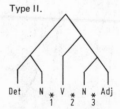

Det   N $_*$ V $_*$ N $_*$ Adj
         1   2   3

Example: La mujer llevaba zapatos negros.
     i.e. the woman was wearing black shoes.

Figure 5. *Sentences used in Experiment 2. Probed positions are indicated by asterisks and numbered in sequence.*

Det = Determiner   *N* = Noun
Adj = Adjective   *V* = Verb

Clearly some explanation of these results, which ran completely counter to what had been expected, was needed. The simplest explanation was that there was something odd about the stimulus sentences. The type II sentences, where the results of the native speakers bore no relationship to the syntactic structure were all characterized by long final Noun Phrases. It was possible that these might be distorting the native speaker results, in that only a small number of Adjectives can appear in initial position in a Noun Phrase. These are mainly numerals and demonstratives, all sets containing a limited number of items, and it was possible that latencies might be affected by having to respond with a member of such a closed set. A further experiment was therefore designed which ruled out this possibility. The sentences used in this second experiment are shown in Figure 5.

These sentence types are shorter than those used in the preceding experiment. They contain only three probe positions, and minimal variations in syntactic structure. In all other respects the procedure in this experiment was the same as in the preceding one.

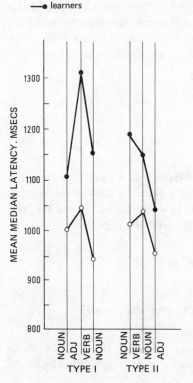

Figure 6. *Mean median latencies for two sentence types. Experiment 2.*

The results of the experiment appear in Figure 6. Once again the native speakers failed to produce any significant difference between the sentence types, while the learner group produced latency patterns that correspond with the pattern predicted by the syntax of the sentences, and produce a significant interaction between probe position and sentence type.

I have no convincing explanation of these findings. There is, however, one possible explanation which deserves some serious consideration. We often assume that experimental results derived from work on English are generalizable to other languages. But there is, of course, no reason why this should be the case, and it is possible that syntactic factors might play a much reduced role in some languages, and that speakers of these languages might rely less heavily on the syntax of their language than speakers of English apparently do. At first glance, it might seem strange to suggest that the grammars of English and Spanish are sufficiently unlike for such a large difference to emerge. There are, however, two rather important differences between the two languages. Firstly, Spanish word order is considerably more flexible than English word order. In particular, though the canonical word order in Spanish is Subject Verb Object (SVO), it is quite frequently the case that the Subject and the Verb are transposed to produce VSO word order. This is a change which is permissible both in speech and writing, and which does not seem to be limited to a small range of registers. Some examples are given below:

(2) Mi padre compró un coche nuevo.
(3) Compró mi padre un coche nuevo.
i.e. My father bought a new car.
(4) La niña empezó a llorar.
(5) Empezó la niña a llorar.
i.e. The little girl began to cry.

The second major difference between Spanish and English is that it is usual in Spanish to omit Pronoun Subjects. So (6) would be the normal unmarked form in Spanish, rather than (7) which is heavily marked and would normally be used only in contrastive contexts like (8).

(6) Compró un coche nuevo.
i.e. He bought a new car.
(7) Él compró un coche nuevo.
i.e. *He* bought a new car.
(8) Ella no tenía dinero, pero él compró un coche nuevo.
i.e. She had no money, but he bought a new car.

The effect of both these differences is to reduce the importance of the major constituent boundary as a feature of sentence structure in Spanish.

In the first case, the MCB is lost as the VP constituent is interrupted by the interpolation of the Subject NP between the V and the Object NP. In the second case too the MCB is lost simply because there is no overt Subject NP, and the sentence consists of a lone VP. All this means that the sequencing of Nouns and Verbs in Spanish is much less reliable as a clue to the syntactic relationships between them than is the case in English, and under these circumstances it seems plausible to suggest that the psychological importance of MCB's will be much reduced in Spanish. This suggestion is further supported by another difference between Spanish and English. In the former language, Verbs carry inflectional endings which change not only to indicate tense, but also to show various characteristics of the Subject Noun Phrase. Such inflections are rare in English, and again would lead one to expect closer psychological links between the Subject NP and its Verb in Spanish, and a further reduction in the importance of the MCB.

The relevance of this discussion to the study of pauses and hesitation phenomena will be apparent. The greater part of this work has been carried out in English, or in closely related languages such as German and French. Speakers of languages which are markedly different from English have scarcely been studied at all. This is a pity, because it is quite likely that pausing and hesitation patterns in these languages could be quite different from those found in English.

Some simple examples should suffice to make this clear. Boomer (1965) claims that many pauses occur after the first word of a clause in English – i.e. after an initial determiner and before the first Noun. In Rumanian, and some other languages, determiners follow their Nouns instead of preceding them, and it seems plausible to imagine that this would lead to quite different pausing patterns in Rumanian. What happens in languages which do not habitually use determiners at all? I have already mentioned the VSO patterning which is found in some Spanish sentences, but many languages have this pattern as their predominating word order. Here again it seems plausible to suppose that the occurrence of a Verb as the first item of most clauses might lead to pausal patterns that differed from those of SVO languages, and the same considerations apply to the other major language type, SOV languages like Japanese. The limited use made in English of inflections might also be expected to influence pausing and hesitation patterns. Inflections play a much more important role in other languages. In Turkish, for instance, a single lexical root can be followed by a whole series of inflectional elements, which change their form depending on the form of the Noun they accompany. It seems likely that linguistic patterns of this sort could have psychological analogues which are not at all comparable with those found in English speakers.

The general point to be made then, is this. There is a strong tendency for psycholinguistics to work within a framework which is defined almost wholly in terms of English. It is important for us to bear in mind that English is not the only language in the world, and that other languages are in some respects radically different from English. Theories derived on the basis of experimental work in English need to be systematically tested against other languages, as it is only in this way that a truly universal psycholinguistics can ever be achieved.

FRANÇOIS GROSJEAN

Comparative studies of temporal variables in spoken and sign languages: A short review[1]

It is only in the last few years that researchers interested in temporal variables have turned to study language in the manual-visual modality: the sign language of the deaf. After a first generation of studies that examined the temporal variables of individual spoken languages (for example, Goldman-Eisler, 1968; Maclay & Osgood, 1959; Blankenship & Kay, 1964 etc.), a good deal of current research is aimed at comparing these variables across spoken languages (Grosjean & Deschamps 1972, 1973, 1975; O'Connell & Kowal, 1972b; Barik, 1977, etc.). This research is developing at a rapid rate and researchers are already starting to uncover those aspects of temporal variables that are language specific and those common to several languages. For example, Grosjean & Deschamps (1975) compared English and French interviews and found that the pause time ratio in the two languages is almost identical (15.5% in French and 16.8% in English) but that this equal pause time is organized differently in the two languages: there are fewer but longer pauses in French whereas in English pauses are more numerous but shorter. Grosjean & Deschamps (1975) accounted for this by showing that speakers of English make use of a pause slot situated inside the VP which speakers of French do not use (23% of all pauses in English were located inside the VP as compared to 9% in French). As more pauses occur in English, the pauses themselves will be shorter and thus the two languages share identical pause times. We can postulate from this that spoken utterances in different oral languages will probably have identical pause time ratios (when such variables as age, sex, linguistic task, situation, etc. are controlled) but that each language will distribute the pause time in such a way that it reflects the linguistic structure of the language.

Grosjean & Deschamps (1975) uncovered another characteristic of temporal variables which is common to English and French and may extend to other oral languages. They found that the grand total of filled pauses *and* drawls was identical in the two languages but that speakers of French produced almost as many drawls as filled pauses whereas English speakers inserted many more filled pauses than drawls. This they explained by the fact that French is largely an open syllable language and speakers are free to lengthen mono- and polysyllabic words when they feel the need to hesitate whereas English is a closed syllable language and speakers must therefore use filled pauses in preference to drawls. Grosjean & Deschamps (1975) conclude that drawls and filled pauses probably have the same hesitation function and that the phonotactic configuration of the different oral languages will lead speakers to use one form of hesitation over another.

Cross-linguistic research on temporal variables is being pursued actively but most researchers have so far limited their comparisons to oral languages that usually belong to the Indo-European group. It is only by extending this comparison to languages in another modality – the manual-visual modality – that truly universal factors will be uncovered. Such languages are the sign languages of the deaf. One of these languages, the sign language used by deaf communities in the United States since the 19th century, known as American Sign Language (ASL), has recently become the object of systematic research by linguists and psychologists (Battison, 1978; Bellugi & Fischer, 1972; Frishberg, 1975; Grosjean & Lane, 1977; Stokoe, 1960; Woodward, 1974). They have shown that the beliefs surrounding sign language (it is a universal language, it is based on spoken languages, it is iconic, it is concrete etc.) are in no way founded. American Sign Language, which should be distinguished from fingerspelling, a visual representation of the English alphabet, is a systematic natural form of symbolical communication among a stable community of users. It has the degree of regularity and structure required of a fully developed language and is not some form of English on the hands. ASL is a different language with different structural principles. For example, a sign in ASL is composed of at least four distinct parameters: shape of the hand, location of the hand, orientation of the palm and movement of the hand. To illustrate this, the sign for the concept GIRL is made with the hand in a fist, the thumb tip brushing down the lower cheek. Experimental evidence that these parameters are perceptually real for signers was obtained in a short-term memory study for signs by Bellugi, Klima & Siple (1975); they showed that a significant number of errors were formational rather than semantic confusions. That the structure of ASL is influenced by the visual mode of the language is intriguing for researchers who are interested in how deeply language structures are rooted in the human being – as deeply as the cognitive structures and processes of the human mind or as superficially as the mode in which the language is communicated.

In the following paper we will present a short review of the studies that have compared temporal variables in English and American Sign Language.

1. Temporal variables at normal rate

Production rate is very different in sign and speech. Grosjean (1979) reports that a speaker produces 2.77 words in the time it takes a signer to produce only one sign (the global physical rates obtained from 5 speakers and 5 signers reading the Goldilocks passage in their native languages were 224 words per minute and 81 signs per minute respectively). But this difference in rate has no effect on the number of propositions per minute produced by speakers and signers. Bellugi & Fischer (1972) found that the length of time per underlying proposition for the two modes was identical. They explained this by the fact that sign language is highly inflected and that it makes considerable use of space and of bodily and facial shifts. What can be expressed in one sign may often take two or three words in English. From this one can postulate that all languages (oral or visual) will be characterized by the same rate of information output if such aspects as age of speaker, linguistic task, situation etc. are controlled.

A second difference between sign and speech is that signers spend more time articulating than do speakers: the articulation time ratio, i.e. the articulation time divided by the total speaking time, is about 88% in sign and 78% in speech (these are averages across the Bellugi & Fischer (1972) and Grosjean (1979) studies). Also, signers articulate more slowly: an average of 1.94 signs per second as opposed to 4.57 words per second. What is interesting however, is that the durational structure of units in sign are influenced by factors which also affect articulation time in speech (Klatt, 1976). The first is production rate. As signing rate was increased in the study conducted by Grosjean (1979), the duration of signs decreased. At a rate of 176 signs per minute, the mean duration of signs was 0.16 sec. As signing rate was decreased, signs were increased in duration: the mean duration of signs at 35 spm was 0.79 sec. Second, the semantic novelty of a sign affects its duration. Signs which occur twice in the same syntactic position are on the average 10% shorter on the second occurrence. Third, signs, like words, are influenced by phrase structure lengthening. It was found that signs at the end of a sentence (as defined empirically by Grosjean & Lane, 1977) are about 12% longer than within sentences.

American Sign Language is characterized by different types of juncture pauses. Covington (1973) lists four different junctures: the internal open juncture which occurs between signs; the single bar juncture which occurs within utterances and during which the hands are held in the position and often the configuration of the last sign (this is by far the most common juncture); the double-bar juncture which occurs within or at the end of an utterance and which marks all questions in ASL and finally, the double-cross juncture which occurs at the end of an utterance and during which the hands move from the active to a rest position. Covington writes, "The functions of the four junctures of ASL closely, though not completely, parallel those of the four junctures of English." As we will see in section 3, this does indeed seem to be the case, but pauses in sign are usually much shorter than in English. Grosjean (1979), who analyzed thè most frequent type of pause in sign – Covington's single bar juncture – reports a mean pause duration of 0.20 sec for sign and 0.46 sec for speech. Thus the small pause time ratio in sign is primarily due to the shorter pauses and not to the smaller number of pauses, which Grosjean (1979) found to be as numerous as in English. An interesting characteristic of all the sign pauses that do not fall into the utterance final category is that the sign preceding the pause remains visible during the pause. As we have just seen, a pause in sign is the momentary cessation of signing with the hands remaining in their signing configuration. This, of course, is very different from what happens in speech where the silence of a pause, taken in isolation, retains no information about the preceding word(s).

Very little is known about hesitation phenomena in sign. No systematic study has examined the sign equivalents of filled pauses, drawls, repeats and false starts. It has been reported that gaze aversion, body shift, raising of the eyebrows are marks of hesitancy in sign, and Bellugi & Fischer (1972) write, "We have seen deaf people hold one hand in a neutral position and wiggle the fingers; perhaps this is one equivalent to 'umm'". Sign informants report that repeats and false starts do seem to occur in sign, but in general hesitation phenomena in this language is in great need of systematic investigation. The findings will help us determine which aspects of hesitation phenomena are modality specific and which are common to all modalities.

2. Temporal variables and change of rate

Grosjean (1979) studied how signers and speakers modulate the component variables of rate (articulation rate, number and length of pauses) when they change their global production rate (signs or words per minute). He found that both signers and speakers cover an identical range of rates when asked to speed up or slow down (signers covered a 2.6:1 range in rate and speakers a 2.7:1 range). In addition, Grosjean reports that signers alter their production rate mainly by modifying their articulation rate and changing their pause time much less. Speakers, on the other hand, primarily change the pause time when asked to speed up or slow down and hardly alter the articulation rate. In addition, when a signer alters his pause time, however little he does so when modifying his physical rate, he alters both the number and length of pauses to the same extent whereas a speaker hardly changes the duration of his pauses and primarily alters the number of pauses. These different strategies were accounted for by the role played by breathing in sign and speech. As signing is an activity that is independent of breathing (Grosjean, 1979), signers will alter their rate mainly by changing the time they spend articulating whereas speakers, especially at slow rate, are compelled by breathing demands to put numerous pauses into their speech and must therefore use this approach to alter their rate. At slow rate, speakers only have enough air to articulate a few words; when this is used up, they must stop articulating and inhale in order to continue articulating. This interaction between breathing and speech also explains why it is that speakers increase and decrease their pause time by altering the number of pauses and leaving the pause durations relatively constant. Inhalation can only take place during the pauses and must be of a minimum duration. As pause durations cannot be compressed beyond a certain point, a speaker will compensate for this by pausing less often but keeping the duration of pauses relatively constant. A signer is not faced with the same constraints and can therefore increase or decrease his pause time, however little he does so, by altering the number and the length of the pauses equally. Were breathing not linked to speech in such a way, we would expect speakers to follow the same strategy as signers when altering their production rate.

3. Distribution of pauses in sign and speech

Grosjean & Lane (1977) found that in sign, as in speech, to a hierarchy of pause frequency and duration corresponds a hierarchy of constituents. The duration of pauses in ASL indicate not only the breaks between simple sentences and between conjoined sentences but also the boundaries between and within the major constituents of these sentences. The grand mean duration of pauses between sentences was 229 msec; between conjoined sentences, 134 msec; between the NP and VP, 106 msec; within the NP, 6; and within the VP, 11 msec. The higher the syntactic order of the break, the longer the pause that occurred at the break.

What is interesting is that when the data are not averaged across sentences, a number of mismatches are found between the constituent structure of the sentence and the pause durations. Grosjean, Grosjean & Lane (1979), (as reported in this volume by Grosjean), first discovered this in a study on speech. They showed that the surface structure of a sentence was a good predictor of the pause data only when sentences and constituents were of equal length. The mismatches that occurred between pause duration and the structural complexity index were due primarily to Ss' concurrent tendency to distribute pauses so as to bisect the sentences and constituents. When constituents are of unequal length, Ss will attempt to displace the pause to a point midway between the beginning of the first constituent (for example, an NP) and the end of the second constituent (for example, a VP), if at that point there occurs a syntactic boundary important enough. It would seem that a compromise takes place between this bisection tendency and the linguistic structure of the sentence. They developed a model to assign to each word boundary in a sentence a predicted share of the total pause duration in light of its structural complexity and its distance from the bisection point. The model accounted for 72% of the total variance in pause time as compared to 56% accounted for by the complexity index alone.

The question for sign now became: does a formal model of syntactic structure alone account for the experimental data obtained from pausing (Grosjean & Lane, 1977), or does the signer, like the speaker, need to make a compromise between two, sometimes conflicting, demands: the need to respect the linguistic structure of the sentence and the need to balance the length of the constituents in the output. Grosjean, Grosjean & Lane (1979) found that their model of performance pause structure in speech predicted the Grosjean & Lane (1977) pause values in sign better than the ASL linguistic structure itself. All sentences five signs or longer were taken from the experimental sign passage and their pause durations in signing were correlated with the complexity indices of the linguistic structure and with values predicted by the performance model. The model was a better predictor than the complexity indices by themselves: $r = 0.85$ as compared to 0.78. Thus signers, like speakers, make a compromise between the need to respect the linguistic structure of the sentence and the need to balance the length of the constituents in the output. Performance structures would therefore be founded in the encoding and decoding of language (be it visual or oral) and not in the properties of any particular communication modality.

It is our hope that researchers interested in cross-linguistic studies of temporal variables will not limit themselves to spoken languages but will take into account all languages – oral and visual. In this way truly universal aspects of temporal variables will be uncovered and accounted for.

Note

1. The writing of this paper was supported in part by grant numbers 768 2530, National Science Foundation, and RR 07143, Department of Health, Education and Welfare.

ROBERT J. DI PIETRO

Verbal strategies: A neglected dimension in language acquisition studies

"Grau, teurer Freund, ist alle Theorie,
Und grün des Lebens goldner Baum."
(Goethe's Faust)

We linguists sometimes suffer from what might be called the philosopher's syndrome. This syndrome is characterized by the formulation of theories about phenomena for which there may not be data. Our competence-orientation directs us first to look inward for explanations of language and then use our speculations to arrange the data of actual speech performance which we subsequently collect. Rationalism abounds in our field and we tend to blur the distinction between theories held about languages and the grammars written of them. The tacit assumption that the rules of grammar should contain all that is significant about a language has influenced much of our work in first and second language acquisition during the last two decades. Many psycholinguists believe that children learn their first language by acquiring rules of increasing complexity as they grow older. Little work has been done on how the child uses his own initiative in creating language form. Instead, the psycholinguist assumes the stance of a spectator who is observing how the child manifests an inevitable and predetermined skill.

Oftentimes, the same attitude is assumed in making postulations about second-language acquisition. If children "acquire rules" in a logical progression, so must learners of a second language acquire the rules of the target language in a comparable way. Some investigators, such as Dulay & Burt (1978), find no significant differences between first and second language acquisition.

The view of language as rational grammar to be achieved has also fostered an approach to second language acquisition known as "error analysis". As recently as three years ago, Pit Corder, one of the outstanding adherents to this approach, maintained that "language learning is no different in kind from any other sort of cognitive learning" (see

Corder, 1975). In the error-analysis approach one uses a grammatical framework around which to classify the types of mistakes made by learners at various stages in the course of instruction. While error analysis makes a valiant attempt to forge a connection between language performance and linguistic competence, it remains indebted to a grammatical format. The spectre of "idealized native speaker" still overshadows error analysis. To dispell this spectre once and for all, we shall have to realize that learning a language––first or second––is *not* just another cognitive process measurable strictly in terms of some criterion of well-formedness. People are more than grammar-machines. While guided by the conventions of their grammars, humans use language to assert participation in a community of fellow beings and to communicate meanings and intentions that are important in many ways beyond exchanging factual information.

The term "verbal strategy" has been used to define how language functions in the service of the human psyche (see, for example, Di Pietro, 1976). Distinguishing between language form and language strategy leads us to formulate two aspects of linguistic competence: artifact and tool (see Di Pietro, 1970). Both aspects are critical to the realization of a full linguistic competence. However, only language as artifact can be cast in terms of grammar. The many communicative and expressive functions of language are better expressed as an inventory of strategies under the heading of "tool".

The tool aspect of language subsumes all verbal devices executed by people in relating to their environment and other people. For those devices which have become conventionalized by society, the term "speech protocol" has been reserved. These protocols include the verbalizations that mark participation in a conversation (such as starting and ending it), the many daily encounters which require passing by someone, introducing oneself to someone, and/or excusing oneself and the recognition of what Goffman (1971) has called the "rites of passage" (changing social status). For example, the speaker of English who finds it necessary to pause while searching for a word may signal his desire to "keep the floor" by repeated utterings of a mid-central vowel (written "uh"). In the Spanish spoken in Latin America, the same protocol of hesitation takes the form "este", repeated several times. In Japanese it becomes "a-no". The above examples are offered as evidence that hesitation formulae are part of the linguistic competence of speakers and are conventionalized in different ways, depending on the language.

In addition to the many other conventionalized protocols in a language such as greetings, leave-takings, and politeness forms, there are strategies which individual speakers create in a personal style. For example, the change-of-subject strategy used to avoid criticism may take any of several forms in English: (1) a direct request to change the subject ("May we change the subject?" or "Let's change the subject") or (2) changing the subject by introducing new subjects and asking the criticizing person his or her opinion about them. Prompting desired invitations or blocking undesired ones can be executed in a number of ways by the individual speaker. In the following illustration, speaker B blocks the attempt made by speaker A to join the group:

Speaker A: Where are you fellows going?
Speaker B: Actually, we're on our way to a party.
Speaker A: Oh, sorry. I'll see you some other time.

The avoidance strategy relies heavily on the word "actually". If Speaker B had omitted it, saying only "we're on our way to a party", Speaker A could have interpreted it as leading to an affirmative answer to his impending request to accompany the group. In fact, Speaker A's initial question is not merely a request for information about the destination of Speaker B and the others in the group. Speaker B interprets it correctly as a request to join and counters it. If we were to restrict our analysis of the conversation to its grammatical (i.e., artifactual) content, we would not be able to establish a continuity which would be logical. "Actually" has no grammatical antecedent in anything that Speaker A has said. By the same token, "Sorry" is not elicited by the grammatical information contained in Speaker B's line. However, if we analyze the interaction strategically, the lines are open to the following paraphrase:

Speaker A: May I join your group?
Speaker B: No, you may not.
Speaker A: I apologize for asking.

For various reasons, people do not make such direct requests as a matter of procedure. Perhaps the psychological damage would be too great.

Many new avenues of research are opened when we begin to consider the tool aspect of language. For example, do children acquire verbal strategies as part of their maturation, together with the grammatical artifact? That is to say, are verbal strategies innate? The question of innateness, as interesting as it is, will have to wait until we have investigated how children at various stages of maturation interact with those around them. The basic data of language use are still missing for each stage. The emergence of each child's *persona* is reflected in the manipulation of language as constrained by variables such as culture, sex and social status.

The adolescent American male who says to his father: "John has a really super new bike" is not just giving linguistic expression to an observation but is making a request for a similar bicycle from his father. Why does this strategy work, when it does work? Part of the answer lies in the child's framing the request in the context of his on-going role relationship with his parent. By calling the father's attention to how another father has provided a gift for another boy, the son "reminds" him of his own responsibility as a provider. The parent to whom such a strategy has been directed must now decide if the withholding of a thing desired by the child violates his role.

In discussing verbal manipulations of all kinds, it is important to distinguish the strategy from the various tactical forms it might take. The strategy illustrated above could have been executed in a number of different ways. A German colleague (Prof. Werner Hüllen of Essen) provided the following alternative tactic used by his own son:

> Son: Schade!
> Father: Was ist schade?
> Son: Daß ich kein neues Fahrrad haben kann.

In this case, the son invites the father to disagree with him. Of course, diagreement would lead to the supplying of a new bicycle by the father, unless some other counter-tactic can be found.

Changing the sex of the off-spring can bring variations on the tactical execution of the same gift-prompting strategy. The following conversation between a 8 year old girl and her father took place in French-speaking Québec:

> Daughter (looking in a store window): Tu sais, Papa, ce lion me fait penser beaucoup à toi!
> Father : Pourquoi?
> Daughter: Parce qu'il est beau et fort comme mon Papa.
> Father: Eh bien, allons acheter ce jou-jou!

It is unlikely that a similar tactic would have been employed by a male child in either English or French. This particular daughter has learned how to use her own sex difference to make her father feel well-suited in the role of male protector and provider.

Cultural constraints vary children's strategies in many ways. In Japan, for example, children are not permitted to initiate conversations with adult strangers. What happens, then, if a child strays away from his/her parents and gets lost? Children in such a difficulty do not have the prerogative of asking an adult stranger for help——unless they can be addressed first. One solution is for the lost child to begin crying. When a concerned adult asks the child what the matter is, the child is then free to speak. This strategy works because crying is not considered a use of language, even though its form can be affected by the conventions of various languages.

Laughter, especially by adults is utilized for many strategic functions. In English, there are three formal parts to the structure of laughter: the vocalic nucleus, the number of times that each segment is uttered and the intonation used. Four different vowels are employed: /a/ as in *ha,* /e/ as in *heh,* /o/ as in *ho,* and /i/ as in *hee* (or *tee*). A single *ha!* (with loud stress and rapidly falling intonation) can represent sarcastic disbelief at what has been said by another. Repeating the same segment, with loud stress on the second one (as in ha, há!) often represents a commentary like "So, I was right after all". The representation of merryment is with the segment *ho* uttered three times *(ho, ho, ho!),* which is reminiscent of Santa Claus. One of the most interesting laughter strategies is *heh, heh!* which a speaker might use in the following type of situation:

A: Hello, John! I haven't seen you in ages!
B: Well, I'm still alive and kicking, *heh, heh!*

There is something "sarcastic" about this kind of laughter to an American speaker of English. Using it is tantamount to expressing one's detachment from the seriousness of what one has said. Most speakers either ignore or have forgotten the derivation of the idiom "still alive and kicking" with its veiled allusion to an ignominious death (such as with animals kicking in the throes of death), but they continue to employ it strategically by marking it with a sarcastic laugh when they apply it to themselves.

The interdependency of laugther und language is evident when we compare laughter strategies across linguistic boundaries. For example, the *hee hee!* laugh serves as a gossipy titter in English, while a formally similar one *(shee, shee!)* is what the Japanese use for signalling the laughter of a giant or monster in a fairy tale.

The planning of a prospectus for the study of verbal strategies in language acquisition should provide for some distinction between devices employed by learners to conceptualize the grammar of the language and those used by them to interact with other people. With regard to grammar-conceptualization, second language learners, as well as children learning their first language, may utilize similar cognitive processes. For example, over-generalization can be observed in the verbalizations of both types of learners. Those learning a second language, however, also experience interference from the knowledge they already possess of the grammar of the first language. While we have no definite statistics as to the actual percentage of errors in second language learning due to interference, pedagogues would be ill-advised to ignore the first language when preparing instructional materials.

In addition to the cognitive strategies used for grammar, first and second language learners also develop tactics for enhancing interpersonal communication. Children learning their first language, for example, often use silence as a way of stimulating adults to persevere in speaking to them.

By breaking their silence in selective response to the range of verbalizations addressed to them, children invite reinforcement of those patterns of adult speech which are most favorable to them. In this way, parents can be led by children to accomodate their own speech patterns to the particular stage of cognitive development of the children. Adults learning a second language may execute a number of different strategies. One common adult acquisitional strategy is to utilize a simple predication with a negated verb in order to elicit an unknown lexeme from a native speaker. Thus, the learner may say, "It's *not* cheap", in order to elicit a response like, "Oh, you mean that it is expensive!".

Skilful second language learners also discover how to say the translational equivalent of "How do you say X in your language?" which can be used with bilingual speakers for vocabulary building. Since second language learners already possess a grammar, they become more aware than first language learners of the potential for entanglement in complex grammatical structures. For this reason, adult second language learners may ask for explanations more frequently than do first language learners.

While much more needs to be said about cognitive strategies in first and second language acquisition, we should also direct our attention to how first language and second language learners utilize language to shape a "persona" (see discussion, above). This term is a convenient one for defining the composite of interactional roles played by individual speakers through both verbal and nonverbal means. The language of the "persona" varies according to the idiosyncratic ways individuals choose to present themselves publically.

The perception by others of what interactional role is being played by an individual does not always match that individual's intentions. The term "interactional ambiguity" can be applied to the situation where a clear communicative function cannot be attached unequivocally to the language being used by a speaker. To give an illustration, the sentence "I wish to give the University a million dollars" said by a businessman to an official of a university might be received in a very different way from how it was intended. Although the speaker may have perceived his role as that of a philanthropist the would-be benefactor might be led to suspect other motives. The knowledge of past speech events involving the businessman might influence the university official's interpretation of the apparent offer being made. Disambiguation of the speaker's intentions must be achieved through information gained both by speech and the other, nonverbal channels, such as intonation and facial expression. There is every possibility that the university official will reach the wrong conclusion about the businessman's intentions. In such a case, communication may continue, but certainly not as either party perceived it.

The ideal enacting of roles in speech events depends greatly on the complementary nature of the roles. An individual who wishes to play the part of a vendor, for example, cannot do so without the cooperation of another individual who wishes to be a buyer. The language of sales transactions is marked by many verbal strategies which have become conventionalized. The salesclerk in an American department store initiates a sales transaction with an expression like "Can I help you?". The potential customer can take this cue to enter into a series of questions about the nature of the object to be purchased, e.g., "How much are these gloves?" or "Do you have size 10?". The intention of each participant to play complementary roles becomes clearer as the conversation evolves. Eventually, they arrive at a point where the actual selling and buying takes place and the interaction is ended.

There are also counterstrategies which can be used to fend off a sales routine. To the salesclerk who asks, "Can I help you?" the person entering the store may answer, "Just looking". Upon hearing this, the salesclerk may retreat and not continue further entreaties or attempt an alternative sales-pitch, such as, "Have you seen the items we have marked down?". If similar attempts at pitching a sale continue, the other person might either be converted into a buyer or invoke a number of new counterstrategies, such as, "I'll call you if I see something I like". The important thing to remember here is that speech events do not always have predictable endings.

In fact, there are even circumstances in which verbalization functions expressively rather than interactionally. As Kursh (1971) points out, the highly emotive language shouted by two persons involved in some sort of altercation has little communicative but much therapeutic value. Neither party may actually hear what the other has said but both will feel better later on for having vented their rage. "White" lies are other uses of language which intercede between speaker's intentions and physical actions which may be violent or otherwise displeasing. A secretary who tells a very angry Mr. Jones that Mr. Smith is "not in" may have saved the latter from physical harm done by the former.

The inventory of verbal strategies needed to play all interactional roles appears to be a very large one. It would include all tactics used to open, continue and conclude conversations, in addition to all the devices one needs to shape and direct discourse to personally desired ends. While much research needs to be done in order to uncover these strategies, we cannot wait to readdress the methodology of second language teaching toward communication. Already several texts to teach English as a second language have appeared which utilize a strategic approach. The course entitled *Mainline Skills* by L. G. Alexander (1976) presents both guided and unscripted dialogues enabling the students to personalize their drills and exercises. In a text called *Insight* by Donn Byrne and Susan Holden (1976), the authors provide photographs of the individuals whose conversations are represented in the lessons. This technique helps remind the students that language is spoken by "real" people for "real" purposes.

Many different classroom practices can be built around verbal strategies. For example, students can be asked to develop a particular interactional role which involves their own judgement as to the desired outcome. A problem such as how to break off an engagement, get a refund from a store, or avoid a criticism can be assigned ahead of time for enactment in class. Different students can be asked to prepare verbal material which might counter the arguments proposed by the other interactants. The class can be asked to discuss and evaluate the performance as an additional conversational exercise. Approaches known as *Community Language Learning* and *Values Clarifications* employ the concept of verbal strategy without making it an explicit goal.

A cursory survey of the coverage of second language textbooks, apart from the strategically oriented ESL texts mentioned above, would reveal very little instructional treatment of the various functions of empty and filled pauses and other paralinguistic phenomena such as laughter and whispering. The sentences given in the text as representatives of performances in the target language are almost invariably "well-formed" (i.e., generated from the body of formal rules which constitute the grammatical artifact). Such sentences are devoid of any indication of the features essential to the dynamics of conversation. Since evidence can be found that pausal phenomena are language-specific but serve essential and universal communicational functions, they cannot be omitted from a course of instruction in a second language.

Just how to teach them is yet to be determined. A start can be made, however, with samples of speech in the target language which are more realistic than the ones now given to students. Several papers given at this workshop are suggestive of ways second language materials can be developed to include strategies of conversation. Wolfgang Klein's study, for example, supplies a running text with several interactants giving and receiving street directions. Already my colleague at Georgetown University, Frederick Bosco, has built lessons around a map and a set of language structures which can be utilized by the students to explain how to get to predetermined geographical locations. While Bosco's language-teaching exercise is directed at the solving of linguistic and cognitive problems, it could be adapted to provide the base for various styles of verbal performance as uncovered by Klein. We who work in second language teaching also need the kind of information about the relationship——or lack of it——between pauses and linguistic structures coming from François Grosjean. Geoffrey Beattie's work on the organization of behavior in conversation and Mark Cook's on the correlation between gaze direction and hesitation have great implications for the articulation of new classroom modeling techniques for natural speech in a second language. Of course, all the studies reported in the contrastive analysis session by Deschamps, Raupach, Faure, Dechert, McLaughlin, and Meara are immediately applicable for the essential information they provide the methodologists about diverse behaviors in first and second language production.

For levels of second language instruction beyond the elementary one we could take a close look at the representation of pausal phenomena in the creative literature of the language. By exposing learners to examples of how an author depicts conversation, they can be given greater insights into the idealized function of the various speech strategies they are to acquire. The hesitation that Dante makes in responding to Cavalcante's anxious query about the fate of his son is an integral part of the text of the *Inferno* and adds considerably to its dramatic effect. The three letters "AOI" written at various points in the medieval French epic, *La chanson de Roland,* remain a curiosity but they may have served as response cues to the audience who were expected to show that they were attending to what was being narrated.

The implications of extending our scope of language beyond the grammatical artifact are numerous. Perhaps the greatest contribution of this workshop on Pausology lies in the view it has given us of language as an organic, highly flexible phenomenon. There can be no question that language serves more than the problem-solving functions of human reason. It is the major tool used to present ourselves to other human beings, binding us together socially and psychologically. We should return to our individual research projects refreshed by the opportunity we have had to exchange ideas about language. We should also have a new respect for the ability of language to elude total explanation, for it lies at the very heart of what Goethe called, "des Lebens goldner Baum".

Final discussion

Chairman and editor   BERNARD J. BAARS

BERNARD J. BAARS (ed.)

On the current understanding of temporal variables in speech

O'Connell/Kowal: During the past three and a half days, we have attended every session of the workshop, have engaged in dozens of discussions in addition to the sessions themselves, and have met each evening to discuss the highlights of the day. We are aware of the fact that it is an impossible task to sum up adequately and accurately the major questions and themes of the conference. Each participant brought a different background and different presuppositions to the workshop. It was our hope that the presentations and informal contacts would generate lively discussions, and the discussions have in fact surpassed our most optimistic expectations. We have asked as many of you as we were able to contact informally to help us in the formulation of this résumé and have endeavored to incorporate your many suggestions into this presentation.

We wish now to present seventeen-and-a-half theses for your consideration. They have been composed to the best of our ability from all the input we have received. There is no pride of authorship. They are presented to foster a final discussion, not to express dogma. If anyone's favorite ideas have been slighted, we apologize beforehand and request emendations, additions, and deletions.

Here are our summary theses:

Thesis 1: The use of the term *pausology* is itself problematic. It seems to connote a non-behavioral subject matter, is neologistic and may foster isolation and unwarranted autonomy. Some term is needed to delimit a discipline preoccupied with temporal dimensions of speech production.

Thesis 2: The *silent pause* stands in urgent need of a definition, both in terms of its physical reality and in terms of its function.

Thesis 3: In general, a *taxonomy of temporal phenomena* of speech production is needed as well as agreement as to inclusion among these phenomena, e.g., laughter, whisper, afterthoughts, and longer parenthetical remarks.

Thesis 4: The evidence clearly indicates that temporal aspects of speech production are *multiply determined:* e.g., by organismic speaker variables. They are also *multiply related:* e.g., to nonverbal behavioral context and prosodic and linguistic context.

Thesis 5: There is no *comprehensive theory of speech production* at this time that is derived from either general psycholinguistics or much less from pausology. Until now the complexity of speech production has not been adequately engaged, either empirically or theoretically.

Thesis 6: Thought in its relationship to speech production is clearly non-continuous and saltatory. Temporal phenomena function therefore both *retrospectively* and *prospectively, proximally* and *distally* with respect to on-going speech.

Thesis 7: *Neurophysiologically* the question of temporal aspects of speech production or the "linguistic act" can be posed as follows: How do we transform muscular representations into speech in real time? How is the speech act represented in the brain?

Thesis 8: Are there some temporal aspects of speech production which constitute *universals?*

Thesis 9: Future research will require that we become more aware of our *historical traditions,* including the mistakes of the past as well as findings.

Thesis 10: There exists an *extraordinary variety of speech genre,* ranging from highly ritualized predetermined speech to free-wheeling conversation. Generalization from one genre to another regarding temporal dimensions must be made with caution.

Thesis 11: As a young science, pausology should be open to *various methodologies* including ideographic and intuitive, experimental and observational, in order to generate and test hypotheses, develop theory and accumulate a normative date base.

Thesis 12: Agreement on the use of *units of speech production* is needed. For reading, the sentence is a noncontroversial unit. For other varieties of spontaneous speech other units have been suggested, including clause, phrase, proposition, perch, topic, idea, intonational and rhythmic units, and episodic units.

Thesis 13: There is empirical evidence for *functional equivalence* and mutual substitution between some temporal phenomena in speech production, e.g., parenthetical remarks and silent pauses.

Thesis 14: Speech production under the pressures of real time indicates some trade off between *errors* and available time.

Thesis 15: Research on temporal dimensions has concentrated for the most part on the speaker and his cognitive and affective processes. The speaker's ability to use temporal dimensions to affect the *hearer* and the hearer's ability to use this input have been neglected.

Thesis 16: Current interest in *second language learning* shows great promise for pausological research.

Thesis 17: *Prescriptive* vs. *descriptive* approaches to the study of temporal aspects of speech production, as well as *linguistic* vs. *psychological* approaches, must be balanced.

Thesis 18: And –– for your final, profound consideration:
Reden ist Silber,
Schweigen ist Gold ––
To err is human.

Baars: Shall we start with Thesis 3? "A taxonomy of temporal phenomena of speech production is needed ..."

Chafe: I understand Thesis 3 to be directed at some sort of initial taxonomy that would say, we do have laughter, and whispers, afterthoughts and so on. At least you can identify them, along with silences and filled pauses and so forth. But we should keep separate the problem of interpretation.

Deese: I think that I am the only one here who has used the term rhetoric in its traditional sense. This taxonomy could well be encompassed under the traditional category of rhetoric. We are really interested in those kinds of phenomena that are excluded from traditional grammar.

Klatt: I wonder whether we should limit ourselves to a taxonomy in terms of phonetic aspects, or whether another one in terms of functional aspects might be as useful and beneficial. Pauses and hesitations, for example, may either be disruptive to effective communication or they may be absolutely necessary to get some message across.

Chafe: Well, I think we have to keep the descriptive and functional aspects apart. As soon as we get into any kind of interpretive taxonomy, you and I are going to have all kinds of disagreements about it ––– but I think that we can fairly well agree on what is a period of silence.

Drommel: When I started to work on pauses in 1969, there was not even a reasonable literature on the problem. Now we have that, but we do not have a consistent theory of pause types which considers all linguistic and paralinguistic aspects of pauses. That, I think, should be the aim of our future work.

Baars: According to Thesis 4, "The evidence clearly indicates that temporal aspects of speech production are multiply determined." Perhaps I should say something about slips of the tongue in this respect. While I have argued that very many slips result from internal competition between speech plans, the opportunities for competition are so ubiquitous in normal speech that I could hardly disagree with this thesis. You can get competition from different items that are retrieved from memory, from stylistic differences, from changing one's mind about a speech plan in the middle of execution, and so on.

Grosjean: There are maybe 40 or 50 different variables that can create silence in speech. A silence may mark the end of a sentence, you can use it to breathe, you can use it to hesitate, there may be ten or fifteen different things happening during that silence.

Kowal: To the more linguistic perspective I would like to add the suggestion that phenomena such as this may function pragmatically as "time-savers" ——— you may use them to fill in when you aren't ready to say something.

Di Pietro: There is one that I would add and that is the interactional type of pause, the dyadic aspect.

Beattie: In social psychology there is a growing literature on the effects of various kinds of hesitations on a listener's judgments of a speaker's credibility. So perhaps we should think not just about how hesitations in speech reflect production processes, but also how they affect a listener's judgments about the speaker.

Good: A recent publication by Labov and Fanshel called "Therapeutic Discourse" goes into that issue quite a bit.

Klatt: I would like to see added to this not only the social aspect but also the personality aspect. It's worthwhile to investigate where personality variables have some impact and influence.

Ozga: I think that we can avoid talking at cross-purposes when we talk about the variables that determine pauses, by stating things clearly according to the principles of old Roman Law, which was given the following form in English: "What was the crime? Who did it? When was it done and where? How done and with what motive? Who in the deed did share?" If you state that at the beginning, you know how to specify the conditions of your data, and you can communicate with other researchers as well. Perhaps we could save time if we could start a workshop like this by stating all those things.

Pribram: I would disagree with the term "multiply determined", I think that temporal phenomena such as pauses are context-sensitive, but that is really something different. Multiple determination is a sort of vague way of talking about it, whereas context-sensitivity in computer language at least, has some very different structural connotations...

Deese: As it does in linguistic theory.

Pribram: As it does in linguistic theory, right. And it isn't just that a lot of social variables are involved, but that there must be some structure ––– neurophysiological structure that is processing it, different from, let's say, a hierarchical structure. There is a difference between just having multiple determination and being context sensitive. Context sensitivity implies a certain graph structure, a weblike graph structure which is not hierarchical, while "having a context" means simply having a class of events which is hierarchically organized.

Deese: A hierarchy is in fact context-free.

Pribram: Right.

Deese: I think that is a very important point, that "multiple determination", and "context sensitivity" are really not the same thing.

Baars: Thesis 5 points out that there is no comprehensive theory of speech production until now, and asserts that the complexity of speech production has not been adequately engaged, either empirically or theoretically.

Laver: Can I say something about this thesis? In part I just don't agree, because there is a richness of phonetic theories about all sorts of aspects of speech signals that we have not discussed here. And there have been very many other temporal variables that have been really rather well studied recently. Things like temporal coordination, for example. I wouldn't wish to say there is a comprehensive theory of speech production available, even from a phonetic view ––– if there were, then all phoneticians would be out of business. But I don't want people to leave with the impression that there isn't more available from phonetic theory.

Di Pietro: What Thesis 5 simply says is that there is no comprehensive theory, and there is no disagreement with that. There is certainly a richness of observations, of course.

Laver: Oh that's true. It also says that "the complexity of speech production has until now not been adequately engaged", and I think that the degree of engagement might be obvious in this room.

Ballmer: I think that one should plead here for a formal theory, but in a hedged sort of way. Of course there are a lot of bad things about formalism, it is used just to impress or to make a lot of fuss about. I think though that the positive aspects are just enormous. There are perhaps two important points to keep in mind when one is using formal theories. The first is that formalism should be intuitively interpretable. It should commit itself intuitively to some empirical issues. You should be able to say that that sign means that there are things out there, otherwise it is intuitively meaningless. Secondly, a formal theory should be algorithmic, in the sense that it provides a mechanism to forecast, to generate predictions. I think that this kind of theory is possible at this stage, and with this in mind we should really plead for such a theory.[1]

O'Connell: Thomas Ballmer is pointing out a place where Sabine Kowal and I have, without wanting to, biased our thesis in a way. I would welcome this addition without further ado. I found the formal approach that he presented yesterday very enlightening, even without understanding all the details.

Wildgen: There are other formal approaches besides those from traditional linguistics. We should not only consider grammar, because in the last few years I have had the impression that grammatical formalisms were not too successful in bringing in information other than traditional linguistic facts.

Pribram: I don't think that theoretical formalism adds anything in the sense of insight unless the insight has been achieved intuitively. Then you may formalize your insights, and have firm ground to stand on.

Ballmer: I think it is true that formalism up to now has not led to real new insights in linguistics. Chomsky for instance just formalized traditional grammar, in a sense. But a theory if it is really good should lead to new insights. If it doesn't do this, it's not really a formal theory. Of course, both Professor Chafe and Professor Pribram are right that theory in language has not been able to do that up to now, but of course in physics, etc., there are well-known examples.

Baars: George Miller published an article a couple of years ago called "Toward a third metaphor for psycholinguistics", in which he argued that psycholinguistics since the 1950's has gone through three stages: first, the information theoretic approach, then the transformational grammar approach, and finally, he would suggest, a computational approach. Each of these stages revolves around a metaphor for human language. I find that attractive, and I would like to pose the question in a slightly provocative way. Is it possible that computational theories should take the place of formal theories?

Chafe: No.

Ballmer: Yes.

Baars: I am glad that provoked something.

Grosjean: Can we end Thesis 5 on a more optimistic note? As John Laver has said, there has been a lot of work in different fields, beyond the very small field of speech production. So let's try to open our eyes to all the work that's been done on other phenomena in speech.

Baars: I think you are making a very good point, and I would like to add something to it. We should not really be pessimistic. If we look at progress in psycholinguistics for example, over the past ten or twenty years, it is clear that there have been failures, and some dead ends, and so on, but it is also clear, I think, that we are immensely more sophisticated today than even five or ten years ago. I think that applies both to theory and empirical methods.

Shall we go on to Thesis 6? "Thought in its relationship to speech production is clearly non-continuous and saltatory. Temporal phenomena function therefore both retrospectively and prospectively, proximally and distally with respect to on-going speech". Some comments?

Klatt: In the speech production of aphasics, the processes are tremendously stretched out, compared to the automatic and fluent speech of normal people. I don't have a rationale yet that would allow me to decide whether the pause works retrospectively or prospectively. I admit that I am really struggling with this concept and I would love to get some help to develop such a rationale. In general, pauses are not only indicative for what follows but also for what is going on in monitoring and assessing what has been produced as well.

I wonder to what degree the participants here have ever had the experience of being surprised about what you said to yourself. Speaking in a stressful situation under all kinds of constraints, speaking in a foreign language even more so, I have quite some experience with this –– and I am quite often surprised to find out what I said.

Drommel: Do you understand yourself?

Klatt: Sometimes I wonder whether others understand me. I think the point is clear. I do not know how to do the study, but I would like to do a study some time on the effects of surprise to your own speech production.

Kowal: Oh, we have done one, our very first one, and it is very obvious that your thoughts run backwards as well as forward.

Pribram: If I am right about there being a frequency encoding in the brain, then the problem of retrospective/prospective doesn't exist in the thought process *per se.* In the brain one has it all of a piece, and once again gets into these context-sensitive kinds of constructions, in which there is no backward and forward. It is only in the "write-out" and "read-out" that one has prospective and retrospective phenomena. The thought process itself is timeless, if you will.

Deese: It seems to me that the main function of consciousness is to monitor speech. I have an example from my own behavior, during my presentation on Tuesday. I was talking in the afternoon, and at one point I said "this morning" ———— I went on, and then paused, I don't know how long, and looked at my watch which was on American Eastern Standard Time. And this long pause was the result of my hearing myself say "this afternoon", and a thinking process triggered by that statement.

McLaughlin: That's an interesting example, because the thought processes questioning the earlier statement might have been going on even while you were speaking. The point is that it isn't just pauses that allow for verbal planning, but even when one speaks one is planning sometimes.

Baars: Thesis 2 reads, "The silent pause stands in urgent need of a definition, both in terms of its physical reality and in terms of its function." Yesterday Dr. Gibbon had what I thought was a very witty definition of the silent pause as a "context-sensitive nothing". Can we have some comment on that?

Klatt: I would like to say something about this quite funny and interesting definition. I could not disagree more with it, because it seems to me that we are all interested in the cognitive aspect of pauses ———— and to consider that as nothing is quite inappropriate. It might be more "all" than "nothing" (but I would not quite suggest that either). So I don't want to get too picky about your definition, but it might show a tendency toward a more acoustic or physicalistic interpretation and measurement. And this is the one tendency that I would most object to.

Baars: Dr. Gibbon, would you like to exercise a right of reply here?

Gibbon: OK, very briefly. Of course the main point of the argument is not the "nothing" but the "context-sensitivity". It seems to me that the context is of course the defining feature, and context can be defined in so many ways, partly in terms of noise and speech on one level, partly in terms of syntactic categories, surrounding segmental categories, syllabic categories, intonational categories and so on. It seems to me that the status of a pause is in a sense secondary. The context needs to be formulated before one can tell where the pause is.

Pribram: "Nothing" does not just mean "no thing", it does not mean emptiness, as any physicist will tell you.

Beattie: It seems to me that the type of researcher and the status of the pause are linked to some extent. There are two very different groups present at this workshop. There is one group that thinks that pauses tell us something about speech processing, and there is another group, I think, that feels that pauses are interesting in themselves. These pausologists think that the pause as a phenomenon is interesting, even when it does not tell us anything about producing or perceiving speech.

Kowal: What we had in mind when we coined this thesis was the follow-ing point. We think that in order to assess the phenomenon as such we need physical measurement, because we have found all along that it's very difficult to be consistent about it without a physical definition (unless you are preoccupied with perceptual processes). That kind of measurement does not say anything about its *function.* So I think the matter of measurement and the question of function should be addressed separately. The one thing I would be cautious about is that one should not try to assess or measure the phenomenon through its function.

Deese: I really balk at a physical definition, because it seems to be entirely arbitrary. You can say we hear pauses 250 milliseconds long, and someone else says 100 or 200 milliseconds. They are all defining their pauses by some physical limit. That is, I think, the important prob-lem, not that pauses are or should be measured physically.

Ballmer: What about considering a pause as a punctuation sign? Nor-mally in linguistics you focus on some theoretical issue when you are able to fix it graphically. So punctuation signs are anchor points or pivots to which you can trace back all the different aspects you are actually about to investigate. Something which is not called a full word, somewhere in between. It may stand at the end of a sentence, at the end of a clause, and so on. But it has a phonological or phonetic, as well as a morphosyn-tactic and a semantic-pragmatic aspect. So it's a real linguistic entity we want to investigate, and how it fits in a grammar is quite an important question.

In the tradition of Pierce, Morris and Carnap, I think we can call this a full sign.

Drommel: Pauses must be considered as context-sensitive variables. There are a lot of factors which influence pauses, and a pause is certainly not nothing. If pauses were nothing, the theory of pause perception would be nonsense ——— pauses are psychological realities. In certain cases they even have phonemic value.

Butcher: I can't really agree about the acoustic establishment of pauses being in some way prior to the functional, descriptive or perceptual. I think that the acoustic variable is only one of a great complex of variables ――― syntactic, affective, social, interactional and so forth. The others, apart from the acoustic variable, are quite sufficient on their own to cause a pause to be perceived. So I think that you can't say we've got to work from the acoustic side or we've got to work from the perceptual side. We have got to work at least from both of these points of view.

One of the most interesting things about pause perception, I think, is to investigate exactly those instances in which the physical and the perceptual don't coincide, where everybody will agree that there is a pause in a text with absolutely no acoustical silence. On the other hand, we have got great long pauses of several seconds which nobody hears. These cases are really the most interesting, and they have implications for the perception of speech and syntactic structure as a whole.

Grosjean: As long as one works with a purely descriptive approach, one will never be able to extract the different factors that are leading to some particular silence. And that's why I'm suggesting a more experimental approach, with definition and control of variables. I don't think there is any real justification for defining pauses according to their length, unless we have some kind of empirical proof of its implications.

Baars: Thesis 7 addresses neurophysiological questions: "How do we transform muscular representations into speech in real time? How is the speech act represented in the brain?"

Pribram: As Professor Chafe said, we have two levels here that we are talking about. One is the temporal aspect of the production and the other is a deeper level, which I think has been missing in this discussion over and over again. People who are talking about context-sensitivity, for example, are not talking about temporal ordering. Context-sensitivity produces a temporal order, but it's at a different level and it has to be inferred from observables.

We are dealing with the problem of coding in general. Temporal phenomena such as pauses are a way of recoding something as well. When you go from a binary system to an octal system, from bits to bytes, what happens is a recombination. There are other things involved, but somehow pauses are very very important in the way we segment things. One of the things that may be happening when we are speaking to each other is that we are using pauses in recoding, and recoding, and recoding as we go along. As I see your faces, I say to myself, "Oh, I'm not communicating when I say it this way", and immediately I recode what I was about to say. That recoding operation is what's indicated by pauses.

Laver: One of the things I took from Professor Pribram's remarks was his description of context-sensitivity. This is essentially a factor of planning: We are using evidence for what goes on on the surface to get to the stream of processes that are going on at a deeper level. And that's not just a limited neurophysiological interest, because it must take into account social factors, psychological factors, all the factors we are interested in. The thing that has made this conference interesting to me, with my specific interests, has been just that --- we have been using surface phenomena to get upstream, to infer how the temporal events have been put together in a cognitive way.

Baars: May I comment on that? It seems to me that you are saying that one function of perceived pauses, at least, is that they demarcate the subjective units in speech. Whether or not there is a physical pause in the speech stream, the perception of pauses tells us something about the "objectification" of speech, the separation of the continuous acoustical stream into perceptual units. A second point I understand from what you just said is that pauses give us a cue about points of highest processing load during the act of speaking.

Drommel: Speech pauses can be clues for the analysis of recoding mechanisms in speech processing, and in that sense they are of greater value than, for example, studying the perception of clicks in speech. Pauses are natural phenomena, while clicks are artificial.

Baars: Thesis 8 asks if there are some temporal aspects of speech production that constitute universals. May we have some comment on that?

Di Pietro: I would like to support the suggestion that we should not only look at traditional linguistic universals across different languages, but also at other temporal aspects of speech production, to see if they are universal or language-specific.

Grosjean: We shouldn't just talk about foreign languages when we think of universals of language. I have been looking at temporal aspects of spoken vs. sign languages, which can be very enriching to see what is specific to the oral modality compared to the manual modality. And many of the so-called universals of language are no longer, to my mind, universals of spoken language only.

Chafe: Has anyone looked at hesitations in sign language?[2]

Grosjean: I have looked at some temporal variables in rather fluent signing, and, for example, you can find an equivalent of final syllable lengthening and semi-vowel duration in American Sign Language. Another thing in ASL is the semantic novelty phenomenon.

Baars: Is there an equivalent of the filled pause in Sign Language?

Grosjean: Yes, for example the equivalent of a silent pause is holding the hands, like that. Now, for the filled pause, those have not been studied very well, but a lot of linguistic units are expressed on the face. I was very interested in the gaze direction studies, because the gaze direction and body movement and head shift are very important to linguistic markers in American Sign Language.

Di Pietro: Pausing occurs also: signers will prolong a sign, they will lengthen it, when they are hesitating.

Meara: May I point out that there is a tremendous difference between American Sign Language and English Sign Language. English Sign Language is written by deaf people. It's quite a different structure.

Grosjean: The general point is a very good one as there are many different spoken languages and of course there are many different sign languages. And it is only by looking at the different spoken languages and different sign languages that one will, hopefully, one day, come to these so-called universals.

Baars: Presumably slips of the tongue are universal as well. I have tried to look at speech errors not really as "mistakes", but as phenomena that reveal something functional about speech production. In the sense that slips are universal, presumably competition between speech plans is also universal. In addition, the whole neglected question of volitional action comes again to the forefront ––– involuntary slips are just not the same as voluntary "errors". Thus I am beginning to think of our work on slips as an investigation of the involuntary component of normal speech. Even error-free speech has this involuntary component.

In general, slips of the tongue are revealing in a way that pauses are not. Slips say something, and if you want to make inferences regarding deeper levels of control in speaking, you have more information to go on.

Thesis 10 points out "... the extraordinary variety of speech genres, ranging from highly ritualized predetermined speech to free-wheeling conversation. Generalizations from one genre to another regarding temporal dimensions must be made with great caution."

Klatt: One instance of this is the following. The research of the St. Louis group has indicated very clearly that authors reading their own poems use different strategies than professional readers or other people. In using different temporal strategies they probably communicate different aspects of the same text.

Gibbon: This dimension of spontaneity vs. predetermined speech underlies a lot of other classifications as well. This is a very important point especially for experimentalists, because the experimental situation by its very nature tends to preclude the use of truly spontaneous speech. This is an artifact of the experimental situation itself. One has to be aware of this dimension of spontaneous vs. predetermined speech or run the danger of creating one's own artifacts.

Baars: There is evidently no disagreement with Thesis 10 then. The next one, Thesis 12, reads: "Agreement on the use of units of speech production is needed. For reading, the sentence is a non-controversial unit. For other varieties of spontaneous speech other units have been suggested …"

Deese: I don't quite know what Sabine Kowal and Dan O'Connell had in mind with "for reading, the sentence is a non-controversial unit". I have been involved in reading research, and I can assure you that the sentence *is* a controversial unit.

Kowal: We meant this just in the sense that you do provide the material for reading and you can define what the sentence is.

Pribram: In writing it is not controversial, but in reading it is.

Deese: Yes, in writing I would say it is non-controversial, or at least less controversial than it is in reading.

Pribram: But in reading we have skipping around and, certainly in rapid reading, we seem to take in things in parallel.

Deese: And in a great deal of text information that turns out to be the case. We have been doing analyses on text-books: algebra text books, biology texts and so on. In some areas less than 50% of the information, measured in terms of the number of semantic propositions, is in well-formed sentences.

O'Connell: I don't think that was what we intended. In another sense the sentence as a unit is completely non-controversial. In a given experiment all we need to do is read the publications of a number of people in this room, and we will see how they accept the empirical definition.

Deese: Reading research people do not necessarily use sentences.

O'Connell: The point isn't whether they use sentences or not but whether they accept the written form as defining a sentence. This seems to me fairly obvious, or am I missing the point? If you don't accept the written form as defining a sentence, you are defining the sentence anew, and I would like to know how you do it. That is the point we are trying to make.

Laver: I suggest that agreement on the use of units is needed. There are two aspects of that. Firstly it is not operational definition that is needed, where in some particular application some local definition is used: It is a matter of all of us, and the rest of the field, being persuaded that there are good grounds for setting up a unit of some specific sort. And the second point springs out of that really. Whatever units are used should be made explicit, and should be given definitions. We heard quite a lot of what you just said, "well, I'll use a traditional definition of unit x whatever that might be". That sidesteps the issue in the most unprofessional way I think.

Bosshardt: If you mean written material, you have punctuation and sign, and in this respect the meaning of "sentence" is perhaps not controversial, but it is if you look on the production side.

Kowal: But people read sentences aloud; that is speech production.

Bosshardt: They are not necessarily producing units identical with the written input.

Kowal: Not necessarily, but when they do produce a sentence, it's easily recognizable as such. I guess that is the point we are making.

Bosshardt: I guess that is the controversy between us. When you say that you can find or define sentences, you should realize that on the response side there is a variability, and the response side does not necessarily correspond with the sentence being read.

Beattie: It seems to me that there is an enormous ambiguity in the experimental literature on hesitation as to what the actual meaning of "units of speech production" actually is. Boomer makes claims about phonemic clauses, Goldman-Eisler regarding temporal cycles, etc., and the implications are really quite different. Some units are found on the basis of a very small amount of partial semantic planning while other claims are made for production units on the grounds that "they are all present in the mind at the same time."

Helfrich: I have a problem in trying to understand the purpose of this thesis. Would you agree that there is not *the* unit of speech production, but rather that there may be various units at various levels, which may be processed simultaneously?

Chafe: Thesis 12 is kind of an extension of Thesis 5, which says that there should be a theory of speech production, and as part of that, that there should be units in such a theory. And that may not be true. There may be not units, although I tend to think that there probably are. But I don't think that until we go a lot further in understanding speech production we can decide what kinds of units there are.

O'Connell: I agree that we should not settle on the unit here but look for whatever proper units there are.

Baars: The next thesis is number 13, and it states that "There is empirical evidence for functional equivalence and mutual substitution between some temporal phenomena in speech production." One instance of this may be competition between speech plans, which can often lead to hesitations, but, as we have shown, also can lead to quite specifically predictable speech errors. In a sense this functional equivalence is another way of talking about the deeper level of analysis mentioned by Professor Pribram ––– that is to say, the deeper level can be viewed as a more abstract description in which lower level phenomena are treated as functionally equivalent, although they may not look the same physically.

Grosjean: I can only agree with this thesis, and I hope that others will go along with the idea that language is very redundant. There are many ways in which we can do many things, and one does not just want to look at a single variable. Very often we have five, six, or seven different ways of marking the end of a certain unit, and we sometimes choose one or several. Thank God it's like that, because language takes place in situations where we need this extreme redundancy.

Baars: A very interesting suggestion has been made for a title for the proceedings of this conference, and I will ask Professor Laver to tell us about it.

Laver: A notion that the organizers already had in mind is not to have a title which is absolutely specific, but broader in scope, able to include pauses and other related phenomena. I would suggest "Temporal Variables in Speech: In Honour of Frieda Goldman-Eisler". She is not only a pioneer, but a person who stands with one foot in the English-speaking world and the other in the German-speaking one, nicely capturing at least two of the languages that are represented here. I wonder if there is general support for this.

O'Connell: I just want to remind people that this fits in with the title of our introductory talk, where we made the best effort we could to express our own very deep gratitude to Frieda Goldman-Eisler, so that mood has already entered into the proceedings of the conference.

Notes

1. On the request of a number of participants Dr. Ballmer extended his "plea for formal approaches":

   "For this conference on Pausology, being heuristically and empirically oriented and advocating a reasonable scepsis towards purely theoretical approaches, it may be helpful to point out what the significance, i.e. merits and limitations, of theoretical considerations are. We should thereby be clear about asking for the minimal requirements a theory should fulfil in order to help heuristic and empirical research. If those are not met by a theory in question – there should be no argument about discarding it right away. If, however, these minimal requirements are met, the theoretical approach has advantages of its own such as being open to intersubjective examination, being precise to a desired degree, being compact and exhibiting last not least a certain beauty and symmetry.

   The minimal requirements one should impose on a theory are (at least) the following. First, its terms and preferably its whole structure should be interpretable intuitively in each relevant aspect with relation to the field in question. In our case of pausology, the terms and structure of an adequate theory should be linguistically, psychologically, sociologically, and biologically interpretable piece by piece. This guarantees the *heuristic* value of a theory. This aspect of heuristic interpretability is often underrated. Secondly, a theory should be algorithmical. There should exist, in other words, the possibility of calculating in the frame of the theory. This requirement provides the basis for *forecasting* and *prediction*. The theory is thus constructive. Thirdly, the results stemming from using the algorithmic mechanisms of the theory should be empirical, in a stricter sense of this word; i.e. the results should be assessed on the basis of conventionally accepted facts only, and not, say, on patching up the theory in the face of discrepancies with those facts. This requirement provides the basis of the (relative) *truth* (soundness) of the theory with respect to the conventionally accepted facts.

   The more differentiated the algorithmically deducable results are the better. Because numerical propositions are more specific than functional correlations, and these are more specific than qualitative judgements, it follows that we should aim at providing theories delivering functional correlations or even numerical propositions. The latter may be too difficult to get at for problems of speech analysis and speech production, at present, but I think it is feasible to deduce functional correlations from theory (cf. Ballmer, this volume)."

2. In response to Wallace Chafe's suggestion François Grosjean agreed to write a survey article on temporal variables in spoken and sign languages (cf. fifth section of this volume).

References

(to Dec. 1978 incl.)

Abbs, B. / Cook, V. / Underwood, M.
  1968   Realistic English 1. London: Cornelsen and Oxford University Press
Abrams, K. / Bever, T. G.
  1969   Syntactic structure modifies attention during speech perception and recognition. Quarterly Journal of Experimental Psychology 21, 280–290
Admoni, V. G.
  1966   Razvitie struktury predlozenija v period formirovanija nemeckogo nacional' nogo jazyka. Leningrad: Izdatel'stvo "Nauka"
Alajouanine, T. / Lhermitte, F. / Ledoux, R. D. / Vignolo, A.
  1964   Les composantes phonémiques et sémantiques de la jargon-aphasie. Revue Neurologique 110, 5–20
Alexander, L. G.
  1976   Mainline Skills. London: Longman
Almeida, A. / Fleischmann, G. / Heike, G. / Thürmann, E.
  1977   Short time statistics of the fundamental tone in verbal utterances under psychic stress. Universität zu Köln, Institut für Phonetik, Berichte 8, 67–77
Argyle, M. / Cook, M.
  1976   Gaze and Mutual Gaze. Cambridge: Cambridge University Press
Austin, J. L.
  1962   How to Do Things with Words. London: Oxford University Press
Baars, B. J.
  1977   The Planning of Speech: Is there Semantic Editing Prior to Speech Articulation? Doctoral Dissertation, UCLA, Dept. of Psychology
         Abstract in: Dissertation Abstracts International 38 (1977) 5, 2392
Baars, B. J.
  (forthcoming) On eliciting predictable speech errors in the laboratory: Methods and results. To appear in: Fromkin, V. A. (ed.): Errors in Linguistic Performance: Slips of the Tongue, Ear, Pen and Hand. New York: Academic Press (tentative title)
Baars, B. J. / Motley, M. T.
  1976   Spoonerisms as sequencer conflicts: Evidence from artificially elicited errors. American Journal of Psychology 89, 467–484
Baars, B. J. / Motley, M. T. / MacKay, D. G.
  1975   Output editing for lexical status in artificially elicited slips of the tongue. Journal of Verbal Learning and Verbal Behavior 14, 382–391

Ballmer, T.T.
   1975   Sprachrekonstruktionssysteme. Kronberg/Ts.: Scriptor
Ballmer, T.T.
   1978   Logical Grammar. Amsterdam: North-Holland
Baranowski, J.M.
   (forthcoming) Temporal dimensions of stutterers' speech at three age levels
Barik, H.C.
   1968   On defining juncture pauses: A note on Boomer's 'Hesitation and grammatical
          encoding'. Language and Speech 11, 156–159
Barik, H.C.
   1977   Cross-linguistic study of temporal chracteristics of different types of speech mate-
          rials. Language and Speech 20, 116–126
Bartlett, F.C.
   1932   Remembering: An Experimental and Social Study. Cambridge: Cambridge Uni-
          versity Press
Bassett, M.R.
   (forthcoming) Little old Snoopy: Narratives by the very young and very old.
Bassett, M.R. / O'Connell, D.C.
   1978   Pausological aspects of Guatemalan children's narratives. Bulletin of the
          Psychonomic Society 12, 387–389
Bassett, M.R. / O'Connell, D.C. / Monahan, W.J.
   1977   Pausological aspects of children's narratives. Bulletin of the Psychonomic Society
          9, 166–168
Bastian, J. / Delattre, P. / Liberman, A.M.
   1959   Silent interval as a cue for the distinction between stops and semivowels in medial
          position. Journal of the Acoustical Society of America 31, 1568 (abstract)
Bastian, J. / Eimas, P.D. / Liberman, A.M.
   1961   Identification and discrimination of a phonemic contrast induced by silent inter-
          val. Journal of the Acoustical Society of America 33, 842 (abstract)
Battison, R.
   1978   Lexical Borrowing in American Sign Language. Silver Spring, Md.: Linstok Press
Bay, E.
   1964   Principles of classification and their influence on our concepts of aphasia. In: De
          Reuck, A. V. S. / O'Connor, M. (eds.): Disorders of Language. Ciba Foundation
          Symposium, London: J. and A. Churchill, 122–139
Beattie, G.W.
   1977   The dynamics of interruption and the filled pause. British Journal of Social and
          Clinical Psychology 16, 283–284
Beattie, G.W.
   1978a Floor apportionment and gaze in conversational dyads. British Journal of Social
          and Clinical Psychology 17, 7–15
Beattie, G.W.
   1978b Sequential temporal patterns of speech and gaze in dialogue. Semiotica 23, 29–52
Beattie, G.W.
   (forthcoming a) Contextual constraints on the floor apportionment function of gaze in
          dyadic conversation. To appear in: British Journal of Social and Clinical
          Psychology

Beattie, G.W.
(forthcoming b) Hesitation and gaze as indicators of cognitive processing in speech. To appear in: Linguistics
(forthcoming c) The role of language production processes in the organisation of behaviour in face-to-face interaction. To appear in: Butterworth, B. (ed.): Language Production. London: Academic Press

Bellugi, U. / Fischer, S.A.
1972 A comparison of Sign Language and spoken language: Rate and grammatical mechanisms. Cognition 1, 173–200

Bellugi, U. / Klima, E.S. / Siple, P.
1974/75   Remembering in signs. Cognition 3, 93–125

Bever, T.G.
1972 Perceptions, thought and language. In: Freedle, R.O. / Carroll, J.B. (eds.): Language Comprehension and the Acquisition of Knowledge. Washington, D.C.: Winston, 99–112

Bever, T.G. / Hurtig, R.R.
1975 Detection of a non-linguistic stimulus is poorest at the end of a clause. Journal of Psycholinguistic Research 4, 1–7

Bever, T.G. / Lackner, J.R. / Kirk, R.
1969 The underlying structures of sentences are the primary units of immediate speech processing. Perception and Psychophysics 5, 225–234

Bierwisch, M.
1966 Regeln für die Intonation deutscher Sätze. In: Studia Grammatica VII. Untersuchungen über Akzent und Intonation im Deutschen. Berlin: Akademie Verlag, 99–201

Blankenship, J. / Kay, C.
1964 Hesitation phenomena in English speech: A study in distribution. Word 20, 360–372

Bolinger, D.L.
1965 Pitch accent and sentence rhythm. In: Bolinger, D.L.: Forms of English: Accent, Morpheme, Order. Cambridge, Mass.: Harvard University Press, 139–180

Boomer, D.S.
1965 Hesitation and grammatical encoding. Language and Speech 8, 148–158

Boomer, D.S.
1970 Review of 'Psycholinguistics. Experiments in Spontaneous Speech' by F. Goldman-Eisler. Lingua 25, 152–164

Boomer, D.S. / Dittmann, A.T.
1962 Hesitation pauses and juncture pauses in speech. Language and Speech 5, 215–220

Boomer, D.S. / Laver, J.D.M.
1968 Slips of the tongue. British Journal of Disorders of Communication 3, 2–11

Bower, G.H. / Springston, F.
1970 Pauses as recoding points in letter series. Journal of Experimental Psychology 83, 421–430

Brazil, D.C.
1975 Discourse Intonation. Discourse Analysis Monographs, 1. Birmingham: English Language Research

344   References

Brazil, D. C.
1978   Discourse Intonation II. Discourse Analysis Monographs, 2. Birmingham: English Language Research
Bredenkamp, J.
1974   Nonparametrische Prüfung von Wechselwirkungen. Psychologische Beiträge 16, 398–416
Broen, P.
1971   A discussion of the linguistic environment of the young language learning child. Paper presented at the American Speech and Hearing Association Meeting, Nov. 1971
Brown, E. / Miron, M. S.
1971   Lexical and syntactic predictors of the distribution of pause time in reading. Journal of Verbal Learning and Verbal Behavior 10, 658–667
Brown, G.
1977   Listening to Spoken English. London: Longman
Brown, R. W.
1973   Schizophrenia, language, and reality. American Psychologist 5, 395–403
Brown, R. W. / Lenneberg, E. H.
1954   A study in language and cognition. Journal of Abnormal and Social Psychology 49, 454–462
Bruce, D. J.
1958   The effect of listeners' anticipations on the intelligibility of heard speech. Language and Speech 1, 79–97
Bryant, E. / O'Connell, D. C.
1971   A phonemic analysis of nine samples of glossolalic speech. Psychonomic Science 22, 81–83
Buswell, G. T.
1935   How People Look at Pictures. Chicago: University of Chicago Press
Butcher, A. R.
1973 a Pausen. Universität Kiel, Institut für Phonetik, Arbeitsberichte 1, 19–39, 83–92, 97–112
Butcher, A. R.
1973 b La perception des pauses. Groupement des Acousticiens de Langue Française: Actes des 4èmes Jornées d'Etudes du Groupe de la 'Communication Parlée' 1973, 371–382
Butcher, A. R.
1975   Some syntactic and physiological aspects of pausing. Universität Kiel, Institut für Phonetik, Arbeitsberichte 5, 170–194
Butterworth, B.
1972   Semantic Analyses of the Phasing of Fluency in Spontaneous Speech. Doctoral Dissertation, University College London
Butterworth, B.
1975   Hesitation and semantic planning in speech. Journal of Psycholinguistic Research 4, 75–87
Butterworth, B.
1976   Semantic planning, lexical choice and syntactic organisation in spantaneous speech. Cambridge University, Psychological Laboratory Internal Report

Butterworth, B.
1977 Hesitation and the production of verbal paraphasias and neologisms in jargon aphasia. Cambridge University, Psychological Laboratory Internal Report

Butterworth, B. / Beattie, G.
1978 Gesture and silence as indicators of planning in speech. In: Campbell, R.N. / Smith, P.T. (eds.): Recent Advances in the Psychology of Language. Vol. 4b: Formal and Experimental Approaches. New York, London: Plenum Press, 347–360

Byrne, D. / Holden, S.
1976 Insight. London: Longman

Carroll, L.
1946 Alice in Wonderland. Cleveland, New York: World Syndicate Publishing Co.

Cattell, J. McKeen
1885 Über die Zeit der Erkennung und Benennung von Schriftzeichen, Bildern und Farben. Philosophische Studien 2, 635–650

Chafe, W.L.
1977 The recall and verbalization of past experience. In: Cole, R.W. (ed.): Current Issues in Linguistic Theory. Bloomington: Indiana University Press, 215–246
1979 The flow of thought and the flow of language. To appear in: Givón, T. (ed.): Discourse and Syntax. New York: Academic Press

Chomsky, N.
1965 Aspects of the Theory of Syntax. Cambridge, Mass.: M.I.T. Press

Christensen, F.
1967 Notes Towards a New Theory of Rhetoric. New York: Harper and Row

Clark, H.H. / Clark, E.V.
1977 Psychology and Language. An Introduction to Psycholinguistics. New York, Chicago, San Francisco, Atlanta: Harcourt Brace Jovanovich

Clemmer, E.J.
(forthcoming) Psycholinguistic aspects of pauses and temporal patterns in schizophrenic speech. To appear in: Journal of Psycholinguistic Research

Clemmer, E.J. / O'Connell, D.C. / Loui, W.
(forthcoming) Readings by church lectors and drama students

Cohen, R. / Engel, D. / Hartmann, P. / Kelter, S. / List, G. / Strohner, H.
1975 Experimentalpsychologische Untersuchungen zur linguistischen Erfassung aphatischer Störungen. Dritter Bericht an die Deutsche Forschungsgemeinschaft. Universität Konstanz

Cook, M.
1971 The incidence of filled pauses in relation to part of speech. Language and Speech 14, 135–139

Cook, V.J.
1968 Active Intonation. London: Longman

Cook, V.J.
1979 Using Intonation. London: Longman

Cooper, F.S.
1976 How is language conveyed by speech? In: Kavanagh, J.F. / Mattingly, I.G. (eds.): Language by Ear and by Eye. The Relationships between Speech and Reading. Cambridge, Mass., London: M.I.T. Press, 25–45

Corder, S. P.
  1975 The language of second-language learners: The broader issues. Modern Language Journal 58, 409–413
Covington, V. C.
  1973 Juncture in American Sign Language. Sign Language Studies 2, 29–38
Cowan, J. M. / Bloch, B.
  1948 An experimental study of pausing in English grammar. American Speech 23, 89–99
Crystal, D.
  1969 Prosodic Systems and Intonation in English. London: Cambridge University Press
Crystal, D.
  1972 The intonation system of English. In: Bolinger, D. (ed.): Intonation. Harmondsworth: Penguin, 110–136, esp. 111–113
Crystal, D. / Davy, D.
  1975 Advanced Conversational English. London: Longman
Cutler, A.
  (forthcoming) Errors of stress and intonation. To appear in: Fromkin, V. A. (ed.): Errors in Linguistic Performance: Slips of the Tongue, Ear, Pen and Hand. New York: Academic Press (tentative title)
Cutler, A. / Foss, D. J.
  1977 On the role of sentence stress in sentence processing. Language and Speech 20, 1–9
Cutler, A. / Isard, S. D.
  (forthcoming) The production of prosody. To appear in: Butterworth, B. (ed.): Language Production. New York: Academic Press
Dale, P. S.
  1974 Hesitations in maternal speech. Language and Speech 17, 174–181
Daneš, F.
  1960 Sentence intonation from a functional point of view. Word 16, 34–54
Dechert, H. W.
  1978 Contextual hypothesis-testing-procedures in speech production. Paper presented at the 5th Congress of Applied Linguistics at Montreal
Deese, J.
  1978 Thought into speech. American Scientist 66, 314–321
Dell, G. / Reich, P. A.
  1977 A model of slips of the tongue. In: Di Pietro, R. J. / Blansitt, E. L., Jr. (eds.): The Third LACUS Forum. Columbia, S. C.: Hornbeam Press, 448–455
Dimond, A. J. / Beaumont, J. G.
  1974 Hemisphere Function in the Human Brain. New York: John Wiley
Di Pietro, R. J.
  1970 Contrastive analysis and linguistic creativity. Working Papers in Linguistics, Honolulu, Hawaii 3, 57–71
Di Pietro, R. J.
  1976 Contrasting patterns of language use: A conversational approach. Canadian Modern Language Review 33, 49–61

Dommergues, J.-Y. / Grosjean, F.
1978 Performance structures in the recall of sentences. University of Paris VIII, unpublished paper
Donovan, A. / Darwin, C.J.
1979 The perceived rhythm of speech. Paper prepared for the 9th International Congress of Phonetic Sciences, Copenhagen
Douglas, R.J. / Pribram, K.H.
1966 Learning and limbic lesions. Neuropsychologia 4, 197–220
Downs, R.M. / Stea, D. (eds.)
1973 Image and Environment. Cognitive Mapping and Spatial Behavior. Chicago: Aldine
Dreyfus-Graf, J.A.
1972 Parole codée (phonocode): Reconnaissance automatique de langages naturels et artificiels. Revue d'Acoustique 21, 3–12
Drommel, R.H.
1974a Probleme, Methoden und Ergebnisse der Pausenforschung. Universität zu Köln, Institut für Phonetik, Berichte 2, 1–60
1974b Die Sprechpause als Grenzsignal im Text. Göppinger Akademische Beiträge. Vol. 89. Göppingen: Alfred Kümmerle, 51–81
1974c Ein Überblick über die bisherigen Arbeiten zur Sprechpause. Phonetica 30, 221–238
Dulay, H.C. / Burt, M.K.
1978 On the relation between second language acquisition and bilingual education. Paper presented at the Georgetown Round Table Meeting, Washington, D.C.
Duncan, S., Jr.
1972 Some signals and rules for taking speaking turns in conversations. Journal of Personality and Social Psychology 23, 283–292
Du Preez, P.
1974 Units of information in the acquisition of language. Language and Speech 17, 369–376
Ehrlichman, H. / Weiner, S.L. / Baker, A.R.
1974 Effects of verbal and spatial questions on initial gaze shifts. Neuropsychologia 12, 265–277
Ekman, P. / Friesen, W.V.
1969 The repertoire of nonverbal behavior: Categories, origins, usage, and coding. Semiotica 1, 49–98
Empson, W.
1961 Seven Types of Ambiguity. Harmondsworth: Penguin
Engelkamp, J.
1973 Semantische Struktur und die Verarbeitung von Sätzen. Bern, Stuttgart, Wien: Hans Huber
Engelkamp, J.
1974 Psycholinguistik. München: Wilhelm Fink
Exline, R.V. / Winters, L.C.
1965a Affective relations and mutual glances in dyads. In: Tomkins, S.S. / Izard, C.E. (eds.): Affect, Cognition, and Personality: Empirical Studies. New York: Springer Publishing Company, 319–350

Exline, R. V. / Winters, L. C.
1965 b Effects of cognitive difficulty and cognitive style upon eye contact in interviews. Paper read to the Eastern Psychological Association

Fairbanks, G. / Hoaglin, L. W.
1941   An experimental study of the durational characteristics of the voice during the expression of emotion. Speech Monographs 8, 85–90

Faure, M.
1978   Les composantes linguistiques, psychologiques et neurologiques du phénomène de l'interruption des phrases dans la langue parlée. Comparaison des phénomènes d'interruption tels qu'ils se produisent en allemand et en français. Interprétation grammaticale du contraste. Thèse de Doctorat, Université de la Sorbonne Nouvelle, Paris III

Fay, D.
(forthcoming) Transformational errors. To appear in: Fromkin, V. A. (ed.): Errors in Linguistic Performance: Slips of the Tongue, Ear, Pen and Hand. New York: Academic Press (tentative title)

Fillenbaum, S.
1971   Psycholinguistics. Annual Review of Psychology 22, 251–308

Fillmore, C. J.
1968   The case for case. In: Bach, E. / Harms, R. T. (eds.): Universals in Linguistic Theory. New York: Holt, Rinehart and Winston, 1–90

Fodor, J. A. / Bever, T. G.
1965   The psychological reality of linguistic segments. Journal of Verbal Learning and Verbal Behavior 4, 414–420

Fodor, J. A. / Bever, T. G. / Garrett, M. F.
1974   The psychology of Language. An Introduction to Psycholinguistics and Generative Grammar. New York, St. Louis, San Francisco, Düsseldorf: McGraw-Hill

Frederiksen, C. H.
1975   Representing logical and semantic structure of knowledge acquired from discourse. Cognitive Psychology 7, 371–458

Freud, S.
1891   Zur Auffassung der Aphasien. Wien: Deuticke

Freud, S.
1901   Zur Psychopathologie des Alltagslebens. Über Vergessen, Versprechen, Vergreifen, Aberglaube und Irrtum. Monatsschrift für Psychiatrie und Neurologie 10

Freud, S.
1904   Zur Psychopathologie des Alltagslebens. Über Vergessen, Versprechen, Vergreifen, Aberglaube und Irrtum, Berlin: S. Karger

Frishberg, N.
1975   Arbitrariness and iconicity: Historical change in American Sign Language. Language 51, 696–719

Fromkin, V. A.
1968   Speculations on performance models. Journal of Linguistics 4, 47–68

Fromkin, V. A.
1971   The non-anomalous nature of anomalous utterances. Language 47, 27–52

Fromkin, V. A. (ed.)
1973   Speech Errors as Linguistic Evidence. The Hague, Paris: Mouton

Fromkin, V.A. (ed.)
  (forthcoming) Errors in Linguistic Performance: Slips of the Tongue, Ear, Pen and
    Hand. New York: Academic Press (tentative title)
Fry, D.B.
  1969 The linguistic evidence of speech errors. Brno Studies in English 8, 70–74.
    Reprinted in: Fromkin, V.A. (ed.): Speech Errors as Linguistic Evidence. The
    Hague, Paris: Mouton 1973, 157–163
Fuller, J.
  (forthcoming) An investigation of natural and monitored sequences by non-native adult
    performers of English. To appear in: Language Learning
Funkhouser, L. / O'Connell, D.C.
  1978 Temporal aspects of poetry readings by authors and adults. Bulletin of the
    Psychonomic Society 12, 390–392
Gardner, R.A. / Gardner, B.T.
  1969 Teaching sign language to a chimpanzee. Science 165, 664–672
Garrett, M.F.
  1975 The analysis of sentence production. In: Bower, G.H. (ed.): The Psychology of
    Learning and Motivation. Vol. 9: Advances in Research and Theory. New York,
    San Francisco, London: Academic Press, 133–177
  1976 Syntactic processes in sentence production. In: Wales, R.J. / Walker, E. (eds.):
    New Approaches to Language Menchanisms. A Collection of Psycholinguistic
    Studies. Amsterdam, New York, Oxford: North-Holland, 231–256
Garrett, M.F. / Bever, T.G. / Fodor, J.A.
  1966 The active use of grammar in speech perception. Perception and Psychophysics 1,
    30–32
Glanzer, M.
  1976 Intonation grouping and related words in free recall. Journal of Verbal Learning
    and Verbal Behavior 15, 85–92
Gnutzmann, C.
  1975 Untersuchungen zu satzphonetischen Erscheinungen in Texten verschiedener
    Redestile. Universität Kiel, Institut für Phonetik, Arbeitsberichte 5, 138–169
Goffman, E.
  1971 Relations in Public. New York: Harper and Row
Goldman-Eisler, F.
  1958a The predictability of words in context and the length of pauses in speech. Lan-
    guage and Speech 1, 226–231
Goldman-Eisler, F.
  1958b Speech analysis and mental processes. Language and Speech 1, 59–75
Goldman-Eisler, F.
  1958c Speech production and the predictability of words in context. Quarterly Journal
    of Experimental Psychology 10, 96–106
Goldman-Eisler, F.
  1961 Hesitation and information in speech. In: Cherry, C. (ed.): Information Theory.
    London: Butterworths, 162–174
Goldman-Eisler, F.
  1967 Sequential temporal patterns and cognitive processes in speech. Language and
    Speech 10, 122–132

Goldman-Eisler, F.
   1968   Psycholinguistics. Experiments in Spontaneous Speech. London, New York: Academic Press
Goldman-Eisler, F.
   1972   Pauses, clauses, sentences. Language and Speech 15, 103–113
Good, D. A.
   1978   On (doing) being hesitant. Pragmatics Microfiche 3.2.
Goodenough-Trepagnier, C. / Smith, F.
   1977   Thematization and intonation in the organization of sentences. Language and Speech 20, 99–107
Goodglass, H. / Kaplan, E.
   1972   The Assessment of Aphasia and Related Disorders. Philadelphia: Lea and Febiger
Goodglass, H. / Quadfasel, F. A. / Timberlake, W. H.
   1964   Phrase length and the type and severity of aphasia. Cortex 1, 133–153
Greene, P. H.
   1972   Problems of organization of motor systems. In: Rosen, R. / Snell, F. M. (eds.): Progress in Theoretical Biology. Vol. 2. New York: Academic Press, 303–338
Grimes, J. E.
   1975   The Thread of Discourse. The Hague: Mouton
Grosjean, F.
   1977   The perception of rate in spoken and sign languages. Perception and Psychophysics 22, 408–413
Grosjean, F.
   1979   A study of timing in a manual and a spoken language: American Sign Language and English. To appear in: Journal of Psycholinguistic Research
Grosjean, F. / Collins, M.
   1979   Breathing, pausing and reading. To appear in: Phonetica
Grosjean, F. / Deschamps, A.
   1972   Analyse des variables temporelles du français spontané. Phonetica 26, 129–156
Grosjean, F. / Deschamps, A.
   1973   Analyse des variables temporelles du français spontané II. Comparaison du français oral dans la description avec l'anglais (description) et avec le français (interview radiophonique). Phonetica 28, 191–226
Grosjean, F. / Deschamps, A.
   1975   Analyse contrastive des variables temporelles de l'anglais et du français: Vitesse de parole et variables composantes, phénomènes d'hésitation. Phonetica 31, 144–184
Grosjean, F. / Grosjean, L. / Lane, H.
   1979   The patterns of silence: Performance structures in sentence production. To appear in: Cognitive Psychology
Grosjean, F. / Lane, H.
   1977   Pauses and syntax in American Sign Language. Cognition 5, 101–117
Grundhauser, R.
   (forthcoming) Idiographic analysis of a five-minute dialogue.
Halliday, M. A. K.
   1967 a Intonation and Grammar in British English. The Hague: Mouton

Halliday, M. A. K.
1967b Notes on transitivity and theme in English. Part 1. Journal of Linguistics 3, 37–81
1967c Notes on transitivity and theme in English. Part 2. Journal of Linguistics 3, 199–244
Halliday, M. A. K.
1968 Notes on transitivity and theme in English. Part 3. Journal of Linguistics 4, 179–215
Halliday, M. A. K. / Hasan, R.
1976 Cohesion in English. London: Longman
Harris, J. W.
1969 Spanish Phonolgy. Cambridge, Mass., London: M.I.T. Press
Harris, K. S. / Bastian, J. / Liberman, A. M.
1961 Mimicry and the perception of a phonemic contrast induced by silent interval: Electromyographic and acoustic measures. Journal of the Acoustical Society of America 33, 842 (abstract)
Harris, Z. S.
1955 From phoneme to morpheme. Language 31, 190–222
Hartmann, R. / Stork, F.
1972 Dictionary of Language and Linguistics. London: Applied Science Publ.
Heike, G.
1973 Phonetische Grundlagen der musikalischen Sprachkomposition. Universität zu Köln, Institut für Phonetik, Berichte 1, 32
Helfrich, H.
1973 Verzögerungsphänomene und sprachliche Leistung beim spontanen Sprechen in Abhängigkeit von Angstbereitschaft und Bekräftigung. Hamburg: Helmut Buske
Henderson, A. / Goldman-Eisler, F. / Skarbek, A.
1966 Sequential temporal patterns in spontaneous speech. Language and Speech 9, 207–216
Henderson, A. / Smith, D. G.
1972 Editing silent hesitation from speech recordings. Behavior Research Methods and Instrumentation 4, 195–196
Hess, W.
1973 Digitale Segmentation von Sprachsignalen im Zeitbereich. In: Einsele, T. / Giloi, W. / Nagel, H.-H. (eds.): Fachtagung 'Cognitive Verfahren und Systeme', Hamburg, 1973. Berlin: Springer, 161–174
Hinrichs, O. / Gonschorek, J.
1971 Ein Sprach-Erkennungsgerät. Nachrichtentechnische Zeitschrift 24, 177–182
Hirsch, E. D.
1979 Measuring the communicative effectiveness of prose. In: Writing. Sponsorship National Institute of Education. Hillsdale, N. J.: Lawrence Erlbaum
Hockett, C. F.
1967 Where the tongue slips, there slip I. In: To Honor Roman Jakobson. Essays on the Occasion of His Seventieth Birthday. Vol. 2. The Hague, Paris: Mouton, 910–936
Hofmann, E.
1977 Sprechablauf und sprachliche Kontrolle bei Paraphasien. Diplomarbeit, Universität Konstanz

Holmes, V.M. / Forster, K.I.
   1970   Detection of extraneous signals during sentence recognition. Perception and
          Psychophysics 7, 297–301
Howes, D.H.
   1967   Hypotheses concerning the functions of the language mechnism. In: Salzinger, K.
          / Salzinger, S. (eds.): Research in Verbal Behavior and Some Neurophysiological
          Implications. New York, London: Academic Press, 429–440
Jaffe, J. / Breskin, S. / Gerstman, L.J.
   1972   Random generation of apparent speech rhythms. Language and Speech 15,
          68–71
Jaffe, J. / Feldstein, S.
   1970   Rhythms of Dialogue. New York, London: Academic Press
James, W.
   1890   The Principles of Psychology. New York: Henry Holt. Reprinted by Dover Publi-
          cations
Janert, K.L.
   1967/68 Recitations of imperial messengers in ancient India. Brahmavidya. The Adyar
          Library Bulletin, Madras 31/32, 511–518
Jarman, E. / Cruttenden, A.
   1976   Belfast intonation and the myth of the fall. Journal of the International Phonetic
          Association 6, 4–12
Jarvella, R.J.
   1970   Effects of syntax on running memory span for connected discourse. Psychonomic
          Science 19, 235–236
Jarvella, R.J.
   1971   Syntactic processing of connected speech. Journal of Verbal Learning and Verbal
          Behavior 10, 409–416
Jarvella, R.J. / Herman, S.J.
   1972   Clause structure of sentences and speech processing. Perception and Psychophy-
          sics 11, 381-384
Jespersen, O.
   1961   A Modern Grammar of English on Historical Principles. London: Allen and
          Unwin
Johnson, N.F.
   1965   The psychological reality of phrase-structure rules. Journal of Verbal Learning
          and Verbal Behavior 4, 469–475
Johnson, N.F.
   1968   Sequential verbal behavior. In: Dixon, T.R. / Horton, D.L. (eds.): Verbal
          Behavior and General Behavior Theory. Englewood Cliffs, N.J.: Prentice-Hall,
          421–450
Johnson, S.
   1967   Hierarchical clustering schemes. Psychometrika 32, 241–254
Johnson, T.H.
   (forthcoming a) Mexican adolescents' narratives.
Johnson, T.H.
   (forthcoming b) Monolingual and bilingual development.

Johnson, T.H. / O'Connell, D.C. / Sabin, E.J.
  1979 Temporal analysis of English and Spanish narratives. To appear in: Bulletin of the
        Psychonomic Society
Jones, D.
  1962 An Outline of English Phonetics. 9th ed. Cambridge: Heffer
Jones, L.V. / Fiske, D.W.
  1953 Models for testing the significance of combined results. Psychological Bulletin 50,
        375–382
Karger, J.
  1951 Psychologische Ursachen von Sprechpausen. Dissertation, Universität Wien
Kendon, A.
  1967 Some functions of gaze direction in social interaction. Acta Psychologica 26,
        22–63
Kendon, A.
  1972 Some relationships between body motion and speech. An analysis of an example.
        In: Siegman, A.W. / Pope, B. (eds.): Studies in Dyadic Communication. New
        York, Toronto, Oxford: Pergamon, 177–210
Kenworthy, J.
  1978 The intonation of questions in one variety of Scottish English. Lingua 44,·
        267–282
Kintsch, W.
  1974 The Representation of Meaning in Memory. Hillsdale, N.J.: Lawrence Erlbaum
Kintsch, W.
  1977 Memory and Cognition. New York, Santa Barbara, London, Sydney, Toronto:
        John Wiley
Kintsch, W. / Kozminsky, E.
  1977 Summarizing stories after reading and listening. Journal of Educational Psycho-
        logy 5, 491–499
Klatt, D.H.
  1976 Linguistic uses of segmental duration in English: Acoustic and perceptual evi-
        dence. Journal of the Acoustical Society of America 58, 1208–1221
Klatt, D.H. / Stevens, K.N.
  1973 On the automatic recognition of continuous speech. Institute of Electrical and
        Electronic Engineers. Transactions on Audio and Electroacoustics. Vol. AU-21,
        No. 3, 210–217
Klatt, H.
  1978a Difficultés rencontrées par les sujets aphasiques lors de la lecture de certaines
        catégories grammaticales. Paper given at the Annual Meeting of the Canadian
        Psychological Association in Ottawa
Klatt, H.
  1978b Die Lesbarkeit von Wörtern als Funktion der grammatischen Wortklasse bei
        Aphasikern. Beitrag zu einer Neudefiniton des Begriffs der Anomie. Archiv für
        Psychiatrie und Nervenkrankheiten 225, 333–348
Klatt, H.
  (forthcoming a) The length of pauses in the reading of aphasics.
Klatt, H.
  (forthcoming b) Psycholinguistik der Aphasie. Frankfurt, Bern, Las Vegas: Lang

Klein, W.
1978 Wo ist hier? Präliminarien zu einer Untersuchung der lokalen Deixis. Lin-
      guistische Berichte 58, 18–40
Klein, W.
(forthcoming) Wegauskünfte. MPG Projektgruppe Psycholinguistik, Ms. To appear in:
      Zeitschrift für Literaturwissenschaft und Linguistik 33
Kleist, H. v.
1965 Über die allmähliche Verfertigung der Gedanken beim Reden. An R[ühle] v[on]
      L[ilienstern]. In: Kleist, H. v.: Gesammelte Werke. Vol. 2. Ed. by Helmut
      Sembdner. München: Carl Hanser, 319–324
Koen, F. / Becker, A. / Young, R.
1969 The psychological reality of the paragraph. Journal of Verbal Learning and
      Verbal Behavior 8, 49–53
Köster, J.-P. / Dreyfus-Graf, J. A.
1975 Optimisation de phonocodes par tests d'intelligibilité avec des sujets allemands.
      Textes des exposés présentés aux 6èmes Journées d'Etude sur la Parole. Groupe-
      ment des Acousticiens de Langue Française, Toulouse. Vol. 1, 405–410; Vol. 2,
      158–159
Köster, J.-P. / Dreyfus-Graf, J. A.
1976 Phonokodes und die Perzeption konstruierter Sprachen. Hamburger Phonetische
      Beiträge 17, 35–82
Kowal, S. / O'Connell, D. C. / O'Brien, E. A. / Bryant, E. T.
1975 Temporal aspects of reading aloud and speaking: Three experiments. American
      Journal of Psychology 88, 549–569
Kowal, S. / O'Connell, D. C. / Sabin, E. J.
1975 Development of temporal patterning and vocal hesitations in spontaneous narra-
      tives. Journal of Psycholinguistic Research 4, 195–207
Krashen, S. D.
1975 A model of adult second language performance. Paper presented at the Linguistic
      Society of America, San Francisco, Winter 1975
Krashen, S. D.
1977a The monitor model for adult second language performance. In: Burt, M. / Dulay,
      H. / Finocchiaro, M. (eds.): Viewpoints on English as a Second Language. New
      York: Regents, 152–161
Krashen, S. D.
1977b Second language acquisition research and second language testing. Paper pre-
      sented at the Convention of the American Council on Teaching of Foreign Lan-
      guages, San Francisco
Krashen, S. D.
1977c Some issues related to the monitor model. In: Brown, H. D. / Yorio, C. / Crymes,
      R. (eds.): Teaching and Learning English as a Second Language: Trends in
      Research and Practice. Washington: TESOL, 144–158
Krashen, S. D.
1978a Second language acquisition. In: Dingwall, W. O. (ed.): A Survey of Linguistic
      Science. 2nd. ed. Stamford, Conn.: Greylock, 317–338
Krashen, S. D.
1978b ESL as post-critical period learning. MEX TESOL Journal 2, 13–24

Krashen, S.D.
  (no date a) Adult second language acquisition and learning: A review of theory and
      application. Unpublished manuscript
Krashen, S.D.
  (no date b) Sources of error and the development of proficiency in adult second language
      performance. Unpublished manuscript
Krashen, S.D. / Butler, J. / Birnbaum, R. / Robertson, J.
  (forthcoming) Two studies in language acquisition and language learning. To appear in:
      ITL. Review of Applied Linguistics
Krashen, S.D. / Sferlazza, V. / Feldman, L. / Fathman, A.
  1976 Adult performance on the SLOPE test: More evidence for a natural sequence in
      adult second language acquisition. Language Learning 26, 145–151
Kuipers, B.J.
  1977 Representing knowledge on large-scale space. MIT AI Laboratory, Technical
      Report
Kursh, C.O.
  1971 The benefits of poor communication. Psychoanalytic Review 58, 189–208
Labov, W.
  1969 The internal evolution of linguistic rules. In: Conference on Historical Linguistics
      in the Perspective of Transformational Theory, UCLA, 1.–2. Feb. 1969, Direc-
      tor: Robert P. Stockwell
Labov, W.
  1972 The transformation of experience in narrative syntax. In: Labov, W.: Language in
      the Inner City. Philadelpia: University of Pennsylvania Press, 354–396
Labov, W. / Fanshel, D.
  1977 Therapeutic Discourse: Psychotherapy as Conversation. New York, San Fran-
      cisco, London: Academic Press
Labov, W. / Waletzky, J.
  1967 Narrative analysis: Oral versions of personal experience. In: Helm, J. (ed.):
      Essays on the Verbal and Visual Arts. Seattle, Wash.: University of Washington
      Press, 12–44
Lakoff, G. / Peters, S.
  1969 Phrasal conjunction and symmetric predicates. In: Reibel, D.D. / Schane, S.A.
      (eds.): Modern Studies in English. Readings in Transformational Grammar.
      Englewood Cliff, N.J.: Prentice-Hall, 113–142
Larsen-Freeman, D.E.
  1976 An explanation for the morpheme acquisition order of second language learners,
      Language Learning 26, 125–134
Lass, R.
  1971 Boundaries as obstruents: Old English voicing assimilation and universal strength
      hierarchies. Journal of Linguistics 7, 15–30
Laver, J.D.M.
  1970 The production of speech. In: Lyons, J. (ed.): New Horizons in Linguistics. Har-
      mondsworth: Penguin, 53–75
  1977a Monitoring systems in the neurolinguistic control of speech production. Paper
      presented at the 12th International Congress of Linguists, Vienna, Austria,
      Aug.–Sept. 1977

Laver, J.D.M.

1977b Neurolinguistic aspects of speech production. In: Gutknecht, C. (ed.): Grund-
begriffe und Hauptströmungen der Linguistik. Hamburg: Hoffmann und Campe,
142–155

Lecours, A.R.

1975   Methods for the descriptions of aphasic transformation of language. In: Lenneberg, E.H. / Lenneberg, E. (eds.): Foundations of Language Development: A
Multidisciplinary Approach. Vol. 2. New York: Academic Press, 75–94

Leeson, R.

1970   The exploitation of pauses and hesitation phenomena in second language
teaching: Some possible lines of exploration. Audiovisual Language Journal 8,
19–22

Leeson, R.

1975   Fluency and Language Teaching. London: Longman

Lehiste, I.

1972   The units of speech perception. In: Gilbert, J.H. (ed.): Speech and Cortical
Functioning. Proceedings of a Symposium held at the University of British Columbia, Apr. 1972. New York, London: Academic Press, 187–235

Lehiste, I.

1977   Isochrony reconsidered. Journal of Phonetics 5, 253–263

Lenneberg, E.H.

1967   Biological Foundations of Language. New York: John Wiley

Lesser, V.R. / Fennell, R.D. / Erman, L.D. / Reddy, D.R.

1974   Organization of the Hearsay II speech understanding system. Institute of Electrical and Electronic Engineers. ASSP-23, No. 1

Levelt, W.J.M.

1969   The perception of syntactic structures. Groningen University, Dept. of Psychology, Heymans Bulletin No. HB-69-31EX

Levelt, W.J.M.

1970   Hierarchical chunking in sentence processing. Perception and Psychophysiscs 8,
99–103

Levin, H. / Silverman, I. / Ford, B.L.

1967   Hesitations in children's speech during explanation and description. Journal of
Verbal Learning and Verbal Behavior 6, 560–564

Lewis, D.

1969   Convention: A Philosophical Study. Cambridge, Mass.: Harvard University Press

Lieberman, P.

1963   Some effects of semantic and grammatical context on the production and perception of speech. Language and Speech 6, 172–187

Lieberman, P.

1967   Intonation, Perception, and Language. Cambridge, Mass.: M.I.T. Press

Linde, C. / Labov, W.

1975   Spatial networks as a site for the study of language and thought. Language 51,
924–939

Lounsbury, F.G.

1954   Transitional probability, linguistic structure, and systems of habit-family hierarchies. In: Osgood, C.E. / Sebeok, T.A. (eds.): Psycholinguistics. A Survey of

Theory and Research Problems. Baltimore: Waverly Press, 93–101. Supplement to: Journal of Abnormal and Social Psychology 49; and in: Osgood, C.E. / Sebeok, T.A. (eds.): Psycholinguistics. A Survey of Theory and Research Problems. Supplement to: International Journal of American Linguistics 20

Luria, A. R.
 1970 Traumatic Aphasia: Its Syndromes, Psychology, and Treatment. Janua Linguarum, Series Maior 5. The Hague: Mouton

Lynch, K.
 1960 The Image of the City. Cambridge, Mass.: M.I.T. Press

Lyons, J.
 1977 Semantics. Vol. 1. Cambridge: Cambridge University Press

MacKay, D.G.
 1970 Spoonerisms: The structure of errors in the serial order of speech. Neuropsychologia 8, 323–350

MacKay, D.G.
 1971 Stress pre-entry in motor systems. American Journal of Psychology 84, 35–51

MacKay, D.G.
 1972 The structure of words and syllables: Evidence from errors in speech. Cognitive Psychology 3, 210–227

MacKay, D.G.
 1973 Complexity in output systems: Evidences from behavioral hybrids. American Journal of Psychology 86, 785–806

MacKay, D.G.
 1976 On the retrieval and lexical structure of verbs. Journal of Verbal Learning and Verbal Behavior 15, 169–182

MacKay, D.G.
 (forthcoming) Speech errors: Retrospect and prospect. To appear in: Fromkin, V.A. (ed.): Errors in Linguistic Performance: Slips of the Tongue, Ear, Pen and Hand. New York: Academic Press (tentative title)

Maclay, H. / Osgood, C.E.
 1959 Hesitation phenomena in spontaneous English speech. Word 15, 19–44

MacNeilage, P.F.
 1970 Motor control of serial ordering of speech. Psychological Review 77, 182–196

Mandler, J.M. / Johnson, N.S.
 1977 Remembrance of things parsed: Story structure and recall. Cognitive Psychology 9, 111–151

Marek, B.
 1975 Derivative Character of Intonation in English and Polish. Doctoral Dissertation, Maria Curie-Skłodowska University, Lublin

Martin, E.
 1970 Toward an analysis of subjective phrase structure. Psychological Bulletin 74, 153–166

Martin, J.G.
 1970 On judging pauses in spontaneous speech. Journal of Verbal Learning and Verbal Behavior 9, 75–78
 1972 Rhythmic (hierarchical) versus serial structure in speech and other behavior. Psychological Review 79, 487–509

358

Martin, J.G.
1975 Rhythmic expectancy in continuous speech perception. In: Cohen, A. / Nooteboom, S.G. (eds.): Structure and Process in Speech Perception. Proceedings of the Symposium on Dynamic Aspects of Speech Perception, held at I.P.O., Eindhoven, Netherlands, Aug. 4–6, 1975. Berlin, New York: Springer, 161–177

Martin, L.W.
1968 Some relations of embedding in English nominals. Paper presented at the 4th Regional Meeting of the Chicago Linguistic Society, 64–65

Massaro, D.W.
1975 Language and information processing. In: Massaro, D.W. (ed.): Understanding Language. New York: Academic Press, 3–28

Mayerthaler, W.
1971 Zur Theorie der Grenzsymbole. In: Stechow, A. v. (ed.): Beiträge zur generativen Grammatik. Schriften zur Linguistik. Vol. 3. Braunschweig: Vieweg, 162–171

McLaughlin, B.
1978a Linguistic input and conversational strategies in L1 and L2. Paper presented at TESOL Convention, Mexico City

McLaughlin, B.
1978b Second-Language Acquisition in Childhood. Hillsdale, N.J.: Lawrence Erlbaum

McLaughlin, B.
(forthcoming) The Monitor Model: Some methodological considerations.

Meringer, R.
1908 Aus dem Leben der Sprache. Berlin: Behr

Meringer, R. / Mayer, K.
1895 Versprechen und Verlesen: Eine psychologisch-linguistische Studie. Stuttgart: Goeschen. New ed., with introduction by A. Cutler and D. Fay: Amsterdam: John Benjamins 1978

Meyer, B.J.F.
1971 Idea Units Recalled from Prose in Relation to their Position in the Logical Structure, Importance, Stability and Order in the Passage. M.S. Thesis, Cornell University (quoted from Meyer 1975)

Meyer, B.J.F.
1975 The Organization of Prose and its Effects on Memory. Amsterdam, Oxford: North-Holland

Meyer-Eppler, W.
1969 Grundlagen und Anwendungen der Informationstheorie. 2nd ed. Berlin: Springer

Miller, G.A.
1953 What is information measurement? American Psychologist 8, 3–11

Miller, G.A.
1956 The magical number seven, plus or minus two, or, some limits on our capacity for processing information. Psychological Review 63, 81–97

Miller, G.A.
1974 Toward a third metaphor for psycholinguistics. In: Weimer, W.B. / Palermo, D.S. (eds.): Cognition and the Symbolic Processes. Hillsdale, N.J.: Lawrence Erlbaum, 397–413

Miller, G.A. / Chomsky, N.
  1963 Finitary models of language users. In: Luce, D.R. / Bush, R.R. / Galanter, E.
        (eds.): Handbook of Mathematical Psychology, 2. New York, London, Sydney:
        John Wiley, 419–491
Miller, G.A. / Galanter, E. / Pribram, K.H.
  1960 Plans and the Structure of Behavior. New York, Chicago, San Francisco: Holt,
        Rinehart and Winston
Miller, G.A. / Heise, G.A. / Lichte, W.
  1951 The intelligibility of speech as a function of the context of the test materials.
        Journal of Experimental Psychology 41, 329–335
Miller, G.A. / Isard, S.
  1963 Some perceptual consequences of linguistic rules. Journal of Verbal Learning and
        Verbal Behavior 2, 217–228
Miller, G.A. / Johnson-Laird, P.
  1976 Language and Perception. Cambridge, Mass.: Harvard University Press
Moerk, E.L.
  1974 A design for multivariate analysis of language behavior and language develop-
        ment. Language and Speech 17, 240–254
Morris, C.
  1946 Signs, Language and Behavior. New York: George Braziller
Motley, M.T.
  1973 An analysis of spoonerisms as psycholinguistic phenomena. Speech Monographs
        40, 66–71
Murray, D.C.
  1971 Talk, silence, and anxiety. Psychological Bulletin 75, 244–260
Mysak, E.D. / Hanley, T.D.
  1958 Aging processes in speech: Pitch and duration characteristics. Journal of Geron-
        tology 13, 309–313
Neisser, U.
  1967 Cognitive Psychology. New York: Appleton-Century-Crofts
Newtson, D.
  1976 Foundations of attribution: The perception of ongoing behavior. In: Harvey, J.H.
        / Ickes, W.J. / Kidd, R.F. (eds.): New Directions in Attribution Research. Vol. 1.
        Hillsdale, N.J.: Lawrence Erlbaum, 223–247
Nielsen, G.
  1962 Studies in Self Confrontation. Copenhagen: Munksgaard
Nooteboom, S.G.
  1969 The tongue slips into patterns. In: Nomen. Leyden Studies in Linguistics and
        Phonetics. The Hague: Mouton, 114–132. Reprinted in: Fromkin, V.A. (ed.):
        Speech Errors as Linguistic Evidence. The Hague, Paris: Mouton 1973, 144–156
O'Connell, D.C.
  1977 One of many units: The sentence. In: Rosenberg, S. (ed.): Sentence Production:
        Developments in Research and Theory. Hillsdale, N.J.: Lawrence Erlbaum,
        307–313
O'Connell, D.C. / Bryant, E.T.
  1972 Some psychological reflections on glossolalia. Review for Religious 31, 974–977

O'Connell, D.C. / Kowal, S.
  1972a Between ... uh ... words. St. Louis University Magazine 45, 23–25
O'Connell, D.C. / Kowal, S.
  1972b Cross-linguistic pause and rate phenomena in adults and adolescents. Journal of
    Psycholinguistic Research 1, 155–164
O'Connell, D.C. / Kowal, S.
  1972c Problems of measurement in psycholinguistic pause and rate research. In: Pro-
    ceedings and Abstract Guide. 20th International Congress of Psychology. Tokyo:
    Science Council of Japan, 348, 386 resp.
O'Connell, D.C. / Kowal, S.
  (forthcoming) Pausology. To appear in: Sedelow, W. / Sedelow, S. (eds.): Computer
    Uses in the Study of Languages. Vol. 3: Cognitive Approaches. The Hague:
    Mouton
O'Connell, D.C. / Kowal, S. / Hörmann, H.
  1969 Semantic determinants of pauses. Psychologische Forschung 33, 50–67
O'Connell, D.C. / Turner, E.A. / Onuska, L.A.
  1968 Intonation, grammatical structure, and contextual association in immediate recall.
    Journal of Verbal Learning and Verbal Behavior 7, 110–116
O'Connor, J.D. / Arnold, G.F.
  1961 Intonation of Colloquial English. A Practical Handbook. London: Longman
Orne, M.T.
  1973 Communication by the total experimental situation. In: Pliner, P. / Krames, L. /
    Alloway, T. (eds.): Communication and Affect. New York: Academic Press,
    157–191
Osgood, C.E.
  1954 Hierarchies of psycholinguistic units. In: Osgood, C.E. / Sebeok, T.A. (eds.):
    Psycholinguistics. A Survey of Theory and Research Problems, 71–73 [cf. Louns-
    bury 1954]
Osgood, C.E. / Sebeok, T.A. (eds.)
  1954 Psycholinguistics. A Survey of Theory and Research Problems. [cf. Lounsbury
    1954]
Ozga, J.
  1975 Paragraph intonation. Paper read at the 8th International Congress of Phonetic
    Sciences, Leeds, Aug. 17–23
Paivio, A.
  1971 Imagery and Verbal Processes. New York, Chicago, San Francisco: Holt,
    Rinehart and Winston
Palermo, D.A.
  1978 Psychology of Language. Glenview, Ill.: Scott, Foresman and Co.
Peirce, C.S.
  1934 Collected Papers. Vols. 1, 2, 5. Cambridge, Mass.: Harvard University Press
Peškovskij, A.M.
  1956 Ruskii sintaksis v naučnom osveščenii ('Russian syntax – scientifically analyzed').
    7th rev. ed. Moskva, 455–461 esp.
Pick, A.
  1931 Aphasie. In: Bethe, A. / Bergmann, G.v. (eds.): Handbuch der normalen und
    pathologischen Physiologie. Bd. 15/2. Berlin: Julius Springer, 1416–1524

Pickett, J. M. / Pollack, I.
  1963 Intelligibility of excerpts from fluent speech: Effects of rate of utterance and
        duration of excerpt. Language and Speech 6, 151–164
Pike, K. L.
  1945 The Intonation of American English. Ann Arbor: University of Michigan Press
  1972 General characteristics of intonation. In: Bolinger, D. (ed.): Intonation. Har-
        mondsworth: Penguin, 53–82, esp. 68–76
Pollack, I. / Pickett, J. M.
  1963 The intelligibility of excerpts from conversation. Language and Speech 6,
        165–171
Pribram, K. H.
  1958 Neocortical function in behavior. In: Harlow, H. F. / Woolsey, C. N. (eds.):
        Biological and Biochemical Bases of Behavior. Madison: University of Wisconsin
        Press, 151–172
Pribram, K. H.
  1961 A further experimental analysis of the behavioral deficit that follows injury to the
        primate frontal cortex. Experimental Neurology 3, 432–466
Pribram, K. H.
  1971 Languages of the Brain: Experimental Paradoxes and Principles of Neuro-
        psychology. Englewood Cliffs, N.J.: Prentice-Hall. 2nd ed.: Monterey, Cal.:
        Brooks/Cole 1977
Pribram, K. H.
  1973a The comparative psychology of communication: The issue of grammar and
        meaning. Annals of the New York Academy of Sciences 223, 135–143
Pribram, K. H.
  1973b The primate frontal cortex – Executive of the brain. In: Pribram, K. H. / Luria,
        A. R. (eds.): Psychophysiology of the Frontal Lobes. New York: Academic Press,
        293–314
Pribram, K. H.
  1977a Brain organization in the construction of values: A sociobiological analysis. In:
        Search for Absolute Values – Harmony Among the Sciences. Proceedings of the
        5th International Conference on the Unity of the Sciences, Washington, D.C.,
        Nov. 26–28, 1977. New York: ICF Press, 641–651
Pribram, K. H.
  1977b New dimensions in the functions of the basal ganglia. In: Shagass, C. / Gershon,
        S. / Friedhoff, A.J. (eds.): Psychopathology and Brain Dysfunction. New York:
        Raven Press, 77–95
Pribram, K. H.
  1977c Peptides and protocritic processes. In: Miller, L.H. / Sandman, C.A. / Kastin,
        A.J. (eds.): Neuropeptide Influences on the Brain and Behavior. New York:
        Raven Press
Pribram, K. H. / Douglas, R. / Pribram, B.J.
  1969 The nature of non-limbic learning. Journal of Comparative and Physiological
        Psychology 69, 765–772
Pribram, K. H. / McGuinness, D.
  1975 Arousal, activation and effort in the control of attention. Psychological Review
        82, 116–149

Pribram, K.H. / Plotkin, H.C. / Anderson, R.M. / Leong, D.
  1977 Information sources in the delayed alternation task for normal and "frontal" monkeys. Neuropsychologia 15, 329–340
Pribram, K.H. / Tubbs, W.E.
  1967 Short-term memory, parsing, and the primate frontal cortex. Science 156, 1765–1767
Quilis, A.
  1964 Estructura del encabalgamiento en la metrica española. Contributión a su estudio experimental. Madrid: Consejo Superior de Investigaciones Científicas
Quinting, G.
  1971 Hesitation Phenomena in Adult Aphasic and Normal Speech. The Hague, Paris: Mouton
Quirk, R.
  1972 The English Language and Images of Matter. London: Oxford University Press
Reich, P.A.
  1975 Evidence for a stratal boundary from slips of the tongue. University of Toronto, Dept. of Linguistics, Feb. 1975
Rochester, S.R.
  1973 The significance of pauses in spontaneous speech. Journal of Psycholinguistic Research 2, 51–81
Rosch, E.H.
  1973 On the internal structure of perceptual and semantic categories. In: Moore, T.E. (ed.): Cognitive Development and the Acquisition of Language. New York: Academic Press, 111–144
Rosenberg, S. / Cohen, B.
  1964 Speakers' and listeners' process in a word communication task. Science 145, 1201–1203
  1966 Referential processes of speakers and listeners. Psychological Review 73, 208–231
Ruder, K.F. / Jensen, P.J.
  1969 Speech pause duration as a function of syntactic junctures. University of Kansas, Bureau of Child Research, training paper No. 42
Ruder, K.F. / Jensen, P.J.
  1972 Fluent and hesitation pauses as a function of syntactic complexity. Journal of Speech and Hearing Research 15, 49–60
Rutter, D.R. / Stephenson, G.M. / Ayling, K. / White, P.A.
  1978 The timing of looks in dyadic conversation. British Journal of Social and Clinical Psychology 17, 17–21
Sabin, E.J.
  (forthcoming) Temporal measurements applied to aphasic speech.
Sabin, E.J. / Clemmer, E.J. / O'Connell, D.C. / Kowal, S.
  (forthcoming) A pausological approach to speech development. To appear in: Siegman, A.W. / Feldstein, S. (eds.): Of Speech and Time. Hillsdale, N.J.: Lawrence Erlbaum
Sachs, J.S.
  1967 Recognition memory for syntactic and semantic aspects of connected discourse. Perception and Psychophysics 2, 437–442

Schank, R.C. / Abelson, R.P.
    1977   Scripts, Plans, Goals and Understanding. Hillsdale, N.J.: Lawrence Erlbaum
Schmerling, S.F.
    1974   A re-examination of "normal stress". Language 50, 66–73
Schneider, W. / Shiffrin, R.M.
    1977   Controlled and automatic human information processing: I. Detection, search,
           and attention. Psychological Review 84, 1–66
Searle, J.R.
    1969   Speech Acts. London: Cambridge University Press
Shiffrin, R.M. / Schneider, W.
    1977   Controlled and automatic human information processing: II. Perceptual learning,
           automatic attending, and a general theory. Psychological Review 84, 127–190
Simon, H.A.
    1974   How big is a chunk? Science 183, 482–488
Stokoe, W.C.
    1960   Sign Language Structure: An Outline of the Visual Communication Systems of
           the American Deaf. Studies in Linguistics. Occasional Papers 8. Buffalo, N.Y.:
           University of Buffalo
Suci, G.J.
    1967   The validity of pause as an index of units in language. Journal of Verbal Learning
           and Verbal Behavior 6, 26–32
Suci, G.J. / Ammon, P. / Gamlin, P.
    1967   The validity of the probe latency technique for assessing structure in language.
           Language and Speech 10, 69–80
Suen, C.Y. / Beddoes, M.P.
    1974   The silent interval of stop consonants. Language and Speech 17, 126–134
Szawara, J. / O'Connell, D.C.
    1977   Temporal reflections of spontaneity in homilies. Bulletin of the Psychonomic
           Society 9, 360–362
Taylor, I.
    1969   Content and structure in sentence production. Journal of Verbal Learning and
           Verbal Behavior 8, 170–175
Tesnière, L.
    1953   Esquisse d'une syntaxe structurale. Paris: Klincksieck
Tesnière, L.
    1959   Eléments de syntaxe structurale. Paris: Klincksieck
Thom, R.
    1974   Modèles mathématiques de la morphogénèse. Recueil de textes sur la théorie des
           catastrophes et ses applications. Paris: Union générale d'éditions
Thompson, S.
    1971   The deep structure of relative clauses. In: Fillmore, C.J. / Langendoen, D.T.
           (eds.): Studies in Linguistic Semantics. New York: Holt, Rinehart and Winston,
           82–87
Thorndyke, P.W.
    1977   Cognitive structures in comprehension and memory of narrative discourse. Cog-
           nitive Psychology 9, 77–110

Tosi, O. I.
    1965 A Method for Acoustic Segmentation of Continuous Sound into Pauses and
          Signals and Measurement of Segment Durations. Doctoral Dissertation, The
          Ohio State University
Trager, G. L.
    1962 Some thoughts on 'juncture'. Studies in Linguistics 16, 11–22
Trager, G. L. / Smith, H. L., Jr.
    1951 An Outline of English Structure. Studies in Linguistics: Occasional Papers 3.
          Norman, Okla.: Battenburg Press
Tulving, E.
    1970 Short-term and long-term memory: Different retrieval mechanisms. In: Pribram,
          K. H. / Broadbent, D. (eds.): The Biology of Memory. New York: Academic
          Press, 7–9
    1972 Episodic and semantic memory. In: Tulving, E. / Donaldson, W. (eds.): Organi-
          zation of Memory. New York: Academic Press, 382–403
Underwood, B. J.
    1966 Experimental Psychology. 2nd ed. Englewood Cliffs, N. J.: Prentice-Hall
Weiner, S. L. / Ehrlichman, H.
    1976 Ocular motility and cognitive process. Cognition 4, 31–43
Weinrich, H.
    1961 Phonologie der Sprechpause. Phonetica 7, 4–18
Weinrich, H.
    1976 Sprache in Texten. Stuttgart: Ernst Klett
Wernicke, C.
    1874 Der aphasische Symptomenkomplex. Breslau: Taschen
Wildgen, W.
    1978a Prolegomena zu einer dynamischen Sprachtheorie. Teil 1: Grundlagen einer
          Theorie der Interkommunikation. Regensburg: Mimeo
Wildgen, W.
    1978b Prolegomena zu einer dynamischen Sprachtheorie. Teil 2: Grundlagen einer
          katastrophentheoretischen Semantik. Regensburg: Mimeo
Wildgen, W.
    (1979 forthcoming) Verständigungstopologie und Verständigungsdynamik. Habilita-
          tionsschrift, Universität Regensburg
Winograd, T.
    1977 Framework for understanding discourse. Stanford University, Artificial Intelli-
          gence Monograph, June 1977
Wode, H.
    1968 Pause und Pausenstelle im Deutschen. Acta Linguistica Hafniensia 11, 147–169
Woodward, J.
    1974 Implication variation in American Sign Language: Negative incorporation. Sign
          Language Studies 5, 20–30
Wunderlich, D.
    1976 Studien zur Sprechakttheorie. Frankfurt/M.: Suhrkamp
Yngve, V. H.
    1960 A model and an hypothesis for language structure. Proceedings of the American
          Philosophical Society 104, 444–466

Zeeman, E. C.
  1977 Catastrophe Theory: Selected Papers 1972–1977. Reading, Mass.: Addison-
        Wesley
Zemb, J. M.
  1968 Les structures logiques de la proposition allemande, contribution à l'étude des
        rapports entre le langage et la pensée. Paris: O. C. D. L.
Zemb, J. M.
  1970 L'apprentissage du français aujourd'hui. Paris: O. C. D. L.
Zemb, J. M.
  1972 a Métagrammaire: La proposition. Paris: O. C. D. L.
Zemb, J. M.
  1972 b Satz, Wort, Rede: Semantische Strukturen des deutschen Satzes. Freiburg, Basel,
        Wien: Herder
Zwirner, E. / Zwirner, K.
  1937 Phonometrischer Beitrag zur Frage der Lesepausen. Archives Néerlandaises de
        Phonétique Expérimentale 13, 111–128

Index of names

(including authors cited)